THE
QUESTION
BOX

THE QUESTION BOX

By

Rev. Bertrand L. Conway
of the Paulist Fathers

With a Preface by

Francis Cardinal Spellman, D.D.

PAULIST PRESS
(Paulist Fathers)
New York, New York

NIHIL OBSTAT: John A. Goodwine, J.C.D.
Censor Librorum

IMPRIMATUR: ✠ Francis Cardinal Spellman
Archbishop of New York

December 28, 1960

Library of Congress
Catalog Card Number: 61-11249

Manufactured in the
United States of America by
Paulist Press, New York, N. Y.

FOREWORD

At the World's Fair in Chicago, 1893, Archbishop Keane, then Rector of Catholic University at Washington, D. C., Father Walter Elliott of the Paulist Fathers, and Father John Driscoll of the Albany diocese took advantage of this international gathering to explain the teachings of the Catholic Church by answering in a kindly manner the problems, difficulties, and objections sincerely presented by men and women of every religious creed.

A Question Box was placed in the Assembly Hall and day after day hundreds of queries on every phase of Catholic belief and practice were submitted. Father Elliott at once grasped the importance and value of this irenic method of religious controversy and adopted it in the doctrinal lectures he later delivered in the diocese of Detroit. Since that time the Question Box has been used extensively and effectively by numerous priests in the instruction of people.

In 1900 Father Alexander Doyle, then Editor of *The Catholic World,* felt the need of a book which would answer the principal questions disturbing American citizens and allay their misgivings about the Catholic Church. He persuaded Father Bertrand Conway, a young Paulist missionary, to devote himself to this challenging project. With enthusiasm, energy, and talent Father Conway produced a summary of Catholic Apologetics which has since been acclaimed in every part of the world.

Father Conway's *Question Box* has enjoyed phenomenal success. The first edition published in 1903 and the second edition in 1929 have sold over 4 million copies. It has been translated into Spanish, French, German, and Flemish. Permission has been given for a Chinese version. No one can estimate the salutary influence this little book has exerted over the years. It has dissipated suspicion and prejudice, dispelled ignorance and error, and helped doubting and inquiring minds to discover the truth about the Catholic Church. It has strengthened wavering Catholics in their Faith, stirred fallen-away Catholics to return to the Church, and initiated innumerable conversions.

On December 8, 1959, Father Conway, at the age of 87 and with almost 63 years of fruitful priestly service to his credit, departed this life after a long illness. As a memorial to his apostolic spirit we at the Paulist Press decided to revise completely his *Question Box* and issue a third edition.

We have eliminated questions that are no longer relevant; edited and updated the material; added popular questions which are being currently discussed; and included entirely new bibliographies of selected books, pamphlets, and magazine articles. For the convenience of the reader we have grouped related questions under definite headings. Paragraphs have been numbered to make the index more serviceable. And we have used larger type for easier reading.

We sincerely thank His Eminence, Francis Cardinal Spellman, for graciously consenting to write a special Preface. We are also indebted to many Paulist Fathers, too numerous to mention by name, who kindly co-operated in the arduous preparation of this edition.

We pray that this *Question Box,* like its predecessors, may by God's grace induce many to explore "the depth of the riches and of the wisdom of God" in which they will find true happiness and by which they will earn a heavenly reward.

JOHN A. CARR, C.S.P.
Executive Publisher

PREFACE

Today, more than at any other time in our history, our fellow countrymen have manifested widespread interest in Catholicism. Men of good will admire the Catholic Church's steadfast adherence to truth, her interest in integral education, her care for the poor and the oppressed, and her dedicated priests, religious and laity who staunchly defend the principles upon which our American democracy has been founded.

Yet, at the same time, enemies of religion are working tirelessly to destroy men's belief in God and His revealed message and to distort the true image of the Catholic Church.

Catholics must, therefore, be well informed about their faith, not only for their own spiritual advancement but also for the enlightenment of those earnestly seeking the fullness of God's truth. They must likewise be equipped to dispel any misunderstandings about the Church and to refute, when necessary, the errors of misguided critics.

It is therefore vitally necessary that there be available a supply of suitable literature for Catholics to place in the hands of inquiring non-Catholics.

The Question Box has been for the past fifty-eight years an invaluable tool in fulfilling such an apostolic need. Indeed, it has become a classic in its kind. Its simple, direct method of question-and-answer presents Catholic teaching with clarity and vigor. Four million copies already have been distributed; countless thousands of souls have had their knowledge of the faith increased, while many un-believers have been brought to the full knowledge and love of Christ. Its influence has been inestimable.

I ask God's blessing upon this newly revised edition of *The Question Box,* and pray that it will continue undi-minished in its influence.

The Feast of St. Joseph
  1961

✠ F. Cardinal Spellman

CONTENTS

PART I
God and the World

What is your opinion of Pantheism and Deism? Are they not much more reasonable than your medieval theism?

[1] Let me say, to begin with, that theism is no more medieval than deism or pantheism. There were deists and pantheists in the Middle Ages as well as among the thinkers of ancient times.

[2] All three of these doctrines refer to the relationship between the world and God, its maker. Deism is a denial of the providence of God; it asserts that after having created the world, God no longer concerned Himself with it. The God of the deists is a disinterested God. Although there are various forms of pantheism, basically it is the doctrine which identifies the world with God. For the pantheists the material world has emanated from the divine substance. Creation is consequently considered by them to be a necessary, and not a free act of God.

[3] The Vatican Council has stated the Catholic position, which is a theistic position, very clearly: "The holy, Catholic, apostolic, Roman Church believes and professes that there is one true and living God, the creator and lord of heaven and earth. He is all-powerful, eternal, unmeasurable, incomprehensible and limitless in intellect and will and in every perfection. Since He is one unique spiritual substance, entirely simple and unchangeable, He must be declared really and essentially distinct from the world, perfectly happy in Himself and by His very nature, and inexpressibly exalted over all things that exist or can be conceived other than Himself.

13

⁴ "Furthermore, by His providence, God watches over and governs all the things that He made, reaching from end to end with might and disposing all things with gentleness (Wis. 8, 1). For 'all things are naked and open to the eyes of Him to whom we have to give account' (Heb. 4, 13), even those things that are going to occur by the free action of creatures."

⁵ Of these three doctrines, theism alone is reasonable. A creator who is not at the same time a conserver is unthinkable. For creation means to produce beings from non-being—from nothing. A being so produced demands, first of all, an almighty creator. For no one but an all-powerful God can bring something from nothing. Secondly, a created being, that is, a being that has begun to exist out of nothing, cannot contain within itself the power to conserve its being. It depends for this conservation of its being on the almighty source of its being, on God. For just as finite things have no reason for coming into being unless we appeal to an omnipotent First Cause, neither do they have any reason for continuing to be unless we appeal to the conserving power of that Cause.

⁶ Nor is it reasonable to hold that the finite world is but an emanation from the infinite God. For this requires us to assert that all the properties of finite things in the material universe are in reality divine properties. This is to include in the notion of the infinite God all the limitations which are characteristic of material things, including the fallibility of the human will. Pantheism is consequently a doctrine which contains contradictory elements. It is merely an attempt to find an easy way of explaining away all the difficulties involved in the notion of creation.

⁷ The scriptural evidence for theism, as opposed to deism and pantheism, is abundant and undeniable. Countless texts could be cited here. For example, when speaking of Jesus, St. Paul states: "All things have been created through and unto Him, and He is before all creatures, and in Him all things hold together" (Col. 1, 16-17). St. Matthew quotes Jesus as follows: "Are not two sparrows sold for a farthing? And yet not one of them will fall to the ground without your Father's leave. But as for you, the very hairs of your head are numbered. Therefore do

not be afraid; you are of more value than many sparrows"
(Matt. 10, 29-31).

*Can reason alone prove the existence of God? If so, why
do so many people persist in denying it? Does not the
Bible command us to believe in the existence of God?
Why then do you Catholics give so much attention to
rational proofs?*

[1] The position of the Catholic Church on the know-
ability of God's existence was clearly defined by the Vatican
Council in 1870: "The same holy Mother Church holds
and teaches that God, the origin and end of all things,
can be known with certainty by the natural light of human
reason from the things that He created: 'for, since the
creation of the world His invisible attributes are clearly
seen . . . being understood through the things that are
made' (Rom. 1, 20); and she teaches that it was, nevertheless, the good pleasure of His wisdom and goodness to
reveal Himself and the eternal decrees of His will to the
human race in another and supernatural way, as the
apostle says: 'God, who at sundry times and in divers
manners spoke in times past to the fathers by the prophets,
last of all in these days has spoken to us by His Son' "
(Heb. 1, 1-2).

[2] Christian thinkers have formulated many rational
proofs for the existence of God. They approach the question from many different points of view and reveal God
to us as the Prime Mover, the First Cause, the Necessary
Being, the One, Perfect Being, the Designer and Orderer
of the Universe, the Origin of Life, the Supreme Lawgiver,
the Ultimate Good, etc. These arguments have a cumulative as well as an individual value, and should be studied
as a whole in order to be fully appreciated. Space does
not permit us to develop them in detail here. But they
may be reviewed in any manual of natural theology. (*See*
Gilson, E., *The Christian Philosophy of St. Thomas
Aquinas.*; Smith, G., *Teaching of the Catholic Church.*

[3] Among these proofs, perhaps the most apt today, when
we are so conscious of the marvels hidden within atoms
and stretching into outer space, is the so-called proof from

order or design. Order and design are seen to be present everywhere in nature. The atomic physicist, for example, tells us that a grain of sand or a speck of dust contains particles so numerous as to outnumber the human inhabitants of the earth. And all these atomic and sub-atomic particles move with unimaginable speeds in a perfectly harmonious mutual motion. These innumerable invisible particles which make up the material universe obey a complex of laws which the atomic scientist has only begun to discover.

[4] Still, the discoveries which he has already made have led him to the brink of travel into outer space. By harnessing the energy which is locked within the atom, science has devised means of propulsion which will inevitably send men hurtling through space to the moon and to other planets. And although space scientists look eagerly forward to the new discoveries which they will make in the far reaches of our universe, they already know much about what they will find there. They will find outer space to be so extended that it will be impractical to measure distance in terms of miles. They have accordingly invented a new measure of celestial distances called the *light year*. One light year is simply the number of miles light travels in one year. Now since light travels at a rate of 186,000 miles each second, one light year is calculated as almost 6 trillion miles. And some stars are hundreds of light years distant from our earth.

[5] Within this vast universe are myriad heavenly bodies, stars like our sun and planets like the earth, all of which move at astounding speeds in unswervable obedience to fixed laws which produce a heavenly harmony so perfect that astrophysicists can predict to the minute, indeed to the split second, astronomical events such as eclipses which will take place thousands of years in the future.

[6] The marvels that modern science has discovered concerning the immensity and grandeur of the universe confirm the truth which the Psalmist uttered centuries before the dawn of the Christian era: "The heavens show forth the glory of God and the firmament declares the work of His hands" (Ps. 18, 2). Indeed, scientists themselves have not hesitated to draw the conclusion which their observa-

tions have made inescapable. In his book, *The Mysterious Universe* (p. 186), the eminent British astronomer, Sir James Jeans, writes: "Today there is a wide measure of agreement, which on the physical side of science approaches almost to unanimity, that the stream of knowledge is heading toward a non-mechanical reality; the universe begins to look more like a great thought than like a great machine. Mind no longer appears as an accidental intruder into the realm of matter; we are beginning to suspect that we ought rather to hail it as the creator and governor of the realm of matter."

[7] The implication in Sir James Jeans' statement that it is only in the 20th century that science has recognized the necessity of looking to God for an ultimate explanation of the universe is misleading. As early as the 17th century, the Father of modern experimental science, Sir Isaac Newton, wrote: "The origin of the material world must be ascribed to the intelligence and wisdom of a most potent Being, always existing and present everywhere, who controls according to His good pleasure, all parts of the universe much more effectively than our soul controls by its will the movements of the body united to it."

[8] As the proof from design brings out clearly the intelligence of God, so the proof from conscience brings out clearly His holiness. What is conscience? It is the human mind, making a practical judgment upon the morality of our every thought, word and deed. It commands us with decision: "This is right; do it. This is wrong; avoid it." And we feel at once an imperative call upon our obedience. Here we are dealing, not with an abstract idea, which the modern mind usually fights shy of, but with a simple, concrete fact, which everyone experiences day by day. There exists within us a strange, mysterious power which is constantly comparing all our actions with an absolute standard of right and wrong, and condemning them without appeal, when they go counter to its ordering. Conscience speaks of a necessary duty that we owe. It brings us face to face with an obligatory law, whose commands are authoritative, final, and unquestioned.

[9] Law implies a lawgiver. A command always implies a superior who issues the command. Who can this Final,

Absolute, Supreme Authority be, save God, the Original Source of all morality, the One Perfect Arbiter of right and wrong? Conscience is merely His voice.

[10] Cardinal Newman puts the argument from conscience well. He writes: "Conscience always involves the recognition of a living object toward which it is directed. Inanimate things cannot stir our affections; these are correlative with persons. If, as is the case, we feel responsibility, are ashamed, are frightened, at transgressing the voice of conscience, this implies that there is One to whom we are responsible, before whom we are ashamed, whose claims upon us we fear. If, on doing wrong, we feel the same tearful, broken-hearted sorrow which overwhelms us on hurting a mother; if, in doing right, we enjoy the same sunny serenity of mind, the same soothing, satisfactory delight which follows on our receiving praise from a father, we certainly have within us the image of some Person to whom our love and veneration look, in whose smile we find our happiness, for whom we yearn, toward whom we direct our pleadings, in whose anger we are troubled and waste away. These feelings in us are such as require for their exciting cause an Intelligent Being. Thus the phenomena of conscience avail to impress the imagination with a picture of a Supreme Governor, a Judge, Holy, Just, Powerful, All-Seeing, Retributive" (*Grammar of Assent*).

[11] If you ask me why some men still persist in denying the existence of God, despite the clear testimony of reason and the general consent of all peoples from the beginning of the world, the answer is not far to seek. Just as the human will can freely and deliberately sin against the light and do the most abominable things, so the human mind can defiantly and illogically deny the most self-evident truths. The Psalmist is right in calling the atheist a "fool" (Ps. 52, 1). St. Paul is right in declaring him "without excuse" (Rom. 1, 20). Personal sin too often blinds man's vision of the unseen world of the spirit. "The sensual man does not perceive the things that are of the Spirit of God, for it is foolishness to him, and he cannot understand, because it is examined spiritually" (I Cor. 2, 14).

[12] Yes, the Bible does command us to believe in the existence of God. We need only recall the first of the Ten

Commandments which God gave to Moses on Mt. Sinai: "I, the Lord, am your God, . . . you shall not have other gods besides Me" (Exodus 20, 2-3). And the Book of Psalms condemns the unbeliever as a fool: "The fool says in his heart, 'There is no God' " (Ps. 52, 1).

[13] Still, the Bible also commands us to be able to explain what we believe to others: "Be ready always with an answer to everyone who asks a reason for the hope that is in you" (I Peter 3, 15). Since it is God, the Creator, who endows man with intelligence, man's use of that intelligence to understand (insofar as he is able), divine truths, can but redound to the glory of God. Far from being opposed to one another, human reason and divine revelation are but two complementary sources of truth.

Do you not make God a mere abstraction existing in the mind by calling Him the absolute, universal being? Are you not fashioning God to the image of man by referring to Him as a personal God?

[1] When Catholics call God the absolute, universal Being, we have in mind a clear-cut distinction between *being* taken as a universal term, and *Being* by which we refer to God. The former word (being) expresses the concept of reality which is totally unspecified; it has the least content of any idea the human mind can form. In this sense it is the poorest of human concepts. The word *Being,* on the contrary, designating the Godhead, implies the fullness of all reality and the infinite unity of all possible perfections.

[2] Because of the limited capacity of the human intellect, we cannot form an adequate idea of the simple totality of God's perfections. Each of the divine perfections is identical with the divine essence and consequently they are not really distinct from one another. But the very make-up of our mind forces us to consider separately and piecemeal what in God is infinite unity and simplicity of essence. We consequently use the term absolute, universal Being to refer to the fullness of divine perfections which are possessed by God in perfect unity.

[3] It is true that all the perfections which we attribute to God are drawn from the finite things of our experience.

But when we ascribe to God a perfection which we find in a creature, such as *intelligence* or *personality,* we are careful not to ascribe it to Him in an identical sense. We attribute human perfections to God only by analogy. For God possesses these perfections in their absolute fullness; man does not. While all our natural knowledge of God is but an analogical knowledge, still this analogy which the human mind is capable of making between creatures and God is the root of the very possibility of our knowing God. It is because we are made in God's image (Genesis 1, 26-27) and not because He is made in ours that it is possible for us to know God in this way.

Why did God make the world? Is it the best world He was able to make? If God is good and all-powerful, why did He not at least make a world in which there would be no physical evil?

[1] Creation is a free act of God. He was not obliged to create the world; He chose freely to do so. And since God is infinite, since His Being and happiness have been boundless from all eternity, He did not stand to gain in any way from His act of creation. Why, then, did He create? St. Thomas Aquinas explains that He willed to communicate His own perfection, His own goodness (Summa Theologiae I, q. 44, a, 4, ad. 3). Goodness tends naturally to diffuse itself. And God who is infinite goodness freely decided to share His goodness with others through the act of creation.

[2] The question of whether or not the world in which we live is the best possible world that God could have created has attracted the attention of philosophers through the centuries. This question cannot be answered with a simple "yes" or a simple "no". Since the world is limited and finite, it can always be added to or improved. In this sense God certainly could have created a "better" world than the one in which we now live. For His power is infinite. But the perfection of the world, as St. Thomas Aquinas points out, must be discussed in terms of what God intended to accomplish by His act of creation (Summa Theologiae, I, q. 50, a. 3, ad 3). He intended the world

to manifest His power and goodness, and insofar as the world conforms to this divine intention, it may be rightfully called the best possible world. Let us point out again, however, that this is not to say that God could not create a greater world than ours. His power is infinite.

³ Some find it impossible to reconcile the presence of physical evil in the world with the omnipotence and infinite goodness of the Creator. As is clear in the story of creation as recounted in the book of Genesis, God created the world for man, and gave man domination over all of nature. Man then sinned against God by disobeying Him and through this *Original Sin* lost for himself as well as for all his descendants the immunity from suffering and death which, till that time, had been his. The Council of Trent states this Catholic doctrine clearly: For through Original Sin Adam "lost for himself and for us the sanctity and justice received from God, and, defiled by the sin of disobedience, transmitted to all mankind death, the sufferings of the body, and sin, the death of the soul." To begin with, then, we see that it was man by misusing his freedom, and not God, who was responsible for much of the evil that we now know has come into the world.

⁴ We may still ask, however, why an all-good God permits evil to continue to exist in the world. Evil is best defined as the absence of a good which should be present. It is not something positive therefore but rather something negative. We call evil a "privation" which means simply the lack of a due good. St. Thomas tells us that "no being can be said to be evil insofar as it is being, but only insofar as it lacks some being; as for example a man is said to be evil insofar as he lacks the being of virtue, and an eye is said to be evil insofar as it lacks the power of sight " (Summa Theologiae I, q. 5, a. 3, ad 2). Now since evil is merely a privation of good, God cannot cause evil as such. He can merely permit it, as in fact He does, to exist in the world. For one who believes in the supernatural destiny of man the fact of physical evil in the world presents little difficulty. As St. Augustine says: "He is powerful enough and good enough to draw good even out of evil" (Enchiridion, ch. 11). Is physical suffering and pain truly an evil? We need only read the eleventh chapter

of his second Epistle to the Corinthians to discover that St. Paul surely did not think so. After recounting the many sufferings which he underwent for the sake of the Gospel, he concludes: "Gladly therefore I will glory in my infirmities, that the strength of Christ may dwell in me. Wherefore I am satisfied, for Christ's sake, with infirmities, with insults, with hardships, with persecutions, with distresses. For when I am weak, then I am strong" (2 Cor. 12, 9-10). How often were the saints desirous of suffering and welcomed it with joy. Sickness has convinced many a man of his utter dependence upon God, and has opened the heart of many a sinner to the consolations of religion. It was, after all, the blood of martyrs which became the fruitful seed of Christians, and it was the tortuous death of our Blessed Savior upon the cross that won salvation for the world. Without suffering we would tend to forget that "here we have no permanent city, but we seek for the city that is to come" (Heb. 13, 14). The supreme value of our spiritual struggle for heaven is the real reason why God permits evil to exist in the world.

Why is it that a good God allows the wicked to prosper in this world, while the good are afflicted with every misery?

[1] As a matter of fact prosperity is not always the lot of the wicked, and misery always the portion of the good. Many good people enjoy health, wealth, social and political preeminence, while many wicked people suffer, even in this life, sickness, poverty, disgrace, imprisonment, and death by capital punishment.

[2] Happiness is not always to be measured by mere externals. The virtuous poor may be happy in the possession of the true faith, and appreciate keenly the consolations of religion, while the wicked rich often find life so empty and profitless, that they kill themselves in despair.

[3] But even if in many instances the wicked prosper, and the good are afflicted, the fact merely proves the existence of an after life, wherein an infinitely just and loving God will right all the inequalities and injustices of this world. This life is a time of trial during which a man must prove himself worthy of the eternal happiness that God metes

out to those who serve Him. The sufferings of the good, therefore, are to be regarded as part of the punishment due their sins, and as a great opportunity of merit, while the prosperity of the wicked is to be looked upon as their reward in this life. "Woe to you rich!" says Christ, "for you are now having your comfort" (Luke 6, 24). And St. Paul says: "For I reckon that the sufferings of the present time are not worthy to be compared with the glory to come" (Rom. 8, 18).

Must Catholics believe in a personal devil? Why did God create the devil? Why does not God, if He is all good, destroy the devil?

¹ Catholics believe that the devil is an angelic person whose will is fixed forever in evil. When God created the angels, He made them good and gave them a share in His own divine life. But before they could enter heaven, they were tested by God. Some of the angels failed the test and sinned grievously against God. They are called evil spirits or "fallen angels." Their leader is named Satan (which in Hebrew means the Enemy), Lucifer, or simply the devil.

² The devil is a spiritual being who has no body and this is why we cannot see him. Because he has intelligence and free will, he is a personal being. He is evil through his own fault. He was good when created by God, but he freely made himself evil by abusing his freedom.

³ The devil is under God's control and cannot act without God's permission. He is allowed to incite us to sin (temptation), to enter human bodies and move the imagination and locomotive faculties (diabolical possession), and to torment people from without (diabolical obsession). However, he has no power over our free will. He can never force our consent to evil. Although the devil is clever and "as a roaring lion goes about seeking someone to devour" (1 Peter 5, 8), we should not be afraid of him for "God is faithful and will not permit you to be tempted beyond your strength, but with the temptation will also give you a way out that you may be able to bear it" (1 Cor. 10, 13).

⁴ If God destroyed the devil, he would violate the precious gift of freedom and deprive man of opportunities for virtue and merit. To destroy free beings would mean God's failure to fulfill the plan of creation. Besides, it is a far greater punishment for the devil to suffer eternally than to be snuffed out of existence. At the Last Judgment God will take from him all power and thrust him back, hopeless and helpless, into hell forever.

Does not the doctrine of the Trinity make three Gods? Where in the Bible can you find this absurd teaching? How can you dare to say that one is three and three are one?

¹ The doctrine of the Trinity is not absurd. It is the most mysterious truth of our faith. We cannot comprehend it for we should need God's own power of understanding to do that.

² The Trinity means that there are three divine persons in one God. "Make disciples of all nations, baptizing them in the name of the Father, and of the Son, and of the Holy Spirit" (Matt. 28, 19). The Father, Son, and Holy Spirit are three persons. The Father has sent His Son into the world (John 3, 16); the Son became man, lived on earth, and died for us (John 1, 14); the Holy Spirit came down upon the Church and is at work making us holy (Acts 2, 4). Each of these persons is truly God, for each has the one same divine nature. Each is infinitely holy and perfect, all-knowing, all-powerful, and eternal. Yet these three persons are only one God. They possess one divine knowledge, one divine love and one divine life.

³ There is no contradiction because the words *one* and *three* do not refer to the same thing. We say there is *one identical nature* completely possessed by *three distinct persons*. It is true that three persons who possess human nature are really three different men because the human nature in each is not numerically the same. But three persons who possess divine nature are not three different gods because the divine nature in each is numerically the same. How this can be we do not know. We accept its truth because we believe Jesus Christ. And we agree with St. Bernard of Clairvaux: "To wish to fathom this

mystery is boldness; to believe it is happiness; to realize it is everlasting life." It is this mysterious truth which distinguishes true Christianity from all other religions.

What is the Natural Law? Can it ever be changed? Why do not all people know and observe it?

[1] God rules all things in this world in accordance with eternal law which is the divine plan for the orderly activity of each thing in conformity with its own nature. When the eternal law guides the movements of irrational beings it is called the law of nature; when it directs the human acts of man it is called the natural law.

[2] Natural law, because it is inherent in man's rational nature, is the rule of right reason. So long as man acts according to right reason he is obeying the natural law, perfecting his nature, and moving to his proper end. And because man's nature cannot essentially change neither can the natural law. The natural law arises out of man's nature. It is simply the way he should act as God has made him.

[3] Everyone is aware of the basic precept of the natural law: do good and avoid evil. By the very fact a person possesses reason he knows this fundamental moral principle. Other precepts of the natural law follow logically from this basic precept and, to make it easier for individuals, God has formulated these natural human precepts in the Ten Commandments. Those who do not believe in God and who desire absolute independence of behavior argue endlessly about what human actions are or are not conformable to man's rational nature. Prejudice and passion often obstruct man's right use of reason and militate against the correct application of the natural law in regard to particular human actions performed under different circumstances.

SELECTED BIBLIOGRAPHY

COLEBURT, RUSSELL. *An Introduction to Western Philosophy.* New York: Sheed & Ward. 1957.

COLLINS, JAMES DANIEL. *God in Modern Philosophy.* Chicago: Regnery. 1959.

CORTE, NICOLAS. *Who Is the Devil?* New York: Hawthorn. 1958.

DANIELOU, JEAN. *God and the Ways of Knowing.* New York: Meridian Books. 1960.

D'ARCY, MARTIN C. *Pain of This World and the Providence of God.* New York: Longmans. 1953.

DOORNIK, N. G. M. VAN. *A Handbook of the Catholic Faith.* Garden City, N. Y.: (Image Books) Doubleday & Co. 1956.

FARRELL, WALTER. *The Devil.* New York: Sheed & Ward, 1957.

GARRIGOU-LAGRANGE, REGINALD. *The Trinity and God the Creator,* 2 *Vols.* St. Louis: B. Herder Book Co. 1952.

——— *God, His Nature and His Existence, 2 Vols.* St. Louis: B. Herder Book Co.

GILSON, ETIENNE. *Elements of Christian Philosophy.* Garden City, N. Y.: Doubleday & Co. 1960.

GUARDINI, ROMANO. *The Living God.* New York: Pantheon. 1957.

JOLIVET, REGIS. *The God of Reason.* New York: Hawthorn. 1958.

KNOX, RONALD A. *The Belief of Catholics.* Garden City, N. Y.: (Image Books) Doubleday & Co. 1958.

LUBAC, HENRI DE. *The Discovery of God.* New York: P. J. Kenedy & Sons. 1960.

MARITAIN, JACQUES. *Approaches to God!* New York: Harper & Bros. 1954.

MESSENGER, ERNEST. ed. *Theology and Evolution.* Westminster, Md.: Newman Press. 1952.

MOUROUX, JEAN. *I Believe.* New York: Sheed & Ward. 1960.

MURPHY, WILLIAM B. *God and His Creation.* Dubuque, Iowa: Priory Press. 1958.

PETIT, FRANCIS. *The Problem of Evil.* New York: Hawthorn. 1959.

PIAULT, BERNARD. *What Is the Trinity?* New York: Hawthorn Books. 1959.

PIUS XII, POPE. *Humani Generis* (Encyclical) in *Four Great Encyclicals.* New York: Paulist Press. 1961.

SHEED, FRANCIS J. *Theology for Beginners.* New York: Sheed & Ward. 1957.

SMITH, RAYMOND. *Establishing the Natural Law.* New York: Paulist Press. 1960.

——— *God Exists.* New York: Paulist Press. 1960.

PART II
Man

May a Catholic believe in evolution? Does not evolution contradict the teaching of the Bible? Can evolution be reconciled with the theistic and Christian theory of life? Has not evolution proved the animal descent of man?

[1] God is the Creator of all things, past, present and future. There can be no existence nor life apart from His causal power. The whole world and each thing in it are to be traced ultimately to God. Consequently, when Sir Julian Huxley dogmatically asserted, "The earth was not created. It evolved. So did all the animals and plants that inhabit it, including our human selves, mind and soul as well as brain and body" (Darwinian Centennial Celebration, Chicago, 1959), we think he was absolutely wrong. Catholics cannot accept his theory of evolution or any other atheistic theory that eliminates God from the evolutionary process.

[2] Evolution is one *possible method* God could have used in the production of living things. He could have, in the beginning, directly created one or several forms capable of evolving or developing into the various species of plants and animals which exist today. Scientists from their study of morphology, comparative anatomy, embryology, palaeontology and allied fields, have found sufficient evidence that evolution is *probable*. Research relating to this scientific hypothesis continues, but at the present time evolution has not yet been established as a scientific fact. There are still many "missing links" which have to be discovered and there are highly respected scientists who doubt if exact proof can ever be found.

³ The evolution of man presents a special problem by reason of his spiritual immortal soul. Catholics deny that the human soul has evolved from the soul of some animal. God directly creates each individual human soul at the moment He infuses it into the zygote produced by the joint action of the male sperm and the female ovum. But what about man's body? Catholics are free to accept its evolution from some pre-existing anthropoid, but they reasonably demand true scientific evidence before assenting.

⁴ The key question of human evolution is, "What is the origin of the body of the first man?" God may have formed it from already existing unorganized non-living matter or He may have used the existing body of an animal. Either method is compatible with the Biblical account because neither the sacred writer nor the Church has defined the precise meaning of the phrase, "slime of the earth."

⁵ The present position of Catholics is clearly expressed by Pope Pius XII in his Encyclical, *Humani Generis*, 1950, "the Teaching Authority of the Church does not forbid that in conformity with the present state of human sciences and sacred theology, research and discussions on the part of men experienced in both fields take place with regard to the doctrine of evolution, insofar as it inquires into the origin of the human body as coming from pre-existent and living matter—for Catholic Faith obliges us to hold that souls are immediately created by God. However, this must be done in such a way that the reasons for both opinions, that is, those favorable and those unfavorable to evolution, be weighed and judged with the necessary seriousness, moderation and measure and provided that all are prepared to submit to the judgment of the Church."

What is the human soul? When is the soul created? Is not the mind composed of a series of successive states? Have animals souls?

¹ The soul is the ultimate principle of our individual conscious life, the principle by which we feel, think and will. It is a substantial principle, subsisting in itself, and thus distinct from an accident, such as color, which is a mode or attribute of something else. The soul is a simple

substance, that is, it is not composed of separate parts; it is also a spiritual substance; its existence is independent of matter.

² The character of the soul is known by its acts. That I am a substantial self is a fact of immediate experience. Father Maher says: "That I am a real being, subsisting in myself; that I am immediately aware of myself as the subject of sensations, feelings and thoughts, but not one of them or all of them; that I am the cause of my own volitions; that I am distinct from other beings; that there is in me a self—that I am an *Ego* which is the center and source of my acts and states, the ultimate ground and subject of my thoughts and affections, is forced upon me by constant, intimate, immediate self-experience, with the most irresistible evidence. If it be an illusion, there is no belief or cognition, however clear or certain, that can claim assent" (*Psychology*, 463).

³ The mind is not composed of a series of successive events or states. On the contrary it has a permanent identity, which ever remains the same during all the varying modes of consciousness. The fact of memory proves this. I am absolutely certain that the *Ego* now writing these lines is the identical *Ego* that wrote the first edition of *The Question Box*. My memory could not give me this absolute assurance of both past and present happenings, if my mind were a mere succession of events or states.

⁴ The soul is a simple, spiritual substance possessing an activity absolutely alien and opposed to the nature of extended and material things. We are capable of forming abstract and universal ideas such as Truth, Goodness and Beauty; we can perceive the rational relations between ideas, making judgments and inferences, and conducting exact processes of inductive and deductive reasoning; we are capable of self-reflection, recognizing with ease the absolute identity of ourselves thinking about something, and ourselves reflecting upon that thinking self; we are possessed of free will, capable of self-determination, and untrammeled in our pursuit of truth, justice and righteousness. The spirituality of our thought, our volition and our self-consciousness is fundamentally opposed in kind to all the properties of things material and extended.

⁵ The animal soul on the contrary is intrinsically and essentially dependent on matter. The animal is incapable of forming abstract ideas, and manifests no spiritual activity whatever. It possesses neither intellect nor free will. It is ruled entirely by instinct and its activity is entirely limited to the sensible and the concrete. The animal soul, or principle of life, is, therefore, incapable of life apart from the body, and perishes with it.

⁶ The human soul is directly created by God. God gives existence to the soul at the very moment when it is to be united to the body produced by generation, because it is designed by God to form with that body one human nature. The Council of Vienne in 1311 defined that "the rational or intellectual soul is directly and essentially the form, that is, the life-giving principle, of the body." The divine origin of the soul is a most fundamental doctrine, which gives the lie direct to the theory of atheistic evolution. It is the basis of human dignity and man's worth.

Does not the soul which is born with the body also perish with it? Can you offer reasonable proof for the immortality of the soul? Did the Jews believe in the immortality of the soul? Why are you opposed to the doctrine of Reincarnation and Spiritism when they admit the immortality of the soul?

¹ Apart from the clear witness of revelation which is contained in both the Old and the New Testaments, there are many reasons which support the belief that the human soul does not perish with the body, but survives the corruption of the body and continues to exist independently.

² Throughout history mankind has universally believed in an after-life. The discovery of ancient tombs both in the Old World and the New has unearthed unquestionable evidence which supports this fact. The respect shown for the bodies of the dead, the religious rites and practices connected with their burial among widely disparate peoples and tribes during all periods of history, including the present, points unmistakingly to a universal belief in the survival of the soul.

³ Furthermore, the strong craving of human nature to

possess lasting happiness which, because of its short dura-
tion, cannot be satisfied in this life, seems to require that
there be a life after death during which this desire will
be satisfied. All men seek happiness; some seek it in
riches and possessions; others in the pleasures of the flesh.
Many men attain a certain amount of happiness in this
life. But sooner or later an awareness of life's incom-
pleteness and vanity comes to every man. He realizes the
truth of St. Augustine's words: "Thou hast made us for
Thyself, O God, and our hearts cannot find rest until
they rest in Thee."

⁴ The fact of conscience may also be offered as a proof
for the immortality of the soul. If there is no future life,
why should any man heed the dictates of his conscience
to do what is right and avoid what is wrong. Why should
he be disturbed, and what man is not, when it reprimands
him for his evil deeds. Why have regard for law if there
is no punishment for the lawbreaker? If life ends with
death, why preach patience to the poor, justice to the rich,
purity to the sensual, or humility to the proud? Man's
natural awareness of the distinction between right and
wrong is an implicit confirmation of the immortality of
his soul.

⁵ Lastly, the fact of the soul's immortality can be demonstrated from the activity of the soul. The activity of any
being reveals its nature. A flower blossoms, a duck swims
and quacks, a dog barks, etc. Accordingly, we can describe
a flower as something which blossoms, a duck as something
which swims and quacks and a dog as something that
barks. Similarly, man is a thinking being. He is capable
of forming abstract and universal ideas such as Truth,
Goodness, and Beauty. He can draw logical inferences
and make judgments from combinations of ideas. He is
also capable of self-reflection, that is, of thinking not
only of beauty, but of reflecting on the fact that he is
presently thinking about beauty. He is even capable of
double and triple reflections, that is, he can think of himself thinking of himself thinking about beauty. Such
activities as these are totally alien to material beings. For
material beings are always individual, never abstract or
universal. Nor is anything material capable of reflecting

upon itself. An eye cannot see itself, nor can a lap sit upon itself. Unlike material beings, the soul is an immaterial or spiritual being. Unlike material beings the soul is not made up of parts; it is rather a simple substance which cannot therefore cease to exist, as all material bodies do, by the separation or disintegration of its parts. Consequently, the soul cannot perish with the body; it survives the phenomenon which we know as death.

⁶Although the Jewish notion of immortality became more and more precise as the history of their people advanced, it cannot be denied that they held a belief in an after-life, however vague, from a very early period. Several pertinent texts can be found in the book of Psalms. Here are two examples: "Therefore my heart is glad and my soul rejoices, my body, too, abides in confidence; because you will not abandon my soul to the nether world, nor will you suffer your faithful one to undergo corruption" (Ps. 15, 9-10). "But God will redeem me from the power of the nether world by receiving me" (Ps. 48, 16).

⁷More precise notions of immortality can be found in some of the later books of the Old Testament. In the second book of Machabees, for example, we find the following passage: "For if he had not hoped that they who were slain should rise again, it would have seemed superfluous and vain to pray for the dead. And because he considered that they who had fallen asleep with godliness had great grace laid up for them, it is therefore a holy and wholesome thought to pray for the dead that they may be loosed from sins" (2 Mach. 12, 44-46; *see* also chapter 7).

⁸In the book of Wisdom, which was written approximately 100 years before the birth of Christ, we read: "But the souls of the just are in the hand of God, and no torment shall touch them. They seemed, in the view of the foolish, to be dead; and their passing away was judged an affliction and their going forth from us, utter destruction. But they are in peace. For if before men, indeed, they be punished, yet is their hope full of immortality" (Wis. 3, 1-4).

⁹Both Reincarnation and Spiritism, though very different from one another, admit the survival of the soul. To this extent they are correct and in conformity with the

Catholic doctrine on this point. Beyond that initial point, however, each of them falls into errors which contradict Catholic doctrine.

10 Reincarnation is the doctrine which teaches that the soul inhabits a plurality of bodies consecutively. It is a very ancient belief and has been found in many parts of the world in almost every period of history. Currently it does not seem to be held to any significant extent anywhere in the world except among the Buddhists and Hindus of India. Belief in the reincarnation of the soul is usually linked to the notion of punishment. This is based on the platonic teaching that the soul is united to matter because of some fault which it committed in a previous existence. This union with matter is an evil for the soul, and the soul's beatitude will consist in finally freeing itself from matter. This is directly contrary to Christian teaching. The Church considers matter to be not an evil but a good, for matter was created by God, and God has created nothing which is not good. Accordingly, the Church teaches the final resurrection of the body and its reunion with the soul for all eternity. Reincarnation also contradicts the Christian teaching that each human soul is directly created by God out of nothing at the moment at which He infuses it into the human body.

11 The Catholic rejects the doctrine of reincarnation first because it contradicts the revealed truth as expressed by the Church, but also because it is a mere hypothesis to the support of which no scientific demonstrations have been brought.

12 Spiritism is the belief in, and practice of, systematic communication with the spirits of the dead. Like Reincarnation it is a very ancient belief and was condemned in the Law of Moses: "Let there not be found among you anyone . . . who consults ghosts or spirits or seeks oracles from the dead." (Deut. 18, 11; *see* also Ex. 22, 17; Lev. 19, 31; 20, 6; Is. 8, 19.) In modern dress it is the same pagan necromancy practiced in pre-Christian times. The alleged communication with the dead is procured through numerous and sometimes extraordinary means: the movement of inanimate objects without physical contact, levitations, spirit photography, table-rappings in answer to

questions, slate-writing, etc. Frequently, civil authorities have exposed such phenomena to be fraudulent. Apart from the possibility of fraud these phenomena may be explained often by natural means such as telepathy or suggestion. The possibility of diabolism cannot be excluded, however, and this lends a most dangerous dimension to the practice of spiritism. Accordingly, the Catholic Church has often condemned it and forbids Catholics to have anything to do with it. A decree of the Holy Office of the Catholic Church dated April 24, 1917, forbids Catholics "to be present at spiritistic communications and manifestations of every kind, with or without a Medium, even though they appear to be good and honest; either by interrogating souls or spirits, or hearing their answers, or by simply looking on, even though one tacitly or expressly protests that he does not wish to have anything to do with evil spirits."

May not the freedom of the will be an illusion and determinism the only true philosophy? Is not your theory of motiveless volition contrary to facts? Is it not true that the strongest motive always prevails?

[1] Free will is the capability of self-determination; it is "that property in virtue of which a rational agent, when all the conditions required to elicit a volition are present, can either put forth or abstain from that volition" (Maher, *Psychology*, 395).

[2] Free will is not "motiveless volition." It does not imply choice *without* motive, but choice *between* motives. It is not true that we always act on the strongest motive, for many men resist time and time again, the onslaughts of a violent temptation. The only reason we can have for calling the motive on which we act the strongest is the fact that we act upon it. The objection is either untrue, or it resolves itself into the harmless statement: The motive which prevails does prevail.

[3] The fact of free will we know by direct consciousness, just as we know our own identity. We are aware that we can freely guide our own thoughts, selecting, if we choose, the least attractive. We are aware that, when two alterna-

tive courses of action lie before us, we can freely deliberate upon their respective merits, reflecting, inquiring, and examining the reasons for each side. We are conscious that our final choice is free: we can purchase a Buick or a Chevrolet car; we can invest our money in railroad stock or industrials; we can resist or consent to an evil thought.

⁴ The moral consciousness of mankind points to the freedom of the will. The sense of moral obligation is written in every man's heart; it is as certain as the uniformity of nature. We know that we are bound to do right and to avoid wrong. We know also that we are free to avoid evil. Is it not unreasonable for the determinist to tell us that these solid convictions are mere illusions?

⁵ Again, we always carefully distinguish between what we do inadvertently and what we do deliberately. No man feels any remorse or compunction for an action he could not possibly avoid. It cannot be imputed to him for either praise or blame. But if having committed a deliberate crime, he afterwards condemns it as sinful and blameworthy, he does so only because he is convinced that he acted freely and without compulsion. The determinist knows nothing of remorse or blame, for as William James says, "He virtually defines the universe as a place in which what *ought* to be is impossible" (*The Will to Believe,* 61).

⁶ The idea of merit supposes free will. "When I have struggled against a difficult temptation, or made some deliberate sacrifice in the cause of virtue, I feel that my act is meritorious, that I have deserved a reward. I may see no prospect throughout my life of receiving the recompense. But I am none the less assured that I have established a right to it, and that such a recompense is just. And this I judge to be so because I believe that act to be free. . . . The good accomplished unwittingly, however useful, is not meritorious on the part of the agent; praise or esteem which I may receive for it, I recognize in my heart to be undeserved" (Maher, *Psychology,* 402).

⁷ No reasonable man can honestly deny that he is not free in some of his acts. All his internal and external experience belies absolute determinism of behavior. Those who today deny human freedom are merely parroting the outmoded scientific theories of the 19th century. They

have failed to keep posted on scientific progress in the 20th century. "Science has no longer any unanswerable arguments to bring against our innate conviction of free will" (James Jeans, *The Mysterious Universe*). "The revolution of theory which has expelled determinism from present-day physics has therefore the important consequence that it is no longer necessary to suppose that human actions are completely determined" (Arthur Eddington, *New Pathways in Science*).

[8] True science refuses to be a hostile witness against man's freedom while true philosophy offers convincing testimony and evidence that man is the master of his life. Both regard determinism as a pessimistic view of man, destructive of morals and praiseworthy accomplishments. Reducing man to a mere automaton and a slave of his physical mechanism and social environment, it denies the essential notion of responsibility for human progress and scorns the free homage of mind, will, and heart which we owe our Creator and Lord.

Catholic philosophers teach us that "death is natural to man" and Catholic theologians tell us that "death is the wages of sin." Can you explain this contradiction?

[1] There is no contradiction. The philosopher looks at the nature of man while the theologian looks at the history of man. By nature man is mortal because he has a body and a soul capable of being separated by outside causes. When this separation actually takes place at death he ceases to be a man. However, when God created the first man he bestowed upon him the gift of immortality, not only for himself but for all his descendants. God would keep man's body and soul together forever. Unfortunately, man lost this special gift by committing Original Sin. Consequently, in the present order of things, in the context of history, man is subject to death not by reason of his nature but because of sin. Had he not used his nature to sin against God, death would have no dominion over him.

[2] Although man lost his immortality, Christ regained it for all men by his conquest of death (death plus resur-

rection). At death man's body dies and decomposes and his soul lives on in hell, purgatory, or heaven. At the *Parousia* or end of the world the resurrected Christ will unite each man's body to his soul. At that moment man will become immortal and he will never taste death again. He will live forever either in hell or in heaven.

SELECTED BIBLIOGRAPHY

AQUINAS, ST. THOMAS. *Soul*. St. Louis: B. Herder Book Co. 1949.

BIOT, RENE. *What Is Life?* New York: Hawthorn Books. 1959.

BRENNAN, ROBERT E. *Image of His Maker*. Milwaukee: Bruce Publishing Co. 1956.

CORTE, NICOLAS. *The Origin of Man*. New York: Hawthorn. 1958.

COLLIN, REMY. *Evolution*. New York: Hawthorn Books. 1959.

HESBURGH, THEODORE MARTIN. *God and the World of Man*. Notre Dame, Ind.: University of Notre Dame Press. 1960.

MORRIS, HILAIRE. *Philosophy for Beginners*. Westminster, Md.: Newman Press. 1960.

MOUROUX, JEAN. *The Meaning of Man*. New York: Sheed & Ward. 1958.

ONG, WALTER J. *Darwin's Vision and Christian Perspectives*. New York: Macmillan. 1960.

PIUS XII, POPE. *Humani Generis* (Encyclical) in *Four Great Encyclicals*. New York: Paulist Press. 1961.

PONTIFEX, MARK. *Freedom and Providence*. New York: Hawthorn Books. 1960.

RUFFINI, ERNESTO. *The Theory of Evolution Judged By Reason and Faith*. New York: J. Wagner. 1959.

SHEED, FRANCIS J. *Theology and Sanity*. New York: Sheed & Ward. 1946.

STAAB, GILES J. *The Dignity of Man in Modern Papal Doctrine*. Washington: Catholic University of America Press. 1957.

STRASSER, STEFAAN. *The Soul in Metaphysical and Empirical Psychology*. Pittsburgh: Duquesne University. 1957.

TEILHARD DE CHARDIN, PIERRE. *The Phenomenon of Man*. New York: Harper & Bros. 1959.

VANN, GERALD. *The Heart of Man*. Garden City, N. Y.: (Image Books) Doubleday & Co. 1960.

WUELLNER, BERNARD J. *A Christian Philosophy of Life*. Milwaukee: Bruce Publishing Co. 1957.

PERIODICALS

Catholic Mind, Vol. 58, Sept.-Oct. 1960: *What About Evolution?*

Catholic Mind, Vol. 57, Nov.-Dec. 1959: *Theology and Evolution.*

PART III
Religion

Is not reason a sufficient guide for a man? What need is there of a divine revelation?

[1] If you grant that God has created man for a supernatural destiny, you must admit that He has revealed that destiny to us, together with the means of attaining it. But a divine revelation is morally necessary to observe even the precepts of the natural law. Reason alone can prove the existence of God, the freedom of the will, and the immortality of the soul. But while some few may attain to a knowledge of moral and religious truth, the majority of mankind need revelation as a sure and certain guide.

[2] The failure of unaided reason to give man an adequate knowledge of his duties toward himself, his fellowmen and God is evident, if we study the history of the pagan nations prior to the coming of Christ. Cicero tells us that nothing was too absurd for a philosopher's creed (*De Div.*, ii., 58), and he often alludes to the ignorance, uncertainty and contradictions of the teachers of his time, as well as to the immoral character of their lives (*Qu. Tusc.*, ii., 4; iii., 12). Skepticism about the gods reigned among the cultured classes, although they defended the immoral, public worship of idolatry as a State necessity, the better to control the people (*De Rep.* 4). Widespread superstition, the usual accompaniment of unbelief, made the trade of augur and soothsayer a lucrative profession, and many truths of the primitive revelation were travestied by the current degrading myths and fables. Plato, one of the greatest of the Greeks, did not hesitate to uphold slavery, to recommend

38

the exposure of sickly children, and to tolerate the grossest form of immorality.

3 "The difficulties," writes Joyce, "in the attainment of the requisite knowledge are insuperable. For men to be able to attain such a knowledge of the natural law as will enable them to order their lives rightly, the truths of that law must be so plain that the mass of men may discover them without long delay, and possess a knowledge of them which shall be alike free from uncertainty and secure from serious error. No reasonable man will maintain that in the case of the greater part of mankind this is possible. Even the most vital truths are called in question. The separation of truth from error is a work involving time and labor. For this the majority of men have neither inclination nor opportunity. Apart from the security which revelation gives they would reject an obligation both irksome and uncertain" (*C. E.*, xiii., 3).

4 Jesus Christ was the answer to the world's longing for a divine, infallible revelation. He taught men clearly the purpose of their existence, the nature of God, and His love for men, the divine meaning of suffering and temptation, the malice of sin and the need of atonement, the sanction of an everlasting reward and punishment. What Christ revealed His Church teaches, as His divine, infallible representative, until He come again.

Cannot a man be moral by obeying his conscience, even if he does not believe in God? Is not virtue its own reward? Is it not enough to obey the positive laws of civil society?

1 No, for conscience is simply the practical reason, determining what is right and wrong in human actions. It is by no means infallible, but may lead men astray in morals, as it may lead them astray in telling them how to invest their money. If you divorce morality from religion, and deny that God is the basis and sanction of the moral law, reason becomes a blind guide, subject to public opinion, caprice, passion or prejudice, and the commanding power of conscience loses its validity and force. Once you admit the existence of God—Creator, Lord and Final End—you admit a Supreme Power possessed of an absolute right to

command an inferior, dependent creature, who in justice is bound to obey his Lord, and fulfill the end for which he was created.

² All law supposes a superior. The modern agnostic theory that each man's reason originates the moral laws by which he is bound, is contrary to reason, revelation and common sense. No man can be superior to himself, or regard himself as his own superior.

³ To ask a man to be moral without believing in God would be something like expecting someone to carry on a business successfully without admitting or accepting a standard for weights, measures or currency. By morality is meant conforming one's conduct to right principles. God alone can and has made known what these principles are and it is He alone who will "render to every man according to his works" (Rom. 2, 6).

⁴ Positive laws of civil society vary both in time and location and they are frequently contrary to the divine law. The same is true of the dicta of any philosophy that substitutes man or the State for God. Hedonism, Communism, Ethical Culture, Humanism, Subjectivism and the rest can neither promulgate or sanction an absolute norm of right living. Without God morality has no stable basis. Even Plato said: "He who destroys religion overthrows the foundation of human society."

⁵ As for virtue being its own reward—a little observation and reflection will reveal that many a virtuous person suffers adversity, even martyrdom; whereas many a rogue enjoys all the comforts of this world.

Is not religion a question of education and environment rather than a matter of intellectual conviction?

¹ It is true that many men are Catholics, Protestants or unbelievers because their parents were so before them, or because of their early training. But the Catholic Church teaches that faith is an act of the intellect based on rational motives of credibility that will stand any test. Given a desire for the truth, a prayerful longing for the grace of God which is never denied those who humbly ask it, a man can readily counteract the false teachings of an irre-

ligious environment or an anti-Catholic education. The Vatican Council thus describes faith: "Seeing that man wholly depends upon God as his Creator and Lord, and seeing that created reason is entirely subject to the Uncreated Truth, we are bound to submit by faith our intellect and will to God the Revealer. But this faith, which is the beginning of man's salvation, the Church confesses to be a supernatural virtue, whereby, with the help of God's grace, we believe what He reveals, not because we perceive its intrinsic truth by the natural light of our reason, but on account of the authority of God, who can neither deceive nor be deceived."

2 If one's education and environment happen to be in accord with divine truth, we are humbly grateful to God, and we do our utmost to live in accord with its teachings. But if, by the grace of God, a man comes to realize that he is an alien to the true Church, he is bound in conscience to search and inquire, until he know the truth of God.

Is not religion a mere question of feeling or emotion? I have been present at revival meetings, and the amount of religion present was in direct proportion to the excitement caused?

1 No, you must not judge Christianity from the excesses of emotional revival meetings. The Catholic Church has always protested against a religion of pure subjective feeling, which, under stress of nervous excitement, makes the emotions take the place of rational supernatural faith.

2a The Catholic Church, while answering every need of the human heart, safeguards her children against all emotional and sentimental delusion, by declaring faith an intellectual act guided by an upright will, and aided always by God's grace. Conversion does not consist in emotional feeling, but in the acceptance of all God's truth on His word, a heartfelt sorrow for sins committed with a confession thereof to the priest as the ambassador of God (*Cf.* 2 Cor. 5, 20).

3 The substitution of sentiment for faith was the great mistake of the 16th century revolt.

*Is it not true that the Christian gospels are based upon
the older religion of Buddhism? Does not the study of
comparative religions prove that Buddhism is in no way
inferior to Christianity?*

[1] It is most illogical to assume that resemblances always
imply dependence. The similarities often cited to prove
that Christianity borrowed from Buddhism, such as the
asceticism of its monks, the celibacy of the clergy and the
like, may be accounted for by the fact that men everywhere
have practically the same experiences, feelings and desires.
The similarities in the lives of our Lord and Gotama are
to be traced to Buddhistic borrowings. For while there is
no evidence whatever to prove the spread of Buddhism
westward to the Greek world as early as the beginning of
the Christian era, it is certain that Christianity reached
India in the first two centuries.

[2] Much of Gotama's life and actual doctrine is mere
conjecture, for the Buddhist sacred books come down to
us for the most part only from the year 300. They are far
inferior to our Bible in spirituality, thought and subject.

[3] Buddhism is far inferior to Christianity as a religion,
for not recognizing man's dependence upon an infinitely
loving God, it makes salvation rest solely on personal
effort. It is utterly lacking in the strong Christian motives
for right conduct, and is at best a selfish utilitarianism. Its
doctrine of *Karma* with its imaginary reincarnations is an
unnatural superstition, adverse to sound morality and true
religion. Its utter pessimism, which declares every form of
conscious existence an evil, is contrary to the instincts of
human nature, and its promise of the unconscious repose
of Nirvana is devoid of the hope and joy of the Christian's
eternal reward of the beatific vision.

*Is not one religion as good as another? Are not creeds in
themselves unimportant, and conduct the one thing essential? Do we not frequently meet men who believe in Christ
and all His teachings, and yet day by day do things that
would bring a blush to a pagan's cheek?*

[1a] One of the most common dogmas outside the Catholic
Church in our day and country is the dogma of indifferent-

ism. The indifferentist will speak patronizingly of religion
as a police force to keep the discontented in check, or as
an outlet for the emotions of pious sentimentalists. He
will praise all religions for the virtuous men they have
produced; he will maintain that intelligence and good
breeding alike call for a kindly toleration toward all creeds
and Churches; he will vehemently denounce the Catholic
Church as bigoted, intolerant and autocratic, because as
the infallible mouthpiece of a divine revelation she claims
obedience under sin. There are many roads, he informs
you, leading to the kingdom of heaven, and an honest
man may travel any one of them with the conviction that
he is pleasing God.

² You meet the indifferentist everywhere. In educational
matters he is a secularist, who marvels at the determined
effort made by Catholics to educate their children in separate Catholic schools; in politics he wants the State to
ignore religion entirely, and becomes indignant when
Church and State work together for the common good;
in social questions he advocates many principles subversive
of Christian morality, and tells the Church to keep her
hands off such questions as divorce, birth control, labor
problems and such like issues. In religion he believes that
all creeds are equally true and equally helpful—perhaps,
down in his heart equally false—and that their acceptance
or rejection is as unimportant as the cut of a man's clothes
or the customs of his peculiar nationality.

³ The Catholic Church condemns in most unequivocal
terms this modern dogma of indifferentism. She asserts
that it is the most subtle enemy of religion, harder to combat successfully than the most bitter prejudice and bigotry.
A man who hates the Catholic Church because he thinks
she stands for everything unintelligent, ignoble and autocratic, may be led to love her, once he learns that he has
been misled by the parents he loves and the teachers he
respects. A good hater like St. Paul, who, as he says himself, acted "ignorantly and in unbelief," became after his
conversion, one of the greatest lovers of Jesus Christ. But
an indifferentist, who declares God indifferent to truth
simply because he himself is indifferent, and who glories
in a self-made religion free of all obligation and restraint,

is hardly apt to consider the claims of a divine, infallible teaching Church, which requires absolute faith in all the revelation of God, and enforces her divine doctrine and law under penalty of sin.

⁴ Is it not strange, however, that the very man who worries night and day over his business troubles, and who sacrifices health and comfort in his pursuit of money, political preferment, or the interests of science should at the same time be utterly indifferent to the truth of God?

⁵ The assertion that one religion is as good as another is irrational. It is a first principle of reason that two contradictory statements cannot both be true. If one is true, the other is undoubtedly false. Either there are many gods or one God; either Jesus Christ is God or He is not; Mohammed is either a prophet or an impostor; divorce is either allowed or prohibited by Christ; the Eucharist is the living Jesus Christ or it is mere bread.

⁶ On this theory a man ought to change his religion as he changes the cut of his clothes, according to his environment. He ought to be a Catholic in Italy, a Lutheran in Sweden, a Mohammedan in Turkey, a Buddhist in China.

⁷ Revelation, if it has any meaning, is a divine message which no one can reject without sin. We must receive it, as the Apostle says, "not as the word of men, but, as it truly is the Word of God" (I Thess. 2, 13). God, a God of Truth, could not possibly have revealed a plurality of religions, or a multitude of varying Christianities. He founded one Church, one Kingdom of God, one Sheepfold, under the perpetual and infallible guidance of Himself and the Holy Spirit.

⁸ Jesus Christ commanded His Apostles to teach a definite Gospel, and condemned those who knowingly rejected it. "Preach the Gospel to every creature. He who believes and is baptized shall be saved, but he who does not believe shall be condemned" (Mark 16, 15-16). He prophesied that many would gainsay His teaching, but He denounced them in unmeasured terms. "Beware of false prophets, who come to you in sheep's clothing, but inwardly are ravening wolves" (Matt. 7, 15).

⁹ The history of Christianity in every age shows how alien to Christ is the dogma of indifferentism, which was

first popularized by the English Deists and the French Rationalists of the 17th century. In the first three centuries the Christian martyrs died by the thousands, rather than save their lives by a profession of indifferentism. Frequently they were asked by friends and relatives to sacrifice to the gods of pagan Rome, or at least to allow their names to be written down as having sacrificed. "What difference does it make?" asked their pagan friends. They answered in the words of Christ: "Therefore, everyone who acknowledges Me before men, I also will acknowledge him before My Father in heaven. But whoever disowns Me before men, I in turn will disown him before My Father in heaven" (Matt. 10, 32-33).

[10] It is one thing for a man to accept the teachings of Christ as true and yet fail to observe these teachings in his conduct. It is quite another thing for an indifferentist to assert that Christ does not care what we believe. How can we please God and do His will on earth if we refuse to believe what He teaches?

Why does the God of truth allow so many religions in the world? As all these religions claim to be true, and a man has not the time to study them all, is not the position of a skeptic or an agnostic perfectly reasonable?

[1] We readily admit that the existence of so many false religions is a great evil, difficult to explain. But because our finite minds cannot fully enter into the secrets of God, must we therefore deny His all-ruling Providence?

The only solution to the problem lies in the mystery of Original Sin, which weakened men's minds and wills, and left them subject to error and sin. St. Paul speaks of pagans who through personal sin "became vain in their reasonings, and their senseless minds have been darkened. For while professing to be wise, they have become fools, and they have changed the glory of the incorruptible God for an image made like to corruptible man and to birds, four-footed beasts and creeping things" (Rom. 1, 21-23).

[2] The existence of many false religions should not cause a thinking man to be a skeptic or an agnostic. A counterfeit coin always points to a true original. There

is always a way of telling the true coin from the false. Divergent views spur on the man of science to further study, so that the working hypotheses of today may become the true facts and certain principles of the morrow.

[3] If a man, therefore, is without faith, he ought not to shrink cowardly from studying the problem of the true religion. His reason will tell him that God exists; that God is good and true and loving: that God has spoken His revelation to the creatures He has made. His reason will tell him that the New Testament is a book unique among all the books of the world, and that Jesus Christ, whose life it records, said things and did things that no mere man could say or do. If he studies conscientiously, and prays humbly and perseveringly for divine guidance, God will give him grace to know which religion is the true one. He is under no more obligation to study them all than the scientist is bound to study the rejected theories of science.

[4] Why not study the one religion which claims to teach the entire content of divine revelation? The Catholic Church has fulfilled the prophecies of the Old Law, she has weathered centuries of persecution, she has proved her divine witness by many miracles, she has won men's intellects by the sublimity of her doctrine, and has won their hearts by the holiness of her teaching and her saints.

Does not the Bible say that "God is not a respecter of persons: But in every nation he who fears Him and does what is right is acceptable to Him" (Acts 10, 34-35)? Does not this plainly imply that a good and charitable pagan like the centurion could be saved without bothering about creeds or doctrines?

[1] There is not the slightest trace of the dogma of indifferentism in this passage. St. Peter is insisting upon the universal character of the Church, and teaching that God excludes no one from His Messianic Kingdom, whether Jew or Gentile.

[2] He does not imply that the pagan is saved by his piety and his natural virtues, but that he is pleasing to God, because he is well prepared to receive the grace of

God, and thus enter His true Church, regardless not of his religion, but of his nationality.

[3] In this same sermon, St. Peter tells his hearers of the necessity of faith and sorrow for sin (Acts 10, 43), and he insists on their belief in Christ's divinity, miracles, death on the cross, His Resurrection, His coming one day to judge mankind, His fulfillment of the Old Testament prophecies (Acts 10, 34-43).

[4] Once Cornelius saw the truth of the Gospel he at once embraced it, and was received into the Church by St. Peter.

Are not all Christians agreed on essentials? I believe in accepting the fundamental teachings of Christ, and setting aside the petty details of dogma.

[1] This distinction between fundamental and non-fundamental doctrines was invented by Jurieu (*Le Vrai Système de l'Eglise*), to offset the evident lack of unity in the Protestant Churches in government, doctrine and worship. It has no Scriptural warrant; it is not mentioned even once in Christian tradition. Indeed its supporters could not agree among themselves either on the criteria required, or on the doctrines to be accepted.

[2] St. Augustine in the 5th century answered this objection in his controversy with the Donatists of North Africa. He writes: "Both of us have baptism, in that we are united. We have the same Gospel; in this we are united. They celebrate with us the feasts of martyrs; in this we also agree. . . . But they are not with us in all things. They are not with us in their schism; they do not agree with us in their heresy. And by reason of those few things in which they are not with us, the many things on which they are avail them nothing" (*The Unity of the Church,* ch. iii.).

Should not a man be perfectly impartial in his study of the Christian evidences, and not be carried away by a wish to believe?

[1a] If by impartiality you mean a mere abstract interest in the problem of religion, the inquirer being perfectly indifferent whether the issue of his search be faith or

agnosticism, I would answer that such an attitude of mind is fatal to all earnest study. For while on the one hand, a thinking man ought not to be carried away by mere feeling, he must realize that he cannot face the religious problem as he would a theorem in geometry. The religious inquirer knows that the result of his search will affect his happiness here and his eternal welfare hereafter.

² The existence of God, the immortality of the soul, the divinity of Christ, the Redemption, the Church, the sacraments, the sanction of reward and punishment—these are truths which must be viewed in their practical bearing. There must be a strong desire to know what reason affirms and what revelation teaches. This supposes a will to believe, which does not make us blindly accept these truths out of mere emotionalism, but makes the seeker after truth careful and critical in his weighing of the evidence.

³ A person who enters the Catholic Church merely from aesthetic or emotional feelings, will rarely persevere. For while the certitude which gives assurance to the claims of faith is subjective, its every element has its objective counterpart. Without solid motives of credibility, such as miracles and prophecy, we cannot have that moral certitude which leads to faith.

What scientific proof is there of the divine origin of Christianity? The facts of science can be proved or tested, but what proof have you of things invisible and incomprehensible? I am willing to accept only what I can prove.

¹ A thinking man who is exercising faith every day in his business, intellectual and social life will not demand of Christianity a proof impossible in the nature of things, but will reasonably investigate the reliability of the authority which claims to voice infallibly the truths of God. He will not ask experimental proof for divine revelation which is over and above reason, but simply ask: What evidence is there that Christ is the Son of God, and His Church divine? He will calmly set aside all passion and prejudice, and study with humility and earnestness the evidences of Christianity: the argument from miracles and prophecy, the absolute perfection of Christ, the unique character of

His sublime teaching, the fact of His Resurrection, the marvelous spread and continuance of His Church despite every obstacle, the testimony of the martyrs, the lives of the Church's saints, and the striking transformation of the world effected by the Gospel.

² We believe that South Africa exists although we may never have been there, and that Caesar or Napoleon lived, although they died many years ago. We accept these truths simply on the authority of others. Although the testimony of men may at times be false because the witness is deceived or a deceiver; yet, no one ought reasonably to reject the principle of human evidence, any more than he ought to reject ocular testimony because a particular individual is short-sighted or color-blind.

³ Indeed, the very man who boasts of accepting nothing unless he can personally prove it, is daily giving the lie to his pet theory. Most of his knowledge depends not on personal investigation, but on the authority of others. No progress would be possible in any science or art unless a man started with the data gathered by his predecessors. Will an historian of universal history be able to read all the original documents? Will a physicist have time to test every experiment of his forebears? Will a lawyer be able to study every case in the reports, a geographer visit every country, a physician experiment with every drug, before he accepts anything as true? Life is too short and facts too many. And yet men illogically reject the idea of authority in religion. Is it not the way that most of us learn everything we know?

⁴ Frequently, too, the same man who accepts without question human, fallible, hesitating and ever varying authority, will refuse assent to a divine, infallible, certain, and unchanging authority. "If we receive the testimony of men, the testimony of God is greater" (1 John 5, 9).

I cannot accept Christianity, because it compels me to believe incomprehensible mysteries. My reason tells me not to believe anything that I cannot comprehend. Is not reason against faith, and must not one bind himself before he can accept such dogmas as the Trinity, the Incarnation, the Atonement and the Eucharist?

[1] You are most unreasonable if in the name of reason you refuse to accept the mysteries of Christianity. For there can be no contradiction between reason and faith, because God is the Author of both natural and supernatural truth. St. Thomas well says: "Although the doctrines of faith surpass the truths of human understanding, there can be no opposition between them. Both proceed from God in their respective orders of grace and nature. And the doctrines of faith become as indubitable through the evidence of the divine authority revealing them, as the primary truths of reason do through their self-evident testimony" (*Contra Gentiles,* i., 7)).

[2] The opposition between science and faith that we hear about so much today is only apparent. It originates either in the errors of scientists who put forth unprovable hypotheses as undoubted facts, or in the mistakes of theologians who teach their private false opinions as Gospel truths. If, as Pope Leo XIII remarked in his Encyclical *Providentissimus Deus,* both would remain within the confines of their own science, real opposition would become impossible.

[3] In fact, reason and faith are helpful to each other. Reason gives faith a solid foundation, so that we are not asked to give a blind assent to truths absolutely unknowable, and it also furnishes us strong extrinsic proofs of the content of divine revelation. Faith on the other hand, as Cardinal Newman says, "furnishes facts to the other sciences, which those sciences left to themselves would never reach; and it invalidates apparent facts, which, left to themselves, they would imagine" (*Idea of a University*).

[4] A moment's reflection will convince you that you are surrounded with mystery in this universe. Mystery is in no way peculiar to religion. Science and philosophy are also faced with mysteries, for man does not know everything about the universe or life. We even speak of the "mysterious universe" and the "mystery of life."

[5] In fact, man only comprehends what he has made himself. He can understand perfectly the mechanism of a watch, because it is his work. But his finite mind cannot comprehend the mysteries of God's world, either of nature

or of grace. Perfect comprehension and perfect intelligence belong to God alone.

[6] Belief in mysteries is of the very essence of religion. A divine revelation which would only tell us what we already know, or what we could readily discover for ourselves, would be utterly useless and meaningless. Only from God Himself can we learn about His inner Being (the Trinity), His Infinite condescension (the Incarnation), and His Infinite love of men (the Atonement; the Eucharist).

[7] Our assent to these dogmas is not a blind assent, but a perfectly reasonable assent, that rests solely upon the authority of God, who has revealed them to us. Unreasonable and blind indeed is the rationalist who, without weighing the evidence, refuses to accept divine truth.

[8] The Catholic's attitude to the supernatural mysteries of Christianity is most reasonable.

Is not faith a mere function of the will? Is it not to trust God to keep His promises?

[1] No, faith is an act of intellect directed by the will. It is to hold something to be true on the word of another. The thing itself does not convince us of its truth but the veracity of the person who tells us. To believe is to accept testimony of people.

[2] Supernatural faith is to believe what God has revealed. Both intellect and will must receive grace from God before a man can make an act of divine faith. "No one can came to Me unless the Father who sent Me draw him" (John 6, 44). Faith in God is a gift. "By grace you have been saved through faith; and that not from yourselves, for it is a gift of God" (Eph. 2, 8). The Vatican Council echoes this teaching of Scripture when it declares, "No person can assent to the Gospel teaching with a view to attain salvation, without the illumination and inspiration of the Holy Spirit."

[3] It is true that the will plays a most important part in the act of faith. Our Lord attributed the unbelief of the Jews to their hardness of heart and their obstinacy of will (Mark 3, 5; 3, 16; Luke 24, 25). A person must have the

will to believe. A good will puts aside all passion, prejudice, and human respect. It resolutely faces the problems of religion and does not cease its pursuit of the truth because the road is beset with difficulties. Many people fail to believe because the truth goes counter to their passions, imposes obligatory laws, demands great sacrifices, and puts definite limits to their independence.

⁴ To trust God to keep His promises is to exercise hope. To accept what God has revealed is to exercise faith.

Did not Luther, in his bold protest against the tyranny of the Catholic Church, uphold the rights of reason?

¹ On the contrary, no one ever rated reason so low as Luther, who believed and taught that Original Sin totally corrupted man and rendered human nature essentially evil. He told his followers at Wittenberg that they must hate reason as their greatest foe. Harnack warns us that "no one can despise reason with impunity, and Luther himself was punished by the darkening of his own views on faith."

² The Catholic Church has always championed the intrinsic worth and dignity of human nature. She proclaims the goodness of reason and free will as precious gifts of God to be used for the glory of God and for the salvation of man. She teaches that Original Sin did not vitiate human nature or destroy man's reason and freedom.

³ Reason is our natural guide to faith. If men could not acquire certitude of the preambles of faith such as the existence of God, the immortality of the soul, the freedom of the will, nor assent to the motives of credibility, the Catholic Church would appeal in vain to an unbelieving world, and the command of Christ to *teach* all nations would be a nightmarish travesty. Without faith it is impossible to please God, but without reason we cannot believe God's divine revelation. Faith is not something irrational; it is "a reasonable service" (Rom. 12, 1).

Does not St. Paul teach that a man is justified by faith? "We reckon that a man is justified by faith independently of the works of the Law" (Rom. 3, 28). And again: "Having been justified, therefore, by faith, let us have peace with God through our Lord Jesus Christ" (Rom. 5, 1).

[1] It is perfectly true that we are justified by faith, but not by faith "alone." We are justified by a faith that works through charity (Gal. 5, 6).

[2] Luther and Calvin held that justification was a purely external process. When the merits of Christ's Redemption were applied to the soul, no internal change took place in the sinner; he did not thereby become any better than he was before. His sins were merely covered by Christ's merits, which were imputed to him as though they were his own. This fundamental heresy, which struck at the very heart of Christianity, has no warrant in either the Gospels or in the Epistles of St. Paul, St. John and St. Peter. The Council of Trent declared against the Reformers that "justification is not merely the remission of sin, but the sanctification and renovation of the interior man by his voluntary acceptance of graces and gifts; whence the unjust is made just, the enemy a friend, that he be made the heir according to the hope of life everlasting" (Tit. 3, 7). . . . We are not merely reputed just (by a legal fiction), the Council adds, "but are so in name and fact, receiving in ourselves, everyone according to his measure, the justice which the Holy Spirit allots to everyone according as He will (1 Cor. 12, 11), and according to everyone's disposition and co-operation. For although no one can be just unless the merits of the passion of Christ be communicated to him, yet this communication takes place in the justification of the sinner when, by the merit of the said holy passion, the charity of God is diffused by the Holy Spirit in the hearts of those who are justified, and *is inherent in them*. Whence in the act of justification, with the remission of his sins, man receives all at once, through Christ, on whom he is ingrafted, the infused gifts of faith, hope and charity. For faith without hope or charity, neither unites man perfectly with Christ, nor makes him a living member of His Body."

[3] St. John describes the grace produced by justification as a new life, really communicated to the faithful (John 3, 5), implying freedom from sin (8, 34-36), and a divine peace that in Christ will overcome the world (14, 27). St. Paul calls our justification the resurrection of the soul (Col. 3, 1), which makes us the adopted sons of God, "heirs

of God, and joint-heirs with Christ" (Rom. 8, 16. 17). He identifies it with our "regeneration and renewal" by the Holy Spirit (Tit. 3, 5), and, in his striking parallelism between the first and the second Adam, he shows that Christ imparts justice to our souls just as truly as Adam transmitted Original sin (Rom. 5, 19).

Does not the Catholic doctrine of merit dishonor the Redemption of Christ, by ascribing salvation to one's personal efforts? Did He not teach that we have no claim to any reward? "When you have done everything that was commanded you, say: 'We are unprofitable servants; we have done what it was our duty to do'" (Luke 17, 10). Does not your teaching imply that God is under obligation to us, as a creditor to a debtor? Is not eternal life our inheritance, and a free gift of God? "For by grace you have been saved through faith; and that not from yourselves, for it is the gift of God; not as the outcome of works, lest anyone may boast" (Eph. 2, 8.9).

[1] Merit is the value attached by God to our good deeds, which we freely perform by the help of divine grace. The Church has always taught that the doctrine of merit rested, not, as Luther falsely asserted, on any absolute right to reward in the works themselves, but on the express promise of God to reward faithful service to Him by grace here and glory hereafter.

[2] It is indeed absurd to speak of God as our debtor, for our deeds can bring Him no advantage. We owe all we have and are to God. But the Scriptures plainly teach that if our good works are freely done in His honor and service, aided always by His divine grace, they are indeed meritorious according to His divine plan. All our merit is primarily His, for He won our right to grace and glory by His infinite merits, when He redeemed us by His passion and death.

[3] Eternal life is our inheritance as adopted sons of God, but it is also our reward. "Knowing that from the Lord you will receive the inheritance as your reward" (Col. 3, 24). Eternal life is a free grace, but that merely proves that grace is necessary to merit it. As St. Augustine says: "When

God crowns our merits, He crowns His own gifts" (*Epis.*, 194, 19).

⁴ The Council of Trent thus states the Catholic doctrine: "Eternal life is to be proposed to those who do good unto the end and hope in God, both as a grace mercifully promised to the children of God through Jesus Christ, and as a reward to be faithfully rendered to their good works and merits, in virtue of the promise of God Himself (2 Tim. 4, 7). . . . For since Christ Jesus Himself constantly communicated His virtue to those who are justified, as the Head to the members (Eph. 4, 15), and as the Vine to the branches (John 15, 4), which virtue always preceded, accompanied and followed their good works, and without which they could be nowise agreeable to God and meritorious; we must believe that nothing more is wanting to the justified, nor is there any reason why they should not be considered as having fully satisfied the divine law, as far as the condition of this life admits, by such works as are done in God, and truly merited the attainment of eternal life in due time, if they die in the state of grace."

Is human nature capable of reasoning about God, or of performing good deeds of itself? Was Calvin right in holding that all *the acts of sinners are sins? Can man of himself work out his own salvation? Can we be certain that we are saved souls?*

¹ The Catholic Church condemns equally the heresy of Pelagius, who taught that human nature of itself could perform all acts necessary to salvation, and the heresy of Calvin who held that *all* the acts of sinners were sins (Council of Trent). She has ever defended the rights of reason and human nature.

² The Catholic Church teaches that a knowledge of God and the moral law is within the reach of our natural powers (Vatican Council). The power of willing and of performing good works is instinctive to man. St. Paul says: "When the Gentiles who have no law do by nature what the Law prescribes, these, having no law are a law unto themselves . . . their conscience bears witness to them" (Rom. 2, 14. 15). God rewards the good deeds of the pagans

(Exod. 1, 21; Ezech. 29, 18), and our Lord recognizes the natural love and friendship of the pagans as something good (Matt. 5, 47).

[3] The grace of God, a supernatural gift bestowed upon us through the merits of Christ's passion and death, is absolutely necessary for us to attain eternal life.

[4] The gift of final perseverance is so much the gift of God, that the Council of Trent taught against Luther that, apart from some special revelation, we can never be sure of it "with absolute and infallible certainty." As St. Paul tells us, "Work out our salvation in fear and trembling" (Phil. 2, 12), and although he says "Be imitators of Me as I am of Christ," he adds: "I chastise My body, and bring it into subjection, lest perhaps after preaching to others I Myself should be rejected" (1 Cor. 4, 16; 9, 27).

How are miracles possible, when we know that the laws of nature are fixed and immutable? Is not a miracle a violation of nature's laws?

[1] It is good at the outset to define our terms. A law of nature is a uniform mode of acting which a natural agent observes under the same circumstances. Thus fire will always burn, and nitric acid will cauterize normal human skin; a broken bone will take some time to knit together; water will freeze at 32 degrees Fahrenheit and boil at 212 degrees; apple trees will bring forth apples, and "great oaks from little acorns grow."

[2] What is a miracle? An event that involves a change in this general order of things. It has been defined as "a sensible fact which is beyond the natural power of every created agency, and which manifests an immediate and extraordinary intervention of divine omnipotence."

[3] When God works a miracle, our scientific knowledge is just as true as it was before. The fact that iron is heavier than water remains generally true, even if God once made an axe-head to float" (4 Kings 6, 5-7); fire will generally burn, even if God once preserved His three faithful followers in Nabuchodonosor's fiery furnace (Dan. 3, 24).

[4] A miracle, therefore, is not a violation of nature's laws. God in certain rare instances simply intervenes to suspend

their ordinary activities for some divine, supernatural purpose.

Do not miracles argue a change in an unchangeable God?
Do they not violate the law of the conservation of energy?

[1] By no means. God knows, once and for all times, from all eternity, when and where He will produce a miracle. He does not make up His mind at the moment the miracle is produced. Being omnipotent and omniscient, God sees in His mind all actual creatures—present, past, and future—together with all the circumstances of their existence and of their actions. A miracle effects a change in the world but not in God.

[2] Only material and bodily things are subject to the physical laws of this world. It is true that we cannot add to the energy of the universe—we can only use it or change it from one form to another. But the universe is not closed to its Creator. It is ever open to His divine action.

May not miracles be due to certain unknown laws of nature? Has not modern science proved that things our forefathers would have deemed miraculous, have now become the commonplaces of everyday experience? Will not the science of the future render all miracles explainable by natural means?

[1a] Some pseudo-miracles of healing, rashly attributed to God's miraculous power, may be explained on the supposition that some unknown law may have produced them. But we know enough of nature's laws to distinguish the real miracle from the counterfeit. We know to a certainty, for example, that blindness is not cured by spittle (Mark 8, 23); that leprosy is not cured by the touch of a hand (Matt. 8, 3); that the dead do not arise at the sound of a voice (John 11, 43); that five thousand people cannot be fed with five loaves and two fishes (Matt. 14, 19).

[2a] The instantaneous character of many of the cures at Lourdes is positive proof against the hypothesis of unknown natural laws. These sick people at Lourdes undergo no sanitorium treatment, but prayerfully and humbly

ask God to work a cure through His Mother's intercession. The many cures effected cannot honestly be denied by any man who carefully weighs the evidence.

If we take into account the general unreliability of human testimony, how can any particular miracle be certainly proved? Does not the evidence in most cases come from simple-minded men, who are really incompetent to judge in such matters?

¹ We readily grant that some simple-minded souls, anxious for a cure, may be deceived regarding the supernatural character of their healing. That is the reason why the *Bureau des Constatations* was established at Lourdes as early as 1867 to distinguish scientifically the true from the counterfeit miracle.

² Since a miracle is a sensible fact, it can be known either by the testimony of the senses, or the testimony of reliable witnesses. The man in the street can testify as well as any scientist to the instantaneous cure of ten lepers (Luke 17, 11), or of a man blind from birth (John 9, 1); to Christ walking upon the sea (Matt. 14, 25), changing the water into wine (John 2, 1-10), or stilling the storm with a word (Matt. 8, 26).

Do not all religions claim their miracles? What special proving power, therefore, have the miracles of Christ and Christianity?

¹ª The alleged wonders of non-Christian religions can all be traced to fraud, hallucination, hypnotic suggestion, psychotherapy or diabolism; they are often absurd, ridiculous and meaningless legends and myths, utterly devoid of authenticity.

²ª Keeping in mind that a miracle is an extraordinary intervention of divine power, it would be unthinkable that the God of truth would show "a sign from heaven" to give support and lend credence to any religious teaching contrary to His revelation.

³ Our Lord Himself warned us that "many false prophets will arise, and will lead many astray (Matt. 24, 11);

and St. Paul tells us of the "lying wonders" of anti-Christ (2 Thess. 2, 9).

⁴ The miracles of Christ and of Christ's Church are, on the contrary, never meaningless or ridiculous, but evidence always of God's omnipotence, mercy, kindness, or justice.

⁵ Our Savior worked miracles to prove His divine mission and to establish the divine character of His revelation. He has allowed His saints to work miracles to prove their divine commission to speak in His name, and to give the world a clear proof of their eminent sanctity.

Must Catholics believe all the miracles recorded in the lives of the saints? I thought the age of miracles ended with the Apostles?

¹ Miracles did not end with the Apostles. Christ Himself promised that miracles would always be a mark of His true Church, and a gift He would always bestow upon His faithful followers, the saints (Mark 16, 17-18; John 14, 12). No unprejudiced man can read the testimony for the miracles of the saints canonized by the Apostolic See, and study the strict rules laid down by Pope Benedict XIV for the Church's guidance, without being convinced of their authenticity. Indeed evidence, which outsiders have considered convincing, has as a matter of fact been rejected by the Congregation of Rites at Rome as untrustworthy. The miracles wrought at Lourdes through the intercession of our Lady are always put to the severest tests of scientific scrutiny.

² Miracles are historical facts, and, therefore, are always to be weighed according to the rules of historical evidence. Catholics are not bound to accept the pseudo-miracles of the medieval chroniclers, or of modern pious sentimentalists, but they strenuously protest against that modern rationalistic prejudice, which refuses to consider any evidence for their happening, because of a false presupposition of their impossibility.

SELECTED BIBLIOGRAPHY

ADAM, KARL. *The Spirit of Catholicism.* Garden City, N. Y.: (Image Books) Doubleday & Co. 1954.

AQUINAS, ST. THOMAS. *Summa Contra Gentiles. On the Truth of the Catholic Church, 5 Vols.* Garden City, N. Y.: (Image Books) Doubleday & Co.

ARADI, ZSOLT. *The Book of Miracles.* New York: Farrar, Straus. 1956.

BARS, HENRY. *The Assent of Faith.* Baltimore: Helicon Press. 1960.

COGLEY, JOHN. (ed.) *Religion in America.* New York: Meridian Books. 1958.

CRISTIANI, LEON. *Why We Believe.* New York: Hawthorn. 1959.

DANIELOU, JEAN. *The Christian Today.* New York: Desclée. 1960.

D'ARCY, MARTIN C. *The Nature of Belief.* St. Louis: B. Herder Book Co. 1958.

DAWSON, CHRISTOPHER. *Religion and the Rise of Western Culture.* Garden City, N. Y.: (Image Books) Doubleday & Co. 1950.

ELIADE, MIRCEA. *Patterns in Comparative Religion.* New York: Sheed & Ward. 1958.

HURLEY, WILFRED G. *The Catholic Way of Life.* New York: Paulist Press. 1957.

JOLY, EUGENE. *What is Faith?* New York: Hawthorn. 1958.

LUBAC, HENRI DE. *Catholicism.* New York: Sheed & Ward. 1950.

MARTINDALE, C. C. *Faith of the Roman Church.* New York: Sheed & Ward. 1950.

NEILL, THOMAS P. *Makers of the Modern Mind.* Milwaukee: Bruce Publishing Co. 1958.

NOYES, ALFRED. *Unknown God.* New York: Sheed & Ward. 1940.

PHILIPPE, MARIE DOMINIQUE. *The Worship of God.* New York: Hawthorn Books. 1959.

PIUS XII, POPE. "The Mystical Body of Christ" (Encyclical) in *Four Great Encyclicals.* New York: Paulist Press. 1961.

TRESE, LEO J. *The Faith Explained.* Chicago: Fides. 1959.

VANN, GERALD. *Morals and Man.* New York: Sheed & Ward. 1960.

WEIGEL, GUSTAVE A. *Faith and Understanding in America.* New York: Macmillan. 1959.

PART IV
Sin

What is sin? Are not all sins equal in the sight of God? Is not this the teaching of the Scriptures? St. James says: "Whoever keeps the whole law, but offends in one point, has become guilty of all" (James 2, 10).

[1] Sin is the conscious and free transgression of the law of God, an express opposition to, and a contempt of, the divine will, a deliberate turning away from God as our ultimate end. It is the greatest of evils, because it deprives God of the honor due Him, and hinders man's attainment of his eternal destiny.

[2] Luther taught that all sins were of equal malice, and the distinction between mortal and venial sins absurd, because he erroneously held that even the smallest sin contained the deadly poison of concupiscence. His teaching was condemned by the Council of Trent. It is also contrary to reason and the Sacred Scriptures. Reason plainly declares there is a clear-cut difference between a sudden outburst of temper due to a nervous strain (a venial sin), and a deliberate sin of murder or adultery (mortal sin).

Are there not certain sins that God cannot pardon? Does not Christ speak of the sin against the Holy Spirit? Does not St. John speak of a "sin into death" (1 John 5, 16-17)? Does not St. Paul teach that "it is impossible for those who were once enlightened . . . and then have fallen away, to be renewed again to repentance" (Heb. 6, 4.6)?

[1a] No sin is unpardonable, absolutely speaking, either by God, or the Church that forgives in God's name. God

wishes all men to be saved (1 Tim. 2, 4), and His mercy is infinite. The contrite sinner will always be pardoned. The texts brought forward have reference to the sinner who refuses to repent, despite the graces God bestows upon him. That person does not actually receive God's pardon, because he does not ask it, or fulfill the conditions necessary for obtaining it.

Must Catholics accept the story of the apple and the serpent in Genesis literally? Why should such a trivial matter as eating an apple be punished so severely?

[1] The third chapter of the Book of Genesis teaches us that our first parents committed the first human sin (Original Sin). It was a grave sin involving pride and its severe consequences affected the whole human race.

[2] Although the writer knew that a sin had been committed, he did not know its exact nature or how it was actually committed. So, being a wise teacher, he described the sin by writing a "doctrinal play" and used his imagination for the setting and dialogue and action. He assigned the principal roles to God, Adam and Eve, and the devil.

[3] The "serpent" was probably introduced because it was familiar to his readers, who would easily recognize its use as an attack on the false forms of Chanaanite worship with its sexual abuses. By introducing the devil in the form of a serpent the writer was able to excoriate the sins of his own age. To the writer the devil was a real person—he chose the serpent as a symbol.

[4] There is no mention of an "apple" in the biblical account. This was introduced into popular thought by a mistranslation of Canticles, 8, 5. The description of the sin is symbolic. It did not consist in the plucking of fruit from a forbidden tree. The "eating" signifies the "sin" and it was the latter that was most serious and not "a trivial matter."

What do Catholics mean by the Fall of Adam? Does not your doctrine of Original Sin imply an unjust God who holds us responsible for Adam's sin?

[1] The Catholic Church teaches that Adam or the first man, as head of the human race, was endowed by God with sanctifying grace and with certain other special gifts, such as freedom from concupiscence, freedom from sickness and death, and knowledge consonant with his unique position. The continued possession of these gifts by Adam and his posterity was dependent on his obedience to a positive command proportionate to his knowledge and strength.

[2] Adam failed God, himself and us by deliberately committing sin. He "fell from grace." His sin was most grievous because there was in him neither ignorance nor concupiscence and he certainly knew what terrible consequences would ensue for himself and us. His was both a personal sin—he actually committed it (Original Sin in Adam)—and a sin of human nature—he committed it as head of mankind (Original Sin in us).

[3] The Council of Trent lists the consequences of Adam's sin as a personal sin: "The first man Adam, having transgressed the mandate of God in Paradise, at once lost the sanctity and justice in which he had been constituted; incurred, through the offense of his prevarication, the anger and indignation of God, and, therefore, the death with which God had previously threatened him, and together with death, captivity under the power of him who thenceforth had the empire of death, that is, of the devil; Adam, through the offense of that prevarication, underwent a complete change for the worse in body and soul."

[4] The same Council states the consequences of Adam's sin as a sin of nature: "If any one assert that the prevarication of Adam was hurtful to himself only, and not to his progeny; and that he lost for himself only, and not for us, the sanctity and justice received from God; or that being himself defiled by the sin of disobedience, he transmitted to all mankind only death and the sufferings of the body, but not the sin which is the death of the soul, let him be anathema, for he contradicts the Apostle."

[5] Original Sin is indeed a great mystery, which the human reason cannot fathom, but it does not imply any injustice on the part of God. Original Sin did not injure man in anything that was natural to him. All the super-

natural and preternatural gifts that Adam lost for himself and for us were not his or ours by right, but were given Adam gratuitously by God, on the one condition that Adam was to obey His easy commandment. "Original Sin is not an evil bias, a tendency to wrong, a taint in spirit or in flesh, a corruption of any part of human nature as such. Concupiscence, the natural activity of instincts or passions not subordinate to reason, is not Original Sin, but a consequence of it, even though it may lead, often enough, to actual sin" (Martindale, *The Faith of the Roman Church,* 84). There would have been injustice only if God had imputed to us another's personal sin, or had deprived us of something due to human nature.

My Church taught me in childhood that dancing, gambling of all kinds, and theater-going were sinful. I still think so after years of experience. Will you explain why your Church is so lenient in such matters?

[1] The Catholic Church teaches that sin is the greatest of evils, and that every Catholic should not only avoid it, but also the occasions of sin. An occasion of sin is an external circumstance, which leads one to commit sin. Any person, place or thing that generally leads us to commit sin becames a proximate occasion, that we are bound to avoid. If not, we freely choose the sin. God delights in seeing His people enjoy themselves in an innocent manner. His Church never has condemned dancing, card playing or theater-going in themselves as evil; she frowns on them only when they become proximate occasions of sin.

[2] Dancing among the Jews usually expressed the people's rejoicing, as the dancing of Mary and the women of Israel after the crossing of the Red Sea (Exod. 15, 20), of Jephte's daughter after her father's victory (Jud. 11, 34), of David before the Ark (2 Kings 6, 12-17). The modern dance for recreation and social fellowship is morally indifferent, although it may become an occasion of sin, if the dance is itself suggestive of immorality, if companions are wicked men and women or if excessive drinking is the rule.

[3] To play games of skill like golf or chess, or games of pure chance like poker or black-jack for a stake, is not in

itself sinful. I may lawfully spend my money for recreation, and give my neighbors some of it, if they prove more skillful or more lucky than myself. A game of poker becomes of interest only when some stake is in sight for the winners. Gaming becomes sinful, if we force a person to play against his will, if we cheat, if we stake money not our own, or use money needed for our debts or for the support of our families.

4 Betting also is not sinful in itself, if the event at issue is really uncertain, if both parties understand the bet in the same way, and if both are prepared to pay if they lose.

5 But all Catholic moralists are agreed that gambling and betting may lead to grave abuse and sin, especially when they are prompted by mere gain. The gambler usually frequents bad company, wastes much valuable time, becomes adverse to hard work, is strongly tempted to be dishonest when luck is against him, and often brings financial ruin upon himself and those dependent upon him.

6 It is also true that many modern movies and plays offend good taste, violate moral standards, and are a waste of time. On the other hand, some movies and plays are not only wholesome and entertaining but also literary masterpieces. Catholics are guided by the Legion of Decency which classifies films suitable for adults and children.

Is an Indulgence a permission to commit sin?

1 No, an indulgence does not refer to sin at all, past, present, or future. It is a remission of the whole or part of the temporal punishment due to forgiven sin, granted by the Pope and the Bishops out of the Church's spiritual treasury, which is made up of the infinite redemptive merits of Jesus Christ, and the superabundant merits of the saints. It is more than the mere remission of canonical works of penance, for it really remits the whole or part of the punishment due the sinner by God, either here or in purgatory.

2 The Council of Trent teaches: "Since the power of conferring indulgences was granted by Christ to the Church, and she has, even in the most ancient times, used this power, delivered unto her by God; the Holy Synod teaches and enjoins that the use of Indulgences for the Christian

people, most salutary, and approved by the authority of Sacred Councils, is to be retained in the Church; and it condemns those who either assert that they are useless, or who deny that there is in the Church the power of granting them" (Sess. xxv.).

[3] This divine power of the Church to grant indulgences may be better understood, if we compare it with the state's custom of pardoning the whole or part of the punishment inflicted by the civil law upon the criminal. The President has the right to grant a complete pardon to any criminal within the confines of the United States; the Governor to any criminal in his state. The state, moreover, remits part of a criminal's punishment for good behavior while in prison.

[4] The state officials may grant a criminal pardon, even if he is not sorry for his crime, out of deference to powerful friends; the Church, on the contrary, never remits the punishment unless the sinner has manifested his sorrow.

By what authority does your Church grant indulgences? Are they mentioned in the Bible? Were they known to the primitive Church?

[1] The power of the keys granted to St. Peter and his successors, and the unlimited power to bind and loose granted to St. Peter, the other Apostles and their successors (Matt. 16, 19; 18, 18) included everything that barred men from heaven, that is, sin and its punishment.

[2] St. Paul exercised this power in the case of the incestuous Corinthian. He first ordered the Church of Corinth to excommunicate him for his sin (1 Cor. 5, 5), and then, after he had manifested his sorrow, the Apostle pardoned him, and remitted his punishment. "Indeed, what I have forgiven—if I have forgiven anything—I have done for your sakes, in the Person of Christ" (2 Cor. 2, 10).

[3a] In the early Church, indulgences were granted by the Bishops, who shortened the severe canonical penances of the time at the intercession of the martyrs, who gave the penitents letters of intercession (*libelli pacis*) (St. Cyprian, *Epis.*, xiii., 2; x., 4; *De Lapsis,* xvi.). That this remission was valid in God's sight is maintained by Tertullian (*De*

Pud., 22). When the era of persecutions was over, the Bishops continued to remit the canonical penances, as we learn from the Councils of Ancyra (314) and Nice (325). From the 8th century onward the severe penances of the early Church were commuted into prayers, fasting, flagellations, pilgrimages to Rome, and to famous shrines like St. Alban's in England and San Juan de Compostella in Spain, almsgiving to churches and hospitals, going on the crusades, and making the jubilee.

Are not pardons sold today in the Catholic Church? Were not indulgences sold all over Europe in the Middle Ages? Did not the Dominican Tetzel, a most wicked man, sell indulgences in Germany in Luther's time?

[1] No, pardons are not sold today in the Catholic Church. It is hard enough to induce some hardened sinners to go to Confession, without charging them for the privilege. A man does not purchase his wife, if at marriage he signs over to her a portion of his property. A Protestant does not purchase a wife for ten dollars, because he gives a fee of that amount to the minister who performs the ceremony.

[2] Catholic historians have frequently mentioned the abuses connected with the preaching of indulgences in the Middle Ages. The medieval pardoner, depicted by Chaucer in the *Pardoner's Tale,* was often an unscrupulous rascal, whose dishonesty and fraud were condemned by the Bishops of the time. It is comparatively easy today to get monies for any charitable enterprise, for we can appeal to thousands by letter, television, radio or the daily press. In the Middle Ages, when men wished to build a church or support a worthy charity, the Bishop or the Pope granted an indulgence, which first of all called upon the people to approach the sacraments of Penance and the Eucharist, and then "to lend a helping hand" in some special work of charity.

[3] While Catholics believe that the building of St. Peter's in Rome was a matter of interest to the whole Catholic world, they heartily condemn the manner of financing the indulgence, and the exaggerations of the preachers in extolling unduly its effects and privileges.

[4] No one believes today the calumnies against Tetzel's character. Luther did not speak the truth when he asserted that "Tetzel sold grace for money at the highest price." As both Pastor and Grisar point out, we must carefully distinguish between Tetzel's teaching with regard to indulgences for the living, and indulgences for the dead. With regard to indulgences for the living, his teaching, as we know from his *Vorlegung* and his *Frankfort Theses,* was perfectly Catholic. He writes: "Indulgences do not pardon sins, but only remit the temporal punishment due to sin, when the sins have been sorrowfully confessed. . . . Indulgences do not detract from the merits of Christ, but substitute for expiatory penalties the expiatory sufferings of Christ. . . . It is a known fact that it is Christian, God-fearing, pious people, and not lewd, idle ones, who are eager to gain an indulgence. . . . For all indulgences are given first and foremost for the sake of God's glory. Consequently whosoever gives alms to procure an indulgence gives primarily for God's sake, seeing that no one can obtain an indulgence, who has not attained to true repentance and the love of God" (Grisar, *Luther,* I., 343).

[5] "As regards Indulgences for the dead," Pastor writes, "there is no doubt that Tetzel did, according to what he considered his authoritative instructions, proclaim as Christian doctrine that nothing but an offering of money was required to gain the indulgence for the dead, without there being any question of contrition or confession. He also taught, in accordance with an opinion then held, that an indulgence could be applied to any given soul with unfailing effect. . . . The Papal Bull of Indulgence gave no sanction whatever to this proposition. It was a vague scholastic opinion, rejected by the Sorbonne in 1482, and again in 1518, and certainly not a doctrine of the Church" (*History of the Popes,* vii., 349). Cardinal Cajetan at the time condemned Tetzel's opinion, and taught that "while we may presume in a general way that God is willing to accept indulgences for the dead, we have no certainty whatever that He does so in any particular case. That is the secret of God alone." In 1477 Pope Sixtus IV had expressly taught that the Church applies indulgences for the dead "by way of suffrage," for the souls in purgatory

are no longer subject to her jurisdiction. They receive indulgences not directly, but indirectly, through the intercession of the living.

Are not indulgences destructive of true religion by making Catholics trust too much in externals, such as the visiting of churches, the reciting of set prayers, and the giving of money to the clergy?

[1]Indulgences are most helpful to true religion, for they are never granted unless one is heartily sorry for his sins, and in the state of grace, or friendship of God. As a matter of fact they develop the sense of solidarity in Catholics by reminding them of the Communion of Saints and the infinite merits of Christ's Redemption, which make them possible. They encourage prayer, fasting, and almsgiving, urge Catholics to frequent the sacraments of Penance and the Eucharist, insist on the frequent visiting of churches where Christ is really present, and foster devotion to the suffering souls in purgatory.

[2] Is it honest to accuse Catholics of externalism, when the motive prompting them to gain indulgences is supernatural, based solely on the justice and mercy of God?

SELECTED BIBLIOGRAPHY

FARRELL, WALTER. *Sin.* New York: Sheed & Ward. 1960.

HASTINGS, CECILY. *The Point of Catholicism.* New York: Sheed & Ward. 1956.

MARITAIN, JACQUES. *Sin of the Angel.* Westminster, Md.: Newman Press. 1959.

O'BRIEN, J. J. *Remission of Venial Sin.* Washington, D. C.: Catholic Univ. of Amer. Press. 1959.

PALMER, PAUL F. *Sacraments and Forgiveness.* Westminster, Md.: Newman Press. 1960.

RONDET, HENRI. *The Theology of Sin.* Notre Dame, Ind.: Fides. 1960.

SHEERIN, JOHN B. *Sacrament of Freedom.* Milwaukee: Bruce Publishing Co. 1961.

VAN ZELLER, PIERRE (ed.). *Approach to Penance.* New York: Sheed & Ward. 1958.

PART V
Jesus Christ

What do Christians mean by the Incarnation? Is this theological subtlety taught in the New Testament? Is it not contrary to reason that God could become man, or a man God? Does not this teaching imply a change in the unchangeable Deity?

[1] The mystery of the Incarnation is the unique and marvelous union of the divine nature and the human nature in the one Person of the Word made Flesh, Christ Jesus. We call this union unique, because no other being is constituted in this way; and marvelous, because it is brought about only by God's infinite power and love.

[2] In the Incarnation the two natures are united in one substantial whole, the divine Person Jesus Christ, as the body and soul, to use an analogy of the Athanasian Creed, are united in one substantial human person. Yet these two natures remain strictly distinct; the lower does not in any way influence the higher, while the higher only influences the lower as it would do even if it were separated.

[3] The mystery lies in the fact that the two natures constitute one single Person, although they are not fused into one single nature. The Word of God takes the place of the human personality, and makes the humanity so completely its own, that this humanity belongs to the Word, and must be adored with Him and in Him.

[4] It is true that the Bible does not contain the precise theological formula of "two Natures in one Person," but it expresses its identical meaning clearly in many a passage. The same Jesus Christ is Son of God and Son of

Man, begotten of the Father from all eternity, and born of the Blessed Virgin in time. In the prologue of his Gospel, St. John states the doctrine with a clearness and a beauty never equaled, "In the beginning was the Word, and the Word was with God; and the Word was God . . . And the Word was made flesh and dwelt among us" (John 1, 1. 14).

[5] St. Paul often teaches that Christ is God and Man at the same time. God sent "His Son in the likeness of sinful flesh" (Rom. 8, 3); "For in Him dwells all the fullness of the Godhead bodily" (Col. 2, 9); "Christ Jesus, who though He was by nature God, did not consider being equal to God a thing to be clung to, but emptied Himself, taking the nature of a slave and being made like unto men" (Philip. 2, 6f.).

[6] Although the Incarnation is indeed a transcendent mystery which never could be discovered by unaided reason, it is not against reason. Reason can prove that Christ claimed equality with God, and that He confirmed His claim to be divine by miracles (*Cf.* John 10, 25).

[7] There is no change whatsoever in God. "God in becoming Incarnate, loses nothing, receives nothing, is not in any way impoverished or enriched, but He terminates, completes and perfects the human nature. The change is in the human nature which is raised up to the divine being, not in the Person who raises it and renders it divine. The eternal does not change on this account any more than the cupola of St. Peter's at Rome changes when seen by the pilgrim for the first time. The change is entirely in the visitor; the monument remains the same, and there only happens to come into being a new reality, namely, the knowledge of the visitor which did not exist before" (Hugon, *The Mystery of the Incarnation,* 45).

Does the Old Testament tell of Jesus the Messias?

[1] Yes, for over two thousand years the prophets of the Old Law declared that God had revealed to them the coming of Jesus, the Messias, who was to be the Redeemer of the world.

[2] God promises a Redeemer to Adam (Gen. 3, 15). He

is to be of the stock of Sem (Gen. 9, 26), of Abraham (Gen. 22, 18), of Isaac (Gen. 26, 4), of Jacob (Gen. 28, 14; Num. 24, 17), of the tribe of Juda (Gen. 49, 8-10; *Cf.* Heb. 7, 14), and of the family of David (Isa. 9, 7; *Cf.* Rom. 7, 3; 2 Tim. 2, 8).

3 The prophets continually style the Messias the Lord (Ps. 2, 2), Jesus or the Savior (Isa. 2, 5; Habac. 8), the Mighty God (Isa. 9, 6), the Emmanuel, or God with us (Isa. 7, 14), the Father of the world to come, the Prince of Peace (Isa. 9, 6).

4 They tell us of His poverty (Ps. 56, 16), His obedience and meekness (Ps. 39, 9; 119, 7), His public preaching (Isa. 9, 1. 2; *Cf.* Matt. 4, 15), His miracles (Isa. 35, 5. 6), His founding of an universal, eternal kingdom (Ps. 44, 7. 8; Ps. 2, 7. 8).

5 They tell us that Christ will be a rock of scandal, and the occasion of ruin for many (Isa. 8, 14; *Cf.* Luke 2, 34), that He will be sold for thirty pieces of silver (Zach. 11, 12), led as a lamb to the slaughter (Isa. 53, 7), to be crucified (Zach. 13, 6), while the people mock Him (Jer. 20, 7; Ps. 21, 8; *Cf.* Matt. 37, 40-42), the soldiers cast lots for His garments (Ps. 21, 19; *Cf.* Matt. 27, 35), and offer Him vinegar to drink (Ps. 68, 22; *Cf.* Matt. 27, 34). His sepulchre shall be glorious (Isa. 11, 10), His body free from corruption (Ps. 15, 10), and He shall dwell at the right hand of God (Ps. 15, 11) to pour forever His Spirit upon all flesh (Joel 2, 28).

6 The prophetical books of the Old Testament are not only a series of accurate and exact predictions of the New Testament—Malachi on the Precursor of Christ, Micheas 5 on Bethlehem, Isaia 7 on the Virgin Birth, Isaia 41 on the miracles, Zacharias on Palm Sunday, Isaia 53 on the Crucifixion and Resurrection — but also the continuous proclamation of God's purpose for Israel and the progressive revelation of God's relationship to the human race. If they were mere predictions, they could be discarded after their fulfillment. But the more we read the prophets the more we understand the deep meaning of their message and how their hopes were realized beyond measure in the birth and mission of Christ. Christ Himself always claimed to have fulfilled the prophecies. He said: "Search

the Scriptures . . . it is they that bear witness to Me" (John 5, 39).

Did Christ ever claim to be God in the Synoptic Gospels? Was not the doctrine of the divinity of Christ borrowed by St. Paul from the pagan mystery religions, or the Jewish Apocalypses?

[1] Yes, Christ claims to be God on every page of St. Matthew, St. Luke and St. Mark. We readily admit that they do not teach the divinity of Christ in so marked and so direct a manner as St. John, for their main purpose was to prove that Jesus is the Christ, that is, the Messias, the descendant and antitype of David, the Expectation and the Hope of Israel. "Whatever deeds or sayings of Christ," says Father Otten, "were calculated to bring out that point clearly and distinctly were appropriately placed in the foreground, while His divine Personality received only such passing notice as was necessary to set forth the full sense of its Messianic character" (*What Think You of Christ?*, 24).

[2] The Synoptics show us Christ claiming to be greater than the temple (Matt. 12, 6), the sabbath (Matt. 12, 8), and the Law (Matt. 5, 27-28). He claims to be superior to the angels (Matt. 13, 41), equal to the Father (Matt. 11, 27).

[3] Christ asserts that he possesses all power on earth and in heaven (Matt. 11, 27; 25, 31; 28, 18) and that it belongs to Him in His own right (Mark 5, 29-32). He freely uses this power to prove His claim of divinity and He offers His many miracles as credentials that He is truly the Son of God. When the Jews questioned His testimony, He appealed to the miracles He had wrought as positive proof of His equality with Jehovah, whom He called His Father (Matt. 11, 4). Whereas human persons perform miracles in the name of God, Christ alone performs them of Himself, "I will; be thou made clean" (Mark 1, 41). Not only does He miraculously heal the blind, the dumb, the paralytic and the leper (Matt. 9, 28. 32. 2; 8, 3) but He raises Himself from the dead (Luke 24, 6).

[4] Then, too, the Synoptics teach that Christ demands absolute obedience and insists on love and service even

unto persecution and death. Father, mother, children, lands, monies—all are to be set at nought when He calls. "He who loves father or mother more than Me is not worthy of Me" (Matt. 10, 37-39). Only God could make such absolute demands upon our minds and hearts.

5 Everyone who reads the Synoptic Gospels acknowledges the surpassing eminence of the character of Christ. But if His claims, miracles and demands are false then He is not a good trustworthy man. As St. John says, "He who does not believe the Son, makes Him a liar" (John 5, 10). But we know that "One there is who is good, He is God" (Matt. 19, 17).

6 St. Paul did not derive his belief in Christ's divinity from human sources. He himself bears witness that he learned it from divine revelation. "I give you to understand, brethren, that the Gospel which was preached by me is not of man. For I did not receive it from man, nor was I taught it; but I received it by a revelation of Jesus Christ" (Gal. 1, 11-12).

7 His testimony is remarkable inasmuch as, before his conversion on the road to Damascus, he deemed it his duty to destroy the work and denounce the name of Jesus, whose divinity he was to proclaim so boldly. He began his public preaching within ten years of the Passion of our Lord, and wrote his first Epistles some twelve years later.

Did not Christ, in refusing the title "good," and ascribing goodness to God alone, by this very fact disclaim divinity? "Why do you ask Me about what is good? One there is who is good, and He is God" (Matt. 19, 17).

1 No, Christ in His answer to the rich young man of the Gospel, neither disclaimed His goodness, nor His divinity. Such questions did not arise either in His mind, or in the mind of His questioner. His words were in no sense a rebuke. He merely wished the young man to realize that God, the Author of the Ten Commandments, was the One Infinite Good. The text that St. Justin had before him makes this clear: "He alone is good, My Father who is in heaven" (*Dial.*, 16, 7).

2 Besides when the young man assured our Lord that

he had kept the Commandments from his youth, Christ advised him, if he wished to be perfect: "Sell all you have, and follow Me." This is a clear statement that following Christ in absolute poverty is a higher service than keeping the Commandments. If Christ were not God, such an exacting demand would be blasphemous.

Does not Christ's cry of despair on the cross prove that He was merely a man, "My God, My God, why hast Thou forsaken Me?" (Matt. 27, 46).

[1] By no means. These words of the dying Christ, quoted from Psalm 21, do not in any way express despair. They simply reveal that God has given over His Son to the cruelty of His enemies. Read this entire psalm which begins with the theme of utter loneliness but which ends in the triumphant fulfillment of prayer. Then listen to our Lord, as He makes His complaint with complete trust in His Father, as He prays earnestly for deliverance, and as He dies uttering joyful words of praise and thanksgiving.

[2] The four Gospels clearly show that this false idea of despair is read thoughtlessly or maliciously into the text. Christ is always represented full of confidence in God, rebuking His disciples for their lack of faith (Matt. 16, 53; Mark 4, 40; Luke 8, 25); the night before He died He had told them "take courage, I have overcome the world" (John 16, 33). On the cross He had promised paradise to the penitent thief (Luke 23, 43), and He had lovingly committed His soul to His heavenly Father (Luke 23, 46). He had freely accepted the chalice His Father gave Him to drink (Luke 22, 42). "He was offered because it was His own will" (Isa. 53, 7).

[3] Some well-meaning but unscholarly preachers of the Gospel have suggested that Christ allowed Himself to experience the torments of hell, as if He were alienated for a time from His Father. Such a view is utterly alien to Catholic teaching. Our Savior, it is true, endured on the cross a mental agony in contemplating the sins of men which far exceeded His physical sufferings, but He knew that He was God's beloved Son, and He always enjoyed to the full the vision of His heavenly Father. The guilt

of actual sin cannot be transferred from one soul to another. To assert that the guilt of men's sins were transferred to our Lord dying on the cross is absurd and blasphemous. *If Christ were really divine how could He undergo temptation? Is not the account of Christ's temptation legendary, or at least a parable He taught to teach His followers how to meet the trials of life?*

[1] It is true that Jesus Christ, the holy and sinless Son of God (*see* John 8, 29; Heb. 7, 26) could never experience, as we do, the inward strife of the flesh and spirit, or the trials that come from errors of the reason or from weakness of the will. But He was true Man and, therefore, was really tempted by the devil (Matt. 4, 1-11). As Adam yielded when he was truly tempted by the devil, so Christ, truly tempted by the devil, triumphed.

[2] The devil, who is a real, clever, angelic person, tempts us by way of suggestion. He tries to persuade us to doubt God's loving care, to be proud and presumptuous of God's help, and to be greedy. These temptations are not sins but suggestions to sin. By making his suggestions to Christ, he was really tempting our Lord to sin. But Christ could not be fooled; He put the devil to rout.

[3] Watching Christ in the face of temptation we can learn how to overcome the temptations of the devil. Notice that the devil may attack us when we are physically weak—Christ had gone without food or drink for forty days—but if we are quick to reject his suggestions we, too, shall not sin. It is comforting to know that "we have not a high priest who cannot have compassion on our infirmities, but one tried as we are in all things except sin . . . for in that He Himself has suffered and has been tempted, He is able to help those who are tempted" (Heb. 4, 15; 2, 18).

Does not the Atonement mean that Christ by His preaching and example delivered men from their sins and taught them how to be saved?

[1a] The preaching and example of Christ are most helpful in enabling one to share in the benefits of the Atonement; but the Atonement itself is something quite distinct

from the preaching and example. By the Atonement is meant the reparation made by Christ for the sins of mankind. One of the consequences of the sin of Adam and Eve was the loss of the happiness of heaven for themselves and for the entire human race; or, as it has been expressed: "the door of heaven was closed." From the very beginning it was revealed that nothing they or their children could do would be sufficient to make adequate atonement and thereby "balance the scales of infinite justifice." God, therefore, promised to send His own Son to assume our nature and take upon Himself this responsibility. Christ, the promised Redeemer, being truly man, could suffer and die for His fellow man; and being at the same time truly divine, His satisfaction for sin would be infinite in value. He did suffer, and upon the cross He gave His life for our salvation. For this reason the cross is sometimes referred to as the "Key of Heaven." The doctrine of the Atonement is brought out clearly in the Gospels and the writings of St. Paul.

² Although Christ made atonement for the sins of all, it does not follow that automatically all will be saved. It is for each individual to prove himself worthy to benefit by the Redemption: "Wherefore . . . work out your salvation with fear and trembling" (Philip. 2, 12).

Was it just for God to punish His innocent Son for the sins of men?

¹ God did not look upon His Son as a sinner or as His foe, for in spite of the fact that Jesus died for our sins, He did not take upon Himself our sins so as to become an object of hatred, as if the Father considered them Jesus' personal sins. No, our Lord remained "holy and guiltless and undefiled, not reckoned among us sinners," (Heb. 7, 26) and therefore He did not have to suffer for Himself. He suffered for us alone, taking upon Himself the penalty or debt, but not the guilt, of our sins. And He *freely* chose to carry out the will of His Father (Mark 10, 45; John 18, 11; Matt. 26, 52-53). So conformed was the human will of Christ to God's will that He not only wanted to die for us, but saw His passion and death as the

very *raison d'etre* of His whole life (Luke 12, 50; Mark 8, 31; Matt. 26, 54). The very fact that this act was so free and done with so much love is what made it so pleasing to the Father. And just as we all sinned and merited punishment by the sin of the first Adam, representative of our human race; so also we are redeemed and restored to the friendship of God by the atonement of Christ, the new Adam and new Head of the race (Rom. 5, 12-21).

Does not your devotion to the Sacred Heart imply the rendering of divine honor to a creature? Does not modern physiology deny the erroneous belief that the heart is the seat of love? Is there any proof of the authenticity of the great Promise? Is it not heretical to hold that one has a certainty of salvation?

[1] The legitimacy of the devotion to the Sacred Heart is understood by all who have a correct knowledge of the dogmas of the Incarnation and the Redemption. Jesus Christ is perfect God and perfect Man in one Divine Personality. The divine Person is united hypostatically not only to the humanity of Christ considered in its totality, but also considered in its several parts, as for instance, His hands, His feet, His precious blood, and His heart. It follows, therefore, that every one of these organic parts is deserving of adoration, not considered in itself, but in view of its union with the Godhead.

[2] The Jansenist theory that a direct adoration of the humanity of Christ or any part thereof is equivalent to rendering divine honor to a creature was condemned by Pius VI. The Sacred Heart of Jesus is worthy of the same worship as His divinity, provided it is worshiped conjointly with His Person.

[3] In this devotion the heart is not viewed as the organ, but only as the symbol of love. Just as the lily represents purity and the scale symbolizes justice, so the heart suggests the thought of love. The Bible speaks of the heart as the ideal seat of the affections (Isa. 65, 14; 1 Tim. 1, 5).

[4] The original letter containing the Great Promise has been lost, but it has come down to us in five different versions. The first is found in the first volume of the 1867

and 1876 Visitandine editions of the *Life and Works of Margaret Mary*; the second in the second volume of the same two editions; the third in the Life by Bishop Languet; the fourth in a manuscript discovered by Father Hamon in 1902, in the library of Joseph Déchelette; the fifth in the annals of the Monastery of Dijon. It is impossible to determine which of these is the original version.

⁵ All the versions agree in insisting upon Holy Communion for nine first Fridays, and in promising the grace of final repentance, and the grace of not dying without the sacraments. Bishop Languet's version declares that after one has complied with the required conditions, he may entertain a hope of receiving the sacraments, and the grace of final perseverance.

⁶ No one has any right to presume that his salvation is secure irrespective of the life he lives in the future, provided he makes the nine Fridays. By the very fact of sinning, he loses his title to this special divine assistance.

⁷ The devout lover of Christ by frequent Communion will be given many graces, which "may lead him to hope for the grace of final repentance," as Bishop Languet says. His words say nothing of an absolute infallible assurance of salvation.

⁸ "The Church has ever cherished devotion to the Sacred Heart and encouraged its spread everywhere. . . . The reason for devotion to the Sacred Heart is not mainly to gain the blessings Christ has promised, but that we should carry out more faithfully our duties to God, namely, the duties of love and expiation, and so promote our own spiritual advancement" (Pius XII, *Encyclical on the Sacred Heart*).

SELECTED BIBLIOGRAPHY

ADAM, KARL. *The Christ of Faith.* New York: Pantheon Books. 1957.

———— *The Son of God.* Garden City, N. Y.: (Image Books) Doubleday & Co. 1960.

AIGRAIN, RENE. *Prophecy Fulfilled.* New York: David McKay. 1958.

ARENDZEN, JOHN P. *Christ is God.* New York: Sheed & Ward. 1958.

BUTLER, BASIL CHRISTOPHER. *Why Christ.* Baltimore: Helicon Press. 1960.

DACHAUER, ALBAN J. *The Sacred Heart.* Milwaukee: Bruce Publishing Co. 1959.

DANIEL-ROPS, HENRY. *Jesus and His Times.* Garden City, N. Y.: Doubleday & Co. 1958.

DURRWELL, F. X. *The Resurrection of Christ.* New York: Sheed & Ward. 1960.

FARRELL, WALTER. *Only Son.* New York: Sheed & Ward. 1953.

FERNANDEZ, ANDRES. *The Life of Christ.* Westminster, Md.: Newman Press. 1958.

FILLION, LOUIS C. *Life of Christ.* 3 Vols. St. Louis: B. Herder Book Co. 1929.

FOUARD, CONSTANT H. *The Life of Christ.* New York: (Angelus Books) Golden Press. 1960.

GLEASON, ROBERT W. *Christ and the Christian.* New York: Sheed & Ward. 1959.

GRAHAM, AELRED. *The Christ of Catholicism.* Garden City, N. Y.: (Image Books) Doubleday & Co. 1957.

GUARDINI, ROMANO. *Lord.* Chicago: Regnery. 1954.

HEINISCH, PAUL. *Christ in Prophecy.* Collegeville, Minn.: Liturgical Press. 1957.

LEBRETON, JULES. *The Life and Teaching of Jesus Christ Our Lord.* New York: Macmillan. 1957.

PIUS XII, POPE. "The Mystical Body of Christ" in *Four Great Encyclicals.* New York: Paulist Press. 1961.

RICCIOTTI, GIUSEPPE. *Life of Christ.* Milwaukee: Bruce Publishing Co. (Popular Ed. 1952)

STIERLI, JOSEF (ed.). *Heart of the Saviour.* New York: Herder & Herder. 1958.

WUELLNER, BERNARD J. *Graces of the Risen Christ.* Milwaukee: Bruce Publishing Co. 1960.

PART VI
The Catholic Church

Did Christ really establish a society which all men were bound to join? or did He not rather insist upon certain spiritual doctrines, which His disciples were to realize as best they could?

[1] Catholics believe with the Vatican Council "that in order to perpetuate the saving work of Redemption, the Eternal Bishop of souls decreed to establish a Holy Church, to which all the faithful might be gathered together by the unity of faith and love, as in the house of God."

[2] The Bible plainly teaches that Christ established a divine society, when He gave the Apostles the power to teach (Matt. 28, 19; Mark 16, 15), to govern (Matt. 18, 18; John 20, 21), and to sanctify the souls of men (Matt. 28, 20; John 20, 22; Luke 22, 19). Christ's true followers are to accept their teaching (Mark 16, 16), obey their commandments (Luke 10, 16; Matt. 18, 17), and to use the divine means of sanctification (John 3, 5; 6, 54) which Christ instituted.

[3] The Church is a divine society, divine in its origin, and supernatural in its end and means. It is, therefore, unfailing and perpetual, always opposed by the world as was Christ, her divine Founder, and always conquering her enemies, as Christ once won the victory of the resurrection through the seeming failure of the cross.

[4] The Church is at the same time a human society, because it consists of human members. That is why scandals, heresies and schisms arise. Christ Himself foretold this, when He compared the Kingdom of God to a field

in which weeds grew together with the wheat; or to a net containing good fish and bad (Matt. 13, 24. 47).

Were not Luther and Calvin right in teaching that the Church was composed only of the just and the predestined? If so, it is visible to God alone.

[1] No, the heretical teaching of Luther and Calvin was condemned by the Council of Trent and again by the Council of the Vatican, which defined as an article of the faith the visibility of the Church. "God established a Church through His Only-Begotten Son, and endowed it with manifest marks of its institution that it might be known by all as the guardian and teacher of the revealed word."

[2] How could our Lord require us to believe under penalty of damnation (Mark 16, 18), and to consider the Christian disobedient to the Church's commands "a heathen and a publican" (Matt. 18, 17), if we could not easily recognize the Church as a visible society? Frequently the New Testament represents the Church as an external, visible society, calling it the house of God (1 Tim. 2, 15), a kingdom (Matt. 4, 23; 13, 24), a field (Matt. 13, 24), a grain of mustard seed that becomes a tree (Matt. 13, 31), a city set on a mountain (Matt. 5, 14), a sheep-fold (John 10, 16), a flock (Acts 20, 28).

[3] St. Paul declares the Church visible to the faithful, so that they may know whom to obey and whom to believe (Eph. 4, 11-14), and to those outside the fold, so that they may accept with certainty a divinely accredited ambassador of the Gospel of Peace (Rom. 10, 14, 15).

[4] The Fathers of both East and West often compare the Church to the sun and the moon, because "she enlightens all under heaven" (Athanasius, *In Ps.* 88, 38), or because as St. John Chrysostom says, "It is easier for the sun to be quenched, than for the Church to be made invisible." They teach plainly the visibility of the Church, when they comment upon "a city set on a mountain cannot be hidden" (Matt. 5, 14); *see,* St. Hilary (*Comm. In Matt.*); St. Augustine (*Epis.,* 52, 1).

*Does not the Catholic Church hinder the direct relation-
ship of the soul to God? Your saint worship is a proof.*

[1] No, on the contrary, her sole aim is to bring souls into
intimate union with God, by having them participate in
the redeeming work of Jesus Christ on the cross—chiefly
by the Mass and the sacraments.

[2] The Church, the Mystical Body of Christ, alone has
the Mass, which renews every day upon our altars the
Sacrifice of Christ on the Cross. It is "a propitiatory Sacrifice," as the Council of Trent teaches (Sess. 12, can. 3),
"whereby God grants grace and the gift of repentance,
and remits crimes and even the greatest sins" (*Ibid.*, ch. 2).

[3] By Baptism a Catholic is united to Christ as the
branch is united to the vine (John 15, 1-6); grace is infused into our souls so that we become "partakers of the
divine nature" (2 Peter 1, 4). By the other sacraments this
personal union is strengthened, deepened and intensified.
Especially in Holy Communion, a Catholic is most intimately joined to Christ, according to His promise, "He
who eats My flesh and drinks My blood, abides in Me
and I in him" (John 6, 57).

[4] The veneration Catholics pay to the saints brings
them closer to Christ, if they but imitate their virtues.
Such veneration is neither worship nor adoration. It is
God alone whom a Catholic adores and worships.

*Is it not a fact that the Catholic Church became corrupt
and so changed by the 16th century, that it no longer
represented the Church that Christ established?*

[1a] No, this is not a fact, although the 16th century reformers made this false assertion, so as to give their followers a pretext for establishing their various separatist
sects. The 19th century modernists, misled by their false
theory of the relativity of truth, have also been compelled
to make the defectibility of the Church the first article of
their rationalistic creed.

[2a] While human societies and States have a natural
tendency to become corrupt and perish in the course of
time, a supernatural divine society like the Catholic Church
cannot fail or become corrupt, for its divine founder, Jesus

Christ, and the Holy Spirit are to abide with it until the end of the world (Matt. 17, 10; John 14, 16). The prophets of the Old Law always declared that the Kingdom of Christ would be a lasting Kingdom (Dan. 2, 44; Isa. 9, 6. 7), a teaching confirmed by Christ in the parables of the weeds (Matt. 13, 24-30.36-43) and the net (Matt. 13, 47-50). Moreover our Lord explicitly promised that "the gates of hell (the power of death or the power of the devil) shall not prevail against it" (the Church).

[3] It is true that parts of the Church may be corrupted by heresy and schism, as in the days of Arianism, of the Eastern Schism, and of the Protestant Reformation. But as St. Cyprian says: "Though tares be seen in the Church, neither our faith nor our charity ought to be impeded, so that we withdraw ourselves from the Church. We ought simply to strive that we may be true wheat; that we may receive fruit according to our labor" (*Epis.* 51). In another letter (*Ad Cornelium,* 55) he tells us that the faithful, who are mindful of the Gospel, ought not to be scandalized if certain proud men leave the Church of God, for some of the early disciples abandoned Christ (John 6, 66), and both He and His Apostles foretold the apostasy of many Christians.

Will you not admit that a Reformation was needed in the 16th century, and that Luther's great reform made people better? Were the Popes of his time, Leo X and Clement VII, at all anxious for reform? How do you account for such a widespread movement against your Church?

[1] Catholics readily grant that a reformation in the lives of many unworthy Catholic clerics and laymen was indeed called for in the 16th century, and historians like Pastor have admitted the worldliness, immorality, nepotism, and avarice that marked many of the clergy (*History of the Popes,* vii., 291-328). Pastor, however, warns us against the unfair exaggerations of bigoted controversialists, and gives us a list of eighty-eight saints and *beati* who died in Italy alone between the years 1400 and 1529 (*Ibid.,* v., 86-88). He says well: "The records of all nations consist of the stories of crimes. Virtue goes quietly on her way; vice

and lawlessness are always making a noise. The scapegoat is the talk of the town; the honest man does his duty, and no one hears of him" (*Ibid.*, 10).

² Catholics, however, hold that a Reformation in the sense of a secession from the Church established by Christ, fostered by kings and princes desirous of the Church's lands and revenues, and denying the divine doctrines, government and worship of the Gospel, could not be of God. The good Catholic remained within the fold, and prayed and worked for reform, like a St. Canisius or a St. Charles Borromeo; the immoral Catholic, like Henry VIII of England, or the Landgrave Philip of Hesse, apostatized.

³ It is true indeed that Leo X (1517-1521) and Clement VII (1523-1534) did not measure up to their task, as Pastor admits (*Ibid.*, vii., 9), but we must not forget that the Council of Trent, which was to bring about the Counter-Reformation, was retarded not by the Popes, but by the princes of the time.

⁴ Döllinger in his book on *The Reformation: Its Interior Development and Effects,* shows from Protestant writers alone that the Reformation in Germany, instead of helping matters, led to intellectual, social, moral and religious deterioration. Luther himself writes: "Now we see the people becoming more infamous, more avaricious, more unmerciful, more unchaste, and in every way worse than they were under Popery." . . . He calls his own town of Wittenberg "a Sodom of immorality," and adds that "although half the town is guilty of adultery, usury, theft and cheating, no one tries to put the law in force" (Grisar, *Luther*, iv., 210, 215).

⁵ The chief cause of the Reformation was the gradual weakening of the bond of Catholic unity and faith during the 14th and 15th centuries. The antipathy to the Holy See on the continent began with Philip the Fair's quarrel with Boniface VIII (1285-1378), and was intensified by the residence of the Popes at Avignon (1309-1376), the rebellion of Louis of Bavaria (1314-1346), and the Great Western Schism (1378-1417). The Black Death (1348-1350), which killed more than one third of Western Europe in two years, had greatly lowered the standard of culture among the clergy, and hastened the development of a

narrow nationalism, which resented the clergy's financial power, and lusted for the wealth the Church had accumulated down the centuries. The weakening of moral discipline among the clergy and people was the chief factor in bringing about the Protestant revolt. A faithful, devout body of Christians, in the first three centuries, died gladly for the faith; the worldly, avaricious, and immoral Christians of the 16th century easily lost the faith that they had ceased to practice.

Did not Savonarola in the 15th century fail to bring about the reform that Luther accomplished in the 16th? Was not Savonarola a precursor of the Reformation?

[1] No, Savonarola was in no sense a precursor of the Reformation, although the Protestants of Germany tried to make the unthinking believe this, by placing the Catholic Dominican alongside the Protestants grouped about the Lutheran memorial at Worms. This calumny has been ably refuted by many scholars, such as Capponi, Dittrich, Frantz, Hergenröther, Pastor, Villari, and others.

[2] In his *Triumph of the Cross*, Savonarola puts apostasy from the Church in the same category as apostasy from Christ (iv., 6), Although some of his works have been placed upon the Index, the greater part of his writings are Catholic to the core.

[3] He had one fault. "In his burning zeal for the reformation of morals he allowed himself to be carried away into violent attacks on men of all classes, including his superiors, and he completely forgot that, according to the teaching of the Church, an evil life cannot deprive the Pope or any other ecclesiastical authority of his lawful jurisdiction" (Pastor, *History of the Popes*, vi., 53). As Cardinal Newman well said: "He thought too much of himself, and rose up against a power which no one can attack without injuring himself. No good can come of disobedience; that was not the way to become the Apostle of either Florence or Rome."

Is not Christ called "the stone that was rejected by you, the builders, which has become the cornerstone" (Acts 4, 11)?

[1] Yes, and rightly so, because He is the Founder of the Church, the Cornerstone of the house of the Kingdom of God. Through His Redemption we are saved, as St. Peter teaches in the very next verse. "Neither is there salvation in any other. For there is no other name under heaven given to men by which we must be saved" (*Cf.* Eph. 2, 20. 22; Matt. 21, 42). These texts do not exclude St. Peter. St. Leo (440-461) answered this objection more than 1,500 years ago. He writes: "You are Peter, that is, whereas I (Christ) am the inviolable Rock; I the Chief Cornerstone . . . nevertheless, you (Peter) are also a rock, because you are consolidated by My power so that, what belongs to Me by My power, may be common to you by being made partaker of them with Me" (Sermon IV, *In Nat. Ord.,* ch. 2).

Does not St. Paul teach that all the Apostles were foundations of the Church? Why do you build it then solely on Peter (Eph. 2, 19-20)?

[1a] They were foundations in the sense that they preached Jesus Christ, whom the prophets foretold. It is obvious that the prophets and the Apostles were not foundations in the same sense. The text reads: "You are citizens with the saints . . . built upon the foundation of the Apostles and prophets."

[2] He could have styled them foundations of the Church had he so willed. St. John did so (Apoc. 21, 14)—for they were the first infallible teachers of Christ's Gospel. Peter was the solid rock upon which they, the foundation stones, were built.

Why do you arrogantly claim that your Church is infallible?

[1b] Because she alone represents Christ, the divine, infallible teacher, in conduct, belief and worship. "I am the Way (conduct), and the Truth (belief), and the Life (worship)" (John 14, 5).

[2b] Reason and revelation alike demand that the teacher of the divine revelation of Christ speak as He did, infallibly, that is, that by divine guidance she be ever kept free from the liability of error.

³ Would a good God, who "wishes all men to be saved and to come to the knowledge of the truth" (1 Tim. 2, 4), fail to provide His revelation with a living infallible witness? Would a just God command us to believe under penalty of hell (Mark 16, 16), and at the same time leave us to the mercy of every false prophet (Matt. 13, 21) and lying teacher (2 Peter 2, 1), preaching a Gospel opposed to His (Gal. 1, 8)?

⁴ No, the Church Christ founded is everywhere spoken of in the New Testament as a divine, infallible teaching authority. Christ says that His Church is like a city firmly built upon a rock foundation, which can never be destroyed by Satan and the powers of evil (Matt. 16, 18; *Cf.* Matt. 7, 24; Ps. 116, 5).

⁵ Throughout the Gospels the mission of the Apostles and their successors is declared identical with the mission of Christ and His heavenly Father. "As the Father has sent Me (to give infallible witness to the truth, John 18, 37; *Cf.* Matt. 1, 38), I send you" (John 20, 21), "He who receives anyone I send, receives Me" (John 13, 20), "He who receives you, receives Me; and he who receives Me, receives Him who sent Me" (Matt. 10, 40; *Cf.* Luke 10, 16; John 12, 44-48; John 15, 20, 24).

⁶ When Christ gave the Apostles their divine commission for all nations until the end of the world (Matt. 28, 20), He promised: "I am with you all days." This phrase is used at least ninety times in the Bible, and outside of the few instances in which it implies a mere salutation (Ruth 2, 4; Rom. 15, 33), it signifies that God will ensure the success of the person's undertaking (Gen. 39, 2; Exod. 3, 12; Jer. 1, 19; Num. 14, 42).

⁷ The Apostles always declare that their teaching is the Word of God (Acts 4, 31; 8, 14; 12, 24; 13, 44; 15, 35; 1 Cor. 14, 35; 2 Tim. 2, 9), which they voice infallibly by the assistance of the Holy Spirit (Acts 2, 4; 4, 31; 15, 25-28; 1 Cor. 2, 4-16), who confirms their witness by miracles (Acts 3, 16; 4, 29-31; 5, 12. 16; 9, 32-42). All other teaching is false and blasphemous, even if it were to come from an angel of God (Acts 13, 18; Gal. 1, 8, 9).

⁸ If you study the writings of the early Fathers of the Church, the various Creeds, and the Councils of the Church

from Jerusalem to the Vatican Council, you must admit that the Church always considered herself infallible, condemning as a heretic outside her fold anyone who denied even one dogma of the Faith. As St. Irenaeus said in the 2nd century: "Where the Church is, there is the Spirit of God, and where the Spirit of God is, there is the Church and all grace. For the Spirit is the truth."

Is not your doctrine of infallibility opposed to freedom of thought? Is not a Catholic hampered in his search for truth by a blind obedience to an infallible Church?

[1] The doctrine of infallibility is indeed opposed to the false freedom of believing error, but not to the true freedom of believing the truth. We have no right to believe what is false, any more than we have a right to do what is evil. Our Savior plainly taught us that error and sin imply not the freedom, but the slavery of the intellect and the will. "You shall know the truth, and the truth shall make you free." "Everyone who commits sin is a slave of sin" (John 8, 32. 34).

[2] A Catholic does not give a blind, degrading obedience to a fallible, human authority, that may ask him to believe without question the most preposterous statements, but a divine authority, that can neither deceive him nor be deceived. "If we receive the testimony of men, the testimony of God is greater," says St. John (1 John 5, 9). He is not hampered in his search for truth, but like the true scientist, builds upon facts and principles he already knows.

[3] Infallibility is the corrective of error in matters of belief, conduct and worship. "It is," as Cardinal Newman says, "a supply for a need, and it does not go beyond the need. Its object is, and its effect also, not to enfeeble the freedom or vigor of human thought, but to resist and control its extravagances" (*Apologia*). It is like radar on the modern ocean liner or jet plane, that points out the true course in the darkness and in the fog.

What do you mean by the holiness of the Church, and why do you claim that she alone has that distinguishing mark? Are there not many devout souls in other religions and other Churches?

[1] Holiness implies nearness to God, the author and source of all holiness (Isa. 6, 3; Apoc. 4, 8). For this reason the Bible calls certain places holy, because God has specially blessed them (Exod. 3, 5; Matt. 4, 5); certain things holy, because they have been dedicated to divine worship (Exod. 29, 29; Heb. 9, 2); and certain persons holy, because they are closely united to God by charity (Tob. 2, 12; Rom. 1, 7; Apoc. 5, 3).

[2] The Catholic Church is holy, because her founder, Jesus Christ, is God, the infinite source of all holiness. He alone could confidently challenge His enemies: "Which of you can convict Me of sin" (John 8, 46)?

[3] The Catholic Church is holy, because of her intimate union with Christ as His Bride (Eph. 5, 23-32) and His Mystical Body (1 Cor. 12, 27; Eph. 1, 22; 4, 11; 5, 30). We are members of His Body, of His Flesh and of His Bones. Catholics are a "chosen people" and a "holy nation," because they are branches of the true Vine, Christ Jesus (John 15, 5). Although men outside her fold may, through invincible ignorance, be members of the Church in desire, and thus share in her divine life, their churches are but withered branches, that do not abide in Him (John 15, 1-6).

[4] The Catholic Church is holy, not because there are no sinners in her fold (Matt. 13, 24-30; 47. 48), but because her one aim is to produce sanctity. "Christ also loved the Church, and delivered Himself up for her that He might sanctify her . . . that she might be holy and without blemish" (Eph. 5, 25-27). The ideal she presents to the world is identical with Christ's: "You therefore are to be perfect, even as your heavenly Father is perfect" (Matt. 5, 48). She has ever taught infallibly the entire Gospel of Christ, for she wished her children to possess "this mind in you which was also in Christ Jesus" (Philip. 2, 5). She has ever interpreted infallibly the commandments and counsels of the Savior, for He said: "If thou wilt enter into life, keep the commandments" (Matt. 19, 17). "Not all can accept this teaching; but those to whom it has been given . . . Let him accept it who can" (Matt. 19, 11. 12). "If thou wilt be perfect, go, sell what thou hast, and give to the poor, and thou shalt have treasure in heaven; and come, follow

Me" (Matt. 19, 21). She has ever infallibly given her children the means of grace instituted by Christ in the Mass and the seven sacraments, whereby the precious blood of Christ shed upon the cross is applied for our sanctification and redemption.

[5] The virtues of Catholics are in exact proportion to their faithful acceptance of her doctrines, their faithful observance of her commandments and counsels, their faithful attendance at holy Mass, and their frequent reception of sacraments. The sinners within her fold, at whom outsiders often point the finger of scorn, are beyond question those very Catholics who disobey her laws, and neglect her sacraments. The accusations of evil-doing that controversialists are fond of making against the Church would be without point, if the Church's teaching were not opposed to the sins they stigmatize.

[6] From the days of the proto-martyr, St. Stephen (Acts 7, 58), the Catholic Church has been the fruitful mother of saints. A body of critical scholars, the Bollandists, have been busy since 1643, transcribing their marvelous lives in some sixty-four folio volumes (Delehaye, *The Work of the Bollandists*). They have died for Christ as St. Peter, St. Paul, St. Polycarp, St. Agnes and St. Cecilia; they have won whole nations to Christ, like St. Patrick, St. Boniface, St. Ansgar, St. Methodius and St. Francis Xavier; they have founded religious orders of men and women that won countless souls to the perfect following of the evangelical counsels like St. Benedict, St. Bernard, St. Francis, St. Dominic, St. Madeleine Barat; they have given up everything this life holds dear to care for the sick (St. Camillus), the poor (St. Vincent de Paul), the prisoners among the Moslems (St. John of Matha; St. Felix of Valois); they have valiantly defended the faith in every part of the world (St. Athanasius, St. Augustine, St. Jerome, St. Ambrose, St. Thomas Aquinas, St. Canisius); they have counseled Popes (St. Catherine of Siena), and led their country to victory against an alien foe (St. Jeanne d'Arc); they have revealed the inmost secrets of the world of spirit (St. Teresa of Avila, St. John of the Cross).

[7] We readily admit that there are many devout souls outside the Catholic Church, as every priest who has had

much experience with converts can bear witness. I have baptized many a Lutheran farmer in the Northwest, who had kept the Ten Commandments faithfully for years, like the young man of the Gospel (Matt. 19, 20), and many a High Church Episcopalian in New York City, who went regularly to Confession and Communion, firmly but erroneously convinced that they were receiving the grace of real sacraments. Their good lives were not due to their heresy or schism, but to the grace of God, who "wishes all men to be saved and to come to the knowledge of the truth" (1 Tim. 2, 4). On questioning them, I found that for years they had been believing many a Catholic doctrine and observing many a Catholic law. They had not sinned against the light, but had acted like St. Paul, "ignorantly, in unbelief" (1 Tim. 1, 13). Once within the fold, they realized that the Catholic Church alone was the one divine school of sanctity.

If your Church is a holy Church, why do you allow adulterers, drunkards and corrupt politicians to be members in good standing? Should not moral character be insisted upon as a qualification of Church membership? Why are there so many poor and ignorant in your Church?

¹ Because the Church is the universal Kingdom of God, divinely commissioned to teach Christ's Gospel to all men— sinner and saint, rich and poor, cultured and uncultured— alike, "There is neither Jew nor Greek; there is neither slave nor freeman; there is neither male nor female. For you are all one in Christ Jesus" (Gal. 3, 28). The Church is not a Church of the elect, as Wyclif taught, or Calvin; nor is she an exclusive club for the outwardly respectable and the well-to-do.

² Sinners are rarely excommunicated from her fold, and only for some flagrant sin, just as traitors and convicted criminals are debarred by the State from citizenship. The adulterer, the drunkard or the corrupt politician is not in "good standing," for he is not permitted to receive Communion, until he manifests a heartfelt sorrow for his sins in the Sacrament of Penance.

³ Christ came into the world for sinners: The angel

Gabriel said to Mary: "Thou shalt call His name Jesus; for He shall save His people from their sins" (Matt. 1, 21). Christ Himself said: "The Son of Man came to save what was lost" (Matt. 18, 11). "I have come to call sinners, not the just" (Matt. 9, 13).

⁴ Christ always speaks of the Church as a Society composed of the good and the wicked. He compares it to a field in which weeds grow with the wheat (Matt. 13, 24-30); to a net containing good and bad fishes (Matt. 13, 47); to a barn containing chaff as well as wheat (Matt. 3, 12); to wise and foolish virgins (Matt. 25, 1-12). St. Paul also speaks of a great house having "vessels not only of gold and silver, but also of wood and clay; and some are for honorable uses, but some for ignoble" (2 Tim. 2, 20). And St. John writes to remind us that we are all sinners: "If we say that we have no sin, we deceive ourselves, and the truth is not in us" (1 John 1, 8).

⁵ I remember meeting in Boston a Unitarian minister from Burlington Vermont, who told me he was about to resign his ministry, because his efforts to gather in the unchurched poor of his city had been met with a decided protest on the part of his wealthy parishioners. The true Church frowns on such narrowness. "As long as you did it for one of these, the least of My brethren, you did it for Me" (Matt. 25, 41). Sinners will remain in the Church until the harvest (Matt. 13, 30), that is, until Christ at the Last Day separates forever the sheep from the goats.

Will you not admit that many of the leaders of your Church — Popes, Bishops and priests — have been wicked men? How can you call such a Church holy?

¹ The Church remains holy, no matter how many of her leaders prove faithless to the Gospel they preach, for these men are cut off from the Church's life by their sins, which can never be traced to her teachings or laws. Would you call an apple tree bad, because you discovered some rotten apples lying on the ground beneath it? No, you judge the tree by the ripening or ripe apples on its boughs. Wicked churchmen will one day have to render a strict account to almighty God for their stewardship, for as Christ said:

"To whom much has been given, much will be required" (Luke 12, 48).

[2] Out of a long line of worthy Popes, a great many of whom are reckoned among the saints, only a few were unworthy of their high office, such as John XII (955-964), Benedict IX (1024-1032), and Alexander VI (1492-1503). But the proportion of unworthy Apostles was one out of twelve. No world dynasty can be compared from the standard of virtue with our illustrious dynasty of two hundred and sixty-two Popes.

[3] At all periods of Church history there have been unworthy Bishops and priests, but as a rule they either repented of their sins before they died, or proved their utter wickedness by apostatizing in times of trial and persecution, or by lapsing into formal heresy and schism.

You claim to have always taught the same doctrines. I can name three new ones in the last century, namely, the Immaculate Conception (1854), Papal Infallibility (1870), and the Assumption (1950). Do you claim to be able to add to the revelation of Jesus Christ? And is not your explanation of "development of doctrine" a mere subterfuge? Finally, is Christ's revelation not sufficiently set forth by the early Church in the Apostle's Creed? Is it not enough to hold the teachings of the first Councils of the Church?

[1] The Catholic Church clearly teaches and firmly holds that after the death of the last Apostle there has been no new public revelation, no objective increase in the deposit of faith. The Catholic Church does not and cannot increase revelation; but what it can and must do is guard and preserve it intact, and strive constantly for a better and deeper understanding of it. What increases, then, is only our explicit understanding of it. The number of dogmas, or explicit formulations of divine revelation increases, but not revelation itself.

[2a] Our Lord committed His message, His revelation to the Apostles—a revelation whose content received added meaning for the Apostles from His acts, gestures, interpretation, etc. And as the foundation stones of the Church

(Eph. 2, 20) they understood the full content of this message, this being possible by the help of a special prophetic
light granted them. In this sense the deposit of revelation
was in the collective intelligence of the Apostles, and fully
illumined by this special light. And so, had events demanded, they could have answered specific questions
regarding Infallibility and other recently defined dogmas.
However, we need not believe that they had clearly thought
out, and formulated in words, a clear expression of all
they understood about Christ's message. Thus, we need
not think that they passed on in an explicit way teachings in regard to the Assumption and the Immaculate
Conception.

³ But they in turn had to pass this deposit of revelation
on to the Primitive Church. This they did by word of
mouth (tradition) and by writings (Scripture). The Christian message was undoubtedly first preached, and then by
way of further instruction the epistles appeared whereas the
gospels could be viewed as condensations of the revelation
being preached. Whether there were explicit teachings
communicated to the Primitive Church orally, that were
not part of the written summaries and explanations (that
is, New Testament writings) is a matter of opinion. But
many of the best authors today think not, holding, rather,
that "Scripture, especially toward the time of its comple-
tion, appears as containing explicitly, certainly not all
revealed truths, but at least the essential ones, the principles, the articles of faith from which the entire deposit
of revelation could, with the help of the Holy Spirit, be
made explicit later on." (Journet, "Scripture and Tradition" in *Dogma of the Immaculate Conception,* p. 12).

⁴ But whereas Scripture, alone, is a non-living thing,
incapable of explaining itself, Tradition, or the collective
understanding of the original deposit of revelation in the
mind of the Church, the living Mystical Body of Christ,
is itself a living, dynamic, vital thing, which, with the
reflection and growth of the whole Body and under the
guidance of the Holy Spirit, must yield new insights, new
depths to the Christian message as written. For while the
Apostles were graced with special illumination to understand the Christian message, it was not so with the Primi-

tive Church. And so it is from this deposit of revelation as possessed by the Primitive Church, and still to a great extent implicit, unformulated, unconceptualized (yet, in which the Church was acutely, if obscurely, aware of unexplored depths), that the development of dogmas takes its rise. Thus it is not the initial message that grows, but only the Church's formulation and explicitation of it. Our understanding of Christ's message will never surpass that of the Apostles, but it can happen that our *formulation* of a particular truth, such as the Assumption, will surpass that which circumstances never led them to formulate in explicit terms.

[5] Dogma is simply a truth of revelation which has been infallibly set forth for our belief by the teaching Church. Two things are necessary:

1. That this truth be contained in the deposit of revelation.

2. That it be so declared by the Church's infallible teaching authority.

[6] The number of dogmas may grow, as also the number of things in which we explicitly believe; but this by no means implies that the Church is teaching new revelation.

[7] The Vatican Council says: "For the Holy Spirit was promised to the successors of St. Peter, not that they might make known *new* doctrines by His revelation, but rather, that with His assistance, they might jealously *guard* and faithfully *explain* the revelation or deposit of faith that was handed down through the Apostles."

[8] The Catholic Church is the Mystical Body of Christ, animated by a life-giving soul which is the Holy Spirit (St. Augustine, Ser. 267). But as life everywhere manifests growth and development, so the living Church must always manifest a constantly expanding growth and corresponding internal development. And Tradition, or the deposit of faith, is, unlike Scripture, the living mind and consciousness of the Church of Christ deeply aware of His revelation. It, too, then, must develop and achieve deeper and clearer expression of its consciousness—always under the guidance of the Holy Spirit and the infallible teaching authority guaranteed to it by Christ.

⁹ Sometimes a truth is easily seen as contained in Scripture (Trinity, necessity of grace, etc.), and its formulation into dogma causes little difficulty. But at other times the infallible guarantee by the Church is the more prominent element, from which we then know that it *must* belong to the deposit of faith. But where and how it is contained in the deposit is not immediately seen. It is implicit in the essence of revelation found explicitly in Scripture, but preserved in the Church's consciousness or living Tradition, in an even more meaningful and pregnant fashion. (This is the case with the Assumption and the Immaculate Conception.) The infallible declaration of the Church that such a truth is part of revelation will suffice for many; but the inquiring mind still seeks to know *how* it is contained, and how explain the development.

¹⁰ Often we can trace the establishment of dogma to the fight against heresy. And while it still remains true that the new formulation, explicitation and clarifications spring from the inner understanding of revelation by the Church, heresy becomes the *occasion* for expressing it. From the very beginning men have tried to read their own heretical opinions into the pages of Scripture, and in this way introduce false teachings regarding the Trinity, Incarnation, Original Sin and the like. But the Church, as teacher and guardian of revelation (Vatican Council) was forced to condemn such error; and this could only be done by defining the doctrine in ever clearer and more definite terms. (E.g., Councils of Nicea, Ephesus, Chalcedon.) This constitutes true development. And we can even explain the emergence of the dogma of papal infallibility as the term of the Church's clarifications in the face of error, about the place of St. Peter and his successors in the Church.

¹¹ But such clarification does not explain *all* development of doctrine. In certain areas, notably with regard to doctrines about the Blessed Virgin Mary, it has come about almost solely as the spontaneous emergence from the Christian consciousness (or Tradition) now more completely understood by a new grasp of what was implicit and unformulated. As if parents confided many things to their children, facts given added meaning by the lives and gestures and attitudes of the parents; and while the children

grasp *some* of it clearly and the rest obscurely, nevertheless, by continual reflection and greater maturity, they begin to realize little by little the full content of this "implicit" teaching.

[12] It appears that this is what happens, for example, in the case of the Assumption. The first clear manifestation of this truth is in the devotional life of the Church and in the testimonies of the Fathers, beginning about the 6th century. Under the guidance of the Holy Spirit and a better understanding of the original deposit of revelation, there begins to emerge the growing conviction that the Assumption of our Lady into heaven is not only true, but a part of the very deposit of revelation, and legitimately grounded in the clearer teachings of Scripture about Mary. And the same Holy Spirit, the Spirit of Truth, brings it about that a false devotion will not persist, while this one grows and becomes the unanimous belief of the whole Catholic world, directed, supported and, finally, infallibly confirmed by the teaching authority of the Church.

[13] Here the primary motive for defining the truth seems to be the fact of its already universal acceptance by the living Church. Says Pius XII in defining the Assumption: "This outstanding agreement of the Catholic prelates and the faithful, affirming that the bodily Assumption of God's Mother into heaven can be defined as a dogma of faith, since it shows us the concordant teaching of the Church's ordinary doctrinal authority and the concordant faith of the Christian people which the same doctrinal authority sustains and directs, thus by itself and in an entirely certain and infallible way, manifested this privilege as a truth revealed by God and contained in the divine deposit which Christ has delivered to His Spouse to be guarded faithfully and to be taught infallibly" (*Munificentissimus Deus*, Eng-Transl., New York: Paulist Press, par. 12).

[14] Thus as Newman says, in regard to the Immaculate Conception: ". . . Catholics have not come to believe it because it is defined, but it was defined because they believed it" And if they believed it, it is because they sensed, obscurely, preconceptually, instinctively, that it was contained in the other truths of the deposit of revelation.

[15] What then of the creeds? As a result of the internal development and clearer understanding of the truths of revelation, and often spurred on by the need to combat heresy, the Church of the first few centuries made a careful formulation of the most basic teachings of Christianity. Grouped together, these formed the creeds, and were a convenient means of securing uniformity in teaching, and a test of orthodoxy for new converts. The principal creeds, the Nicene, the Athanasian and the Apostles' (the last two in their present form are no earlier than the 5th or 6th century) remain for us today much revered summaries of the essential truths of Christianity. But they do not contain the dogmas which became explicit only later. And it is as illogical to refuse acceptance to later definitions as to accept the Nicene Creed and refuse belief in the later Athanasian Creed. For all the creeds and dogmas spring from the one original deposit of revelation and are guaranteed by the same infallible teaching authority of the Church, under the guidance of the Holy Spirit.

[16] In summary, then, when the Church defines a doctrine, she does not create new revelation. She simply declares infallibly that this belief is part of the original deposit of revelation taught by Jesus Christ and the Apostles.

Is there not a great difference between the faith of a learned and the faith of an ignorant Catholic?

[1] No there is not. The trained theologian or apologist may know more facts, and have a greater grasp of the principles of philosophy or theology, but his faith is identical with the faith of the most illiterate peasant. Both believe the same Gospel of Christ in its entirety, and for the same reason — the authority of God, witnessed unto them by the divine, infallible teaching of Christ's one true Church.

Does not the Catholic Church insist upon an outward uniformity with her laws rather than upon fidelity to conscience? Did not Luther reinstate conscience in its rights?

[1a] No, we answer to both questions. Conscience is a dictate of the practical reason, deciding that a particular action is right or wrong. It is the voice or ambassador of

God, making known to us His eternal law, and applying it in our every day life. Pope Innocent III taught plainly: "Whatever is done contrary to conscience leads to hell" (*Decret.*, Lib. ii., tit. 3, ch. 3).

² The Catholic Church has always taught that conscience, the authoritative guide of our moral conduct, requires us to submit to all properly constituted authority especially to the divine authority of Christ's Church Luther, by substituting fallible private judgment for the infallible common judgment of the Church in matters of faith and morals, left conscience to itself, or referred it to his own teaching, that is, his peculiar interpretation of the Scriptures. Mere subjectivism became the guide of himself and his followers.

³ The Church does not usurp the office of the individual conscience, but refers it to the divine tradition of faith and morals, taught by Jesus and the twelve Apostles. She has never been content with mere formalism or "an outward holiness by works," as Luther styled it, but has always insisted upon the virtues of faith, hope, love of God and the neighbor, urging men to live a supernatural, interior life of grace.

If I, as a Lutheran, have taken an oath at my confirmation to die in the Church of my baptism, can I honestly go against that oath and become a Catholic? I believe that the religion of my parents is good enough for me.

¹ As soon as you believe that the Catholic Church is the one true Church, the oath you took in good faith as a Lutheran is no longer binding. An oath to do wrong is sinful and of no effect, whether it be an oath like Herod's which brought about the death of John the Baptist (Matt 14, 7-10), or an oath to remain in known heresy and schism

²ª If your parents were poor, would that prevent you from trying to better your condition? Not in the slightest degree. As soon as you become convinced of the poverty of the partial Gospel you possess, you must, as a thinking man, better your spiritual condition by accepting without question Christ's one true Gospel.

My mother—a good soul and a sincere Protestant—assures me that it will break her heart if I become a Catholic. I believe all the teachings of your Church, but find it hard to grieve one dear to me by becoming a convert.

[1] The true Christian ought not to hesitate a moment about joining the Catholic Church, once he is convinced of the truth of her divine claims. To be false to conscience is to imperil the salvation of your soul. Our Lord said plainly: "Therefore, everyone who acknowledges Me before men, I also will acknowledge him before My Father in heaven. But whoever disowns Me before men, I in turn will disown him before My Father in heaven" (Matt. 10, 32-33).

[2] Our Lord knew full well that converts would often meet bitter opposition on the part of their relatives and friends, when they contemplated entering His true Church, but He clearly taught that He must come first. "For I have come to set a man at variance with his father, and a daughter with her mother. . . . He who loves father or mother more than Me is not worthy of Me" (Matt. 10, 35. 37).

[3] The Fourth Commandment, "Honor thy father and thy mother," does not require obedience to parents, when they command something contrary to God's law, for as St. Peter says: "We must obey God rather than men" (Acts 5, 29). Children, after reaching the legal age of maturity, need not obey their parents when they propose to marry, to enter religion, or to follow the dictates of their conscience in embracing the true faith.

I envy my Catholic wife and little ones, saying their prayers morning and night with simple faith in God and in Jesus Christ. I would give a great deal to believe as they do, but I honestly cannot. Will God damn me forever for something I cannot help?

[1a] God, who is Infinite Justice and Holiness, condemns only those who knowingly sin against the light; that is, men who know His divine truth and deliberately reject it, and who know His divine law, and deliberately refuse to obey it. The Catholic faith is a gift and a grace of God,

which He gives to all men who are rightly disposed to receive it. The very fact that you earnestly desire to believe, is a sure sign that your present state of mind will not be permanent.

² Pray daily for this most precious gift, for our Lord has promised, "If you ask the Father anything in My name, He will give it to you" (John 16, 23).

³ First of all ask God pardon for your sins, for sinfulness blurs the spiritual vision of many an unbeliever. "The sensual man does not perceive the things that are of the spirit of God, for it is foolishness to him, and he cannot understand, because it is examined spiritually (1 Cor. 2, 14). It is frequently a short step from the Confiteor to the Credo; from the act of sorrow to the act of faith. "If anyone desires to do His will, he will know of the teaching whether it is from God" (John 7, 17).

⁴ Remember that reason, God's own light within the soul, is a gift of God as well as faith. Reason can prove the existence of God, and if you weigh the many arguments which any priest will develop for you, you will soon be convinced of their cumulative force. Reason is also able to study the Scriptures, the history of the Church, and the many proofs from prophecy and miracles attesting the divinity of Jesus Christ, the Son of God.

⁵ Read a life of Jesus Christ and sooner or later the conviction will come that He is God, calling for the perfect submission of your intellect and will. Only one Church —the Catholic Church—dares teach as He taught with divine infallible certainty; only one Church claims His divine pardoning power over the sins of men; only one Church is founded on Peter, the Rock, teaching everywhere the same Gospel that Jesus and the Apostles gave the world.

⁶ Do not expect to comprehend the mysteries of the Gospel, for God's revelation cannot be fully grasped by any finite intellect. Do not look for mathematical evidence in matters of faith, for God could not promise you a reward for a forced assent to His truth. He demands of us a free and a willing service. Do not be dismayed by difficulties.

⁷ As Cardinal Newman said: "Ten thousand difficulties do not make one doubt."

What are the conditions of entrance into the Catholic Church? Must a convert from one of the other Churches be rebaptized, and confess the sins of a lifetime?

[1] The Catholic Church requires of all adults, who seek admission into her fold, a supernatural sorrow for all past sins, and a firm belief in all the teachings of Christ and His Apostles, as handed down from the beginning by the written and the unwritten tradition of Christ's one divine Church. Converts are required to study carefully under the guidance of some priest an approved catechism, that is, a brief summary of Catholic belief and practice.

[2] A member of one of the other Churches is always asked to make a profession of faith with his right hand on the book of the Gospels before he is baptized.

[3] If the convert has already been validly baptized, he is bound only to confess the mortal sins he has knowingly and willingly committed since his Baptism. If there is doubt of the validity of his Baptism, he is baptized conditionally with the words, "If you are not baptized, I baptize you in the name of the Father, and of the Son, and of the Holy Spirit." He then receives the sacrament of Penance conditionally after confessing all the mortal sins he has knowingly and willingly committed during his whole life. This is to make sure he is in the state of grace with all his mortal sins forgiven. If he has never been baptized, he simply receives the sacrament of Baptism which cleanses his soul of all sin.

[4] Ordinarily, a priest keeps the convert under instruction from three to six months. During this period the convert usually attends Sunday Mass, prays daily and observes the laws of fast and abstinence.

Are not converts to your Church required, by the profession of faith they make on entering it, to hate their relatives and friends?

[1a] No, they are asked to detest heresy, which is a denial of God's truth, and to detest schism, which is a withdrawal from Christ's one true Church (Matt. 7, 15; 12, 25); they are not, and cannot be, asked to hate anyone.

[2] The love of all the brethren is a proof of our love of

God. The First Commandment according to our Lord was: "Thou shalt love the Lord thy God. . . . And the Second is like it, Thou shalt love thy neighbor as thyself. There is no other commandment greater than these" (Mark 12, 29-31). And St. John teaches: "If anyone says 'I love God,' and hates his brother, he is a liar. For how can he who does not love his brother, whom he sees, love God, whom he does not see" (1 John 4, 20).

[3] A convert on the contrary will love his relatives and friends more than ever, because he has drawn nearer to God. He will pray for their conversion daily, and offer up many a Mass and Communion that they too may see the light, and be given the grace not to be "disobedient to the heavenly vision" (Acts 26, 19).

Do not converts to your infallible Church have to surrender their reason? Your Church is a spiritual despotism.

[1] No, the Catholic faith is most reasonable, for the ultimate authority on which we believe is the voice of God speaking to us through the Church. As Orestes Brownson says: "It is not the Church that establishes spiritual despotism; it is she who saves us from it. Spiritual despotism is that which subjects us in spiritual matters to a human authority, whether our own or that of others; and the only redemption from it is having in them a divine authority. Protestants themselves acknowledge this when they call out for the pure word of God. The Church teaches by divine authority; in submitting to her we submit to God, and are freed from all human authority. She teaches infallibly; therefore, in believing what she teaches, we believe the truth, which frees us from falsehood and error, to which all men without an infallible guide are subject, and submission to which is the elemental principle of all spiritual despotism" (*Works*, x., 128).

[2] Brownson's friend, Father Hecker, the founder of the Paulist Fathers, thus answers our questioner: "It was one of the happiest moments of our life, when we discovered for the first time, that it was not required of us to abandon our reason, or to drown it in a false excitement to be a religious man. That to become a Catholic, so far from

being contrary to reason, was a supreme act of reason"
(*Questions of the Soul,* 286; *Aspirations of Nature,* chs.
xxiii., xxiv.).

[3] I might cite the evidence of hundreds of converts who
give the same testimony regarding the freedom a Catholic
enjoys. The late Msgr. Ronald Knox writes: "I had been
encouraged to suppose, and finally prepared to find, that
the immediate result of submission to Rome would be the
sense of having one's liberty cramped and restricted in a
number of ways, necessary no doubt to the welfare of the
Church at large, but galling to the individual. . . . The
curious thing is that my experience has been exactly the
opposite. I have been overwhelmed with the feeling of
liberty—the glorious liberty of the sons of God. . . . It was
not until I became a Catholic that I became conscious of
my former homelessness, my exile from the place that was
my own" (*Spiritual Aeneid,* 247, 249).

*Does your Church approve of bringing people into her fold
by force, as happened in the days of Charlemagne, of Louis
XIV, and the Kings of Spain with regard to the Jews and
Moors?*

[1] No, the Church is in no way responsible for the actions of Catholic sovereigns, who from motives of policy,
avarice or mistaken zeal used force in bringing about conversions. Alcuin and Arno of Salsburg severely blamed
Charlemagne for his enforced conversion of the pagan
Saxons; Pope Innocent XI rebuked Louis XIV for his cruel
dragonnades, and asked James II to interpose his good
offices on behalf of the oppressed French Huguenots; Sixtus
IV continually denounced the arbitrary cruelty and injustice of the Spanish Inquisition (Alzog, *Church History,* ii.,
122; iii., 284; Pastor, *History of the Popes,* iv., 399-402).

[2] The teaching of the Church on this matter is plainly
set forth in the writings of Tertullian, Origen, St. Cyprian,
Lactantius, St. Hilary and others. Tertullian writes: "It is
a fundamental human right, a privilege of nature, that
every man should worship according to his convictions.
It is assuredly no part of religion to compel religion. It
must be embraced freely and not forced" (*Ad Scapulam,*
ii., ch. ii.).

SELECTED BIBLIOGRAPHY

BELLOC, HILAIRE. *Characters of the Reformation*. Garden City, N. Y.: (Image Books) Doubleday & Co. 1958.

BOUYER, LOUIS. *Christian Initiation*. New York: Macmillan. 1960.

BURGGRAFF, ALOYSIUS J. *Handbook for New Catholics*. New York: Paulist Press. 1960.

CAVANAUGH, JOSEPH H. *Evidence for Our Faith*. Notre Dame, Ind.: University of Notre Dame Press. 1959.

CONGAR, MARIE J. *The Mystery of the Church*. Baltimore, Md.: Helicon Press. 1960.

DE LA BEDOYERE, MICHAEL. *The Meddlesome Friar and the Wayward Pope*. Garden City, N. Y.: Hanover House. 1958.

DOUILLET, JACQUES. *What Is a Saint?* New York: Hawthorn Books. 1958.

HUGHES, PHILIP. *A Popular History of the Reformation*. Garden City, N. Y.: (Image Books) Doubleday & Co. 1960.

JOURNET, CHARLES. *The Church of the Word Incarnate*. New York: Sheed & Ward. 1955.

KAISER, EDWARD G. *Sacred Doctrine*. Westminster, Md.: Newman Press. 1958.

LECLER, JOSEPH. *Toleration and the Reformation*. New York: Association Press. 1960.

LUBAC, HENRI DE. *Splendor of the Church*. Sheed & Ward. 1956.

LUCAS, HENRY S. *The Renaissance and the Reformation*. New York: Harper & Bros. 1960.

MITCHELL, JOHN D. (ed.). *The Parish Priest's Guide to Inquiry Classes*. New York: Paulist Press. 1960.

NEILL, THOMAS P. *History of the Catholic Church*. Milwaukee: Bruce Publishing Co. 1957.

NOORT, GERARDUS C. VAN. *Christ's Church*. Westminster, Md.: Newman Press. 1957.

OTT, LUDWIG. *Fundamentals of Catholic Dogma*. St. Louis: B. Herder Book Co. 1957.

PIUS XII, POPE. "The Mystical Body of Christ" in *Four Great Encyclicals*. New York: Paulist Press. 1961.

RIDOLFI, ROBERTO. *The Life of Girolamo Savonarola*. New York: Alfred A. Knopf. 1959.

ROSS, WILLIAMSON. *The Beginning of the English Reformation*. New York: Sheed & Ward. 1957.

WEIGEL, GUSTAVE. *A Catholic Primer on the Ecumenical Movement*. Westminster, Md.: Newman Press. 1957.

PART VII
The Papacy

Is there any Biblical proof that Christ made Peter the first Pope? Were not all the Apostles equal?

[1] The Catholic Church believes that St. Peter was the chief Apostle, exercising by Christ's appointment the supreme power of governing His Church. The Vatican Council says: "If anyone says that Christ the Lord did not constitute the Blessed Peter prince of all the Apostles and head of the whole Church militant; or if he says that this primacy is one of mere honor and not of real jurisdiction received directly and immediately from our Lord Jesus, let him be anathema."

[2] On three different occasions Christ speaks of the primacy of St. Peter over the twelve Apostles.

[3] 1. After St. Peter had acknowledged His divinity, Christ promised him a reward in the following words: "I say to thee, thou art Peter, and upon this rock I will build My Church, and the gates of hell shall not prevail against it. And I will give thee the keys of the kingdom of heaven; and whatever thou shalt bind upon earth shall be bound in heaven, and whatever thou shalt loose upon earth shall be loosed also in heaven" (Matt. 16, 18-19).

[4] (a) The metaphor of the rock is easily understood. Christ the rock, the chief cornerstone of the Church (Eph. 2, 20; Matt. 21, 42), promises to make Peter the rock, on which His Church (1 Cor. 3, 9) is to be built. He is addressing him alone ("I say to *thee*"), not the other Apostles. Our Lord has in mind the wise man of His own parable (Matt. 7, 24). The rock foundation of a building gives it unity, strength and stability; it holds all the various

107

parts of the building solidly together. In a society this is effected by the authority of the head, by whom unity is forever preserved.

⁵ (b) Christ then gives the reason why He intends to build His Church upon the rock, Peter, namely, "that the gates of hell shall not prevail against it." Whether hell means the hell of the damned or the realm of death, the meaning is obvious. The Church of Christ is to withstand forever the attacks of every foe within or outside her fold.

⁶ (c) The symbol of the keys, in the East, always implied power and authority, and the giving of the keys the transfer of that authority. Even in our day when we wish to honor a visitor of prominence, we give him the keys of the city. When we sell a building, we give the keys to the new owner the day the title passes. When Eliacim was appointed over the palace in the place of Sobna, we read: "I will place the key of the house of David on his shoulder; when he opens, no one shall shut, and when he shuts, no one shall open" (Isa. 22, 22).

⁷ (d) "Binding and loosing" among the Rabbis of our Lord's time meant to declare something "prohibited" or "permitted." Here it plainly means that St. Peter, the steward of the Lord's house, the Church, has all the rights and powers of a divinely appointed steward. He does not, like the Jewish Rabbis, declare probable, speculative opinions, but he has the right to teach and govern authoritatively, with the certainty of God's approval "in heaven." The member of the Church that refuses to obey is to be regarded as "a heathen and a publican," as Christ says in a similar passage (Matt. 18, 17). A lawgiving power is certainly implied by these words.

⁸ 2. The night before He died Jesus said to St. Peter: "Simon, Simon, behold, Satan has desired to have you, that he may sift you as wheat. But I have prayed for thee, that thy faith may not fail; and do thou, when once thou hast turned again, strengthen thy brethren" (Luke 22, 31-32). Satan had desired to try the Apostle, as once he tried the patriarch Job (Job 1, 11-12). Christ tells St. Peter that, although He prayed for all the Apostles (John 17, 9), He prayed especially for him (Luke 22, 31), that he might strengthen the others.

[9] 3. After the Resurrection, Christ bestowed upon St. Peter the primacy He had twice promised. His words are: "Simon, son of John, dost thou love Me more than these do?" He said to Him, "Yes, Lord, thou knowest that I love Thee." He said to him, "Feed My lambs." He said to him a second time, "Simon, son of John, dost thou love Me?" He said to Him, "Yes, Lord, Thou knowest that I love Thee." He said to him, "Feed My lambs." A third time He said to him, "Simon, son of John, dost thou love Me?" Peter was grieved because He said to him for the third time, "Dost thou love Me?" And he said to Him, "Lord, Thou knowest all things, Thou knowest that I love Thee." He said to him, "Feed My sheep" (John 21, 15-17).

[11] Indeed the pre-eminence of St. Peter is suggested in many a passage in the New Testament. His name is changed at his first meeting with Christ (John 1, 42), thus indicating the office of rock foundation, which was to be given him later on. He is always named first in the lists of the Apostles (Matt. 10, 2; Mark 3, 16; Luke 6, 14), and always regarded as their leader (Matt. 17, 1, 23-26; 26, 37-40; 14, 22; Mark 5, 37; 9, 1; Luke 5, 2-10; 8, 45). After the Resurrection he presides at the election of Matthias (Acts 1, 22); he is the first to preach the Gospel (Acts 2, 14); he is the first to work miracles (Acts 3, 6); he is the judge of Ananias and Sapphira (Acts 5, 1-10); he is the first to declare the universality of the Church's mission (Acts 10), and the first to receive a pagan convert (Acts 10); he presides at the Council of Jerusalem (Acts 15).

Does not the rock mean Christ (Matt. 16, 18)? We read in the Bible, "and the rock was Christ" (1 Cor. 10, 4).

[1] Christ is the rock, primarily; He is the divine Founder of the Church. Peter is the rock, secondarily; he is the Head of the Church by divine appointment of Christ. Peter is dependent on Christ; he is "the rock and foundation of Christ" (St. Cyprian, Theophylact, *In Lucam,* 22). Both Christ *and* Peter are "rocks" but in different senses.

[2] Modern Biblical scholars agree that in Matt. 16, 18 the word "rock" refers to St. Peter. All admit the divine appointment of Peter but they argue as to the nature of the

appointment—was it a personal one to Peter alone or could he pass it on to his successors?

³ In his first Epistle to the Corinthians, St. Paul is referring to an event recorded in Exodus 17, 6f. The rock struck by Moses is called "spiritual" because it typified Christ. As water flowed from the material rock for the refreshment of the Jews so blood flowed from Christ, the rock, for the salvation of men.

If St. Peter was the chief Apostle why do we read that "there arose also a dispute among them (the Apostles), which of them was reputed to be the greatest" (Luke 22, 24)?

¹ The Apostles might have been ignorant of the primacy of Peter before the resurrection, just as they were ignorant of the passion and resurrection of our Lord (Matt. 16, 23; 20, 17-19). Our Lord could have ended the dispute in a moment, had He declared that no one would be the chief or the greatest Apostle in His Church. On the contrary, He implies that there would be a ruler among them, not lording it like the pagan kings over their subjects, but making authority a means of serving the brethren. He Himself gave the example: "Even as the Son of Man has not come to be served but to serve" (Matt. 20, 28). "I am in your midst as He who serves" (Luke 22, 27).

² In fact, He plainly points out that one is chief among them, for He says: "Let him who is greatest among you become as the youngest, and him who is the chief as the servant" (Luke 22, 26).

If Peter was infallible, why did he deny the Savior (Matt. 26, 70; Mark 14, 66-72)?

¹ᵃ The infallible primacy was not given to St. Peter until after the Resurrection (John 16, 16), and, moreover, infallibility has no reference to the personal errors or sins of individual Popes. It is noteworthy that St. Mark's Gospel, which is the testimony of St. Peter, emphasizes more than the other three Gospels, the human weaknesses and sins of the chief Apostle. In his humility St. Peter records to the

utmost detail his triple denial of Jesus, while at the same time he altogether omits the great promise recorded by St. Matthew in chapter 16.

Did not James preside at the Council of Jerusalem, and give the definite sentence? How then was Peter chief Apostle?

[1] St. Peter, not St. James, presided at the Council of Jerusalem. The question at issue was whether the Gentiles were bound to obey the Mosaic Law. Paul, Barnabas, James and the rest were present as teachers and judges, just as Bishops were present at the Vatican Council, but Peter was their head, and the supreme arbiter of the controversy, as Pius IX was in the 19th century.

[2] St. Peter spoke first and decided the matter unhesitatingly, declaring that the Gentile converts were not bound by the Mosaic Law. He claimed to exercise authority in the name of his special election by God to receive the Gentiles (Acts 15, 7), and he severely rebuked those who held the opposite view (Acts 15, 10). After he had spoken "the whole meeting quieted down" (Acts 15, 12). Those who spoke after him merely confirmed his decision, mentioning like Paul and Barnabas the miracles wrought by God on their missionary journeys, or suggesting, like James, that the Gentiles respect the scruples of the Jewish converts, by abstaining from the things they detested (Acts 15, 20, 21).

Did not St. Paul refuse to acknowledge St. Peter as his superior, when he "withstood him to his face" (Gal. 2, 11)?

[1a] St. Paul's rebuke of St. Peter, instead of implying a denial of his supremacy, implies just the opposite. He tells us that the example of St. Peter "compelled" the Gentiles to live as the Jews. St. Paul's example had not the same compelling power.

[2a] The rebuke, however, did not refer to the doctrine, but to the conduct of St. Peter, as Tertullian says (*De Praes.*, 23). St. Peter had not changed the views he had himself set forth at the Council of Jerusalem (Acts 15, 10). But at Antioch he withdrew from the table of the Gentiles, because he feared giving offense to the Jewish con-

verts. They at once mistook his kindliness for an approval of the false teaching of certain Judaizers, who wished to make the Mosaic Law obligatory upon all Christians. His action was at most imprudent, and calculated to do harm because of his great influence and authority. St. Paul, therefore, had a perfect right to uphold the Gospel liberty by a direct appeal to St. Peter's own example and teaching.

[3] The duty of fraternal correction (Matt. 18, 15) may often require an inferior to rebuke a superior in defense of justice and truth. St. Bernard, St. Thomas of Canterbury and St. Catherine of Siena rebuked Popes, while fully acknowledging their supreme authority.

How can you claim that St. Peter was Bishop of Rome when most scholars deny that he was ever in Rome?

[1] St. Peter (c. 42-67), who had received from Christ jurisdiction over the whole Church, was the first Bishop of Rome. The date of his arrival, the length of his residence, and the details of his Apostolic activity remain more or less uncertain, but modern scholarship regards as certain that Peter was in Rome and that he was martyred there.

[2] Peter himself witnesses to his presence in Rome when in his first Epistle he tells us that he is writing from Babylon, a word that was figuratively used for Rome in Apostolic times (1 Peter 5, 13). Elliott, a Protestant, thus comments, "We have to remark that the city of Babylon was certainly not the seat of a Christian community; that no ancient record has the slightest trace of St. Peter's presence or work in Chaldea; that all ancient authorities are unanimous in asserting that the later years of his life were passed in the West of the Roman Empire. On the other hand, Babylon was well known in Asia Minor during the lifetime of St. John as the symbolical designation of Rome. . . . Accordingly, we find an absolute consensus of ancient interpreters that Babylon must be understood as equivalent to Rome" (*Speaker's Commentary*).

[3] The Fathers of the first four centuries frequently speak of the labors of St. Peter in Rome and his martyrdom there. They repeatedly bear witness to Peter as Bishop of Rome. St. Irenaeus refers to "that greatest, most ancient

and most illustrious Church, founded and constituted at Rome by the glorious Apostles, Peter and Paul, with which every Church must agree" (*Adv. Haer.*). St. Cyprian calls Rome "the Chair of Peter, and the ruling Church, whence the unity of the priesthood has its source" (*Ad Cornel.*). Eusebius in his *History* states that "Linus was the first after Peter who obtained the Episcopate of the Church of the Romans."

4 Modern scholars, Catholic, Protestant, and Rationalist, offer convincing authoritative testimony that St. Peter was truly the Bishop of Rome.

5 Cave writes: "That Peter was at Rome, and held the See there for some time, we fearlessly affirm with the whole multitude of the ancients. We give witness above all exception, derived from most remote antiquity." And he proceeds to quote St. Ignatius, Papias, St. Irenaeus, Dionysius of Corinth, Clement of Alexandria, Tertullian, Caius of Rome and Origen (*Historia Literaria,* i.).

6 Dr. Lardner writes: "It is the general, uncontradicted, disinterested testimony of ancient writers in the several parts of the world—Greeks, Latins, Syrians" (*History of the Apostles,* ch. xviii.).

7 Pearson writes: "Since it has been handed down from almost the beginning that St. Peter preached the Gospel in Rome, and there suffered martyrdom, and since no one has ever affirmed that either Peter or Paul was crowned with martyrdom elsewhere, I think, with full security, faith may be given to this account. For who would believe that so great an Apostle could have died in such obscurity as that no one ever recorded the place of his death?" (*Minor Theological Works,* iii., 34; Vacandard, *Etudes de Critique,* iv., 3-12.)

8 It is remarkable that none of the Eastern schismatics who seceded from Rome from the 5th to the 11th centuries ever denied the Roman Episcopate of St. Peter. They could easily have done so to put forward a plausible reason for their schism, but they never dreamed of using so impossible an argument. It was only for controversial purposes that in the 13th and 14th centuries the Waldenses and Marsiglio of Padua contested this historical truth.

[9] Finally, the Vatican Council defined as an article of Catholic faith that "St. Peter still lives, presides and judges in the person of his successors, the Bishops of Rome."

[10] During the last twenty years (1940-1960), excavations under the Altar of the Confession in St. Peter's Basilica have produced archaeological discoveries as evidence that the Apostle Peter had been buried there.

[11] A Greek inscription dating to about 160 A.D. states that "Peter is within." From this and many other inscriptions it becomes clear that, at least since the middle of the 2nd century, the faithful have been convinced that St. Peter's tomb was in the place marked by the chapel under the present papal altar. Dr. Margherita Guarducci, the distinguished Italian archaeologist and foremost authority on the epigraphy of the excavations, states: ". . . we can now say that in the investigation of St. Peter's tomb, Science has come to the aid of Faith. This happy alliance has placed on age-old tradition a strengthened and renewed seal of irrefutable Truth" (*The Tomb of St. Peter, 183*).

Granted that Peter was the chief Apostle and head of the Church in the beginning, how can you prove that his power was handed down the centuries? Was there any exercise of the papal supremacy during the first three centuries?

[1] The Vatican Council teaches as an article of faith that the Pope is the legitimate successor of St. Peter. "If any one says that the Roman Pontiff is not the successor of Blessed Peter in the primacy, let him be anathema."

[2] The primacy of St. Peter was not a personal privilege, like the power of working miracles, but an essential part of Christ's Church, the rock on which it was built. As long as the Church was to last—till the end of the world—Peter was to reign in an unbroken succession of Bishops of Rome. The House of God will always need its *foundation*; the House of God will always need a *confirmer of the brethren*, and a *shepherd* to guide and rule them.

[3] Many of the documents of early Church history were destroyed during the pagan persecutions of the first three

centuries, but ample records remain to show that the Bishops of Rome exercised the supreme power of teaching, ruling and judging. Before St. John died, Pope Clement of Rome (90-99) of his own accord wrote to the Christians of Corinth, urging concord and submission to their ecclesiastical superiors. There is no record of the Apostle John intervening, although Ephesus was easier of access than Rome. The Corinthians accepted Rome's message and legates gladly, and the Pope's letter was placed almost on a level with the Sacred Scriptures for nearly a century (Clement, *Ad Cor.*, i., 1, 2, 44).

[4] Pope Victor (189-198) at the close of the 2nd century summoned the Bishops of the time to come together in councils to determine the date of celebrating Easter. The Asiatics accepted the Jewish Pasch for their feast, while Rome observed it on the Sunday after the Jewish Pasch. Although the Council of Asia appealed to St. John and St. Philip as their authorities together with Papias and St. Polycarp, the Pope threatened the Bishops with excommunication, unless they abandoned their custom. Could there be a more striking evidence of his realization of his supreme authority? Who but the supreme Bishop would have dared to separate Bishops from the unity of the whole Church? No other Church ever claimed such power.

[5] St. Irenaeus, Bishop of Lyons, wrote in 180 his well known treatise against the Gnostics of his time. In it we find a clear assertion of the unity of the Church's teaching, and the supremacy of Rome, the guardian of the Apostolic tradition, over all other Churches. He says: "Indeed, the superior pre-eminence of that Church is such that every Church—I mean the faithful of any country whatsoever—necessarily agrees with her, that is, every Church in any country in which the Apostolic tradition has been preserved without interruption" (*Adv. Haer.*, iii., 3).

[6] In the year 256 a conflict arose between Pope Stephen (254-257) and St. Cyprian, Bishop of Carthage, on the question of baptisms conferred by heretics. Rome considered these baptisms valid, while Carthage declared them invalid. Despite the fact that St. Cyprian with his Bishops in Council refused to give up his custom, Pope Stephen (254-257)

insisted upon the *traditional* teaching, and threatened the opposing Bishops wih excommunication, as Pope Victor had done in the Easter controversy.

⁷ The Archbishop of Alexandria, Dionysius (195-265), was accused at Rome of heresy with regard to the Blessed Trinity. Pope Dionysius (259-268) asked him to explain his words, which he did in his reply to the Pope, and in the four books of his *Refutation and Apology* (Athanasius, *De Sent. Dion.*, 13, 18). The Pope asked him not to reject the term consubstantial, although the word did not become classical until the following century. The Archbishop, in modifying his language, showed that he was really orthodox, and thereby recognized the authority of the Bishop of Rome to call him to account.

Does not the primacy of the Pope destroy the power of the individual Bishops?

¹ No, it does not, for the individual Bishops are successors of the Apostles, and therefore enjoy true jurisdiction within their own territory, and to a certain extent over their own subjects, even outside their dioceses. As legislators they can enact binding statutes, and dispense from their observance. They cannot, of course, make laws contrary to the laws of the Universal Church, any more than a governor of the United States can order his legislature to go counter to the Federal Government. The Bishop is also judge in his own diocese, and the source of jurisdiction in the sacrament of Penance. His court is the court of first instance, although appeals are allowed to the higher courts of the Metropolitan and the Pope. He is also the authoritative teacher, exercising this office by his own preaching, the issuing of pastoral letters, and the controlling of the preaching of his clergy, the doctrine set forth in published works, and the teaching of his schools and seminaries.

² As far as orders are concerned, the Pope holds only an equal place with other Bishops, but in matters of jurisdiction he enjoys supreme, universal and immediate jurisdiction over the whole Church and every member of it. This supremacy is not given by the cardinals who elect him, but immediately by God. The Pope is the Church's supreme

and infallible teacher, its supreme legislator, and its supreme judge.

[3] Pope Gregory states the Catholic doctrine of the primacy in many passages of his letters. He calls the Apostolic See of Rome "the head of the faith," and the "head of all the churches," because "it holds the place of Peter, the Prince of the Apostles." "All Bishops," and he expressly mentions Constantinople, "are subject to the Apostolic See." It has always been the teaching of the Church that the Bishops are not mere agents of the Pope, but by divine institution true successors of the Apostles. Pope Leo XIII echoes in the 19th century the words of Gregory I in the 7th century: "Although the power of Peter and his successors is complete and supreme, it is not the only power. He who made Peter the foundation of the Church, also selected the twelve, whom He called Apostles. Just as the authority of Peter must be perpetuated in the Roman Pontiff, so also the ordinary power of the Apostles must be inherited by their successors, the Bishops. Hence the order of Bishops pertains of necessity to the very constitution of the Church" (*On the Unity of the Church*).

How can a mere man be infallible? Is that not a prerogative of God alone?

[1] God alone is essentially infallible, for, as the Absolute Truth, He cannot deceive or be deceived. God can, however, make the Pope infallible as His representative upon earth, in order to safeguard His divine revelation. That He has done so is proved by the Sacred Scriptures and by the history of the Church.

What do Catholics mean by the infallibility of the Pope? How can you prove it a part of the Gospel teaching?

[1a] The Vatican Council thus defined the doctrine of Papal infallibility:

"Faithfully adhering to the tradition received from the beginning of the Christian faith . . . we teach and define that it is a dogma divinely revealed that the Roman Pontiff, when he speaks *ex cathedra,* that is, when in discharge of the office of pastor and teacher of all Christians, by virtue of his supreme Apostolic authority, he defines a doctrine regarding faith and morals to be held by the Universal Church, by the divine assistance promised him in the Blessed Peter, is possessed of that infallibility with which the divine Redeemer willed that His Church should be endowed for defining doctrine regarding faith and morals; and that, therefore, such definitions of the Roman Pontiffs are irreformable of themselves, and not from the consent of the Church."

² The Pope, therefore, is infallible only:

1. When he speaks *ex cathedra,* that is, when he speaks officially as supreme pastor of the Universal Church. He is not infallible as supreme legislator, supreme judge or supreme ruler. He is not infallible as a simple priest, local Bishop of Rome, Archbishop of the Roman Province, Primate of Italy, or Patriarch of the West.

2. When he defines a doctrine regarding faith and morals. To define a doctrine means to settle it definitely, finally, irrevocably. To omit to define a doctrine might do incalculable harm or imply culpable neglect on the part of a Pope, but it would not be inconsistent with infallibility.

3. When he speaks of faith and morals, which includes the whole content of divine revelation, or the deposit of faith, as St. Paul calls it (Matt. 28, 20; 1 Tim. 6, 20; 2 Tim. 1, 14). It follows logically that the Pope is also infallible in judging doctrines and facts so intimately connected with revelation, that they cannot be denied without endangering revelation itself.

4. When he intends to bind the whole Church. This intention of binding all the faithful must be clearly expressed.

³ Once we admit that the Church is infallible, it follows naturally that its head and mouthpiece must likewise be infallible. For if Peter and his successors, could as supreme pastors teach false doctrine, they would cease to be the rock foundation on which the Church was built; the gates of hell would prevail contrary to Christ's promise; error would be sanctioned in heaven; the faith of the brethren would not be strengthened; the flock of Christ would not be fed with the true food of divine faith (Matt. 6, 18. 19; Luke 22, 31. 32; John 16, 16. 17).

Does infallibility mean that the Pope can do no wrong?

[1] It does not. Infallibility does not mean that the Pope is incapable of committing sin. He may commit sin like any other Catholic, and he is bound like any other Catholic to use the same divine means of pardon, the sacrament of Penance. Infallibility is not a personal, but a divine, official prerogative, given by Christ to Peter and his successors to keep them from error in teaching truths men must believe to be saved.

Does not your infallible Pope make wrong right by his power of dispensation?

[1a] He does not. A dispensation is the relaxation of a law in a particular case and granted by an authorized legislator for good and sufficient reasons. The law itself still remains in force, although an individual or many are exempted from observing it on a special occasion. For example, the Pope dispenses all Catholics from the law of Friday abstinence when Christmas falls on Friday.

[2] The Pope can dispense from all ecclesiastical laws, even if they have been passed by a General Council, because he is the Supreme Legislator of the Church. In fact, he has power to modify or even abolish any Church law. However, he cannot dispense from the natural and divine law. Pope Clement VII refused Henry VIII's application for divorce because Henry was validly married to Catherine of Aragon. Pius VII refused Napoleon's request for his brother Jerome's divorce because Jerome had been validly married to Miss Patterson, a Protestant of Baltimore. These Popes had to refuse for they had no power of dispensation in these cases.

Does the Pope confess his sins to a priest? Why should the ruler submit to his subject? By going to confession does not the Pope show that he is not really infallible?

[1b] To be infallible does not mean to be impeccable or to be sinless. The Pope is human and subject to daily temptations. If he sins mortally, the only way he can be forgiven is by receiving the sacrament of Penance. The

Pope knows that Jesus Christ wants it this way and that the priest in the confessional acts in the name and with the power of Christ. "Whose sins you shall forgive, they are forgiven" (John 20, 23). The Pope does not relinquish his office or diminish his authority any more than Christ did when He was baptized by John the Baptist.

[2b] It is customary for the Pope to confess frequently, even daily, not because he commits many sins but because he desires to obtain the grace of the sacrament, to guide and strengthen him in ruling the Church.

How could Pope Liberius be infallible, when we know that he subscribed to an heretical Arian Creed, and broke with Athanasius, the great defender of the Nicene Creed?

[1] Of Liberius we know little more than the two facts that he was exiled by the Emperor Constantius for his refusal to condemn St. Athanasius, and that after his death his orthodoxy became the subject of long and bitter dispute. While Liberius was in exile, Constantius placed Archdeacon Felix on the papal throne; and when Liberius returned (after his rumored repudiation of Athanasius) the emperor proposed that Felix should co-operate with Liberius in the government of the Church. But the Romans, shouting "One God, one Christ, one Bishop," drove Felix from the city; and the Senate condemned him to perpetual banishment. This antipope Felix has sometimes been confused with an earlier Felix, a Roman martyr, and on this account has been falsely represented as a saint.

[2] The doctrinal controversy was occasioned by the statement of certain writers, including St. Jerome, who affirmed that Pope Liberius was allowed to return from exile, only after he had signed an Arian formula. The truth is that he signed, *not an heretical Arian Creed,* but the compromise formula of the Third Council of Sirmium. This contained no direct attack upon the orthodox faith, although it purposely omitted the Greek word, *omoousios,* which had been used by the Council of Nice. Liberius was told that this word was being interpreted to spread the heresies of Sabellius and Photinus. Lest his action be misunderstood, Liberius added a positive declaration safeguarding

the consubstantiality (true natural sonship with identity of nature) of the Son with the Father.

³Pope Liberius was no heretic. Nevertheless, in his eagerness to return from exile and govern the flock of Christ, he manifested a weakness of character which was in sharp contrast to his unyielding support of Athanasius, two years before at Milan. St. Athanasius defended his friend by saying that Liberius' signature was forced from him under threat of death (*History of the Arians,* 41). That this was true is evidenced by the glowing testimony of the Fathers and Popes of the 4th century. They speak of Liberius in the highest terms, praising both his holiness and his orthodoxy, namely, St. Ambrose, St. Basil, Pope Siricius, and Pope Anastasius.

Does not the condemnation of Pope Honorius by the 6th General Council in 680 prove that the Bishops of that time had no idea of papal infallibility?

¹ It proves nothing of the kind. Here is a summary of the relevant facts in the case. Pope Honorius reigned from 625 to 638. During these years the Church in the Byzantine Empire was split into factions over a theological controversy. The debated question was: is it more correct to use the formula, "one operation" or the formula, "two operations" when speaking of Christ's human activity and divine activity?

² Archbishop Sergius, Patriarch of Constantinople, corresponded with Pope Honorius in an effort to settle the question and to reconcile the parties involved. He suggested that as it was only a war about words, Honorius should outlaw both expressions and forbid further public discussion. After stating that it would be better to avoid both expressions, Honorius added in his reply, "We acknowledge one will of our Lord, Jesus Christ." This declaration (it is obviously heretical; since Christ is truly God and truly man, He has both a divine will and a human will) only fanned the fires of controversy. It gave rise to a new heresy that wracked the Eastern Church for the next forty years, namely, the heresy of Monothelitism (one will in Christ).

[3] Later, Sergius composed an explanation (*Ecthesis*) which the Emperor Heraclius published in 638, at the same time ordering all his subjects to avoid both the expressions "one operation" and "two operations" and to recognize one will in Christ. We cannot determine how Honorius would have reacted to this pronouncement, because he was dead when the imperial edict appeared. However, the next two Popes, Severinus and John IV, condemned the *Ecthesis* and the Emperor repudiated it before his own death in 641. In his condemnation, Pope John IV asserted that "one will" is an inaccurate phrase, but he exonerated Honorius by explaining he had used it in an orthodox sense, namely, to deny that Christ has two *contrary* wills.

[4] In 648 the Emperor Constans II, as a substitute for the *Ecthesis,* published another document called the *Type,* which did not discuss the controverted doctrine, but which forbade anyone to use either the expression "one will" or the expression "two wills."

[5] Both the *Ecthesis* and the *Type* were condemned by Pope Martin I in the Lateran Council of 649. In retaliation, Constans had the Pope arrested, dragged to Constantinople, and exiled to the Crimea where, after much suffering, he died in 655.

[6] The 6th General Council at Constantinople in 680 ended the long debate by condemning all those who held the doctrine of "one will," including Pope Honorius, "We anathematize Honorius who did not attempt to sanctify this Apostolic Church with the teaching of Apostolic tradition, but by profound treachery, permitted the teaching to be polluted." Pope Leo II confirmed the Council's decision.

[7] This condemnation by the Council has nothing to do with papal infallibility, for Honorius did not issue a solemn definition of faith for the whole Church; and it is only in such definition that papal infallibility is exercised. As to the charge that Honorius personally believed a false doctrine, we must remember that his letter to Sergius did not explicitly affirm a heresy; that learned theologians of the time considered Honorius to be personally orthodox; that the Council of Constantinople did not accuse Honorius of imposing heretical doctrine in his official capacity but of

fostering heresy by his negligence; that Pope Leo II approved the condemnation because Honorius had not "extinguished the flame of heretical doctrine from the beginning, but rather had fanned it by his negligence." Leo censured him not so much for what he did but for what he had failed to do, for negligence of duty rather than for teaching heresy.

[8] The history of this celebrated case shows that the Bishops were keenly aware of papal infallibility. Their understanding of this doctrine accords with the definition of the Vatican Council. The very fact that the Bishops sent the decrees of the Council of Constantinople to Pope Leo II for ratification in order to make them binding clearly proves that they had a true notion of papal infallibility.

Did not the Popes forge at Rome a series of documents known as the False Decretals in order to have a basis for their usurped supremacy? Did not Pope Nicholas I (858-867) use them in support of his new claim to rule the other Churches?

[1] The False Decretals did not originate in Rome, but in a city of France—either Rheims or Tours—about the year 850. In view of the anarchy which followed the death of Charlemagne (800-814), the unknown compiler of these decrees sought to free the clergy from metropolitan and lay aggression. Many of these documents are authentic letters of the Popes, for example, Leo I (440-461), although ascribed to Popes living in a previous century.

[2] They introduced nothing new in the essential government of the Church, but aimed throughout at protecting the Bishops from the unjust accusations of lay princes, and the injustice of imperious prelates like Archbishop Hincmar of Rheims. It was precisely because they introduced no novel legislation that they were so readily and so universally accepted.

[8] That they did nothing to enhance the supremacy of the Pope is admitted today by most scholars. Pope Nicholas I indeed knew of their existence, but he never used them himself. Rome, in fact, outside of one citation by

Pope Adrian II (867-872) on a minor matter, utterly ignored them until the time of Leo IX (1049-1054).

⁴ Their authenticity was questioned, long before the Reformation, by Catholic theologians and canonists, Peter Comestor (1178), Godfrey of Viterbo (1180), Stephen of Tournai (1203), Nicholas de Cusa (1431), and Juan de Torquemada (1468). The Church saw the False Decretals come and go with the greatest equanimity, for she knew that the papal claims could be proved independently of the forgeries of a well-meaning but dishonest 9th century French canonist.

Was not the line of papal succession broken during the Great Western Schism which lasted for forty years (1378-1417)?

¹ No, it was not. There can be no doubt that the actual papal succession passed through either the Roman or the Avignon line. Today, the official Vatican lists, as well as most historians, recognize the legitimacy of the Roman line.

² Barely a year after he had restored the papal residence to Rome ending the long "Avignon Captivity," Pope Gregory XI died on March 27, 1378. The Roman populace, fearful that the French majority in the sacred college of Cardinals would elect one of their own nationality and remove the Papacy once more to Avignon, gathered in large numbers before the conclave, clamoring for "a Roman Pope or at least an Italian." The Cardinals did not fully accede to the people's wishes, but did elect unanimously on April 8 an Italian, the Archbishop of Bari, who took the name Urban VI. Though the election took place under very peculiar circumstances, there can be no question that the cardinals fully recognized Urban as the rightful Pope: they informed the six absent Cardinals of his selection, they celebrated the Holy Week liturgy with him, and they requested benefices from him.

³ By August 2, the Cardinals had come to regret their choice. Immediately after his election, Urban began to act strangely and imprudently, rebuking the Cardinals in public and even attempting physical violence against one of them. The Cardinals knew very well that they could

not depose a Pope. The only possible loophole in canon law was a provision that the election of a Pope under the influence of force and fear was null and void. Accordingly, the Cardinals issued a manifesto declaring Urban's election invalid because it had been held with a threatening Roman mob just outside the doors. Every one of the Cardinals rejected Urban and on Sept. 20 elected Clement VII. Certainly if Urban had acted more tactfully after his election, whatever misgivings anyone may have had about its legitimacy, the second election would never have taken place. What made Clement's position so impressive was that he received the approbation of every one of the Cardinals.

[4] With conflicting arguments and testimony hurled back and forth, it was practically impossible for outsiders to know the real facts in the case. The nations divided on political lines. England, most of Germany and Flanders acknowledged Urban, while France, Scotland and Spain acknowledged Clement. Theologians, canonists and even saints divided on national lines—St. Catherine of Siena adhered to Urban and St. Vincent Ferrer upheld the French Clement.

[5] Historians today with all the evidence at their disposal generally agree that Urban VI was the legitimate Pope. The true succession continued through his successors, Boniface IX, Innocent VII, and Gregory XII. Clement VII and his successors, Benedict XIII, Alexander V, and John XXIII were really anti-Popes, although it was practically impossible to be sure of this fact during the schism.

[6] This Great Schism was not a schism in the ordinary sense of the term, because neither side questioned the unity of faith or the supremacy of the Pope. The only problem was to determine who was the legitimate Pope. In 1876 there was considerable doubt in these United States regarding the validity of the election of President Hayes. Suppose a civil war had broken out between Democrats and Republicans on this question. Both sides would have admitted that there was a real President elected, but they would have differed as to which one had been legitimately elected. So in the Great Western Schism. All Catholics believed that there was a real Pope; but they could not know which was the lawfully elected one. The succession

went on uninterruptedly through the Roman line, and all controversy on the matter was settled by the Council of Constance which elected Martin V (1417-1431).

[7] It is interesting to note that Cardinal Roncalli took the name of John XXIII. His choice of name makes it clear that in the history of the Church no *true* Pope had ever previously reigned as John XXIII.

[8] Catholics readily admit the scandalous and tragic events of the Great Schism. It harmed the prestige and authority of the Papacy and prepared the way for the 16th century revolt. On the other hand, it manifested the enduring divine character of the Papacy. Could any mere human institution survive such confusion over leadership or triumph over such internal insurrection?

How was Pope John XXII infallible when he taught that there are two heavens, one for the faithful who are saved and one for the elect who are predestined?

[1] Pope John XXII neither believed nor taught this heretical doctrine. There is only one heaven for all the saved. Nevertheless, he was involved in another controversy and accused of heresy.

[2] In 1274 the second Council of Lyons defined that the just enter heaven *soon* after death. A theological debate arose over the meaning of the word "soon," and this debate was not officially and finally settled until 1336. Some theologians equated "soon" with "immediately" and claimed that the just enter heaven instantly or right away after death. Others argued for a "delayed heaven" and held that the just, although saved, are not granted the beatific vision for some time after death. In fact, some asserted that no human souls, except those of Christ and the Virgin Mary, enjoy the vision of God until the last day when their bodies will be united to their souls.

[3] Before his election as Pope, John wrote a book in which he stated that the souls of the blessed do not see God right after death. He seems to have favored the view that the just are first given the face-to-face vision of Christ in whose humanity they see God somewhat obscurely. Then

finally, perhaps at the last judgment, they receive the full reward of the true beatific vision.

⁴ In 1333, when John was Pope, an assembly of theologians of Paris affirmed the opinion opposed to John's teaching and asked him to confirm their view. He repudiated his former opinion and declared himself in agreement with the Parisian theologians. On December 3, 1334, at a Consistory of Cardinals, he solemnly professed that "the souls separated from the body and fully purified are now in heaven and see God and the divine essence face to face and clearly." Two years later, on January 29, 1336, Pope Benedict XII officially put an end to the controversy by defining the true doctrine.

⁵ John's erroneous teaching in no wise impairs papal infallibility. Firstly, he wrote as a private theologian free to express his personal opinion on a controverted subject, for the Church had not yet defined the point at issue. Secondly, as Pope, he never imposed his personal view on the Universal Church as a matter of faith. Instead, he was persuaded by the sound reasoning of Parisian theologians to change his position and to subscribe to orthodox doctrine.

Did not the Council of Constance in 1415 teach that a General Council was superior to the Pope? How do you explain this in view of your doctrine that Rome never changes, or that General Councils never err?

¹ The primacy of the Popes has always been the teaching of the Catholic Church. The Pope, as the Head of the Church and the chief Bishop, alone has the right to convoke a General Council, and alone has the authority to give its decrees binding force. The General Councils have always acknowledged the primacy of the Popes—Ephesus (431) and Chalcedon (451) as well as Trent (1545-1563) in the 16th and the Vatican (1870) in the 19th.

² At Ephesus the Bishops assembled clearly acknowledged the primacy of Pope Celestine I (422-432). The Pope wrote to St. Cyril of Alexandria ordering him to excommunicate Nestorius if he did not repent, and sent to the Council three legates, who were to act as judges, confirming everything that St. Cyril did, as representative of the Apos-

tolic See. He also wrote directly to the Council, declaring that he was certain they would assent to the condemnation of Nestorius which he had already pronounced. His legates were well received, and his orders obeyed to the letter. One of the legates asserted his primacy: "There is no doubt that the holy and most blessed Peter, Prince and Chief of the Apostles, received the keys of the kingdom, and that until the present time he always lives and judges in his successors."

[3] At Chalcedon, the papal legate, Bishop Paschasius, presided in the place of Pope Leo I (440-461), and condemned Dioscorus in his name. The Council received with enthusiasm the Pope's dogmatic letter to Flavian of Constantinople, saying: "That is the faith of the Fathers, that is the faith of the Apostles . . . Peter has spoken by Leo." The Bishops finally wrote the Pope to confirm their decrees. He did so with the one exception of the twenty-eighth canon, which had been passed in the absence of his legates. He rejected it, because the Eastern Bishops falsely ascribed the primacy of the Popes to the political position of Rome, led by their desire to make the See of Constantinople superior to the other Eastern patriarchates.

[4] The Council of Constance in its third, fourth and fifth sessions did erroneously declare that the Council was above the Pope, but these decrees never received the force of law in the Church, and were deliberately set aside as null and void by Pope Martin V on April 22, 1418, and by Pope Eugenius IV on July 22, 1446, as "detrimental to the rights, dignity and supremacy of the Holy See." The Council became a General Council only in its last sessions when the newly elected Pope, Martin V, presided, and when he and his successors approved it with the exception of its anti-Papal heresy.

[5] Gerson himself admitted that his views were due "to the confused state of opinion resulting from a season of protracted schism, and that they denied the universally accepted doctrine of Papal supremacy" (*De Potes. Eccles.,* xii.). Common sense might have told him that a body without a head could not be a living organism. He and his friends were undoubtedly intent upon ending the abnormal state of affairs occasioned by the great Western

Schism (1378-1417). Three Popes were claiming the Papacy, and no one knew with certainty which was the true one. All were unwilling either to abdicate, or submit their claims to arbitration. The only possible solution of the difficulty seemed to be the submission of their claims to the decision of a Council. The great mistake of the theologians of Constance was to give their practical scheme for ending the schism the force of a dogmatic truth, applicable at all times and under all circumstances. The Council of Florence in 1439 decided finally the true position of the Pope. "We define that the Holy Apostolic See of the Bishop of Rome possesses a primacy throughout the whole world; that the Roman Pontiff is the successor of blessed Peter, Prince of Apostles; that he is the true Vicar of Christ, the Head of the Universal Church, and of all Christians, the Father and Teacher of all Christians; that to him was given in blessed Peter, by our Lord Jesus Christ, the fullness of power to feed, to rule and to govern the Universal Church."

Was there not at one time a female Pope, Johanna?

[1] No, there never was a woman Pope. This fable is mentioned first in the 13th century by two Dominicans, John de Mailly and Stephen de Bourbon, who placed her pontificate in 1100, and by the Papal chamberlain, Martin of Troppau, who says she was Pope in 855. It originated either in a rumor concerning a woman patriarch of Constantinople spoken of by Pope Leo IX in 1053 in a letter to Cerularius; in a medieval satire ridiculing the domination of Theodora and her two daughters in the 10th century; or in the survival of a local Roman folk-tale connected with an ancient pagan monument, discovered during the pontificate of Sixtus V (1585-1590) in a street near the Colosseum.

[2] The legend was generally accepted during the 14th and 15th centuries, but from the days of Pope Pius II (1458-1464) it has been universally rejected as unhistorical. Protestant and rationalistic scholars alike agree in rejecting it: Bayle, Basnage, Blondel, Burnet, Bochart, Cave, Chamier, Casaubon, Dumoulin, Gibbon, Gieseler, Leibnitz, Mosheim, Neander, De Thou.

[3] Not one historian mentions the woman Pope from the 10th to the 13th century, which is good evidence of her never having existed. Chronology settles the question, for the two dates assigned to her pontificate are impossible. Leo IV died July 17, 855, and was immediately succeeded by Pope Benedict III (855-858). We have coins with the images of Pope Benedict III and the Emperor Lothair, who died September 28, 855, and a charter for the Abbey of Corvey issued by Benedict III on October 7, 855. There was no interregnum between these two Popes. The other date, 1100, is out of the question, as Pope Paschal II reigned from 1099 to 1118.

Does not your teaching of infallibility give the Popes today the power they exercised in the Middle Ages of deposing sovereigns, and freeing subjects from their allegiance?

[1] The deposing power exercised by the Popes in the Middle Ages has nothing whatever to do with the dogma of infallibility. Pope Pius IX answered this objection in a letter to the Roman Academy, July 20, 1871. He said: "This right has without doubt been exercised by the Supreme Pontiffs from time to time in crucial circumstances; but it has nothing to do with Papal infallibility, neither does it flow therefrom, but from the authority of the Pope. Moreover, the exercise of this right in those ages of faith, which regarded the Pope as the Supreme Judge of Christendom, and recognized the great advantages of his tribunal in the great contests of peoples and of sovereigns, was freely extended by public jurisprudence and the common consent of nations to the most important interests of States and their rulers. But altogether different are the conditions of the present time; and malice alone can confound things so diverse, namely, the infallible judgment concerning the truths of divine revelation, with the right which the Popes exercised in virtue of their authority, when the common good demanded it."

[2] No Pope today would dream of exercising the deposing power, because, as Pius IX well said, modern conditions are altogether different. In medieval times, a united Christendom granted the Popes this power for the general good.

[8] Do not forget, however, that the principle of a religious qualification for sovereignty is still maintained by some nations even to this day. The King of England, for example, must be a member of the Protestant Church by Established Law, even though he rules over an Empire, the vast majority of which is Pagan, Mohammedan, Jewish and Catholic. According to English law, he would be deposed, were he to become a Catholic, a Jew or a Mohammedan.

Were the Popes infallible when they ordered Europe to exterminate the Moslems in the medieval crusades, promising heaven to all who died fighting the infidels? Were not the Crusades mere marauding expeditions, undertaken for gain and conquest under the semblance of piety?

[1] The infallibility of the Pope is not involved in their encouragement of the crusades against the Moslems. The Popes are infallible only when they define matters of faith and morals for the Universal Church.

[2] Answering the appeals of the Emperor of Constantinople and the Christians of the East, the Popes, as heads of a united Christendom, ordered Europe to undertake a crusade against the Moslems, who had profaned the holy places of Palestine, and massacred and enslaved thousands of native and visiting Christians. Pope Urban II, in his speech at the Council of Clermont, November 27, 1095, did not promise heaven to every combatant, but freed from canonical penalties all who took the cross "from motives of earnest and sincere devotion." An Indulgence was granted, that is, a remission of the punishment due forgiven sin, to every crusader who "died truly penitent" (Alzog, *Church History,* ii., 250).

[3a] It is perfectly true that some crusaders were actuated by motives of glory and of gain. Some of the nobles hoped to carve out a princedom in the East; some merchants made fortunes in transporting the troops and selling them supplies; some peasants were anxious to escape from the burdens of serfdom. But the main body was inspired by religious motives; to free the sepulchre of Christ from profanation, and to succor their persecuted brethren. The word "crusade" even to our day has always been associated with a high ideal of service for the brethren.

How could one infallible Pope, Eugenius IV (1431-1447) condemn Joan of Arc (1412-1431) to be burned as a witch, while another Pope, Benedict XV, declared her a saint in 1919?

[1] Pope Eugenius IV knew nothing of the trial and condemnation of St. Joan of Arc by the scoundrel Bishop Cauchon of Beauvais, for a month before her death he makes no mention of it in a letter to his legate in France, Cardinal de Sainte-Croix, asking him to bring about peace between the Kings of France and England (Raynald, *Annales Eccles.*, 1431). It is true that the Maid of Orleans appealed to the Pope during her trial, but her unjust judges, under English influence and in English pay, denied her appeal, knowing to a certainty that Rome would recognize at once the invalidity of their mock trial.

[2] St. Joan of Arc was captured before Compiègne by the bastard of Wandonne, a vassal of John of Luxembourg, who sold her to the English for about $100,000 (490,000 N.F.). The English regent, the Duke of Bedford, acting for his ten-year-old nephew, Henry VI, ordered Cauchon, the Bishop of Beauvais, to try her for heresy and witchcraft, declaring that even if she were acquitted, "it was his intention to take back and regain possession of the said Joan." It was against international law to put St. Joan to death for having defeated the English in battle; they had no alternative but to hold her for ransom, or keep her a prisoner until the end of the war. To have her condemned by an ecclesiastical tribunal, all the members of which were all highly paid political partisans, would restore the confidence of the English soldiers, and compromise the French King, Charles VII, as an accomplice of "a disciple of Satan, and an imp of hell."

[3] Bishop Cauchon and his infamous judges found no difficulty in declaring St. Joan guilty of every conceivable crime—"contempt of her parents, presumption, lying, superstition, despair and attempted suicide, bloodthirsty passion, diabolism, idolatry, heresy and schism." They next staged a travesty of a public adjuration, so that immediately after they might make her innocent and necessary assumption of male attire in prison the basis of a charge of relapse into

heresy—which implied the stake. That they were pronouncing judgment according to orders received and paid for is evident from the fact that the judges received letters of indemnity from the King of England on June 12, 1431.

[4] Nineteen years later, when the English had been driven from France, the ungrateful Charles VII, who had deserted St. Joan in her hour of trial, suffered remorse of conscience, and signed a warrant, ordering a trial of rehabilitation (February 14, 1450). Five years later, November 5, 1455, the revision proceedings were opened in Paris, with the approval of Pope Calixtus III. The sentence was declared null and void on every count, the following illegalities being proved to the hilt, namely, that the presiding judge was her mortal enemy, and therefore should not have been allowed to preside; that all evidence favorable to the accused was purposely suppressed; that she was illegally detained in a lay prison before and after judgment; that she was refused an advocate, although a minor; that her examinations were utterly unfair and tricky; that the questions proposed to her were unduly obscure and intricate; that false counsel was given her by pretended friends, the better to bring about her death sentence; that the summary of the twelve articles was falsified, and never submitted to her; that her appeal to the Pope was disallowed, while her judges falsely stated that she was unwilling to submit to the Church; that a pretended adjuration was substituted for the six-line paper submitted to her; that the second hasty trial was illegal and based on false pretenses; that she never was condemned by the civil judge, etc. The annulment of St. Joan's unjust sentence was declared solemnly at Rouen, July 7, 1456, a sentence confirmed in our days by Leo XIII, Pius X and Benedict XV, who in turn declared her venerable, blessed and a saint.

How could such an anti-Papalist as Aeneas Sylvius, an immoral man and an immoral writer, become Pope? Was not his change of views due solely to his promotion to the Papacy?

[1] It is true that Aeneas Sylvius was Chief Abbreviator at the schismatical synod of Basle, which fought Pope Euge-

nius IV (1431-1447) and maintained the superiority of a General Council over the Pope. He also for a time entered the service of the anti-Pope, Felix V. It is true that his private life as a layman was not above reproach, and that he wrote many a page in the spirit of the pagan Renaissance.

[2] But he sincerely repented of his sins, and in 1444, a year before his ordination, he most humbly begged pardon of the Pope, in a document that has come down to us, and was graciously received at the time (Pastor, *History of the Popes,* i., 340, 348). The Pope in answering him said: "Holy Mother Church is inexorable to one who denies his fault, but never refuses absolution to the penitent."

[3] Aeneas Sylvius became Pope in 1458. Seven years later he issued his famous Bull of Retraction, in which he strongly repudiated his erroneous teaching on the Papacy, and in another document condemned his erotic writings. He says: "Misled, like St. Paul, we have said, written and done much that is worthy of condemnation, and in ignorance have persecuted the Church of God and the Roman See. Therefore we now pray: Lord, forgive us the sins of our youth. . . . We are therefore obliged to imitate St. Augustine, and retract our errors. We exhort you then to give no credit to those earlier writings which oppose the supremacy of the Roman See, or contain anything not admitted by the Roman Church. . . . To St. Peter alone did the Savior give the plenitude of power; he and his lawful successors are the only possessors of the primacy. If you find in the Dialogues, in our letters, or in our other works anything in opposition to this teaching, reject and despise it. Follow that which we now say; believe the old man rather than the youth; do not esteem the layman more highly than the Pope; cast away Aeneas, hold fast to Pius" (Pastor, *ibid.,* iii., 283). He had realized his error long before he became Pope, for in this very document he mentions a letter of retractation which he had sent to the Rector of the Academy of Cologne, in August, 1447.

How could an immoral and worldly Pope like Alexander VI (1492-1503) be infallible? Are not the attempts of Catholic historians to whitewash him palpably dishonest?

[1] *Infallibility,* freedom from error in defining to the world a solemn truth, and *impeccability,* freedom from sin, are two totally different things. While we naturally expect the Popes to be of the highest moral character—and most of them have been—the official prerogative of infallibility has nothing whatever to do with the Pope's personal goodness or wickedness.

[2] Our Lord told the Jews that the personal unworthiness of the Scribes and Pharisees in no way nullified their true teaching. "All things, therefore, that they command you, observe and do, but do not act according to their works" (Matt. 23, 3). The notion that a temporal or an ecclesiastical superior loses his authority while he is in the state of mortal sin, was an error of Wyclif, condemned by the Church in the 14th century.

[3] It is true that in the latter half of the 19th century certain Catholic writers tried to whitewash Alexander VI, namely, Bernacchi, Chantrel, Leonetti, Nemée, Ollivier and others. But it is not fair to style them dishonest, for a Catholic naturally feels called upon to defend the honor of the Pope, as any true man feels bound to defend his mother's good name. Call them unscholarly, if you will, or ignorant, but remember that we hold with Pope Leo XIII: "The Church has no need of any man's lie." The most scholarly Catholic historian of the Popes, Ludwig Pastor, grants that Alexander lived the immoral life of the secular prince of his day, both as Cardinal and as Pope (*History of the Popes,* v., 363; vi., 140); that he obtained the Papacy by the rankest simony (*Ibid.,* v., 385); and that he brought his high office into disrepute by his unconcealed nepotism and lack of moral sense (vi., 139). He frees him, however, from the calumnious charges of incest and poisoning (iv., 135).

[4] We must not forget that there was a Judas among the Apostles, and that our Lord prophesied that weeds would grow up with the wheat until the Last Day (Matt. 13, 24-30). It is true that the personal holiness of priest or Pope is helpful as an example to non-Catholics and an encouragement to the faithful. But "just as the intrinsic worth of a jewel is not lessened by an inferior setting, so the sins of a priest cannot essentially affect his power of offering

Sacrifice, administering the sacraments, or transmitting doctrine (*Ibid.*, vi., 14).

By what right did Pope Alexander VI (1492-1503) divide the Spanish and Portuguese possessions in the New World? Was this not an unwarranted assumption of power?

[1] Catholic Europe before the Reformation regarded the Pope as the Supreme Court of international law, just as the World Court is regarded today. The aim of the Pope's Bull, *Inter Caetera*, May 4, 1493, was not, as some have pretended, to give away lands that he owned or claimed, but to mark the limits within which the two nations, Spain and Portugal, could operate without coming into conflict. He was merely selected as arbiter, just as Pope Leo XIII was chosen arbiter by Bismarck in his dispute with Spain over the Caroline Islands in 1883.

[2] John II of Portugal (1481-1495) was thus enabled to maintain good relations with Castile. The Pope's decision drew an imaginary line 360 leagues west of Cape Verde, the Spaniards acquiring the right to all lands lying to the West, and the Portuguese acquiring those to the East. That is why most of the coast line of Brazil discovered in 1500 fell to Portugal, while the rest of America and the West Indies fell to Spain. The Pope's action by preventing war between the two countries, aided greatly in the work of colonization.

If you claim that the Popes are infallible, how can you reconcile the contradictory decrees of Clement XIV suppressing the Jesuits, July 21, 1773, and Pius VII restoring them, August 7, 1814?

[1a] The papal Briefs suppressing and restoring the Jesuits are mere disciplinary and administrative measures that must be judged on their merits. The Pope is not infallible as supreme legislator and judge, but only as supreme teacher of faith and morals. He has a perfect right to institute, suppress, and restore any religious order, but one need not be a Jesuit to consider the action of Clement XIV imprudent and unjust.

[2a] The Jesuits had been expelled from Portugal in 1759, from France in 1764, from Spain and Naples in 1767, be-

cause the Bourbon princes were jealous of their influence and covetous of their possessions. In 1773, Clement XIV unfortunately yielded to political pressure and issued his Brief of Suppression. The Jesuits, however, had a staunch defender in the person of Catherine II of Russia. She saved them from canonical extinction and maintained their corporate existence by refusing to allow publication in her territories of the Brief of Suppression. Nevertheless, outside her jurisdiction "the Jesuits died without a murmur, and in this silence they were true to their lifelong training. They proved to the world the solidity of virtue that reigned throughout the Order, and showed that their doctrine of 'blind obedience' was not a matter of mere words. . . . They had preached sermons in every part of the world, but never one like this" (Campbell, *The Jesuits*).

[3] Alzog, in his *Church History*, thus speaks of the Brief of Suppression: "Clement XIV would have shown himself at once more prudent and more just had he said to the Jesuits what Pius IX did on a similar occasion in 1848. 'In many countries,' said he, 'they are not willing to tolerate you, or have you remain. Very good, then; withdraw from persecution for the present, and wait the return of better days.' Had he done this he would not have given a quasi-indorsement to *charges that never were proved.*"

[4] In 1801 Pius VII restored the Society in Russia and in 1803 permitted the English Jesuits to affiliate with the Russian community. In 1804 he extended the Russian community to Naples and in 1814 he restored the Society to full religious and canonical status all over the world. In his Bull of Restoration, Pius VII wrote that "the Catholic world unanimously demands the re-establishment of the Society of Jesus," and he adds, "I would consider myself guilty of a grievous sin in the sight of God, if I did not answer this world-wide appeal."

Why do Catholics defend the temporal power of the Popes? Did not Christ say: "My Kingdom is not of this world" (John 18, 36)? Should not the Pope have voluntarily given up the Papal States in 1870 for the sake of a united Italy? Does not the settlement of the Roman Question imply the denial of religious liberty to non-Catholics in Italy?

[1] The Church is indeed a spiritual kingdom established solely for the salvation of mankind. The temporal power of the Popes which lasted for centuries, was not at all necessary for their spiritual power, because that persists of its own divine right, guaranteed as it is by the abiding presence of Christ and the Holy Spirit. The Church ruled in Christ's name with full authority in the first three centuries, while the pagan Emperors were doing their utmost to destroy it. But Catholics have always maintained that to carry on effectively their supreme, world-wide jurisdiction as Vicars of Christ, the Popes ought not to be subject to any secular prince. As Pius IX declared in 1849: "Peoples, kings and nations would never turn with free confidence and devotion to the Bishop of Rome, if they saw him the subject of a sovereign or government, and did not know him to be in possession of his full liberty. There would always arise in them a strong suspicion and a continued fear that the Pope in his acts yielded to the influence of the sovereign and the government in whose territories he dwelt. Under this pretext the decrees of the Pope would oftentimes be disobeyed" (Allocution, April 20, 1849).

[2] The Protestant French historian, Guizot, writes: "The union of the spiritual and the temporal power in the Papacy did not arise from the systematic development, either of an abstract principle, or of ambitious aims. Theories and ambitions may have been mixed up with it, but that which has really produced the civil power of the Popes, is necessity; an increasing, unceasing necessity. . . . The donations of Pepin and Charlemagne were nothing but the coping stones in the structure which began long before, and was supported by the good sense of the people and the favor of kings" (*L'Eglise et la Societé*, 72, 142).

[3] The temporal power of the Popes, consecrated by a tenure of over one thousand years, ended when the Italian troops entered Rome on September 20, 1870. The Popes protested against the robbery of their States by Italy; first by refusing to accept the Law of Guarantees, and secondly, by remaining prisoners within the Vatican, thus preserving their dignity and their honor intact.

[4] The Popes refused to accept the Law of Guarantees of May 13, 1871, and the money indemnity it allowed for the

spoliation of the Papal States, because it was a unilateral and not a bilateral contract—an Italian law pure and simple, which a new Parliament could apply, interpret, modify and suppress at will. It in no way guaranteed the Pope's liberty and independence.

⁵ There was no chance of a reconciliation between the Popes and Italy so long as the liberals were in power. With the coming of Mussolini the whole situation changed. From the very outset of his régime he determined to settle the Roman Question, and the powers he possessed as dictator gave him the opportunity that no Italian statesman, dependent upon a Parliament, could ever have had. The negotiations for both Treaty and Concordat began as early as the summer of 1926, Barone acting for the Government and Pacelli for the Pope. Over one hundred conferences were held between 1926 and 1928, the Pope himself considering every detail in the twenty-nine audiences he granted to Pacelli. The final draft was completed on November 22, 1928, and on February 11, 1929, the Treaty and Concordat were signed by Cardinal Gasparri and Mussolini.

⁶ The Treaty proper, which consists of a preamble and twenty-seven articles, establishes the independence of the Holy See. While leaving unchanged the religious freedom guaranteed to non-Catholics by the Constitution, it makes the Catholic religion the sole religion of the State, recognizes the sovereignty of the Holy See "as an inherent attribute of its nature," erects the Vatican State as free and independent, declares the person of the Pope sacred, settles the status of the Cardinals, Vatican officials and diplomatic agents, and enacts laws concerning passports, customs, property rights, etc. The Treaty ends with the Pope's recognition of the legitimacy of the dynasty of Savoy, and his solemn declaration that he is fully satisfied with the independence guaranteed him for the carrying out of his spiritual primacy. The Roman Question is finally settled.

⁷ Pius XI, in his charge to the Lenten preachers in 1929, said with regard to the small territory he had demanded for the Vatican City. "We would show in the most certain manner that no earthly cupidity moves the Vicar of Christ, but only the consciousness of that which it is impossible to yield; because such a territorial sovereignty is a condi-

tion universally recognized as indispensable to every true sovereign jurisdiction. The least amount of territory, then, that is sufficient to support that sovereignty itself; so much territory without which it cannot exist, because having nowhere to rest. . . . We are glad to see the material earth reduced to the minimum terms, which can and ought to be spiritualized by the immense, sublime, and verily divine spirituality which it is destined to sustain and serve."

[8] In these wise words the Pope answers those unthinking bigots who keep repeating our Lord's words: "My kingdom is not of this world." It is true that the Pope is a King of a little strip of territory in Italy, but if he is King *in* this world, he is not *of* it, for he demanded his Kingship only as a means for the indispensable exercise of his spiritual office.

Is not your Pope the antichrist of St. Paul and St. John? Does he not wear the number 666 in his belt, the mark of the Beast?

[1] No, the Vicar of Christ upon earth is not antichrist, nor does he wear the number 666 in his belt. The Reformers of the 16th century borrowed their calumny of the Pope antichrist from the Albigenses, the Waldenses, Wyclif and Huss. On the continent Luther, Calvin, Zwingli, Bucer and Beza, and in England Cranmer, Latimer, Ridley and Tyndale sponsored this absurd lie, hoping by a bitter anti-Catholic slogan to wean the people away from all consideration of the Papal claims. No non-Catholic scholar of repute today would dream of calling the Pope antichrist, for the Papacy has won the respect and esteem of the world by its uncompromising defense of the divinity of Christ and His entire Gospel.

[2] If our Lord was called Beelzebub by the anti-Catholics of His day, is it not natural to expect, as He Himself said, that His disciples and Vicar should be maligned by the anti-Catholics of all ages (*see* Matt. 10, 25).

SELECTED BIBLIOGRAPHY

BREZZI, PAOLO. *The Papacy, its Origins and Historical Evolution.* Westminster, Md.: Newman Press. 1958.

CHAPMAN, JOHN. "The Condemnation of Pope Honorius." *Dublin Review,* July, 1906, Jan., 1907.

CONGAR, MARIE J. *After Nine Hundred Years.* New York: Fordham University Press. 1959.

—— *Christ, Our Lady and the Church.* Westminster, Md.: Newman Press. 1959.

FLICHE, A., and MARTIN V. (eds.). *Histoire de l'Eglise.* Paris: Bloud & Gay. 1934.

GUARDUCCI, MARGHERITA. *The Tomb of St. Peter.* New York: Hawthorn Books, Inc. 1960.

HEFELE, CHARLES J. *A History of the Councils of the Church.* 5 Vols. Edinburgh: T. & T. Clark. 1909.

HUGHES, PHILIP. *A History of the Church.* Vol. II. New York: Sheed & Ward. 1947.

JEDIN, HUBERT. *Ecumenical Councils of the Catholic Church.* New York: Herder & Herder. 1960.

KIRSCHBAUM, ENGELBERT. *The Tombs of St. Peter and St. Paul.* New York: St. Martin's Press. 1959.

KUHNER, HANS *Encyclopedia of the Papacy.* New York: Philosophical Library. 1958.

McSORLEY, JOSEPH. *Outline History of the Church by Centuries.* St. Louis: B. Herder Book Co. 1954.

ORMESSON, WLADIMIR. *The Papacy.* New York: Hawthorn Books. 1959.

PIUS XII, POPE. *Humani Generis* (Encyclical) in *Four Great Encyclicals.* New York: (Deus Books) Paulist Press. 1961.

SCOTT, S. HERBERT. *The Eastern Churches and the Papacy.* London: Sheed & Ward. 1928.

ULLMANN, WALTER. *The Origins of the Great Schism.* London: Burns, Oates & Washbourne. 1948.

PART VIII
The Sacraments

Do Catholics believe that God's gifts and graces are limited to the seven sacraments? Is not your sacramental teaching medieval? What did primitive Christianity know of the scholastic terms of "matter" and "form"? Are not the sacraments hindrances to real religion, making it dependent upon a meaningless ritual?

[1] The very definition of a sacrament proves that it is not a meaningless ritual, for a sacrament is a visible sign instituted by Christ, signifying and producing sanctifying grace in the soul. Three elements constitute a sacrament:

1. The visible sign; namely, the external washing of water (by pouring, sprinkling or immersion) in Baptism with the invocation of the Blessed Trinity aptly signifies internal cleansing of the soul from original and actual sin.

2. The producing of interior grace; namely, Baptism produces sanctifying grace in the soul, so that "by water and the Spirit," as our Lord taught, we are supernaturally born into the kingdom of God (John 3, 5).

3. The institution of Christ; namely, the Apostolic commission includes the command to baptize (Matt. 28, 19).

[2] God's grace, although it ordinarily comes to us by Christ's institution through the Mass and seven sacraments, is not denied to a non-Catholic who does not know of their existence, or to a Catholic who cannot receive them because no priest is available at the hour of death. God gives sufficient grace to everyone to be saved, "wishes all men to be saved and to come to the knowledge of the truth" (1 Tim. 2, 4). Many a High Church Episcopalian convert has asked

me whether the graces he felt he had received in past communions were a mere mockery. "Not in the least," I answered, "for you have been making spiritual communions in good faith, even though you did not realize that your minister was a mere layman going through an empty form."

3 It is true indeed that the terms "matter" and "form" were not applied to the sacraments until the 13th century, but the idea conveyed by these words dates from St. Augustine (Tract. 80, *In Joan.*, 3). These philosophical terms were borrowed from Aristotle, and their use confirmed by the Councils of Constance, Florence and Trent. They do not imply, as some non-Catholics seem to imagine, that the sacraments are material, corporeal things. What they mean is that just as bodies are composed of two constituents, the one indeterminate and the other determining, so too in the sacraments two elements, the one indeterminate and the other determining, can be distinguished; and these may rightly be called "matter" and "form." In Baptism, the washing with water is the "matter," while the words used in baptizing (I baptize you in the name of the Father, and of the Son, and of the Holy Spirit), which show why the water is being used, and what it symbolizes, is the "form."

4 It is of faith that Christ instituted the seven sacraments (Trent), but it is also clear from the history of both East and West that He did not determine, except in a most general way, the matter and form of certain sacraments such as Confirmation, Orders and Extreme Unction. He allowed the Church to determine them with precision.

5 The sacraments, instead of being hindrances to religion, are on the contrary the greatest possible divine helps to sanctify our souls, for they apply the infinite merits of Christ's Redemption to us. When we are dead in sin they give us the divine life in the Sacraments of the Dead (Baptism and Penance), and, when we are in the state of grace, they give us the divine life more abundantly (John 10, 10) in the Sacraments of the Living (Confirmation, Extreme Unction, Orders, Matrimony and the Holy Eucharist).

6 Christianity is a sacramental religion. Christ is God and Man. The Word was made Flesh and dwelt among us that the sons of men might through His passion and death

become the sons of God. His Church is visible and invisible, with a divine and a human element. We, the members of the Church, are not disembodied spirits, but creatures of body and soul. We, therefore, naturally expect the life of the Church to be a supernatural life so given by Christ, as to make visible human things at once the signs and the causes of things invisible and divine. The ritual of the sacraments cannot be meaningless, for they all signify the grace of God, and effect it in our souls.

Did not the Catholic Church invent at least some of the seven sacraments? If Christ really instituted them, why do we find so many different ways of administering them in East and West?

[1] It is of faith that Christ instituted the seven sacraments (Council of Trent). The Church has no power whatever to institute a sacrament, because the sacraments produce supernatural grace in the soul. "None but God can cause grace, since grace is nothing else than a participated likeness of the divine nature" (2 Peter 1, 4; *Summa Theol.* III, Q. 62, a. 1). God alone therefore can institute a sacrament (*Ibid.*; Q. 64, a. 2).

[2] The diversity of practice at different times in the Church (Holy Orders), and even today in the East and West (Confirmation, Penance) proves only that Christ did not prescribe the precise material sign (made up of *matter* and *form,* in theological language) to be used in all of the sacraments. As the Council of Trent says: "The Church has always had the power to determine or to change things in the administration of the sacraments when it judges that such a procedure would be more useful for those who receive the sacraments or would contribute more to the honor of the sacraments themselves, in accordance with different circumstances, *always keeping the substance of the sacraments the same."*

[3] The Church, then, cannot touch the *substance* of the sacraments, that is, whatever Christ Himself instituted. Now what Christ desired was the granting of special graces for definite human needs, and this under appropriate visible signs of these special graces. Whether He chose to

specify also the details about the mode is not essential to the notion of sacrament.

⁴ The make-up or composition of the visible sign (oil and definite words for Extreme Unction) may be modified by the Church—as long as the essential signification is preserved. The Church has the power—at least where Christ did not specifically indicate them (in the Eucharist and Baptism)—to change the "matter and form" provided they still combine to form this sign (of cleansing, strengthening, etc.) to which Christ attached His grace.

I believe that there are but two sacraments, Baptism and the Lord's Supper, and that your other five sacraments are a corruption of the Apostolic teaching. How can you prove that there are seven sacraments?

Do you find seven sacraments mentioned either in the Bible or in the documents of primitive Christianity? Was not the number seven fixed at a very late date—the 12th century?

¹ The Catholic Church has always held to the *existence* of the seven sacraments, although the *name* "sacrament" was not always or exclusively used only for them. The New Testament mentions all seven sacraments more or less explicitly. (Baptism: John 3, 5; Confirmation: Acts 8, 15-17; Eucharist: Matt. 26, 26-28; Penance: John 20, 23; Holy Orders: 2 Tim. 1, 6; Matrimony: Eph. 5, 31-33; Extreme Unction: James 5, 14-15.) Nevertheless, it is true that the Bible nowhere draws up a list of them and tells us that there are seven and no more. We frankly admit the necessity of the living Church (which received and began to use these sacraments) and its authority in this matter of the sacraments. Christ entrusted to His Church all His seven sacraments just as He entrusted the Bible to her safekeeping; but while she daily used these means of grace and salvation, she did not at once delve into the exact nature and definition of these realities.

² One by one we find the sacraments mentioned by the early Fathers of the Church. Most of their writings were of a very practical nature, intended to instruct the catechumens and the faithful, or to refute points under fire by the heretics. And so we find the Apostolic Fathers, such as

St. Justin, mentioning frequently Baptism and the Eucharist to refute the calumnies of the pagans. Tertullian a hundred years later speaks also of Confirmation and Penance.

³ In the 3rd century the baptismal controversy made writers of both East and West discuss the conditions necessary for the validity of Baptism, Confirmation, Holy Orders and the Eucharist. Writers in the 4th century like St. Cyril of Jerusalem wrote treatises on Baptism, Confirmation and the Eucharist for the instruction of the catechumens. The Donatist controversy led St. Augustine to treat of Baptism and Holy Orders, while the Pelagian heresy compelled him to prove that the sanctity of Marriage could be reconciled with the propagation of Original Sin. He mentions six of the seven sacraments. The seventh, Extreme Unction, is described by his contemporary, Pope Innocent I (401-417), in his letter to Decentius of Gubbio. By the 5th century, therefore, we meet with all the seven sacraments in the writings of the Fathers. And so accepted was the teaching, that the heretical Nestorians and Monophysites, who broke from the Church about that time, have preserved to this day the doctrine of the seven sacraments (influenced, no doubt, by later Western theology but accepting nothing they did not consider absolutely in harmony with their traditions).

⁴ Yet even in systematic treatments of the sacraments the Fathers did not come to any agreement on the precise meaning of a sacrament. There were many rites in the Church, and the Fathers as yet had no criterion to distinguish those which are productive signs of grace (sacraments) from those which are simply signs (sacramentals). Thus, according to the best opinion the term "sacrament" (from "sacrum" meaning "holy thing") was used to designate anything that was holy, either because it was the *subject* of holiness, or because it was a *sign* of holiness, or because it was the *cause* of holiness, in other words, whatever had a relationship to holiness. Consequently, in the early Church, the term "sacrament" was much more widely applied than simply to the seven things of which we speak today.

⁵ Augustine was the first to attempt to define a sacrament; for him it was "a sacred sign," the emphasis being

on the idea of signifying; then with the Middle Ages, and more precisely with Peter Lombard in the 12th Century, another aspect was emphasized too; namely, that this sign be *causative* of grace; hence, a material thing that not only is a *sign* of holiness or grace, but also *causes* it. And of all the rites used in the Church, it was recognized that only seven could any longer be classified according to this definition. The realities did not change in any way, but we admit that the Church has limited the name to these seven realities left to her by Christ which alone are both signs and causes of grace.

⁶ It was only some 350 years later that the Reformers began to question not just the name, but the very reality which the Church had held fast to from the beginning. They all agreed in rejecting the number seven. And, Luther, who first accepted three, Baptism, Penance and the Lord's Supper, finally came to agree with Calvin in reducing the number to two, Baptism and the Lord's Supper. It was against them that the Council of Trent reaffirmed the traditional teaching that "there are neither more nor less than seven sacraments."

⁷ The attitude of the Eastern Orthodox Church at this time confirms the teaching of Rome. The Reformers were attempting a rapprochement with the Orthodox, but in 1576 the Patriarch of Jerusalem refused all offers of union with the Lutherans because of their denial of the seven sacraments. And later, in 1638, a synod of Constantinople condemned Lukaris for his Lutheran and non-Apostolic teaching of only two sacraments, and declared explicitly that seven sacraments were instituted by Jesus Christ.

Why do Catholics believe that Baptism, Confirmation and Holy Orders cannot be repeated?

¹ Because, as the Council of Trent teaches, they impress upon the soul a *character,* that is, a spiritual and indelible sign by force of which the sacrament cannot be repeated. The character of each of these sacraments places a distinctive mark upon the soul of each recipient. Baptism marks him forever as a member of Christ, a Christian; Confirmation marks him as a soldier of Christ; and Holy Orders, as

a priest of Christ. Even should he desert Christ, these marks will remain—to his added shame. Thus, each of these sacraments places the recipient in a distinctive class, rendering repetition superfluous, and bestowing on him both power to receive new graces and functions and power to carry out obligations of his new status.

[2] The doctrine of sacramental character has become increasingly clearer with theological study, yet it can be traced back to the very beginnings of Christianity. It is explicitly held by all from the Middle Ages, at which time the terminology regarding the sacraments was clarified. St. Thomas defines character as "a seal by which the soul is marked so that it may receive or bestow on another, things pertaining to divine worship. . . . It is specifically the character of Christ, to whose character the faithful are likened . . . a certain participation in the priesthood of Christ." (*Summa Theol.* III, q. 63, art. 3, ad. 2.)

[3] But this doctrine was even explicit as far back as St. Augustine. He taught that Baptism, even when received by heretics and schismatics must not be repeated, (*Epis.* 22, 2) because the convert has received in Baptism "the character of the Lord" (*Epis.* 173, 23). This character, imprinted and engraved on the one baptized (*Ad Caes.* 2) cannot be lost. It is even had when grace is not received. It is comparable to the distinctive mark of a brand upon sheep, an image engraved upon a coin, the sort of indelible tattoo (*Contra Epist. Parm.* 2, 13, 29) with which Roman soldiers were permanently marked as soldiers of their emperor (for example, the letter "D" was affixed to the hands of soldiers under emperor Domitian). Thus even desertion cannot efface this mark.

[4] Augustine uses the word "character" only of Baptism, but the doctrine it embodies he applies also to Holy Orders. Writing against the Donatists, he invokes the *constant tradition* of the Church which forbade re-ordination of Bishops validly ordained by unworthy ministers. The reason: the priestly character is given by God once and for all, and irrevocably, because the priest's action is at all times the action of Christ Himself (*In Joan.* 5, 15).

[5] There is plenty of testimony in pre-Augustinian times of the doctrine of sacramental character. But it is mostly

found in the Fathers' frequent comparisons of the "seal" of the sacrament to military tattooing of soldiers, branding of animals, the imprint of a ring or seal, and to the image on a coin. *See* Leeming, *Principles of Sacramental Theology*, pp. 162-183.)

[6] The scriptural evidence is implicit only. Though Eph. 1, 13 and Eph. 4, 30 speak of being "signed" or "sealed" by the Holy Spirit, the primary reference is to the presence of the Holy Spirit and his action through grace. However, the Fathers of the Church did not hesitate to apply these texts also to the seal of the baptismal character.

Do not Catholics attribute a magical effect to the sacraments by teaching that they confer grace of themselves? Isn't that what the mysterious phrase "ex opere operato" means?

[1] Not at all. The Catholic Church condemns magic as a mortal sin against the virtue of religion, and brands it as an immoral attempt to work miracles by the power of the devil. We call an action magical, when an insufficient cause is expected to produce a higher effect, that is, to claim that a pen could write poetry by itself; or when something material and created is regarded as producing *of itself* a spiritual effect, and to claim that the sacraments all by themselves could produce grace.

[2] If a pen wrote poetry all by itself, it would be magical. But if used in the hand of a poet it becomes an instrument in the production of what we call an instrumental cause of the poetry. Catholics claim no more for the sacraments. They do not cause spiritual effects all by themselves, but only as divinely intended instruments of God. God is the principal cause; the sacraments are *instrumental causes* of grace. (This is not to say that God provided for no direct granting of graces. He did, notably through a prayer).

[3] "Ex opere operato" (literally, "from the work performed") means that whatever grace is received in virtue of receiving this sacrament is received through the instrumentality of the sacrament itself that is received, and not through the personal worth of the recipient. One's personal dispositions are a necessary *condition,* not a cause. Thus we

do not receive grace "no matter what our state of soul," but if the dispositions be correct, then reception of the sacraments will—by the wish of Christ in instituting them—be the instrumental means of infallibly producing God's grace within us.

I believe that the sacraments merely serve to strengthen faith, and that they have no intrinsic power. Are not the sacraments "mere tokens of the divine promise that sins were to be forgiven by faith" (Luther)?, "mere messengers announcing to men God's deeds of kindness" (Calvin)?, "mere signs of Christian profession" (Zwingli)?

[1] No, these teachings of the Reformers were explicitly condemned by the Council of Trent. It is of faith that the sacraments contain the grace they signify, and confer that grace on those who do not place an obstacle thereunto, and that grace is conferred by the sacraments of themselves *ex opere operato. (See ¶3, p. 149)*

[2] The New Testament always represents the sacraments as efficacious means for the forgiveness of sins and the imparting of the grace of God. St. Peter tells the convert Jews that they must do penance and be baptized "in the name of Jesus Christ for the forgiveness of your sins, and you will receive the gift of the Holy Spirit" (Acts 2, 38). Ananias says to the convert Saul of Tarsus, "Get up and be baptized and wash away thy sins, calling on His name" (Acts 22, 16). St. Paul in many passages speaks of the efficacy of Baptism, which cleanses us from all sins, gives us salvation "by the bath of regeneration and renovation by the Holy Spirit," so that we may "walk in newness of life," having become "a new creation" and adopted sons (Titus 3, 5; Rom. 6, 4; Gal. 6, 15).

In view of your doctrine that the administration of a sacrament depends upon the intention of the minister, how can anyone ever be certain of having received a sacrament?

[1] The Catholic Church, believing in the objective efficacy of the sacraments, regards the minister as one who represents Christ and acts in His name. The minister, therefore, must conform his will to the divine will; as a

minister of God's Church he must have "at least the intention of doing what the Church does" (Council of Trent). Such a doctrine is self-evident. How can a priest absolve a penitent, if he does not intend to do so? How can two parties to a marriage give a valid consent, if they have no intention to marry? A right intention is therefore an essential element of the sacramental idea.

[2] To withhold deliberately one's intention would be a sin of such malign malice, that we think it beyond the average sinner's thought. We have a perfect trust in God's general providence, and a perfect confidence in the Church's extreme watchfulness with regard to the administration of the sacraments, that frees us from all worry in the matter.

Does your Church teach that Baptism is absolutely necessary for salvation? Do you therefore put all who die without Baptism in hell? Why condemn pagans who have never heard of Baptism, or children, who through no fault of their own die unbaptized, to eternal damnation?

[1] It is of faith that Baptism is a necessary means of salvation (Council of Trent). The words of Christ are plain: "Unless a man be born again of water and the Spirit, he cannot enter into the kingdom of God" (John 3, 5). He commanded the Apostles to baptize all nations, and promised salvation to all who believed and were baptized (Matt. 28, 19-20).

[2a] The Catholic Church does not condemn everyone to hell who has not been baptized with water. She mitigates the apparent harshness of her doctrine by teaching that in case of urgent necessity the Baptism of desire will suffice (Council of Trent). This is the doctrine of the Fathers of the Church. St. Ambrose says in his sermon on the Emperor Valentinian II, who died a catechumen: "I hear you express grief that he did not receive the sacrament of Baptism. Tell me, what else is there in us except the will and petition? But he had long desired to be initiated before he came to Italy, and expressed his intention to be baptized by me as soon as possible. . . . Has he not, therefore, the grace which he desired? Surely he received it because he asked it" (*De Obitu Valent.*, 51). St. Augustine says the

same: "I find that not only suffering for the name of Christ can supply the defect of Baptism, but even faith and conversion of heart, if there be no time for celebrating the sacrament" (*De Bapt.*, iv., 22).

[3] The Baptism of blood, or martyrdom for Christ, was also regarded by the Fathers as an equivalent for Baptism of water. St. Augustine writes: "To all those who die confessing Christ, even though they have not received the bath of regeneration, martyrdom will prove as effective for the remission of sins, as if they were washed at the baptismal font" (*De Civ. Dei.*, xiii., 2).

[4] Adults who die without the knowledge of the Gospel are saved by the merits of Christ, if they die in perfect charity or are perfectly contrite for their sins. This includes the implicit desire of Baptism, which is defined as a state of mind in which a man would ardently long for Baptism, if he knew that it was necessary for salvation.

[5] Children dying unbaptized are indeed deprived of the beatific vision of God in heaven, but they do not incur the punishment of hell, which is due only to actual sin. Their deprivation of heaven is not unjust on God's part, for the glory of heaven is a free, supernatural gift, in no way due to human nature. It is highly probable that they enjoy a natural happiness, as St. Thomas teaches (IV Sent. II, dist. 30, Q. 2, ad. 5).

Is there any difference between the Baptism of John the Baptist and Christian Baptism? Is it sufficient to baptize one in the name of Jesus Christ, as we read in Acts 2, 38?

[1] The Council of Trent defined an essential difference between the Baptism of John (Matt. 21, 25) and the Baptism instituted by Christ (John 3, 5; Acts 2, 38). John's Baptism, although superior to the legal purifications of the Jews (Ex. 30, 17-21), was essentially distinct from and inferior to Christian Baptism. As St. Thomas says, "it prepared men for grace, leading them to faith in Christ, and exciting them to sorrow for their sins" (*Summa Theologiae*, III, Q. 38, art. 3). Christian Baptism forgives sins and bestows the gift of the Holy Spirit, blessings which the Baptism of John did not do, as he himself confessed, "I have

baptized you with water, but He (Christ) will baptize you with the Holy Spirit" (Mark 1, 8). This is why St. Paul at Ephesus gave Christian Baptism to the Jews who had been baptized by John. They had not received the Holy Spirit (Acts 19, 2-5).

[2] Baptism "in the name of Jesus Christ" refers to Christian Baptism as contrasted with the Baptism of John. These people were not baptized with the invocation of Christ, but in the faith and by the authority of Christ. They were baptized in the name of the Blessed Trinity according to the instructions of Christ, "Go, therefore, and make disciples of all nations, baptizing them in the name of the Father, and of the Son, and of the Holy Spirit" (Matt. 28, 19).

As a Baptist I hold that immersion is the only true Baptism. Was not immersion the practice of the primitive Christians?

[1] Baptism by immersion has always been considered by the Catholic Church as valid, provided the one baptizing pronounces the Trinitarian formula, "I baptize you in the name of the Father, and of the Son, and of the Holy Spirit." The washing with water, whether accomplished by immersion, pouring, or sprinkling, accompanied by the invocation of the Blessed Trinity constitutes valid Baptism.

[2a] Although the early Christians may have waded into a body of water to be baptized, archaeology offers convincing evidence that their baptism was not by immersion. Duchesne writes, "We constantly see representations of the celebration of Baptism on monuments. . . . But do we ever see total immersion, the neophyte plunged into the water so as to disappear completely? Such a thing is never seen. This immersion is never to be met with in the mosaics of ancient churches, in the paintings of the catacombs, in ordinary pictures, domestic objects, glasses, spoons, etc.; it is never sculptured or engraved on marble. In all such ancient monuments the neophyte appears standing, his feet in the water, but the greater part of the body out of the water, while water is poured on his head with the hand or with a vase. This is Baptism by infusion, not

by immersion" (*Churches Separated from Rome*). It seems improbable that the 3,000 converts of St. Peter on Pentecost were baptized by immersion (Acts 2, 41). Neither was immersion practical in the home of Cornelius (Acts 10, 47-48) nor in the prison at Philippi (Acts 16, 33).

[3] Catholics do not claim that Baptism by immersion was never practiced in the Church. However, they deny that immersion was ever the only method. In the 1st century the *Document of the Twelve Apostles* mentions infusion as well as immersion. Tertullian describes Baptism as "a sprinkling with any kind of water" (*De Bapt.*) and St. Augustine says that Baptism forgives sins even if the water "merely sprinkles the child ever so slightly" (In Joan.). In the 13th century, St. Thomas tells us, immersion was the common practice but that "Baptism can also be conferred by sprinkling and pouring" (*Summa Theologiae,* III, q. 66, art. 3).

[4] The very fact that Baptism is necessary for salvation proves that immersion is not the only valid method. Are men in prison, the sick and dying, children just born, and people of the desert to die without Baptism because the absence of enough water makes immersion impossible?

[5] Christ commanded Baptism by water. He did not prescribe the manner of applying water but left its administratino to the prudent judgment of the Church. The present law for Catholics makes Baptism by pouring obligatory. Immersion and sprinkling, though valid, are forbidden.

Can anyone administer the sacraments? May a person who is not a Catholic or who is a sinner validly baptize? What do you think of the custom in some of our city hospitals of agnostic and Jewish doctors baptizing Catholic children?

[1] To administer the sacraments validly, Baptism and Matrimony excepted, the person must be an ordained representative of Jesus Christ and authorized by the Church to act in the name of Christ. Baptism is an exception because it is absolutely necessary for salvation. In urgent cases, any person can baptize, although its solemn administration requires someone in Holy Orders. As the contract and sacrament are identical in the sacrament of Matrimony,

the contracting parties are the sole ministers of the sacrament.

²ᵃ People who are not Catholics or who are sinners may validly baptize, for the validity of the sacrament does not depend upon the orthodoxy or the holiness of the person baptizing. This has been the traditional teaching of the Church.

³ᵃ The custom of the physicians you mention is most praiseworthy. Carefully instructed by Catholic priests or nurses, these doctors validly baptize, for they have the intention of doing what the Church does. They perform a most charitable act for which God surely will bless and reward them.

Is not Baptism a mere external ceremony of initiation into the Christian fellowship? Are parents bound to give Christian names to their children at Baptism? May a Protestant be a sponsor for a Catholic child?

¹ Baptism is much more than an initiation ceremony. "Do you not know that all we who have been baptized into Christ Jesus have been baptized into His death? . . . for he who is dead is acquitted of sin. But if we have died with Christ, we believe that we shall also live together with Christ" (Romans 6, 3. 7f.).

² The Catholic Church teaches that Baptism cleanses from all sins, original and personal. "There is therefore now no condemnation for those who are in Christ Jesus" (Romans 8, 1). It remits not only the eternal penalties of sin, but also all temporal punishments, so that "in those who are born again, there is nothing that God hates . . . nothing whatever to retard their entrance into heaven" (Council of Trent).

³ Baptism is a new creation, a second birth, for we are "born again of water and the Spirit" (John 3, 5). It confers sanctifying grace on the soul, making it a partaker of the divine nature (2 Peter 1, 4), a friend of God (John 15, 14), and an adopted child of God (Romans 8, 15); it also imparts the virtues of faith, hope, and charity (1 Cor. 13, 13) and transforms us into living temples of the Holy Spirit (1 Cor. 3, 16).

⁴ Baptism effects our reconciliation in Christ and our incorporation into the Mystical Body of Christ. "All you who have been baptized into Christ have put on Christ" (Gal. 3, 27); "we were all baptized into one Body" (1 Cor. 12, 13). By imprinting an indelible character on the soul which forever distinguishes it from the unbaptized, Baptism makes us members of the Church, capable of receiving the other sacraments, and able to worship God.

⁵ Baptism is a holy event that foreshadows heaven as our destiny. It directs us to our supernatural end. It is the beginning of eternal life, the seed of grace which one day will blossom into the blessed fruit of heavenly glory.

⁶ Catholic parents are obliged to give Christian names to their children at Baptism. When they refuse, the pastor is bound to add a saint's name to the name proposed by the parents and to record both names in the baptismal register. The Church wants the person baptized to imitate the virtues of the saint chosen and to have the saint as a protector during life.

⁷ Only a Catholic may be the sponsor for a Catholic child, for it is his duty to see that the child is brought up a good Catholic if the parents neglect this obligation. The sponsor or godparent contracts a spiritual relationship with the person baptized; they cannot marry without a dispensation. Although Protestants cannot act in an official capacity, they are most welcome to attend the baptismal ceremony.

Does not the Bible require faith and repentance preparatory to Baptism? How can babies repent and believe (Acts 2, 38)? There is no mention of infant Baptism in the Bible. Did the early Church believe in infant Baptism?

¹ The text cited is irrelevant, for it simply declares that faith and sorrow for sins committed are required of adult converts seeking admission into the Church. The Catholic Church teaches that same doctrine today. There is no express mention of the baptizing of infants in the New Testament, but it is at least probable that there were infants among the whole families that were baptized by St. Paul (Acts 16, 15; 1 Cor. 1, 16). Infant Baptism is necessary

because they have contracted the guilt of original sin which Baptism alone can remit (John 3, 5).

² The early Fathers are unanimous in insisting upon infant Baptism, basing it on the universal command of Christ to all (Matt. 28, 19; John 3, 5), and on its divine power to cleanse from original sin. St. Irenaeus (140-205) writes: "He came to save all who through Him are born again unto God; infants, and children, boys and youths, and elders" (*Adv. Haer.,* Lib. ii., ch. xxii.). Origen (185-255) declares infant Baptism an Apostolic institution (*Epis. ad. Rom.,* Lib., v., 9), and necessary to cleanse infants from Original Sin (*In Lev.,* viii., 3). St. Cyprian and the Bishops of the Third Council of Carthage (253) taught that children should be baptized as soon as possible after birth. Their Baptism was not to be deferred until the eighth day, as some maintained. This is a faithful echo of the teaching of the Apostles, as St. Augustine remarked (*Epis.,* cxliv., 23).

³ The Council of Milevis (416) taught the necessity of infant Baptism, and this doctrine was repeated in the Councils of Fourth Lateran, Vienne, Florence and Trent.

Why do you rebaptize Protestants when they enter your Church?

¹ª We do not rebaptize them, as Baptism can be received only once. (*See* ¶1, p. 147). We baptize converts conditionally, only when a prudent doubt exists about the validity of the former Baptism. The form is: "If you are not baptized, I baptize you," etc. If the first Baptism was valid, the conditional Baptism is not a sacrament.

What passage in the Bible proves that the sacrament of Confirmation was instituted by Christ? Can you prove that it is a sacrament distinct from Baptism? Was not the laying of hands (Acts 8, 17) a conferring of special gifts, such as healing, speaking with tongues, etc.?

¹ The institution of the sacrament of Confirmation by Christ is nowhere expressly stated in the New Testament. But Catholics are certain that it is a divinely instituted sacrament and distinct from Baptism. They know this by

the infallible affirmation of the Church (Council of Trent) and by the solid testimony of the Fathers of the Church.

[2] We know that Christ promised the Holy Spirit to those who believed in Him (John 7, 37-39; 14, 6; 15, 26; 16, 7). And He fulfilled this promise, for the Apostles "were filled with the Holy Spirit" on Pentecost (Acts 2, 4), and both John (7, 38) and Peter (Acts 2, 38) declare that this Pentecostal gift was intended for all Christians. Other allusions to Confirmation, more or less clear, are found in 2 Cor. 1, 21-22; Eph. 1, 13; Tit. 3, 5; 1 John 2, 20, 27.

[3] The Holy Spirit was imparted by the laying on of hands, a sacramental rite *distinct* from Baptism for it could only be done by an Apostle or one of their successors. For if the baptizer was an Apostle he immediately confirmed afterwards (Acts 19, 6); but if others baptized the baptized person awaited the coming of an Apostle or other Bishop (for example, the Samaritan whom Peter and John confirmed had already been baptized by Philip in Acts 8, 14. 18). Such an important rite distinct from Baptism and performed only by the Apostles and their successors could only have stemmed from Christ Himself. Although the Holy Spirit is given in Baptism initially, Christ promised Him in a special way; and if this laying on of hands is not the fulfillment of the promise, then what is? There is no other answer.

[4] St. Jerome (d. 419) speaks of Confirmation being given by the Bishops of his time, calling it the custom of the Churches "that upon those who have been baptized by the presbyters and deacons, the Bishop hastens to impose hands" (*Dial. adv. Lucif.*, 9). Two hundred years before, St. Cyprian (d. 258) said: "Two sacraments preside over the perfect birth of a Christian, the one regenerating the man, which is Baptism, the other communicating the Holy Spirit" (Epist. 72; and in Epist. 73 giving our interpretation of Acts 8).

[5] Tertullian (d. 222) is the first of the Fathers to make any explicit mention of Confirmation as distinct from Baptism, probably because both were carried out by the Bishop in the same ceremonies; Confirmation through an imposition of hands which immediately followed the baptismal anointing: "After having come out of the bath, we are

anointed thoroughly with a blessed unction according to the ancient rule. . . . Next to this, the hand is laid upon us through the blessing, calling upon and inviting the Holy Spirit" (*De Bapt.* 8, written about 198 A.D.).

[6] This laying on of hands did not mean simply the bestowing of extraordinary gifts, as is proved by the fact that these gifts were sometimes given without any external rite (Acts 10, 44), and did not always appear with Confirmation (1 Cor. 12, 30). The charisms or gifts were granted to some people in order to help spread Christianity more easily during those crucial early years. And if the rite of imposing hands did not cease to be practiced in spite of the disappearance of the charisms, is it not precisely because these charisms were not regarded as its essential object? The essential thing was, and is, the *inner* strengthening of the Holy Spirit to make of us mature Christians and soldiers of Christ, ready to profess and defend our faith in Him.

How is the sacrament of Confirmation given? Is it necessary for salvation? What is its effect? Can a priest ever confer it?

[1] Confirmation is given by the Bishop and consists in the imposition of hands (essentially the imposition bound up with anointing itself), and the anointing with chrism, a mixture of olive oil and balsam, which is specially blessed by the Bishop on Holy Thursday. The words spoken by the Bishop as he anoints the forehead with chrism are: "I sign you with the sign of the cross, and confirm you with the chrism of salvation, in the name of the Father, and of the Son, and of the Holy Spirit." Confirmation is not necessary for salvation, but the Council of Trent urges all to receive it: "In a matter so full of holiness through which the divine gifts are so liberally bestowed, the greatest care should be taken to avoid all neglect."

[2] Its effects are an increase in grace (as in all the sacraments) and a special effect of strengthening us in the faith. By Confirmation the work begun by Baptism is completed. Baptism gives us the essential supernatural life (grace, virtues, gifts of Holy Spirit) necessary for salvation, whereas

Confirmation increases this life to the level of adult Christian living. In each we receive the Holy Spirit; and as the Spirit of God, He imparts to us the life of God. He does this in Baptism by imparting this life to be lived on a *personal* level. "Unless a man be born again of water and the Spirit, he cannot enter into the kingdom of God" (John 3, 5). But alongside this interior and personal life, we need to live an outward-going Christian social life; and it is strength for this kind of life that is given by the Holy Spirit in Confirmation, which makes us *witnesses* of Christ. Thus, Confirmation gives us the Holy Spirit not only that we may live by Him—which is the effect of Baptism—but that we may profess our Christianity before a world that needs Christ, but often hates Him. Confirmation even provides the strength for martyrdom. Thus, it helps us not just to submit passively to sufferings for Christ's sake, but to be apostles, witnesses (witness means "martyr"), soldiers of Christ before the world. (*See* Roguet: *Christ Acts Through Sacraments,* p. 68.)

[3] The Bishop is the ordinary minister of this sacrament, the only one who can administer it by reason of office. Down through the years, however, the Popes have at times granted simple priests delegation to do it, making them "extraordinary" ministers of the sacrament. Such delegation (at least by tacit permission) explains how it is that in the Eastern Church priests are the usual ministers (though still not "ordinary" ministers). Then, in 1946, Pope Pius XII granted to all *pastors,* by reason of holding this position, delegation to administer Confirmation to those in their territory who are in danger of death from sickness, whenever the presence of the Bishop cannot be had (AAS, 38, 1946, 350s).

What constitutes the sacrament of Penance?

[1] On the part of the priest the *absolution*: "I absolve you from your sins in the name of the Father and of the Son and of the Holy Spirit." On the part of the penitent, *contrition,* that is, sorrow of heart and detestation of sin committed, with the resolve to sin no more; *confession,* that is, the declaration of sins to a priest with the purpose

of obtaining forgiveness; and *satisfaction,* that is, the payment of the temporal punishment due forgiven sins (Council of Trent).

How do you prove from the Bible that the Catholic Church has the power to forgive sin?

[1] Christ promised St. Peter and the Apostles the power to forgive sin (Matt. 16, 18; 18, 18), and fulfilled that promise on the first Easter evening (John 20, 21-23).

[2] The power of the keys implied supreme jurisdiction over the whole Church, and necessarily included the power to forgive sin, because sin alone excludes men from the kingdom of heaven. God ratified this power in St. Peter, the other Apostles and their successors, when He said: "Whatever thou shalt bind on earth shall be bound in heaven, and whatever thou shalt loose on earth shall be loosed in heaven" (Matt. 16, 19).

[3] This promise was fulfilled when Christ said: " 'As the Father has sent Me, I also send you.' When He had said this, He breathed upon them, and said to them, 'Receive the Holy Spirit; whose sins you shall forgive, they are forgiven them; and whose sins you shall retain, they are retained' " (John 20, 21-23).

[4] Why had the Father sent Him? To save sinners by pardoning their sins. "I have come to call sinners, not the just" (Matt. 9, 13). "I was not sent except to the lost sheep of the house of Israel" (Matt. 15, 24). "The Son of Man came to save what was lost" (Matt. 18, 11). "Thou shalt call His name Jesus; for He shall save His people from their sins" (Matt. 1, 21). "Jesus Christ came into the world to save sinners" (1 Tim. 1, 15).

[5] He frequently pardoned sinners; namely, Magdalen (Luke 7, 47), the woman in adultery (John 8, 11), Zacchaeus (Luke 19, 9), the man sick of the palsy (Matt. 9, 2), the thief on the Cross (Luke 23, 43). The pardoning power which He exercised He bestowed upon His Apostles. As the Father had sent Him to pardon, so He sent them to pardon in His Name. "Receive the Holy Spirit," said Christ, because forgiving sins implies the giving of the

spiritual life of grace to the sinner, and making him a temple of the Holy Spirit (1 Cor. 3, 16).

[6] Sins are not to be pardoned lightly, but after careful judging of the dispositions of the sinner. If he is sorry for his sins, he is forgiven by the Apostles and by God; if he refuse to repent, his sins are not forgiven by the Apostles, or by God. They are retained.

[7] Was this pardoning power to cease with the Apostles? By no means. The very nature of the Church, which is the representative of Christ to continue His work until the end of the world (Matt. 28, 20), proves that the pardoning power was not a personal gift to the Apostles, but a permanent institution, to last as long as there were sinners in the world (Council of Trent).

Was not the practice of auricular Confession introduced by Innocent III at the Fourth Lateran Council in 1215, as Calvin maintained? Did the early Christians believe that the Church had the pardoning power?

[1] No, the Council of Trent expressly mentions this statement of Calvin as "a vain calumny," and adds: "The Church did not, through the Lateran Council, ordain that the faithful of Christ shall confess—a thing which it knew to be necessary and instituted of divine right—but that the precept of Confession should be complied with at least once a year."

[2] Confession is not a human institution of Pope or Council, but a divine institution observed in the Church from the beginning. "If anyone denies either that sacramental Confession was instituted, or is necessary for salvation, by divine right, or says that the manner of confessing secretly to a priest alone, which the Church has observed from the beginning, and doth observe, is alien from the institution and command of Christ, and is a human invention, let him be anathema" (Council of Trent).

[3] No one denies that Confession today is observed as a divine law everywhere in the Catholic Church, and that it has been universally observed in both East and West since the 12th century. If a Pope or a General Council had instituted such a distasteful duty, there would have been a

general protest against it at some period in Church history. There is no such record.

⁴ The Eastern Orthodox Church, which first separated from Rome in the 9th century, and the Lesser Eastern Churches which seceded in the 5th, have all retained Confession as a divine institution.

⁵ The medieval penitential books contain practical directions for hearing Confessions; they urge the confessor to warn the penitent not to conceal his secret sins of even thought and desire, but to confess them as if he were speaking to God. The oldest, the penitential of Vinnianus (570), comes from Ireland, and the most influential was the penitential of the Greek Archbishop Theodore, Archbishop of Canterbury (690). St. Columbanus introduced these books into France at the beginning of the 7th century (615).

⁶ St. Gregory the Great (590-604) in his homily on John 20, 23, writes: "The Apostles, therefore, have received the Holy Spirit in order to loose sinners from the bonds of their sins. God has made them partakers of His right of judgment; they are to judge in His name and in His place. The Bishops are the successors of the Apostles, and, therefore, possess the same right." The Bishop must be just in exercising his power to retain or remit sins in God's place. He must know the sins that have been committed, and what penance the sinner has performed for them. He can obtain the exact knowledge of the penitent's sins only through Confession, and, therefore, Confession is a necessary corollary of the judicial character of the Bishop's sentence. If the Bishop has the obligation of judging, he must have a knowledge of the case to be judged. St. Gregory calls upon the sinner to make this necessary Confession with his own lips and of his own accord; an humble and sorrowful Confession is the beginning of the sinner's spiritual resurrection. It is the duty of the ministers of the Church to free the sinner from his bonds, which is accomplished by the priest's absolution. A tremendous ministry this, for the confessor is responsible for the forgiveness he may unjustly accord or refuse. All the essentials of the sacrament of Penance are contained in these words (*Hom.* xxvi.): Confession, Contrition, Satisfaction and Absolution.

⁷ St. Leo the Great (440-461) writes: "God in His abun-

dant mercy has provided two remedies for the sins of men; that they may gain eternal life by the grace of Baptism, and also by the remedy of Penance. Those who have violated the vows of their Baptism may obtain the remission of their sins by condemning themselves; the divine goodness has so decreed that the pardon of God can only be obtained by sinners through the prayers of the priests. Jesus Christ Himself has conferred upon the rulers of the Church the power of imposing canonical penance upon sinners who confess their sins, and of allowing them to receive the Sacraments of Christ, after they have purified their souls by a salutary satisfaction. . . . Every Christian, therefore, must examine his conscience, and cease deferring from day to day the hour of his conversion; he ought not to expect to satisfy God's justice on his deathbed. It is dangerous for a weak and ignorant man to defer his conversion to the last uncertain days of his life, when he may be unable to confess and obtain priestly absolution; he ought, when he can, to merit pardon by a full satisfaction for his sins" (*Epis.*, cviii.).

[8] These words are so plain that some Protestants have traced the origin of Confession to St. Leo the Great. It is good to note that when he speaks of "the prayers of the priests" he is not referring to any prayers the priest might offer up for sinners, but to the priestly absolution in the sacrament of Penance which in his time was used in the form of a prayer. This is still the custom of the Eastern Churches.

[9] St. Augustine (354-430) tells the early Christians "not to listen to those who deny that the Church has the power to forgive all sins" (*De Agon. Christ*, 3; Ser. 295, 2). He compares the sinful conscience to an abscess filled with pus, the priest to a surgeon, and Confession to the lancing of the abscess, whereby the pus is driven forth. He warns sinners not to delay their Confession to the hour of death, because at that time they may be unable to confess their sins to a priest (*In Ps.*, lxvi., 5; Ser. 393).

[10] St. Ambrose (340-397) declares that priests pardon all sins, not in their own name, but as "ministers and instruments of God" (*De Poen.*, i., 2).

Where in the Bible is auricular Confession taught?

[1] Auricular Confession is nowhere expressly mentioned in the Bible, but Christ Himself divinely commanded it by giving His Apostles the power to remit and retain sins (John 20, 23). The sacrament of Penance is a judgment, requiring on the part of the priest-judge an accurate knowledge of the nature, number and circumstances of the sins committed. This can be known only through the penitent himself, who is at once defendant, prosecutor and witness in this divine, secret tribunal (Council of Trent). In a word the sinner must lay bare his soul to the priest, so that he may be able to know the state of his conscience, and, convinced of his sorrow, give him a fitting and an adequate penance.

Do not the words "whose sin you shall forgive" in John 20, 23 simply mean the declaration that sins are forgiven, or the power to preach the Gospel?

[1a] No, both these interpretations of the Reformers were expressly condemned by the Council of Trent. "The absolution of a priest is not a bare ministry only, whether of announcing the Gospel, or of declaring that sins are forgiven, but it is after the manner of a judicial act, whereby sentence is pronounced by the priest as a judge."

[2] This is clear from the words of Christ, who gave the Apostles the power either to bind or loose; either to forgive or to retain sins (Matt. 16, 19). Christ does not say a word about *declaring* sins forgiven, or lead us to believe that forgiveness of sins is merely the power to preach the Gospel.

Does not the confessional give the priest too much power, and enable him to interfere with a man's private affairs?

[1b] Not at all. His only power is a power delegated by Christ, whose minister he is (1 Cor. 4, 1) to forgive sins in His name, and to advise, warn, threaten and encourage souls in their daily conflict with temptation and sin. He has no right whatever to pry into a penitent's private affairs. He can question him only about sin and its occasions, and the more intelligent and careful the sinner's confession, the less will he be questioned by his confessor.

²ᵇ The priest undoubtedly has the right to declare the moral law authoritatively, and to enforce obedience to the commandments of God and the precepts of the Church under penalty of denying absolution. He has no right whatever to enforce his private opinions upon his penitent.

Why do you not allow Confession to be optional?

¹ Because the sacrament of Penance is necessary of divine right, as the Council of Trent teaches. As Jesus Christ established the pardoning power for the forgiveness of post-baptismal sin, every Christian is bound to be pardoned in the way He divinely appointed.

² St. Augustine thus answers this question. He says: "Do penance, as it is done in the Church, in order that the Church may pray for you. Let no one say to himself: 'I do penance secretly before God; God knows it, and He will forgive me, because I am doing penance in my heart.' Has it, therefore, been said without reason: 'Whatever thou shalt loose on earth shall be loosed also in heaven.' Have the keys been given to the Church of God in vain? Are we to frustrate the Gospel and the words of Christ?" (Ser. 392.)

How can a priest listen year after year to the recital of sins without his own mind becoming corrupted?

¹ᵃ Because God gives His priests special graces to keep their minds and hearts pure, especially by means of daily Mass, daily reading of the breviary, and frequent confession. The priest, moreover, listens to the sins of men like another Christ, with sympathy and love for the repentant sinner, who causes "joy in heaven . . . more than ninety-nine just who have no need of repentance" (Luke 15, 7). The more he understands the malice of sin, and its evil effects upon the sinner, the more he hates it as the world's greatest evil.

²ᵃ Does the judge on the bench or the physician in the city hospital become corrupt, because he comes in daily contact with sin and the effects of sin? No reasonable man would say so. The heart becomes corrupt only by constantly yielding to temptation.

Is a priest always bound to keep secret the sins revealed to him in confessions? Ought he not be obliged to give a murderer up to justice?

[1] Yes, a priest is bound by the natural law, the divine law and the law of the Church to keep absolutely secret whatever he hears in Confession. As early as the 6th century the Second Synod of Dovin in Armenia decreed: "A priest who reveals the confession of the penitents shall be deposed with anathema." The Fourth Lateran Council (1215) commanded confessors "not to betray the sinner in any manner, whether by word or sign or in any other way," and decreed that priests guilty of this crime "be deposed from their office, and imprisoned in a monastery for life." Canon Law says: "The priest, who dares break the seal of Confession directly, shall incur excommunication reserved in most special manner to the Holy See." Priests are forbidden even to speak about what they have heard in Confession, whether in private conversation or in sermons, no matter in what form or under what pretext this is done. (*Instruction of Holy Office,* June 19, 1915.)

[2] This law admits of no exceptions. A priest may not break the seal of Confession, either to save his own life or his own good name, to save the life of another, or to further the aims of justice. This is eminently reasonable, for no criminal would dream of going to Confession, if he knew the confessor were bound to reveal his crime to the State authorities. The civil courts recognize the confessor's privilege of silence both here and abroad. It was embodied in the law of New York State in 1828 on occasion of the trial of the Jesuit, Father Kohlmann, who refused to reveal in court information he had received under the seal of Confession.

Does not Confession weaken character? Is not Confession an incentive to sin by making forgiveness easy?

[1a] No, on the contrary, Confession strengthens character by its insistence upon supernatural motives for sorrow, and prevents many a sin, making the sinner realize its heinousness in the sight of God, and its disastrous consequences here and hereafter.

[2] If Confession were an incentive to sin, how is it that wicked Catholics, who give the lie to the Church by their daily lives, rarely go to Confession, while the most virtuous Catholics go frequently? How is it that Catholic fathers and mothers are glad when their children go often to Confession, and are sorrowful when they neglect this important duty? How again can you account for the countless thousands of sinners won back to God by means of good, contrite confessions?

[3] It is much easier to confess one's sins to God, for then the sinner may easily crave pardon without fulfilling the necessary conditions. The confessor reminds the sinner that he cannot pardon him, unless he atones for the past by restoring his neighbor's good name or property, unless he is sorry from a supernatural motive, and unless he promises to avoid in the future all the proximate occasions of sin. All priests know that hardened sinners find this difficult, for at times they will depart unabsolved rather than promise amendment.

[4] We readily admit that some Catholics go to Confession in a mechanical, perfunctory manner, without realizing the dignity and sacred character of this divine sacrament. We know, too, that after Confession they continue doing things that would bring the blush of shame to the cheek of a decent pagan. But a Catholic yields to the temptations of the world, the flesh and the devil (Matt. 13, 22), not on account of the sacrament of Penance, but because he has proved remiss in his promise of amendment.

Do you believe that a Catholic is damned if he cannot go to Confession before death, no priest being available? How about non-Catholics who do not believe in Confession?

[1] No, God never asks us to do what is morally impossible. A Catholic in grievous sin, who cannot obey the divine law of Confession because no priest is at hand, is bound to make an act of perfect contrition, which at once reconciles him to God. A non-Catholic, who is invincibly ignorant of the divine character of the sacrament of Penance is pardoned in the same way.

Is not Confession degrading and unmanly?

[1] Confession is not degrading, but on the contrary is one of the noblest acts of the true Christian, for it proves his willingness to be reconciled to God in the way He divinely appointed. It is indeed humiliating, but humility is a Christ-like virtue, especially calculated to conquer the pride of sin. Jesus said: "Learn of Me, for I am meek and humble of heart" (Matt. 11, 29). The proud Pharisee who boasted of his good deeds was not pleasing to God, but the humble publican, who struck his breast, saying: " 'O God, be merciful to me, a sinner,' . . . went back to his home justified . . . for he who humbles himself shall be exalted" (Luke 18, 13—14).

[2] Confession is not unmanly, for it calls for every manly quality: intelligence, courage, humility, energy, and determination.

Do Catholics have to pay for Confession?

[1a] No. To administer the sacraments for money is simony, a grievous sin expressly forbidden by canon law. A Protestant once assured me that his Catholic servant had often asked money from him to pay for her Confession. One evening he followed her to find out whether she was going directly to church, as she had declared. He found her going to a theater instead. She had simply used his anti-Catholic prejudice as a means of extorting money.

I could never kneel down to a fellow man and confess all my sins. That is asking too much of flesh and blood.

[1b] Whether you find Confession an easy or a difficult matter is not the question. The true Christian simply asks: Is Confession a divine commandment, inasmuch as Christ gave the pardoning power to His priests? You are not asked to confess your sins to an ordinary man, but to a priest, who is divinely commissioned for the purpose, and carefully trained by many years of study and prayer for this unique ministry. Read Cardinal Manning's *Eternal Priesthood,* or Cardinal Gibbons' *Ambassador of Christ,* if you really desire to know what the priesthood really means.

²ᵇ Confession indeed is difficult for the hardened sinner who does not wish to give up his wicked life, but it is full of joy and consolation to the repentant sinner, as any Catholic can tell you. A non-Catholic who is wont to confess his sins to God—and he often forgets to do even this—may, as an outsider, consider Confession to a priest a most harrowing experience, but converts, who have tasted its divine consolation, soon learn to welcome it. Many a convert after his first Confession has said to me: "Father, it was not so hard after all." Do you expect God to pardon you without the slightest suffering or mortification? Do you think your pride can be cured without the least evidence of humility?

How can our sins be forgiven by merely telling them to a priest?

¹ Our sins cannot be pardoned by merely telling them to a priest. The sacrament of Penance also requires Contrition or sorrow for sin, and satisfaction or atonement for sin.

² The Scriptures teach plainly that God will not forgive the sinner, unless he is truly sorry for his sins (Acts 2, 37). The sinner's sorrow must be a true sorrow of the mind and will; it must embrace every grievous sin; it must be supreme, hating sin as the greatest of evils; it must be inspired by supernatural grace, and based on faith, "the beginning, root and foundation of all justification" (Council of Trent). The detestation of sin may arise from various motives; the vileness of sin itself, the fear of hell and punishments (imperfect contrition), or the perfect love of God (perfect contrition).

³ Perfect contrition "reconciles man with God before the sacrament of Penance is actually received" (Council of Trent), although it necessarily includes the desire of receiving the sacrament. This is evident from our Lord's words: "He who has My commandments, and keeps them, he it is who loves Me. But he who loves Me will be loved by My Father, and I will love him" (John 14, 21). Imperfect contrition or attrition suffices for the valid reception of the sacrament of Penance. The Scriptures often appeal to the

fear of God to deter men from their sins. Our Lord said: "Do not be afraid of those who kill the body . . . but be afraid of Him who is able to destroy both soul and body in hell" (Matt. 10, 28). The Council of Trent declared that this fear "is a gift of God and an impulse of the Holy Spirit."

⁴ Not only must the sinner be truly sorry for his sins, he must also make satisfaction for them. Even when sins have been pardoned by God, there often remains the liability to temporal punishment to atone for the injury done Him, and to bring about the sinner's reformation. God often requires satisfaction of the sinner for the transgression of His laws, both natural and supernatural. The impure man may be forgiven his sin, and yet be punished for his immorality by ill health; the murderer may be pardoned his crime, and yet have to expiate it in the electric chair. The Scriptures tell us that God pardoned Adam his disobedience, the Israelites in the desert their murmuring and idolatry, Moses his lack of faith, and David his murder, adultery and pride; but they were all severely punished by Him. St. Paul also speaks of sickness and death as temporal punishments for unworthy communions (1 Cor. 11, 30-32).

⁵ The acceptance of the penance given in Confession is proof of the sinner's good will, and entitles him to the benefit of the sacrament. It is given, as the Council of Trent says, "not only for the healing of the soul's weakness (a medicine of infirmity) and the preservation of a new life, but also for the avenging and punishing of past sins." All the temporal punishments for sin are not necessarily forgiven by the sacrament of Penance; some may remain to be remitted by prayer, fasting and almsgiving. This teaching is based on the Scriptures, which mention the fasting of the Ninivites (Jonas 3, 5), the prayers and penance of Manasses (2 Paral. 33, 12, 13), and the almsgiving of Job 4, 11.

⁶ St. Augustine (354-430) writes: "Man is forced to suffer even after his sins have been forgiven, though it was sin that caused him to fall into such misery. For the punishment outlasts the guilt, lest the guilt should be accounted slight, if with its forgiveness, the penalty also came to an end" (*In Joan.*, cxxiv., 5).

If, as you claim, you possess the Apostolic power of pardoning sin, why do you priests not also possess the power to work miracles, which Jesus conferred upon the Apostles (Matt. 10, 1. 8; Mark 16, 17-18; Luke 9, 2; John 14, 12)?

[1] Whereas the pardoning power is an essential part of the threefold divine commission of teaching, pardoning and sanctifying the souls of men, the extraordinary gift of miracles is not essential. Christ gave the Apostles the power to perform miracles, to prove that the Kingdom of God was at hand, and they were His accredited messengers. He promised this gift to His Church forever as a characteristic mark of her holiness, and the holiness of her saints.

Why do Catholics believe that they receive the living Christ in Holy Communion?

[1a] Catholics believe in the Real Presence of Jesus Christ in the Holy Eucharist, because He promised to give His Flesh as food and His Blood as drink (John 6, 48-70); because He fulfilled this promise at the Last Supper (Luke 22, 19-20); because St. Paul declares this was the belief of the Apostolic Church (1 Cor. 10, 16; 11, 27-29); because the early Fathers explicitly taught that the Eucharist was "the flesh and blood of the Incarnate Jesus" (St. Justin, *Apol.,* i., 66); because Christ's infallible Church solemnly defined this doctrine. "The Holy Synod teaches . . . that in the august sacrament of the Holy Eucharist, after the consecration of the bread and wine, our Lord Jesus Christ, true God and Man, is truly, really and substantially contained under the appearance of those sensible things. . . . If anyone denies that in the sacrament of the most Holy Eucharist are contained truly, really and substantially the body and blood, together with the soul and divinity of our Lord Jesus Christ, and consequently the whole Christ; but says that He is therein only as a sign, or a figure or virtually, let him be anathema" (Council of Trent).

Ought not the sixth chapter of St. John to be interpreted figuratively? Does not the phrase "to eat flesh" signify belief in the divinity of Christ? Why do Catholics take the sixth chapter of St. John literally?

[1] Catholics make a distinction between the first part of Chapter 6 (vv. 26 to 51), wherein Christ speaks of Himself figuratively as the bread of heaven, a spiritual food to be received by faith, and the second part (vv. 51 to 59), wherein He speaks literally of His Flesh and Blood as a real food, and a real drink.

[2] A careful study of the whole chapter calls for a literal interpretation of the words to "eat the flesh of the Son of Man, and drink His blood" (John 6, 54). Christ makes a clear-cut distinction between three kinds of bread: the bread or manna of the desert (Exod. 16, 15; John 6, 49), given by Moses to the Jews in the past to nourish the body; the bread of heaven or the bread of life (John 6, 32. 35), Christ Himself, given by the Father in the present to the Jews as an object of faith; and the bread of life, Christ Himself in the Eucharist, to be given in the future by Christ for the life of the world (John 6, 52).

[3] Again a figurative interpretation is impossible, according to the rules of language. If a figure of speech has a definite meaning, we cannot use it in a new sense, merely for purposes of controversy.

[4] To eat one's flesh was a familiar figure among the Jews of old, as it is a common figure among the Arabs of today, but it always means to do a person some serious injury, especially by calumny or by false accusation. Is it not absurd to imagine that our Lord would promise eternal life and a glorious resurrection to those who calumniated Him?

[5] To drink one's blood was also a familiar figure among the Jews, but it always meant a chastisement of God (Isa. 49, 26; Apoc. 16, 6) upon His enemies, a meaning impossible here. Drinking blood was expressly forbidden by the Jewish law (Gen. 9, 4), and was therefore regarded as a heinous crime (1 Kings 14, 33).

[6] The Jews certainly understood our Lord literally, for they said: "How can this man give us His flesh to eat?" (John 6, 53). Our Lord's reply to them proves that He meant them to do so. We must remember that Christ, like every good teacher, made two kinds of answers to men who objected to His teaching. If they did not understand His meaning, He explained His doctrine more fully. In this

way He explains Baptism to Nicodemus (John 3, 3-5), the possibility of the rich man being saved (Matt. 19, 24-26), the fact of Lazarus' death (John 11, 11-14), the idea of freedom (John 8, 32-34).

⁷ When His hearers understood His teaching but refused to accept it, He repeated His teaching with even more emphasis. Thus He insisted upon His power to forgive sins, when the Scribes accused Him of blasphemy (Matt. 9, 2-7), and insisted upon His being Eternal, when the Jews said He was not yet fifty years old (John 8, 56-58).

⁸ In like manner He acted with the Jews who objected to His teaching about the Real Presence. When they objected: "How can this man give us His flesh to eat?" He did not explain His doctrine in a figurative sense, but He repeated the doctrine that gave offense in a most emphatic manner. He puts His doctrine in the form of a precept: "Unless you eat the flesh of the Son of Man, and drink His blood, you shall not have life in you"; and declares "My flesh is food indeed, and My blood is drink indeed." He tells them that this eating and drinking is a pledge of everlasting life, a bond of intimate union with Him, a pledge of supernatural life here and of resurrection hereafter (John 6, 54-59).

⁹ When many of the disciples still refused to accept this doctrine, saying: "This is a hard saying. Who can listen to it?" (John 6, 61), Christ did not retract His words, and say that He spoke merely in figure. On the contrary, He rebuked them for their lack of faith, and asked them to accept His words, because He came from heaven, and would one day ascend "where He was before." The unbelieving Jews walked no more with Him, but the faithful Apostles, who did not comprehend the mystery of the Holy Eucharist, humbly accepted Christ's word. Peter answered for them: "Lord, to whom shall we go? Thou hast the words of eternal life, and we have come to believe that Thou art the Christ, the Son of God" (John 6, 62-70). The early Fathers hold that the Body of Christ is really present in the Eucharist; they cite the doctrine of the Real Presence to refute the various heresies of their time on the Incarnation; they expressly deny that the Eucharist is a mere figure of Christ's body; they assert that Christ is received in

Communion, physically and corporeally. St. Ignatius writes: "They (the Docetae) abstain from the Eucharist and prayer, because they confess not that the Eucharist is the flesh of our Savior Jesus Christ, the flesh which suffered for our sins, which the Father in His mercy raised up" (*Ad Smyrn.*, 7).

[10] St. Justin writes: "We have been taught that the food over which thanksgiving has been made by the prayer of the word which came from Him—by which (food) our blood and flesh are nourished by transmutation—is both flesh and blood of the same Incarnate Jesus" (*Apol.*, 1, 65-66).

Ought not the words of Christ at the Last Supper be interpreted in a figurative sense (Matt. 26, 26-28; Mark 14, 22-24; Luke 22, 19-20; 1 Cor. 11, 23-25)?

[1] The Catholic Church has always interpreted the words: "This is My body; This is My blood," which occur in the four accounts of the Last Supper, in a strictly literal sense (Council of Trent). No explanation of these simple words can make their meaning clearer. Christ says that what He holds in His hands is His Body and we, like the Apostles, humbly accept His word. The literal sense is the obvious sense, and was so understood from the beginning. The denial of the Sacramentarians came over 1500 years too late, and went counter to the constant voice of Christian tradition. By the year 1577 there were some 200 different interpretations of these words current among the Reformers, which proves how hard pressed they were to defend their arbitrary explanations. Luther till the very end of his life maintained the literal interpretation of these words against the Sacramentarians, Zwingli, Carlstadt, and Œcolampadius, although like all heretics, he illogically waged bitter war against the Sacrifice of the Mass. In fact he said he was tempted to deny the Real Presence in order "to give a great smack in the face of popery," but the teaching of the Bible and all antiquity were too strong in its favor.

[2] A figure of speech is always known to us either from the nature of the case, or from the usages of a language. For example, I may refer to a man's cunning by calling him a fox, or to his bravery by calling him a lion. Again

I may hold in my hand a photograph of the President of the United States, and say: "This is the President of the United States." In both instances my meaning will be evident at once. But in no way is bread the fitting or possible symbol of the human body. Christ plainly excluded any possibility of a figurative meaning to His words when He said: "The bread that I will give is My flesh for the life of the world" (John 6, 52). St. Luke's account tells us that Christ spoke of His body as "given for you," and of His blood as "shed for you" (Luke 22, 19-20). Therefore the body given to the Apostles was the same body that was crucified on the cross, and the chalice contained the same blood that was shed for our sins.

[3] The words of the institution were spoken on the night preceding our Lord's passion and death. The Holy Eucharist was His last will and testament (Luke 22, 20). It was a sacrament and a sacrifice to be celebrated in His Church until the end of time (1 Cor. 11, 26). The words of a will should be clear, and interpreted in their natural, literal sense (Gen. 49, 29). Would Christ, the infinite God and lover of souls, use a figure of speech that would deceive millions of His followers for all time, and lead them into the very idolatry He came to abolish? The sacraments and sacrifices of the Old Law were established in plain terms. Why not then the more important sacrament and sacrifice of the New Law, which Christ was leaving us as a pledge of our supernatural life here and hereafter (John 6, 58-59).

[4] St. Paul certainly interpreted the words of the institution literally. He writes: "The cup of blessing that we bless, is it not the sharing of the blood of Christ? And the bread which we break, is it not the partaking of the body of the Lord?" (1 Cor. 10, 16). He is contrasting the Jewish and the pagan sacrifices with the sacrifice of the Christians, and arguing against any participation in the pagan sacrificial banquets. The reason given is that partaking of the consecrated cup unites us to the blood of Christ, and partaking of the consecrated bread unites us to the body of Christ. If the pagan banquet and sacrifice are real, so are the Christian sacrament and sacrifice.

[5] He states the doctrine of the Real Presence even more plainly in 1 Cor. 11, 27-29. He writes: "Therefore whoever

eats this bread or drinks the cup of the Lord unworthily, will be guilty of the body and the blood of the Lord. But let a man prove himself, and so let him eat of that bread and drink of the cup; for he who eats and drinks unworthily, without distinguishing the body, eats and drinks judgment to himself."

[6] If our Lord is not present in Communion, these words of the Apostle are utterly meaningless. Because Christ is really present, the Apostle warns the sinner to cleanse his conscience of sin, for an unworthy Communion merits God's condemnation or judgment. We must distinguish this body of the Lord from all other food, and therefore come to Communion with a conscience clear of grievous sin.

Is not the Lord's Supper a sacrament? Why then do you call it the Sacrifice of the Mass? It seems to me that the Sacrifice of the Cross is sufficient for true Christianity.

[1] The Lord's Supper is a sacrament *and* a sacrifice. As a sacrament it contains the real body and blood of Christ under the sign of bread and wine. As a sacrifice it is the prolongation of the Sacrifice of the Cross.

[2] On the night He was betrayed, our Blessed Lord offered Himself to His heavenly Father under the appearance of bread and wine as a sacrifice for sin. By consecrating the bread and wine separately He clearly manifested the bloody separation of His body and soul on the cross. Furthermore, He left this visible unbloody sacrifice to His Church and He commanded the Apostles and their successors to offer the same sacrifice "from the rising of the sun to the going down" (Malachias, 1, 10-11.). "Do this in remembrance of Me" (Luke 22, 19).

[3] The Sacrifice of the Mass does not replace or substitute for the Sacrifice of the Cross. Rather it is a true and proper sacrifice in which Jesus Christ, through the priest, offers Himself a most acceptable victim for sin to the eternal Father, by an unbloody immolation as He once did upon the cross by a bloody immolation. Only the manner of offering is different. For on the cross and in the Mass it is the one same victim, Jesus Christ, who is offered by Himself.

[4] The Eucharistic sacrifice is the means established by Christ Crucified to impart to us the saving virtue of the cross for the remission of the sins we daily commit. The sacrifice of the altar is the supreme instrument whereby the merits won by the Redeemer upon the cross are distributed to the faithful: "as often as this commemorative sacrifice is offered, there is wrought the work of our Redemption" (*Roman Missal*, Secret of 9th Sunday after Pentecost). Instead of implying that the physical death of Christ is not sufficient, the Catholic Mass " 'rather proclaims and renders more manifest its greatness and necessity,' as the Council of Trent declares. By its daily immolation it reminds us that there is no other means of salvation except in the cross of our Lord Jesus Christ" (Pius XII, Encyclical, *Mediator Dei*, 1947).

Did not Christ say of Himself figuratively "I am the Door" (John 10, 9), "I am the true Vine" (John 15, 1)? Might He not, therefore, call the Eucharist His body only in figure?

[1a] "I am the Door" (or Vine) does not mean I represent, or am the figure of the door (or vine), for our Lord certainly did not intend to make Himself the symbol or figure of material objects. The context in both cases makes our Lord's figurative meaning clear. Just as one enters a house through a door, so we have access to the Father through Him. "If anyone enter by Me he shall be safe" (John 10, 9). Just "as the branch cannot bear fruit of itself unless it remain on the vine, so neither can you unless you abide in Me" (John 15, 4).

Is not the doctrine of the Real Presence impossible? How can the eternal God be contained in the wafer Catholics receive in Holy Communion?

[1] The doctrine of the Real Presence is undoubtedly a great mystery like Creation, the Blessed Trinity and the Incarnation, but it is not impossible, because it does not imply any self-contradiction. If God can create the universe out of nothing, why cannot He change the substance of bread and wine into His body and blood? The true follower of Christ does not ask how can this man give us His

flesh to eat (John 6, 53), but accepts Christ's word humbly (John 6, 67-70). The Apostles who had witnessed the transubstantiation of water into wine at Cana in Galilee (John 2, 1-11), and the feeding of the five thousand with five barley loaves and fishes (John 6, 1-14) never questioned Christ's power to change bread and wine into His flesh and blood.

² Non-Catholics declare the doctrine of the Real Presence impossible, because they think it involves a self-contradiction. They suppose that it requires the same thing to be both bread and not bread at the same time. This is not the Catholic teaching. After consecration the species of bread is not really bread, but the body of Christ, for the substance of the bread has been changed into the substance of Christ's body. What is not changed are the "accidents or the sensible qualities of the bread; namely, its color, taste," etc. But the reality of a thing lies in its substance, the invisible part of it, not in the accidents, or visible part. St. Cyril stated this clearly: "Being fully persuaded that what seems bread is not bread, even though it seems so to the taste, but Christ's body; and what seems wine is not wine, even though the taste will have it so, but Christ's blood."

³ The substance of Christ's body in the Eucharist has none of the sensible qualities of a human body; it is not extended so as to occupy space, although it is united with accidents which do occupy space. Contrary to physical laws, as the Catechism of the Council of Trent says, "they subsist of themselves, inhering in no subject." It would, therefore, be wrong to say: "The body of Christ is round" or "The blood of Christ has a light color," for these expressions are to be used with regard to the accidents alone. This is certainly a mysterious doctrine, hard to understand, because there is nothing like it in all our experience. But the mysteries of Christianity are all unique, because they pertain to divine things. We accept them on the testimony of God (1 John 5, 9), and on the infallible witness of Christ's divine Church.

Was not your doctrine of transubstantiation invented by the Council of Trent? Can it be proved from the Bible or from the teaching of the Primitive Church?

[1] The word "transubstantiation" is not older than the 11th century, but the idea is clearly taught in the Bible and in the early Fathers. The Council of Trent thus defines the way in which Christ is really present in the Holy Eucharist: "By the consecration of the bread and of the wine a conversion is made of the whole substance of the bread into the substance of the body of Christ our Lord, and of the whole substance of the wine into the substance of His blood; which conversion is by the Holy Catholic Church suitably and properly called transubstantiation."

[2] By this definition the Council condemned the Lutheran doctrine of consubstantiation, that the substance of bread and the body of Christ exist together; the Calvinistic doctrine of a virtual or dynamic presence, whereby the efficacy of Christ's body and blood is communicated from heaven to the souls of the predestined and the Zwinglian idea of a mere memorial supper.

[3] The words of institution, "This is My body," plainly imply that what Christ held in His hands must have ceased to be bread, and must have become His body. As there was no change in the accidents or appearances of bread and wine, the change must have been what the Church fittingly calls transubstantiation.

[4] St. Ambrose teaches transubstantiation when he asks: "Cannot, therefore, the words of Christ, who was able to make something out of nothing, change that which already exists into something which it was not before? . . . What we effect (by consecration) is the body taken from the Virgin" (*De Myst.*, ix., 51).

[5] St. Augustine writes: "That which is seen on the table of the Lord is bread and wine; but this bread and this wine, when the word is added, becomes the body and blood of the Logos" (Ser. 5).

[6] St. Cyril writes: "As a life-giving sacrament we possess the sacred flesh of Christ and His precious blood under the appearances of bread and wine" (*In Luc*, xxii., 19). "What seems to be bread is not bread, but Christ's body; what seems to be wine is not wine, but Christ's blood."

[7] All the ancient liturgies, Eastern and Western, plainly teach transubstantiation. The following prayer is from the liturgy of St. Basil: "Make this bread into the precious

body of our Lord and God and Redeemer Jesus Christ, and this chalice into the blood of our Lord and God and Savior Jesus Christ, which was shed for the life of the world."

Does not the doctrine of the Real Presence contradict the evidence of my senses? What I see and taste is merely bread and wine.

[1] It does not, for what we see and taste after the consecration are the accidents or appearances of bread and wine, which have not been changed. The senses tell us nothing regarding the substance of bread and wine before consecration; they tell us nothing of the body and blood of Christ which is present after consecration.

[2] The senses judge only of appearances, and, therefore, may often lead us to make false inferences. I apparently see the sun rising in the East and setting in the West, but science with its Copernican system of astronomy corrects that mistake.

[3] Reason and revelation are our guides to divine truth; not feeling or sense impressions. If Christ declared that He would give us His flesh to eat and His blood to drink, we must accept His word, no matter how mysterious or incomprehensible the doctrine appears to be.

How can the body of Christ be in so many places at once? How can Christ be in heaven, and at the same time in all the churches of the world?

[1a] The Council of Trent has defined this multilocation of the body of Christ. "For neither are these things mutually repugnant—that our Savior Himself always sits at the right hand of the Father in heaven, according to the natural mode of existing, and that, nevertheless, He is in many other places, sacramentally present to us in His own substance, by a manner of existing which, though we can scarcely express it in words, yet by the understanding, illuminated by faith, we can conceive, and ought most firmly to believe, is possible to God."

[2] Father Dalgairns thus answers this question: "The whole question resolves itself into this—can a body be un-

extended? Who will say that God cannot take from a body the property of extension? What contradiction is there in it? Is it not easy for us to conceive substance without extension? If we take to pieces the idea of substance, we shall find that it is quite independent of quantity, on which extension depends; for the smallest grain of gold is as really and substantially gold, as all the precious metal contained in the whole universe. Again, quantity is a sensible thing which is seen by the eye and felt by the touch; but as for substance, it is revealed to us by the mind alone. Let God but only reduce a body to the state of pure substance, and it ceases at once to be extended, without ceasing to be a body. It is by extension that a body becomes subject to the laws of space; take extension away, and it partakes at once of some of the prerogatives of spirit.

[3] "This then is what God has done to the body of Jesus in the Blessed Sacrament. It has ceased to be extended, and all at once it is freed from the fetters which bound it to place. It is not so much that it is in many places at once, as that it is no longer under the ordinary laws of space at all. It pervades the Host like a spirit. It uses, indeed, the locality formerly occupied by the bread, in order to fix itself in a definite place, but it only comes into the domain of space at all indirectly through the species, as the soul only enters into its present relations with space through the body. Who will say that this involves contradiction, or that it is beyond the power of omnipotence?" (*The Holy Communion*, i., 35, 36.)

Why do you go counter to the Bible (John 6, 54; 1 Cor. 11, 27. 29) and the institution of Christ (Matt. 26, 27), by denying the cup to the laity in Communion? Did not Christ plainly say: "All of you drink of this?" Does not the Catholic Church deprive the people of half the Lord's Supper contrary to the practice of the Primitive Church?

[1] The Catholic Church, in prescribing Communion under one kind at the Councils of Constance and of Trent, did not in any way go counter to the teaching of Christ or St. Paul, or in any way destroy the essence of the sacrament of the Holy Eucharist. The Council of Trent teaches:

"Laymen, and clerics when not celebrating, are not obliged by any divine precept to receive the sacrament of the Eucharist under both kinds, neither can it by any means be doubted, without injury to faith, that Communion under either kind is sufficient for them unto salvation."

[2] It is easy to understand how Protestants who do not believe in the real objective presence of Christ in the Holy Eucharist, and who do believe that the essence of the sacrament consists in eating mere bread and drinking mere wine, should insist on receiving under both kinds. Catholics, however, who believe that the Eucharist is the living Jesus Christ, are certain that they receive not His body alone under the form of bread, nor His blood alone under the form of wine, but His body, blood, soul and divinity under either form (Council of Trent). The communicant, who receives under one kind, receives the same living Christ as he who communicates under both kinds.

[3] The sixth chapter of St. John presents no difficulty, for as the Council of Trent pointed out, the Lord promised the same reward for Communion under one kind as under both. He who said, "Unless you eat the flesh of the Son of Man, and drink His blood, you shall not have life in you" (John 6, 54), also said, "He who eats this bread shall live forever" (John 6, 59); and He who said, "He who eats My flesh and drinks My blood has life everlasting" (John 6, 55), also said, "The bread that I will give you is My flesh for the life of the world" (John 6, 52); and, finally, He who said, "He who eats My flesh, and drinks My blood, abides in Me and I in him" (John 6, 57), said, nevertheless, "He who eats this bread shall live forever" (John 6, 59).

[4] When Christ said to the Apostles, "All of you drink of this" (Matt. 26, 27), He was speaking not to the laity, but to priests, who in celebrating Mass, as He ordered, always partake of Communion under both kinds. The Eucharist is both a sacrament and a sacrifice. For the Sacrifice of the Mass a double consecration is necessary, for it is the Sacrifice of the Cross. Its Priest is the Priest of Calvary, its Victim is the Victim of Calvary, and its mode of offering is a mystic representation of the blood-shedding of Calvary. Protestants, having abolished the Mass, do not understand the Catholic doctrine of Communion.

[5] St. Paul in his letter to the Corinthians is insisting primarily upon the necessity of the Christian receiving Communion with a heart cleansed of sin. He merely mentions the fact that the early Christians usually received under both kinds, which nobody denies. He says expressly that it is sacrilegious to receive Communion under either form, if one is in mortal sin: "Whoever eats this bread or drinks the cup of the Lord unworthily, will be guilty of the body and the blood of the Lord" (1 Cor. 11, 27). The reading *"or* drink" has such overwhelming evidence in its favor, that the Revised Version has corrected the erroneous *"and* drink" of the King James version of the Bible.

[6] While Communion under both kinds was the common custom for twelve centuries—it is still so in the East—the Church always approved the concurrent custom of receiving the Holy Eucharist under either kind. Communion under the form of bread was common practice in the Primitive Church. Both Tertullian (*Ad Uxorem,* i., 5) and St. Basil (*Epis.* xciii.) tell us that the early Christians took Holy Eucharist under the form of bread to their homes, and gave themselves Communion before breakfast.

[7] The present law of receiving Communion under the form of bread dates from the Council of Constance in 1414, which condemned the Hussites of Bohemia for teaching that the cup was absolutely necessary. This law was confirmed by the Council of Trent, which condemned the false teaching of the Reformers on this point. Long before the law was passed, however, the custom of receiving Communion under the form of bread had become widespread for practical reasons. These "grave and just reasons," mentioned by the Council of Trent, were: the risk of spilling the precious blood; the difficulty of reserving Communion under the species of wine; the dread of drinking from a chalice touched by infected lips; the cost of obtaining wine for thousands of communicants.

[8] Were any doctrine involved, no difficulty would have prevented the Church from insisting upon the observance of a divine law. As it involved merely a question of discipline, she was ever ready, as the guardian of the sacraments, to adapt her laws for their administration to the changing conditions of the times.

What constitutes the sacrament of Holy Orders in your Church? How do you prove it a sacrament of Christ? When was the priesthood established, and by what particular ceremony?

¹ The Council of Trent teaches: "If anyone says that Order, or sacred ordination, is not truly and properly a sacrament instituted by Christ the Lord; that it is a kind of human figment devised by men unskilled in ecclesiastical matters; or that it is only a sort of rite for choosing ministers of the word of God and the sacraments; let him be anathema." "If anyone says that by these words: 'Do this in remembrance of Me' (Luke 22, 19) Christ did not constitute the Apostles priests, or did not ordain that they and other priests offer His body and blood, let him be anathema."

² At the Last Supper, Jesus Christ, the High Priest of the New Law according to the order of Melchisedech (Ps. 109, 4; Heb. 7, 11), instituted as a permanent and official act of worship the Eucharistic Sacrifice which He had just offered, and in commanding His Apostles to do what He Himself had done, He gave them the power to do what He commanded, that is, to offer this self-same sacrifice as the representatives and sharers of His Eternal Priesthood.

³ Although most likely Christ made His Apostles priests without any special ceremony (Bellarmine, *De Sac. Ord.,* i., 2), the Acts of the Apostles and the Epistles of St. Paul mention all the elements of the sacrament of Holy Orders; the external symbolic rite of the imposition of hands and prayer; the internal grace given by this rite; and its institution by Christ.

⁴ The external sign is the imposition of hands. Paul and Barnabas ordained priests for the different Churches. "And when they had appointed presbyters for them in each Church . . . they commended them to the Lord in whom they had believed" (Acts 14, 22). St. Paul counsels Timothy who was a Bishop, "Do not lay hands hastily upon anyone" (1 Tim. 5, 22).

⁵ St. Paul also teaches that the imposition of hands communicates internal grace, "Do not neglect the grace that is in you . . . with the laying on of hands of the presbyterate"

(1 Tim. 4, 14). "I admonish you to stir up the grace of God which is in you by the laying on of my hands" (2 Tim. 1, 6).

[6] Christ instituted Holy Orders because "He Himself gave some men as Apostles, and some as prophets, others again as evangelists (preachers), and others as pastors and teachers, in order to perfect the saints for a work of ministry, for building up the body of Christ" (Eph. 4, 11-12).

[7] St. Gregory of Nyssa (395) writes: "The same power of the word renders sublime and honorable the priest, who, by the newness of ordination, has been singled out from the multitude; he who was yesterday one of the people suddenly becomes a commander, a presiding officer, a teacher of righteousness, and the dispenser of hidden mysteries" (*Orat. in Bapt. Christi*).

[8] St. Augustine (354-430) places Holy Orders on a level with the sacrament of Baptism. "Each is a sacrament, and each is given to man by a certain consecration: Baptism when a man is baptized, the other when he is ordained; and for this cause, in the Catholic Church, neither can be repeated" (*Contra Epis. Parmen.*, ii., 13).

[9] The Council of Trent declares that Holy Orders is proved a sacrament "on the testimony of the Scriptures, the Apostolic tradition, and the unanimous consent of the Fathers."

Is there the slightest proof of Episcopacy in the early Church? Were not Bishop and presbyter synonymous terms in the New Testament?

[1] The Catholic Church teaches that it possesses a divinely instituted hierarchy of Bishops, priests and deacons; that Bishops are superior to priests, and have the power of confirming and ordaining (Council of Trent). The existence of these Orders is very clear at the beginning of the 2nd century, in the letters of St. Ignatius of Antioch (d. 110). By then the terms "bishop" (*episcopus,* meaning originally "superintendent") and "presbyter" (originally meaning "elder") were applied to distinct members of the hierarchy, the first applying exclusively to the Bishop and the second to simple priests. And by then, too, we find

one Bishop at the head of each Church (monarchical episcopate) with priests and deacons under him. But was all
this as clear in the first Christian communities?

2 In the New Testament and during the 1st century,
the terms "bishop" and "presbyter" are used interchange-
ably to designate the *same* persons (*see* Acts 20, 17. 28;
1 Tim. 3, 1-7 and Tit. 1, 5-9; Tit. 1, 5. 7). Who, then, were
these "bishop-presbyters"? Very few think they were *all*
Bishops; a good number of scholars say *some* of them were
Bishops such as the college of presbyters in 1 Tim. 4, 14;
but it seems better to say that *all of them were simple
priests* without power of ordaining—the characteristic function of a Bishop.

3 Who, then, were the successors of the Apostles, with
power of governing the Church and of ordaining priests?
They were people who did not have, at first, the name
"bishop" at all—men such as Timothy and Titus (much
like Apostolic Delegates), and probably select persons such
as Barnabas, Manahen and Simeon called Niger from the
groups with special charisms, known as Apostles (in a
broader sense), prophets and doctors. (*See* 1 Cor. 12, 28;
Eph. 4, 11-12; Rom. 12, 6-7.)

4 With the death of the Apostles, these successors were
to assume the full role of founding Churches, organizing
and ordaining. Thus, in accord with the mission they received from Christ to spread the Church and assure its
continuance until the end of time, the Apostles established
this law of succession, so that after their deaths others with
power to ordain would continue to supply the Churches
with priests and deacons (St. Clement of Rome, *Ad Cor.*
44, 1-3).

5 It seems certain that in the beginning the newly
founded Churches did not have at their head one Bishop,
with priests and deacons under his jurisdiction. The
Apostles were not attached to any particular Church permanently, nor were the delegates and successors mentioned
above. They were all missionary Bishops, each Apostle
in charge of a large territory, the others helping the
Apostles.

6 But by the end of the 1st century we find our present
day arrangement of one Bishop in each Church (mon-

archical episcopate). This simply means that the successors of the Apostles found it wise—due to the rapidly expanding Church, threats of persecution, etc.—to establish themselves permanently in one center, and consecrate other Bishops for the larger centers.

[7] St. Ignatius of Antioch gives us irrefutable testimony to the divine origin of the episcopacy. "Whoever is sent by the Master to run His house, we ought to receive him as we would receive the Master Himself. It is obvious, therefore, that we ought to regard the Bishop as we would the Lord Himself" (Eph. 6, 1). The Council of Trent is merely summing up all of tradition in saying that the episcopacy is divinely established, or as Ignatius puts it, Bishops "are sent by the Master."

[8] Ignatius also affirms in the clearest words the monarchical episcopate at his time—an arrangement that must have been well established already. "For there is one flesh of our Lord, Jesus Christ, and one chalice that brings union in His blood. There is one altar, as there is *one Bishop* with the priests and deacons." (*Philad.* 4, 1; *see also Magn.* 2; 6, 1;13, 1; *Thrall.* 3, 1; 7, 1; *Smyrn.* 8, 1; *Polyc.* 6, 1.)

[9] Even during the lifetime of St. John we can see in the Churches founded by him the change from the Apostolic and missionary stage to the settled and episcopal stage. The "angels" of the Churches of Asia (Apoc. 1-3) are, if not the Bishops themselves, at least the personifications of the Churches, whose unity is concretized in the Bishop.

[10] Two things are certain then: first, the legitimate transmission of Apostolic power to successors; and secondly, the existence of a single Bishop in each Church by the end of the 1st century.

Why did Pope Leo XIII declare Anglican Orders null and void?

[1] Pope Leo XIII declared in his *Apostolicae Curae,* September 13, 1896, that "Ordinations carried out according to the Anglican rite have been and are absolutely null and utterly void." His condemnation rests on theological, not historical, grounds: the inherent defect of *form* in the

Edwardine Ordinal used in the consecration of Parker in 1559; and the defect of *intention* in those using it.

[2] He calls attention to the fact that his predecessors, Popes Julius III and Paul IV, gave identical decisions regarding the invalidity of Anglican Orders, when the case came up during the reign of Mary Tudor, and that for three centuries the Catholic Church had always ordained absolutely all convert Anglican ministers.

[3] The key passage explaining the action of the Holy See is found in Chapter 33 of the *Apostolicae Curae*: "Connected, therefore, with this inward defect of form, is a defect of intention, equally necessary for the existence of a sacrament. Concerning the mind or intention in itself, which is something internal, the Church does not pass judgment; but she is bound to judge of it insofar as it is externally manifested. Now, if a person has seriously and duly used the proper matter and form for performing or administering a sacrament, he is by that very fact presumed to have intended to do what the Church does. This principle is the basis of the doctrine that a sacrament is truly a sacrament even if it is conferred through the ministry of a heretic or unbaptized person provided the Catholic rite is used. But if, on the contrary, the rite is changed with the manifest purpose of introducing another rite which is not accepted by the Church, and of repudiating that which the Church does and that which by Christ's institution belongs to the nature of the sacrament, then it is obvious, not only that the intention necessary for a sacrament is absent, but also that an intention is present which is contrary and opposed to it."

[4] It is well to recall that the 39 Articles recognize only two sacraments, Baptism and the Lord's Supper, and that the sacrificial character of the latter is denied explicitly in the Articles and implicitly in the Ordinal itself. Moreover, when one remembers how for cenuries English Protestants mocked and outlawed the Mass and the Catholic priesthood, it would be an astonishing paradox if, since 1552, the English Protestant Church had itself been not only making sacrificing priests indistinguishable from Catholic priests in respect of their office, but had actually been *meaning* to do so. And yet the whole modern Anglican

contention that the Church of England has Catholic Orders depends on the position that this *was* the meaning and intention of the Ordinal of 1552.

[5] In 1897 the Archbishops of Canterbury and York wrote the letter *Saepius officio,* as the official reply of the Anglican Church. They argue that the Preface to the Ordinal of 1552 provides a clear public statement of objective or formal intention. Thus the official case for the Anglicans rests on the Preface.

[6] On July 5, 1955, the Upper and Lower Houses of the Canterbury and York Convocations fully recognized the *validity* of South Indian Orders; yet the Church of South India has no Preface to its Ordinal which approximates quite closely the Anglican Ordinal. In fact, the South Indian Church does not commit itself "to any particular view or belief concerning Orders of the ministry . . . and in making this provision for episcopal ordination and consecration . . . declares that it is its intention and determination . . . to secure the unification of its ministry, but that this does not involve any judgment upon the validity or regularity of any other form of the ministry" (*The Constitution of the Church of South India,* Christian Literature Society for India, 1952).

[7] By recognizing South Indian Orders as fully equivalent to Anglican Orders, the Anglican episcopate has officially admitted, in effect, that the Preface to the Ordinal does not really matter, that it does not mean what they previously claimed in 1897, and that it might just as well never have been written. Their action confirms what the Popes have been maintaining throughout the controversy. Hugh Williamson writes, "Until July 5, 1955, I, in common wih every other Anglo-Catholic priest, was content to rest on the argument that the Preface to the Ordinal of 1552 . . . could be (because there was no expressed intention otherwise) interpreted in the Catholic sense. It allowed us to hold—so we said—that if St. Peter was a sacrificing priest, the late Bishop Barnes, whatever his private views, was a sacrificing priest. That argument is now impossible, for, on July 5, 1955, the whole Anglican episcopate officially attached to the rite a specific meaning which destroys

every vestige of orthodox intention" (quoted in *Anglican Orders,* Stephenson, 1956).

Why are not women ordained in your Church as well as men? Were not deaconesses ordained in the Primitive Church?

[1a] Because such ordinations are contrary to the will of God, as manifested in both the Old Law and the New. Our Lord selected twelve men as His Apostles, and they in turn selected men as their successors. St. Paul excluded women from all share in liturgical functions, forbidding them to teach (1 Tim. 2, 12) or even to address the assembled faithful (1 Cor. 14, 34, 35).

[2a] The deaconesses of the early Church were specially blessed, but they were never ordained, as St. Epiphanius (315-403) expressly states (*Adv. Haer.,* 79, 3). They maintained order in church among the women, instructed them in the faith as many Sisters do today, and attended them at Baptism. They ceased to exist by the 8th century.

Why do Catholics call their priests "Father," when Christ said: "Call no one on earth your father; for one is your Father, who is in heaven" (Matt. 23, 9)?

[1] Catholics call their priests Father, because the priest is the ordinary minister of Baptism, which gives them the new birth of supernatural grace (John 3, 5).

[2] Christ was not finding fault with the use of the terms "Rabbi" or "Father" in themselves, but was teaching us that God alone, the Father of us all, is the source of all authority, and at the same time rebuking the Pharisees for their indomitable pride (Matt. 23, 2-10). It is absurd to interpret our Lord's words literally, for we have a perfect right to call our fathers and teachers by their just title. The early Christians never interpreted these words literally, for St. Paul calls Timothy his son (Phil. 2, 22; 1 Tim. 1, 2), and he calls himself the spiritual father of those whom he had converted. "For although you have ten thousand tutors in Christ, yet you have not many fathers. For in Christ Jesus, through the Gospel, did I beget you" (1 Cor. 4, 15).

I believe that anyone who is filled with the Apostolic spirit has the right to preach the Gospel. Does not the Bible say that every Christian is a priest?

[1] No one has the right to teach the Gospel authoritatively or carry on its sacred ministry unless he is divinely commissioned as a successor of the Apostles or has been ordained to the priesthood by the sacrament of Holy Orders. "And no man takes the honor to himself; he who takes it is called by God, as Aaron was" (Heb. 5, 4). "How are men to preach," asks St. Paul, "unless they be sent?" (Rom. 10, 15). Notice how Paul begins his letters to the Churches, "Paul, an Apostle, sent not from men nor by man, but by Jesus and God the Father" (Gal. 1, 1). "Paul, an Apostle of Jesus Christ by the order of God our Savior and of Christ Jesus our hope" (1 Tim. 1, 1). "Paul, an Apostle of Jesus Christ, by the will of God" (2 Tim. 1, 1).

[2] In the Catholic Church there is the official priesthood of Orders and the priesthood of the laity. Ordained men and baptized people by the indelible character of the sacraments of Orders and Baptism participate in the priesthood of Christ but in different ways. This is why St. Peter (1 Peter 2, 9) and St. John (Apoc. 1, 6) refer to Christians as priests. The priest of Orders, however, alone has the power to govern, to teach, to administer the sacraments, to change the bread and wine at Mass into the true body and blood of Christ, and to forgive sins. The lay-priest has the right to worship God as Father by reason of Baptism and to offer at Mass the sacrifice of praise and expiation with the ordained priest and in union with him.

[3] Pope Pius XII clearly distinguishes the two kinds of priesthood: "Only to the Apostles, and henceforth to those on whom their successors have imposed hands, is granted the power of the priesthood . . . the visible external priesthood of Jesus Christ is not handed down indiscriminately to all members of the Church in general, but is conferred on designated men, through what might be called the spiritual generations of Holy Orders . . . qualifying them to perform those official acts of religion by which men are sanctified and God is duly glorified. . . . The fact that the faithful participate in the Eucharistic sacrifice does not

mean that they are also endowed with priestly power. . . . We must not forget that the priest acts for the people only because he represents Jesus Christ. . . . Hence, he goes to the altar as the minister of Christ, inferior to Christ but superior to the people." (Pius XII, Encyclical, *Mediator Dei*, 1947.)

Why are Catholic priests forbidden to marry? Is there any Biblical warrant for clerical celibacy as a dogma of the Gospel? Were not the priests of the Primitive Church married? How long has celibacy been enforced in your Church? Are not the Eastern priests allowed to marry?

[1] Clerical celibacy is not a precept of the divine or natural law; neither is it a dogma of the Catholic Church. It is simply an obligatory law of the Western Church, imposed with a view to the dignity and duties of the priesthood.

[2] Voluntary celibacy was commonly practiced by the faithful as early as the 2nd century both in the East and in the West: in Syria, Asia Minor, Greece and Rome. Wherever Christianity spread, thousands of generous souls spontaneously followed not merely the commandments of the Lord, but the three evangelical counsels of poverty, chastity and obedience.

[3] If thousands of these early Christians voluntarily practiced celibacy "for the kingdom of God," in imitation of Christ and His Virgin Mother, was it not imperative that their leaders—Bishops, priests and deacons—should themselves give an example of perfect Christian asceticism?

[4] As a matter of fact, many of the clergy in the first three centuries did observe celibacy, although at that time no law of the Church enforced it. Tertullian, in order to deter a widow from a second marriage, reminds her of the number of those in sacred Orders who had embraced continence, and had chosen God for their spouse.

[5] In the 4th century the celibacy of the clergy is mentioned by Eusebius (*Dem. Evang.*, i., 9; 260-340), St. Cyril of Jerusalem (*Cat.*, xii., 25; 315-386), St. Jerome (*Ad Vig.*, ii.; 340-420), and St. Epiphanius (*Adv. Haer.*, lix., 4; 315-493). They tell us that it was commonly practiced in the

East, in Egypt and in Rome; that it was held in high honor by the Church; that it enabled the clergy to devote themselves wholeheartedly to their sacred ministry.

⁶ The earliest law enforcing celibacy was passed by the Council of Elvira in Spain about the year 300. Bishops, priests and deacons were to be deposed, if they lived with their wives and begot children after their ordination. A similar decree was enacted by a Roman Council under Pope Siricius (384-399), who wrote letters to Spain and Africa insisting upon its observance. A few years later Pope Innocent I (402-417) wrote similar letters to Bishops Victricius of Rouen and Exuperius of Toulouse. By the time of Leo the Great (440-461) the law of clerical celibacy was obligatory throughout the West.

⁷ The Eastern Churches followed a less strict line of development. The Council of Ancyra in Galatia (314) permitted deacons to marry, if before their ordination they declared their intention of not leading a life of celibacy. The Council of Neo-Caesarea in Cappadocia (315) forbade priests to contract a new marriage under penalty of deposition. The Council of Nice (325) refrained from passing any law of celibacy but forbade the clergy to have in their houses any woman who might excite suspicion about their morals; mothers, sisters and other relatives were excepted. The Apostolic Constitutions (400) forbade Bishops, priests and deacons to marry after their ordination but permitted them, if married, to keep their wives. The sixth canon indeed forbade Bishops and priests to put away their wives "under pretext of piety."

⁸ The custom of insisting upon a celibate episcopate in the East became a law under the Emperor Justinian (527-565). The custom also of allowing priests and deacons to live with the wives they had married before ordination became general about the middle of the 7th century, and was solemnly sanctioned by the Council of Trullo in 692.

Is not celibacy impossible, as the history of Confession down the ages amply proves? Is not celibacy against human nature? I think priests ought to marry, because the father develops a finer and kindlier nature, and by his personal experience can teach religion with greater force.

[1] Celibacy is not impossible, and the history of Western Christendom bears witness that it has been kept by an overwhelming majority of priests.

[2] But even in the lawless period that followed the break-up of the Empire of Charlemagne, the Church always held aloft the high standard of clerical celibacy, and denounced most vehemently clerics who were faithless to their vows. When concubinage had become widespread on the continent, God raised up holy and energetic Popes to combat the immorality of unworthy Bishops and the unworthy clergy serving under them. Leo X (1049-1054), St. Gregory VII (1073-1085), Urban II (1088-1099), and Calixtus II (1119-1124), made a determined fight against clerical concubinage, and the reform they inaugurated was permanent. The decree of the First Lateran Council (1123) which declared the marriages of all in Holy Orders invalid was the high water mark of the law of celibacy in the West. Laxity of observance at certain periods will, of course, be admitted by any candid historian, but no one who knows the facts can deny that the law of celibacy has been faithfully observed from the 4th century by the vast majority of the clergy of the West.

[3] Celibacy is not impossible, for the grace of God is given abundantly to all His priests to keep them chaste. Daily Mass, the recitation of the divine Office, the frequent meditation on divine truths, the consolations of the confessional, the intimate contact with the sick and dying—all these are aids to keep every priest faithful to his vow. He is not chosen lightly for his sacred office, but is watched over for years by intelligent and pious seminary professors, who, only after a most careful judgment, declare him worthy of the sacred ministry.

[4] A little common sense is all that is needed to answer the charge that celibacy is impossible. Would you dare say that all unmarried people find it impossible to be chaste? Are your own unmarried children, sisters, widowed cousins, maiden aunts and bachelor uncles all impure? Are all husbands, who for certain reasons are separated for a long period from their wives, bound to commit adultery? To claim that celibacy is impossible is a libel on the purity

of thousands of men and women. Impure men make the statement because they rashly judge others by their own wicked lives. Good people believe this calumny out of inbred prejudice.

⁵ Some declare that celibacy is against nature. They are right, if by nature they mean the corrupt and sensual inclinations of man's lower nature, which, as St. Paul says, is continually fighting "against the law of my mind" (Rom. 7, 23). They are wrong, if they mean that all men must marry to be pure. There are thousands of pure men and women, who remain celibate out of mere natural affection for their own flesh and blood. Frequently there is nothing supernatural in their sacrifice. We have known men who have remained unmarried merely to satisfy their mother's strongly expressed—though utterly selfish—desire. We have known women who have joyfully taken a dead mother's place to provide for a large family of younger brothers and sisters. Can you honestly call their unselfishness and devotion unnatural?

⁶ The scandals of history which some controversialists quote as an indictment against celibacy prove nothing whatever. A married clergy, whether in schismatic Russia, Lutheran Germany, or the United States, has not been free from scandals.

⁷ Practically speaking, the Catholic Church knows from long experience that a celibate clergy can do more effective work for God's people than a married clergy. An unmarried priest is freer and more independent than a minister with a wife and family. Protestants have often admitted this to me, when arguing for a celibate ministry, either in poor country parishes, or in the foreign mission field.

⁸ In view of the statistics of the law courts, it is rather futile to argue that a married man necessarily develops a finer and a kindlier nature than the celibate. The true priest is the most kindly of mortals—beloved by both young and old, rich and poor, cultured and uncultured alike. To say that a priest should marry in order to teach religion with greater efficiency is about as sensible as to order a physician to taste every drug himself, before he can prescribe correctly for his patients.

Did not God command us "to increase and multiply"? If a person does not marry, is he not committing a sin?

[1] God spoke these words to Adam as the Head of the human race, invoking a general blessing upon mankind which was to spread everywhere by the divine institution of marriage (Gen. 1, 23). The obligation does not rest on any particular individual but on the human race as a whole.

[2] Consequently, a person who chooses to remain unmarried does not violate this command of God. There is no danger of the race dying out from celibacy, because the vast majority of men and women marry and have children. In fact, the world today is faced with a serious overpopulation problem.

Does not St. Paul say: "It is better to marry than to burn" (1 Cor. 7, 9)?

[1a] In verses eight and nine St. Paul expressly declares that he is addressing the unmarried. He first advises them to remain unmarried, if they feel called, as he was, to follow Christ in the practice of celibacy. "I say to the unmarried and to widows, it is good for them if they so remain, even as I." But he immediately adds that if they are remaining unmarried in order to lead a sensual life, or if they are continually subject to carnal desires, they had better marry, "for it is better to marry than to burn," that is, with evil desires.

Does not your law of celibacy belittle marriage?

[1b] Not in the slightest degree. Because the Catholic Church exalts celibacy, she by no means belittles marriage. On the contrary, she regards marriage as one of the seven sacraments instituted by Jesus Christ, a sacrament, holy in all its relations. She strongly condemns adultery, divorce, polygamy and race suicide as essentially opposed to the Christian Gospel. Virginity is for the few, while marriage is for the many; both are holy, although in different ways. The outside Churches which have ignored Christ's counsel of virginity, have at the same time degraded marriage by their denial of its sacred character, and by their pagan

views of divorce and family limitation. The Catholic Church has always been loyal to the teaching of Christ.

Was not St. Peter a married man? Does not your Church place an impossible burden on its clergy by its law of celibacy?

[1] Whether St. Peter was married or not is irrelevant, for clerical celibacy is not a divine law but a Church law which dates only from the 4th century. It does not depend on precedent; it is founded on the Church's judgment that it can best fulfill its divine mission on earth with an unmarried clergy than with priests having wives and children. It is simply a practical measure which permits priests to devote their full time exclusively to the sacred ministry of Christ. "He who is unmarried is concerned about the things of the Lord, how he may please God. Whereas he who is married is concerned about the things of the world, how he may please his wife" (1 Cor. 7, 32-33).

[2] Clerical celibacy is not an intolerable or impossible burden for God does not allow the priest to be tempted above that which he is able and God gives him divine grace to be faithful to his vow. History offers proof that celibacy is practical. If it were an impossible burden, the Pope would abrogate the law. After all, he, too, observes it.

Who instituted marriage? How can you prove from the Bible that marriage is a sacrament? Did any of the early Fathers consider it one of the seven sacraments?

[1a] God Himself instituted marriage when He declared, "a man leaves his father and mother, and clings to his wife, and the two become one flesh" (Gen. 2, 24).

[2a] Until the time of Christ marriage was a sacred contract freely entered into by the parties and binding until death. It was Christ who raised marriage to the dignity of a sacrament. He made the contract an external sign of internal grace which would confer on the baptized husband and wife supernatural strength to discharge the duties of their new state in life.

[8] St. Paul teaches that the holy union of husband and wife is like the union of Christ and His Church. "Love your wives just as Christ also loved the Church . . . that He might sanctify her . . . even thus ought husbands also to love their wives as their own bodies . . . the two shall become one flesh. This is a great mystery—I mean in reference to Christ and to the Church" (Eph. 5, 25-32).

[4] St. Augustine asserts that "a sacrament is recommended to believers in wedlock" by St. Paul (*De Nupt. et Concup.* 1, 10). In another passage he admirably sums up the belief of the Primitive Church:

"These are the blessings of matrimony on account of which matrimony itself is a blessing: offspring, conjugal faith, and the sacrament. By conjugal faith it is provided that there should be no carnal intercourse outside the marriage bond with another man or woman; with regard to offspring, that children should be begotten of love, tenderly cared for and educated in a religious atmosphere; finally, in its sacramental aspect, that the marriage bond should not be broken and that a husband or wife, if separated, should not be joined to another even for the sake of offspring. This we regard as the law of marriage by which the fruitfulness of nature is adorned and the evil of incontinence is restrained" (*De Gen. ad litt.,* 9, 7, 12).

[5] In a Christian marriage the matter and form of the sacrament are contained in the consent of the man and woman expressed externally by words and signs. The ministers of the sacrament are the parties themselves. The priest is the Church's official witness before whom and two other witnesses all valid marriages of Catholics must be performed.

Is not marriage a contract? Why then do you keep calling it a sacrament?

[1] Marriage is both a contract and a sacrament. The free consent of the man and woman expressed externally by words and signs constitutes the contract. But Christ made the contract an outward sign of internal grace. He took the marriage contract itself and attached to it what

was not there before, namely, internal grace. In this way, he made marriage a sacrament.

[2] By the contract, the parties mutually give and pledge themselves to each other in an unbreakable union with new rights and duties. By the sacrament, Christ gives the husband and wife rich graces so that they may be true to each other until death and carry out faithfully and lovingly the duties of their union.

[3] When two unbaptized persons marry validly, their marriage is a lifelong binding contract. It is not, however, a sacrament because baptism is a necessary condition for the administration and reception of the sacrament of marriage. When two baptized persons marry validly, their marriage is not only a contract but also a sacrament. We call it a Christian marriage.

Why does the Catholic Church arrogantly claim the sole control over Christian marriage? By what right does the Catholic Church pretend to declare marriages valid or invalid, independently of the State?

[1] There is no arrogance in the Church's claim. While never interfering with the State's right with regard to the civil consequences of marriage, the Catholic Church claims the entire control over Christian marriage because it is a sacrament, and all the seven sacraments have been divinely committed to her care. As the representative of Christ, she has the right to decide whether error, force or fraud has annulled a marriage contract; she has the right to limit the competency of certain parties to marry, namely, those under age, those closely related, those in Holy Orders; she has the right to safeguard her children from making unhappy marriages by her impediments of disparity of worship, of abduction and of crime.

[2a] Some civil jurists argue that the State has absolute power over the contract while the Church's power is limited to the administration of the sacrament. The truth is that in a Christian marriage the contract and the sacrament are inseparable because the contract itself has been raised by Christ to the dignity of a sacrament. "To decree and ordain concerning the sacrament is, by the will of Christ

Himself, so much a part of the power and duty of the Church, that it is plainly absurd to maintain that even the very smallest fraction of such power has been transferred to the civil ruler" (Leo XIII, Encyclical, *On Christian Marriage*).

³ From the very beginning the Church has always exercised her control over marriage independently of the State, thus saving the faithful from the tyranny of civil, anti-Christian legislation. Instead of being actuated by arrogance and a lust for power, she has, despite the strong pressure of powerful rulers, ever kept loyal to the trust given her by her divine Founder.

⁴ The Council of Jerusalem repudiated licentious and free love (Acts 15, 29); St. Paul condemned the incestuous marriage of the Corinthian (I Cor. 5, 5); Ignatius, Justin, Athenagoras, and Tertullian publicly denounced as adulterous certain marriages which had been sanctioned by Imperial law; and the Popes have withstood powerful rulers who sought with threats to obtain the Church's approval of their divorces. The Church deserves no small thanks for defending the sanctity of marriage and for protecting not only religion but civilization from the destructive forces of immorality.

⁵ Many non-Catholics, disgusted with the lax views so prevalent today, will heartily endorse the words of Pope Leo XIII, "All rulers and administrators of the State who are desirous of following the dictates of reason and wisdom, and anxious for the good of their people, ought to make up their minds to keep the holy laws of marriage intact, and make use of the proffered help of the Church for securing the safety of morals and the happiness of families, rather than suspect her of hostile intention." (Encyclical, *On Christian Marriage*)

Why is marriage called "the lay sacrament?"

¹ Because the contracting parties administer the sacrament to each other. The priest is the official representative of the Church and the chief official witness to the sacrament of Matrimony. He alone can carry out its solemn ceremonies, and give at Mass the nuptial blessing, which

every Catholic ought, if possible to receive. But because the contract and the sacrament are identical, and because the matter and form of the sacrament are contained in the contract, the priest cannot be the minister of this sacrament.

What is a morganatic marriage?

[1] A morganatic marriage is a marriage contracted between a man of royal birth and a commoner, with the express understanding that the wife and children will be content with only a certain portion of the paternal inheritance. It is a valid marriage like any other marriage, differing solely in the civil effects which involve a renunciation of the husband's rank, titles, and properties.

If a Catholic receives the sacrament of Matrimony in the state of mortal sin, is it a valid marriage?

[1a] Yes. The marriage is valid but the Catholic commits a sacrilege. The marriage ceremony is not to be repeated because the contract was entered validly. The Catholic must receive absolution in the sacrament of Penance and be restored to the state of grace before he can derive the sacramental benefits of his marriage.

Is polygamy allowed by the Gospel as Luther and the Reformers taught, when they permitted the Landgrave of Hesse to have two wives? Was Calvin right when he condemned the polygamous marriages of the patriarchs as adulterous?

[1b] Both Luther and Calvin were heretical in their teachings on polygamy. While the original condition of marriage was monogamous, as Pope Nicholas (858-867) taught (*Ad Cons. Bulg.*), God granted a dispensation to the patriarchs, and tolerated the practice of polygamy (Deut. 21, 15-17). The Gospel absolutely forbids polygamy, as we learn from the words of Christ and St. Paul (Matt. 19, 4-6; Rom. 7, 2). The Council of Trent condemned the Reformers who held "that it is lawful for Christians to have several wives, and that this is prohibited by no divine law." The early Fathers are unanimous in condemning polygamy.

²ᵇ St. Ambrose (340-397) writes: "It is not lawful for you to take a wife while your wife is alive. To seek another while you have your own, is the crime of adultery" (*De Abraham*, 7).

Luther, Melanchthon and Bucer wrote Landgrave of Hesse that the divine law gave a general sanction to polygamy, and, acting on their advice, he took a second wife, Margaret von Sale. The Reformers urged him to keep this second marriage secret for fear of scandal, and because it clearly violated the Imperial law of the time. Bucer advised Philip, if any difficulty arose with the Emperor, to meet the problem by a downright lie. The Protestant historian, Köstlin, says of their disgraceful action: "Philip's bigamy is the greatest blot on the history of the Reformation, and remains a blot in Luther's life, despite everything that can be alleged in explanation or excuse" (Grisar, *Luther*, iv., 13-70).

Why does the Catholic Church absolutely prohibit divorce? Is it not cruel and heartless to compel a woman to live with a drunken, adulterous husband, who refuses to support her? Would it not be more reasonable to allow exceptions in certain cases, as all modern States do?

¹ Our Lord's teaching that Christian marriage is indissoluble is clear. He said to the Pharisees who questioned Him about the lawfulness of divorce: "Have you not read that the Creator, from the beginning, made them male and female, and said, 'For this cause a man shall leave his father and mother, and cleave to his wife, and the two shall become one flesh'? Therefore now they are no longer two, but one flesh. What therefore God has joined together, let no man put asunder." When the Pharisees asked Him why then did Moses allow divorce, Christ answered that the Mosaic bill of divorce was contrary to the primitive law of indissolubility, and was granted only "by reason of the hardness of your heart" (Matt. 19, 4-8).

² St. Paul compares Christian marriage to the indissoluble union of Christ with His Church (Eph. 5, 24), and expressly states that death alone can dissolve the marriage bond. "For the married woman is bound by the Law

while her husband is alive; but if her husband die, she is set free from the law of the husband. Therefore while her husband is alive, she will be called an adulteress if she be with another man" (Rom. 7, 2-3). "But to those who are married, not I, but the Lord commands that a wife is not to depart from her husband" (1 Cor. 7, 10-11).

[3] The words of Christ and St. Paul are most clear. They stigmatize the remarriage of either husband or wife with a third person as adultery (Matt. 10, 11; Luke 16, 18); they declare that if a just cause for separation exists, the parties must remain single or become reconciled (1 Cor. 7, 10); they assert that death alone can dissolve the marriage bond (Rom. 7, 2; 1 Cor. 7, 39).

[4] Separation from bed and board is permitted for weighty reasons, as the Council of Trent teaches. The Church would consider continual drunkenness or adultery weighty reasons.

[5] The State is no guide in the matter of divorce, as St. John Chrysostom remarked over a thousand years ago. He writes: "Do not cite the civil law made by outsiders, which command that a bill be issued and a divorce granted. For it is not according to these laws that the Lord will judge thee on the Last Day, but according to those which He Himself has given" (*De Lib. Rep.*).

Why does not the Catholic Church allow divorce on the grounds of adultery? Did not Christ Himself allow it (Matt. 5, 32; 19, 9)? I have been told it was permitted in the early Church and that even today some Catholics obtain a civil divorce.

[1] The Catholic Church never allows divorce (separation with the right to marry again) on the grounds of adultery because Christ absolutely forbade divorce with no exceptions (Mark 10, 11-12; Luke 16, 18).

[2] Neither of the passages cited in the question gives permission for divorce. "But I say to you, that everyone who puts away his wife, save on account of immorality, causes her to commit adultery; and he who marries a woman who has been put away commits adultery (Matt. 5, 32). "And I say to you, that whoever puts away his wife, except for

immorality, and marries another commits adultery; and he who marries a woman who has been put away commits adultery" (Matt. 19, 9). In these passages Christ is clearly teaching that a man who puts away his wife for adultery does not *cause* her to commit adultery because she has already committed it and that one has the right to separate from the adulterous partner. If Christ had sanctioned divorce, He would have been plainly contradicting Himself.

[3] The early Fathers unanimously taught that adultery never justifies divorce:

[4] Hermas (160 A.D.) writes: "If a man have an adulterous wife, let him put her away, and let the husband remain by himself. But if he put his wife away and marry another, he also commits adultery (*Mand.*, iv., 4).

[5] St. Justin Martyr (165) writes: "Whoever marries a woman that has been put away by another, commits adultery" (1 *Apol.*, i., 15).

[6] St. Clement of Alexandria (150-216) writes: "The Bible declares it to be adultery, if a person marries another while his or her partner is still alive" (*Strom.*, ii., 23).

[7] St. Jerome (340-420) writes: "As long as the husband is alive, even though he be an adulterer . . . and is deserted by his wife for his crimes, he is still her husband, and she may not take another. . . ." (*Epis.*, 55.)

[8] Catholic husband or wife, with prior permission of the Bishop, may simply separate from the party guilty of adultery. In rare instances, as a last resort, the Bishop may permit the injured party to obtain a civil divorce. In all such cases, however, both parties remain truly married. Neither may marry again nor keep company with the opposite sex.

Does not St. Paul permit divorce among Christians (1 Cor. 7, 12-15)?

[1] In this passage, St. Paul is not discussing Christian marriage, but the natural marriage of the unbaptized. He plainly teaches that a marriage between two unbaptized persons may be dissolved, if husband or wife is converted to the faith, while the unbaptized party refuses to live with the convert in peaceful wedlock. He says: "If any brother has an unbelieving wife and she consents to live with him,

let him not put her away. . . . But if the unbeliever departs let him depart. For a brother or sister is not under bondage in such cases, but God has called us to peace" (1 Cor. 7, 12-15).

[2] This is known in canon law as the Pauline Privilege. Before it can be used, the convert must find out:

1. Whether the unbaptized partner is willing to receive Baptism, for in that case the marriage remains intact.

2. Whether the unbaptized party is willing to live in peaceful wedlock without blaspheming the Creator; that is, without intending to pervert or tempt the Christian to mortal sin. If after due inquiry, technically called interpellation, these questions are answered in the negative, the Pauline Privilege may be used, and a new marriage contracted, which *ipso facto* dissolves the old. The laws governing this matter are found in canons 1120-1127 of the Code (Ayrinhac, *Marriage Legislation in the New Code*, 288-303).

[3] Although natural marriage is in itself indissoluble, it can be dissolved by God, who permitted divorce in the Old Law and the Pauline Privilege in the New.

Did not Pope Alexander VI grant a divorce to Lucrezia Borgia? and another divorce to Louis XII of France? Did not Pope Clement VIII grant a divorce to Henry IV of France? Did not Pope Pius VII grant a divorce to the Emperor Napoleon, and again to his brother Jerome?

[1] No, in not one of these cases was a divorce granted by the Pope.

[2a] The marriage of Lucrezia Borgia to Giovanni Sforza was annulled in 1497 on the plea that it had never been consummated, as we learn from a letter of Cardinal Ascanio Sforza to Ludovico Il Moro, cited by Pastor (*History of the Popes*, v., 520). Pastor calls this annulment "a disgraceful affair" as Sforza's testimony was forced upon him by his relatives, and Lucrezia had in view at the time her second marriage with Alfonso, the natural son of Alfonso II.

[3] Louis XII's marriage with Jeanne of Valois was annulled in 1498 by a judicial commission appointed by the Pope. The King swore that the marriage had never

been consummated; that he had married Jeanne only because forced to do so by her father, Louis XI; that they were related in the fourth degree of consanguinity; that there was a diriment impediment of spiritual relationship, Louis XI having been his godfather (Maulde, *Jeanne de France; see* Pastor, *History of the Popes,* vi., 57).

[4] The marriage of Henry IV and Marguerite de Valois was annulled by a Papal commission, composed of the Cardinal de Joyeuse, the Nuncio at Paris, and the Archbishop of Arles, because they had been married by Cardinal de Bourbon without having received the necessary dispensations from consanguinity and spiritual relationship (Henry II, her father, had been godfather of Henry of Navarre), and because Marguerite had given a forced consent, under pressure of Catherine de Médicis and her son, Charles IX.

[5] Pope Pius VII did not grant a divorce to Jerome Bonaparte. On the contrary, he pronounced his marriage in 1803 with Miss Patterson, a Protestant girl of Baltimore, to be perfectly valid according to the laws of the Catholic Church. In a long letter in answer to the Emperor, the Pope declared that the four reasons he had advanced for nullity were irrelevant. The marriage was annulled March 21, 1805, not by the Pope, but by the French State, in order that Jerome might marry a German Princess.

[6] Pope Pius VII had nothing whatever to do with the annulment of Napoleon's marriage with Josephine de Beauharnais, as it was never referred to him by Josephine, or by the French ecclesiastical courts, which alone took cognizance of the case.

[7] Napoleon was married to Josephine during the French Revolution, March 9, 1796, in a civil ceremony. On the eve of the coronation, December 1, 1804, the Pope declared that he would take no part in the ceremony, unless Josephine's scruples concerning her civil marriage had been set at ease by a religious marriage. The Emperor consented, and Cardinal Fesch married them secretly without witnesses in the Tuileries, after he had obtained all the necessary dispensations from the Pope.

[8] Five years afterwards, in 1809, Napoleon determined to divorce Josephine, because she had not given him an

heir. He called a family meeting at Fontainebleau, induced her to consent to a divorce, and soon after had it declared by the French Senate. His aim was to marry the Czar's sister, and, when that plan failed, to marry Marie Louise of Austria. But Catholic Austria insisted—for form's sake at least—upon the Emperor's religious marriage being annulled. Instead of appealing to the Pope, who is the ordinary judge of the marriage cases of sovereigns, Napoleon preferred to have his wishes carried out by subservient ecclesiastical courts, which he felt confident would do his bidding. Had not the Pope excommunicated him? Had not the Pope refused his request for Jerome's divorce?

He gave the matter in hand to his arch-Chancellor Cambacérès, who submitted the case to the diocesan ecclesiastical court of Paris. He placed before them sworn affidavits from Cardinal Fesch, Berthier, Duroc and Talleyrand, who testified that Napoleon had told them that he had never given consent to the religious marriage, but went through it merely to satisfy the scruples of Josephine.

⁹ The diocesan court declared the marriage null, because of the absence of the parish priest and two witnesses, alleging dishonestly "the difficulty of having recourse to the Pope, to whom it has always belonged in fact to pronounce upon these extraordinary cases." Three days later, the metropolitan court pronounced the marriage null, not only on account of the absence of the parish priest, but also on the plea that the Emperor had not given consent.

¹⁰ Anyone who impartially weighs all the testimony will stigmatize this decree of nullity as unjust and unwarranted by the facts.

¹¹ In the first place Cardinal Fesch, as he says himself, had asked the Pope for all the necessary dispensations. It is a mere quibble to state, as the Church court did, that he obtained them as Grand Almoner, and not as parish priest and witness. For the Pope knew all the facts in the case from Josephine herself, and the saintly Pontiff was not the man to consent to a mock marriage. He certainly possessed the full power to dispense from the law of the Council of Trent. We know the exact words of the Catholic ritual used on the occasion, and we know further that a marriage certificate was given to the Empress by the Cardinal.

[12] Secondly, the diocesan court rejected the plea of non-consent as ridiculous, although the metropolitan court falsely asserted that it had agreed with its findings in the matter. No impartial court would have considered for a moment the affidavits of such servile courtiers as Duroc, Berthier, Talleyrand, and the Emperor's uncle, Cardinal Fesch. Their affidavits are so much alike, that they bear on their face evidence of having been framed by the same hand. They knew the testimony the Emperor required of them, and they also knew that, if it were not given, they would suffer dire punishment at his hands. To what extremes this unscrupulous autocrat could go, they had learned from his cruel imprisonment of Pope Pius VII. They would soon have another example of his anger when defied, in the punishment he was to mete out to the thirteen honest "Black Cardinals," who protested against his invalid marriage with Marie Louise of Austria.

[13] We regret that Josephine never appealed her case to Rome, as Ingeburga appealed to Celestine III against the French church courts, who had unjustly annulled her marriage with Philip Augustus.

Is it not true that while your Church theoretically prohibits divorce, she practically allows it by her system of annulments and dispensations? What difference practically is there between a divorce and an annulment? What about your Church's setting aside the marriage of the Duke of Marlborough and Miss Vanderbilt? and the marriage of Marconi and Miss O'Brien?

[1] It is not true. The Catholic Church never grants a dispensation from the divine or the natural law, but only from a law of her own making. She never, like the modern State, declares a valid marriage null and void, but asserts by her annulment that a so-called marriage never actually took place. Is there no difference between tearing up a genuine fifty-dollar bill (the State divorce) and declaring another fifty-dollar bill a counterfeit (the Church annulment)?

[2] For good canonical reasons the Catholic Church grants a dispensation for a man to marry his first cousin, his sis-

ter-in-law, or one unbaptized; but she never grants a dispensation for a man to marry a second woman while his first wife is living, or to marry his daughter, his sister, or one who is impotent.

³ The Marlborough-Vanderbilt marriage was declared null by the Church, after it had been proved conclusively that it was the result of compulsion. The law is clear: "A marriage is invalid, if entered into because of violence or grave fear, inflicted unjustly and from without" (Can. 1087).

⁴ The Marconi-O'Brien marriage was declared null, because both parties made its dissolubility a strict condition of their consent. The mother of Miss O'Brien refused at first to let her daughter marry, if the bond were to be considered indissoluble, for, she argued, many marriages turn out badly. Mr. Marconi made an express agreement with the mother, the daughter and the entire family, whereby he stated that either party could sue for divorce, if at any time he or she thought fit. This was in evident contradiction to the law of the Catholic Church, which states (Canon 1086, No. 2): "If either party or both by a positive act of the will exclude the marriage itself . . . or any essential property of marriage, the contract is invalid."

When a person has his marriage annulled by the Church does he also get a civil divorce?

¹ If the Church declares a marriage null (no true marriage), the person must obtain a civil divorce before marrying again. Failure to do so could result in a charge of bigamy by the State. The Church ordinarily does not declare a marriage null until the civil divorce has been obtained.

Why is your Church so bitterly opposed to mixed marriages? If you consider them evil, why do you allow exceptions for money? Must a non-Catholic be baptized in order to marry a Catholic? May the parties to a mixed marriage have a Catholic ceremony first, and then be married by a minister to please the parents who are non-Catholics? Why must all *children be brought up Catholics? Why do you not have mixed marriages in church?*

[1] The Catholic Church has prohibited mixed marriages from the earliest times, as we learn from the laws passed by the Councils of Elvira (300), Laodicea (343-389), Hippo (393) and Chalcedon (451).

[2] The chief reason for the prohibition is the danger of loss of faith on the part of the Catholic party and the children born of the marriage. Frequently a bitter unbeliever or a Protestant manifests his hatred of the Church after marriage, and by ridicule, bad example, and moral pressure of various kinds, occasions the apostasy of a weak-minded, ill-instructed or careless partner. The Catholic Church in the United States loses thousands annually by mixed marriages. If the danger of perversion is proximate, such marriages are forbidden even by the divine law.

[3] The influence of an unbelieving non-church-going parent, especially a mother, in the open questioning of all things Catholic, will naturally prove a hindrance to the children's faith and devotion, unless it is strongly counteracted by the Catholic parent, the Catholic school, and the Church. Frequently, too, the Catholic parent dies, and the non-Catholic remarries, bringing up the children in an alien faith.

[4] The different religious beliefs of the parents often cause discord in the home, especially when the non-Catholic is dominated by bitter, prejudiced relatives. Serious trouble too may arise from the divergent moral views on such important matters as divorce, family limitation, and the vital necessity of Catholic education for the children.

[5] The Catholic Church never grants a dispensation unless for just and grave reasons. The non-Catholic party need not be baptized, but he must give guarantees in writing that the danger of the Catholic party's perversion will be removed. Both parties also must promise that all the children will be baptized and brought up as Catholics. The Church has no option in this case, for she is bound by the divine law to do all in her power to prevent her children losing the faith.

[6] Canon law expressly forbids a Catholic to give or renew his matrimonial consent before a non-Catholic minister. Catholics doing so by the very fact incur excommunication, for such action is an open profession of heresy

or schism. We must not sacrifice principle merely to please the unthinking, and if, the first marriage is considered binding until death, why should a sensible person go through a second meaningless ceremony? In countries that insist upon their citizens going through the formality of a civil marriage, a Catholic is bound to obey the law to insure civil privileges. The civil marriage is then to be regarded merely as a legal formality; it has no religious significance whatever.

[7] It is not true that the Church charges for dispensations. The Council of Trent decreed that marriage dispensations, if granted at all, should be granted gratuitously. The same law has been frequently promulgated by the Popes and the Sacred Congregations. All that is permitted is a small donation for chancery expenses, and the poor are expressly dispensed even from this financial burden.

[8] Mixed marriages are permitted to take place in church. There is, however, no Mass nor do the parties receive the nuptial blessing. Only a simple ceremony is allowed.

Can a Catholic marry an active Mason or Communist?

[1a] Yes. The Bishop, however, must give permission and the priest must witness the ceremony. Catholics are forbidden to marry members of societies condemned by the Church because of the danger to their faith and morals. The Bishop can permit such marriages only for grave reasons, and provided there is assurance that the Catholic's faith will not suffer and that the children will be raised as Catholics.

Is the marriage of a Catholic valid if performed by a Protestant minister or a justice of the peace? By what right did the Pope interfere with the marriages of Protestants in his Ne Temere decree of 1908? Why does your Church forbid people to marry their relatives? Why cannot the sponsor marry the baptized person?

[1] The *Ne Temere* decree of Pope Pius X, which became effective on April 19, 1908, and is binding on all Catholics, declares, "Only those marriages are valid which are contracted before the parish priest or the local ordinary, or a

priest delegated by either of them, and at least two witnesses." It is not the pastor or the Bishop of the parties
who has proper jurisdiction but the pastor of the parish or
the Bishop of the diocese in which the marriage takes place.
Consequently, the marriage of a Catholic, if performed by
a Protestant minister or a justice of the peace, is not valid.

2 Pius X did not legislate for Protestant marriages. He
simply laid down the law for Catholics. Two Protestants
who marry before a minister or justice of the peace are
truly married and such a marriage binds until death.

3 The Church forbids a Catholic to marry near relatives
such as a first or second cousin, uncle, aunt, nephew, or
niece. This law prevents unnecessary "inbreeding." Bio-
logically and psychologically, it is preferable for a person
to marry someone who is not a relative. God Himself condemns the union of brothers and sisters as incestuous except when absolutely necessary to continue the human race
as was the case with the children of Adam and Eve. For
serious reasons the Church dispenses from her own law.

4 A sponsor at Baptism becomes the spiritual godfather
or godmother of the baptized person. This spiritual relationship is the basis for the legislation of the Church.

*What is the position of the Catholic Church on birth con-
trol? Do you think the Church will change its laws to meet
the conditions of modern living?*

1 The Catholic Church brands as gravely sinful any
artificial process of contraception. She condemns all techniques devised by human artifice to frustrate the conjugal
act either in its exercise or in its effects. Pope Pius XI
stamped as a sin against nature "every use of marriage,
whatever it may be, in which the exercise of this act is
deprived by man of its power to beget life" (Encyclical
Casti Connubii). Artificial birth control disrupts the order
of creation, violates the law of God, and vitiates the process
of nature. It seeks sexual pleasure for its own sake while
deliberately frustrating the purpose for which God intended the pleasure.

2a Catholic theologians distinguish two ways in which the
sexual act is deliberately frustrated in its natural power

to generate life. The first method is the exercise of the generative act in such a way as to preclude the immediate purpose to which it is ordained by nature, that is, the transfer of semen. For example, extra-vaginal semination or condomistic intercourse vitiates the marriage act in its very operation. The second method nullifies the remote natural effects of the conjugal act by preventing fertilization. Spermicides, expellents, and drugs are used to forestall pregnancy. Both methods, regardless of the specific devices employed, are gravely sinful.

[3] The Church will never change her moral teaching because it is based on the law of God and on human nature. Moral principles are valid at all times and in all societies.

Is it true that Catholic married couples are obliged to have as many children as they possibly can? Is the begetting of children the only purpose of marriage?

[1] The Catholic Church teaches that the procreation and education of children constitute the *primary* end of marriage. This is the principal purpose of marriage, but not its sole purpose. Marriage also perfects husband and wife in mutual love and devotion and protects them against concupiscence. This mutual perfecting and complementing of the married couple are secondary ends and must be subordinated to the primary end.

[2] The Church has never obliged Catholics to have as many children as they possibly can, irrespective of circumstances. She does, however, urge married couples to have a wholesome attitude toward children and to accept the obligations and duties of parenthood. She warns them against that selfishness which simply does not want children because of the pain and inconvenience of bearing them, the trouble of raising them, and the financial difficulties of educating them. Although the Church outlaws contraceptives to prevent conception, she wisely counsels continence when serious medical, eugenic, economic, or social conditions warrant the limiting and spacing of children.

[3a] The Church is most understanding and sympathetic about the real problems of married life in the concrete. Nevertheless, her *ideal* is the large family because it is a

psychological fact that, other things being equal, character formation is better achieved in the large family than in the small family. Family life is happier and more congenial. There is greater opportunity for helpfulness, generosity, social adaptability, and genuine love. Children are a blessing to the family and a boon to the nation. They are born to people not only the earth, but heaven as well.

By its bitter unyielding opposition to birth control measures your Church is callously sentencing millions of starving people to senseless poverty and death in the overpopulated areas of the world. How can Catholics who worship a loving God be so indifferent to such tragic suffering?

[1] Catholics are not indifferent to the terrible suffering that afflicts the overpopulated areas of the world. They are bound to do all they can to improve conditions. They desire the use of all human means to help these people, but in conscience they cannot approve means which violate the natural law and offend the loving God who created all of us.

[2] The "population explosion" is a most difficult, complex, and pressing problem that has no easy solution. Birth control is no panacea, for it disregards the psychological, economic, and social factors involved. An immoral means can never solve the problem.

[3] Although demographers present conflicting data as to the actual facts, we are acutely aware of a population crisis in certain distressed areas. And if these people are to be truly helped there must be a concerted organized effort on the part of all nations to pool their resources and relieve the situation. Increased production and more widespread distribution of food, construction of better housing facilities, use of modern agricultural techniques, more opportunities for employment—these are some of the things that must be done. Individuals, agencies, and governments must ceaselessly apply themselves to the solution of the problem. No one can blind himself to the horrible plight of these afflicted people nor deny the moral obligation of remedying the manifold disease.

[4] The advocates of birth control falsely believe that

theirs is the only solution and that eugenic education will solve the problem. They berate the Catholic Church as hostile to scientific progress and as unsympathetic to the alleviation of poverty and starvation. The Church is deeply concerned and sincerely desires to reduce the sufferings of mankind. She is not opposed to birth control and family planning so long as *morally licit* means are employed. She believes that it is more worthy of man and more in keeping with the dignity of human nature that people be educated to control rationally the exercise of the sex act than that they be taught the application of contraceptives. She is not so naïve, however, as to believe that even *legitimate* birth control can erase poverty and starvation from the earth. That is why she strongly urges not only proper education but that all the newest scientific advances that have been made in psychology, economics, sociology, and engineering be directed in a vast effort toward an effective solution of worldwide overpopulation—an effort she prays God will bless with success.

I understand that the Catholic Church opposes birth control and family planning. Yet some of my neighboring Catholics tell me they practice the "rhythm method." Are these Catholics disobeying the Church?

¹ The Catholic Church opposes *artificial* birth control. She forbids the use of man-made means which frustrate either the natural operation of the sex faculty or the natural processes leading to fertilization.

² The "rhythm method" is not an artificial means of preventing birth. Rather it is man's discovery of human nature's own way of limiting offspring. The couple simply space the marriage act to harmonize with the sterile periods in the wife's cycle. During the fertile periods they exercise rational control of the sex appetites by abstaining from physical intimacy. The natural law does not demand that sexual intercourse must always be inseparably joined to the procreation of children.

³ Although the Catholic *ideal* is fertility, not sterility, there are practical realistic circumstances which make it permissible, advisable, or even obligatory for married

couples to limit the number of children. Catholics may use the "rhythm method" when *both* parties are *willing* and *able* and when there is *good reason* for avoiding childbirth. Selfishness, however, can never be the determining motive.

4 When circumstances warrant and the necessary conditions are fulfilled, Catholic married couples may practice permanent or periodic continence for preventing births and planning families.

How can Catholic women practice the "new method" of painless childbirth? The Bible flatly declares, "in pain shall you bring forth children" (Gen. 3, 16). Science has no right to make painless what God wants painful in punishment for sin.

1 Modern medical authorities contend that childbirth, being a natural normal function, should and can take place without needless pain. They have developed a new method which eliminates the use of drugs or hypnosis. They teach the expectant mother to co-operate with nature.

2 The mother is carefully instructed on the natural processes of childbirth; she is taught to relax mentally and physically while in labor; and she is trained to exercise freely the muscles of the uterus to ease the process. Co-operation with, rather than resistance to, nature is stressed and encouraged. The happy result is the substitution of calm confidence for anxious fear.

3 The method is scientifically sound and morally acceptable. There is no violation of human nature. And no less an authority than Pope Pius XII assures us that this method is compatible with the Book of Genesis, "in punishing Eve, God did not wish to forbid—nor did He forbid —mothers to make use of means which render childbirth easier and less painful. One must not seek subterfuge for the words of Sacred Scripture. They remain true in the sense intended and expressed by the Creator; namely, motherhood will give the mother much suffering to bear. In what precise manner did God conceive this chastisement and how will He carry it out? Sacred Scripture does not say" (*Address to European Obstetricians and Gynecologists,* Jan. 8, 1956).

Why not be honest and admit that the majority of Catholics really favor artificial birth control? Your Church denies them the right to do their own thinking and to express their opinions. This is not freedom but coercion.

[1] Why limit your charge to birth control? No doubt, a poll would reveal that public opinion is largely in favor of remarriage after divorce, adultery, fornication, mercy-killing and similar sins. Counting noses or heads cannot change the goodness or badness of actions. The morality of human conduct is not to be judged by what an individual's happiness may seem to require nor from statistics of what people like or do, but from what, according to the design of the Creator, they ought to do. Morality cannot be determined by majority vote.

[2] The Catholic Church refuses to be influenced by public opinion on matters of faith and morals. She follows Christ and not the majority—this is why she is unpopular. To allow Catholics to decide the morality of birth control by vote would be to deny that the Catholic Church infallibly speaks in the name of Christ who founded it as the "pillar of truth." Catholics are Catholics because they freely believe that neither Christ nor His Church can err. To them voting on moral issues would be a denial of their religious beliefs and principles. When a sincere Catholic practices artificial birth control, he knows he is doing something wrong. He has no need of "a show of hands."

[3] Although the Church demands that Catholics assent to the immorality of birth control, she never forces anyone to be a Catholic or to remain a Catholic. Then too, on matters which do not relate directly to revealed faith and morals, the Church allows her members freedom of thought and expression. There is wide divergence of opinion among Catholics on many controversial issues that are being currently debated in philosophy, theology, psychology, psychiatry, sociology, economics and politics. But all Catholics freely and gladly submit to the Church when she speaks as Christ in teaching the eternal unchanging truth.

May a Catholic woman use new drugs that are advertised as "safe" for birth control practice?

¹ᵃ The search continues for the easiest and safest way to prevent pregnancy. In recent years several drugs such as hesperidin and progesterone have appeared on the market. The latest pill is Enovid which has proved 100% effective in tests conducted over a four-year period. In fact, it has been approved as safe by the Food and Drug Administration (FDA) and can only be purchased on a doctor's prescription. It is reported that some of these drugs *regulate* more definitely the menstrual cycle and cure pathological conditions while others *interfere* with the production of ova.

²ᵃ Catholics must be guided by the moral principle that if these drugs or pills directly produce sterility either temporarily or permanently their use is immoral. A Catholic woman should not use these drugs before she has consulted her confessor.

I cannot understand your opposition to artificial insemination. You want married couples to have children, yet you would deprive the wife of having a child of her own flesh and blood.

¹ The desire of a husband and wife for a child is good and commendable. But such a desire cannot transform an unlawful means into something morally good. The end can never justify the means.

² The Church teaches that artificial insemination of a wife with donor's seed (A.I.D.), or with husband's seed apart from conjugal intercourse (A.I.H.), is a violation of the integrity of marriage. The biological act of generation may not be divorced from the intimacy of the marriage act itself, because marriage does not confer a right to children, but to conjugal intercourse conducive to generation. Artificial insemination bypasses the marriage act and the wife is made pregnant by the injection of semen previously obtained from her husband or from a donor. Both the ejection and injection of semen take place outside sexual intercourse.

³ Donor-insemination has become a filthy business enterprise. Semen is collected into "banks" and sold at high prices. These males function as stallions begetting children

they never know and for whom they accept no responsibility. They gladly accept the possibility of parenthood, but shirk parental obligations. A Chicago judge recently ruled that donor-insemination constitutes grounds for judicial separation under the same conditions as ordinary adultery.

Will you please explain the difference between direct and indirect abortion? Why is the former never allowed?

[1] Abortion is the interruption of a pregnancy before the fetus is viable. The supposition is that the fetus is still alive and that the placenta is still attached to the mother. To expel a dead fetus is not an abortion.

[2] An abortion is called direct when the interruption of pregnancy is intended either as an end (that is, to avoid caring for children, a pregnant woman takes a drug to induce abortion) or as a means to some other end (that is, to protect her good name, a pregnant unmarried woman takes a drug to induce abortion). On the other hand, an abortion is called indirect when the interruption of pregnancy is the undesired but unavoidable effect of a procedure which is immediately intended and directed to accomplish some other good purpose (that is, to stop a hemorrhage which also results in abortion).

[3] Direct abortion is never morally permissible. It is a direct attack on innocent life and the person involved becomes an unjust aggressor. It violates the command of God and the law of nature, "Thou shalt not kill." The life of the mother and child is equally sacred and no one has the power, not even public authority, to destroy it.

[4] Indirect abortion may be permitted for a sufficiently serious reason (that is, when a cancer operation is really necessary to save the life of the mother). There is no intention to kill the mother or the child.

Why do priests anoint Catholics with oil when they are dying? Does not St. James in his Epistle (5, 14-15) refer to the miraculous power of healing in the early Church, and not to a sacrament of Christ?

[1a] Because, as the Council of Trent teaches, "this Sacred Unction of the sick was instituted by Christ the Lord as

a true and proper sacrament of the New Law, insinuated indeed (that is, prefigured) in Mark 6, 13, but recommended and promulgated to the faithful by James the Apostle. 'Is any one among you sick? Let him bring in the presbyters of the Church, and let them pray over him, anointing him with oil in the name of the Lord. And the prayer of faith shall save the sick man, and the Lord will raise him up, and if he be in sins, they shall be forgiven him' (James 5, 14-15). In which words, as the Church has learned from Apostolic tradition, received from hand to hand, he teaches the matter, the form, the proper minister, and the effect of this salutary sacrament."

[2] St. James' words clearly describe all the essential characteristics of a sacrament. The anointing with oil, like the ablution in Baptism, is a visible act, while the prayer of faith said over the sick man is the form. The Apostle ascribes internal grace to the external rite, namely, salvation, upraising or bodily cure, and above all, the forgiveness of sins. The divine institution is implied in the words, "in the name of the Lord," that is, either by Christ's command, or by His power. Only God can make a visible sign bring about the forgiveness of sins.

[3] St. James is not speaking of a miraculous gift of healing bestowed upon disciples who were not priests, but of a permanent divine institution to be administered by a priestly ministry. Freeing one from physical evils is not "saving" him in the Gospel sense, as we learn from other passages in this same Epistle. Restoration of health may follow the spiritual benefits of the anointing, when, as the Council of Trent says, "it is conducive to the soul's salvation," but it is only a secondary effect of the sacrament.

If Extreme Unction is a sacrament, why is it never mentioned until the 12th century?

[1] It is not true that the sacrament of Extreme Unction is never mentioned until the 12th century. It is true that the early Fathers do not speak of it as often as they speak of Baptism, Penance or the Eucharist, but this can readily be understood. In the first place we have lost all but a few fragments of the commentaries on the Epistle of St.

James by Clement of Alexandria, Didymus, St. Augustine and St. Cyril of Alexandria. The earliest commentary we possess dates from the 8th century, St. Bede's (735). Extreme Unction was always looked upon as a complement of Penance, and it was given in the early days, as now, just before the Viaticum. Even in our time we speak of a person receiving the Last Sacraments, without expressly mentioning Extreme Unction, and we have in every language five hundred treatises on the Eucharist compared to one on Extreme Unction. We must also take into account the doctrine of development, which declares it absurd to require the early Church to speak in the language of the Council of Trent. The Church was content to rest upon the text of St. James, which clearly taught the sacramental efficacy of Extreme Unction, and she anointed the dying for centuries before her sacramental theology was systematized by the scholastics.

[2] The first express mention of the term "Extreme Unction" is to be found in the statutes attributed to Sonnatius, Bishop of Rheims (600-631). One of them reads: "Extreme Unction is to be brought to the sufferer who asks for it, and the priest is in person to look after and visit him, thus animating and duly preparing him for future glory."

How is Extreme Unction given, and what are its effects? Is not this sacrament apt to frighten people to death at a critical moment?

[1] The sacrament of Extreme Unction consists in the anointing of the sick man's eyes, ears, nose, mouth, hands and feet with olive oil blessed by the Bishop, the priest saying: "Through this holy unction and His most tender mercy, may the Lord pardon thee whatever faults thou hast committed by sight, hearing, smell, taste, touch and walking." When death is imminent, and there is no time for all the anointings, one on the forehead will suffice, with the words: "By this holy unction may the Lord pardon thee whatever faults thou hast committed." The sacrament is given only to those who are dangerously sick, and is never administered to soldiers going to battle, or to criminals about to be executed.

[2] The three effects of the sacrament are: the strengthening of the soul to bear one's sickness more patiently, and to resist the temptations of the devil; the restoring of the person's health, if that be conducive to his soul's salvation. A Sacrament of the Living, it supposes sanctifying grace in the soul which receives it. But if the sick man is unable to confess his grievous sins, and has only imperfect sorrow for them, it also forgives them.

[3] To defer Extreme Unction until the last moment out of fear that it may frighten our sick relatives is sinful, for this sacrament may and often does help him to recover his health. In any case it is a divine sacrament intended for the dying, and should, if at all possible, be administered before the patient becomes unconscious. We do not hesitate to call in another doctor for consultation, even though our action may frighten the sick man. Why, then, hesitate to call in the divine Physician, when the soul is about to enter into eternity?

SELECTED BIBLIOGRAPHY

ACKEN, BERNARD VAN. *The Holy Eucharist*. Westminster, Md.: Newman Press. 1958.

CLYNES, RAPHAEL. *Liturgy and Christian Life*. Paterson, N. J.: St. Anthony Guild Press. 1960.

DANTEC, FRANCOIS. *Happy Homes*. Westminster, Md.: Newman Press. 1960.

DONLAN, THOMAS C. *Christ and His Sacraments*. Dubuque, Iowa: Priory Press. 1958.

——— *Toward Marriage in Christ*. Dubuque, Iowa: Priory Press. 1957.

ELLARD, GERALD. *Christian Life and Worship*. Milwaukee: Bruce Publishing Co. 1956.

EVANS, ILLTUD. *One in Christ*. Chicago: Fides. 1957.

HEENAN, JOHN C. *Confession*. New York: Sheed & Ward. 1957.

HENRY, ANTONIN M. *Christ in His Sacraments*. Chicago: Fides. 1958.

HOWELL, C. *Of Sacraments and Sacrifice*. Collegeville, Minn.: Liturgical Press. 1952.

KELLY, GEORGE A. *The Catholic Marriage Manual*. New York: Random House. 1958.

LECLERCQ, JACQUES. *Marriage, a Great Sacrament*. New York: Macmillan. 1957.

LEEMING, B. *Principles of Sacramental Theology.* Westminster, Md.: Newman Press.

LECUYER, JOSEPH. *What is a Priest?* New York: Hawthorn Books. 1959.

LITTLEDALE, A. V. (trans.). *Confession.* Chicago: Fides. 1960.

McAULIFFE, C. R. *Sacramental Theology.* St. Louis: B. Herder Book Co. 1958.

MARTIMORT, AIME G. *In Remembrance of Me.* Collegeville, Minn.: Liturgical Press. 1958.

MASURE, EUGENE. *The Sacrifice of the Mystical Body.* Chicago: Regnery. 1957.

NICOLAS, MARIE J. *What is the Eucharist?* New York: Hawthorn Books. 1960.

O'MAHONY, PATRICK J. (ed.). *Catholics and Divorce.* New York: T. Nelson. 1960.

PALMER, P. *Sources of Christian Theology.* Vol. 1 (Sacraments and Worship). Westminster, Md.: Newman Press. 1957.

PIUS XI, POPE. *Casti Connubii* (Encyclical on Marriage). New York: Paulist Press.

PIUS XII, POPE. *Four Great Encyclicals.* New York: (Deus Books) Paulist Press. 1961.

RISK, JAMES E. *Marriage-Contract and Sacrament.* Chicago: Callaghan & Company. 1957.

ROGUET, A. M. *Christ Acts Through the Sacraments.* Collegeville, Minn.: Liturgical Press.

SATTLER, HENRY V. *Together in Christ.* Washington: National Catholic Welfare Conference, Family Life Bureau. 1960.

SHEERIN, JOHN B. *Sacrament of Freedom.* Milwaukee: Bruce Publishing Co. 1961.

STEPHENSON, ANTHONY A. *Anglican Orders.* Westminster, Md.: Newman Press. 1956.

TAILLE, MAURICE DE LA. *Mystery of Faith* (2 Vols.). New York: Sheed & Ward. 1950.

THOMAS, JOHN L. *The Catholic Viewpoint on Marriage and the Family.* Garden City, N. Y.: Hanover House. 1958.

—— *Marriage and Rhythm.* Westminster, Md.: Newman Press. 1957.

VAN ZELLER, HUBERT. *Approach to Penance.* New York: Sheed & Ward. 1958.

VEUILLOT, PIERRE (ed.). *The Catholic Priesthood according to the Teaching of the Church.* Westminster, Md.: Newman Press, 1958.

PART IX
The Commandments of God

Why do Christians pray to God to inform Him of what He already knows? Does He not appreciate their needs without their informing Him in wordy petitions?

¹ We do not pray to inform God of our needs, or to instruct Him what to do, for the all-knowing God knows the inmost secret of every heart and all its needs. We pray to God because we desire to acknowledge His power and goodness, because we feel our utter dependence upon Him, and because He Himself taught us to pray by word and by example.

² Jesus Christ taught us to hallow God's name, and to do God's will perfectly on earth as it is done in heaven; He taught us to pray for temporal and spiritual favors, such as the grace to overcome temptation, the forgiveness of our sins, and the grace of final perseverance (Matt. 6, 9-13; Luke 11, 1-4). He promised to receive our prayer when it came from a loving heart (Matt. 5, 23-24), saying to us: "Ask, and it shall be given you; seek, and you shall find; knock, and it shall be opened to you" (Matt. 7, 7). For "if you, evil as you are, know how to give good gifts to your children, how much more will your heavenly Father give the Good Spirit to those who ask Him?" (Luke 11, 13.) And again: "Whatever you ask in My name, that I will do. . . . If you ask Me anything in My name, I will do it" (John 14, 13. 14).

³ He began His public ministry with a forty days' prayer (Mark 1, 35); He spent whole nights in prayer (Luke 6, 12); He prayed when He performed miracles (Matt. 14, 19;

John 11, 42); He prayed in His agony in the garden (Matt. 26, 39-41), and on the cross for Himself and for His executioners (Matt. 27, 46). We not only ask God for favors, as He Himself taught us to do, but we adore Him, praise Him, thank Him for His favors, and ask Him pardon for our sins.

Why are not all our prayers answered, as the Lord promised (John 14, 13)?

¹ If we pray humbly (Ps. 1, 19; Luke 11, 5-8) and perseveringly (Matt. 14, 22-28; Luke 11, 5-13; 18, 1-7) for spiritual blessings that will ensure our soul's salvation—the grace to resist temptation, the pardon of sin, and the grace of final perseverance—God will answer us.

² If we ask spiritual blessings for others, God will pour forth His grace in abundant measure, but the sinner we pray for may resist God's grace even to the end. God will never force the human will, for He demands a free, not a forced service.

³ If we pray for temporal blessings, such as health, success, and fortune, God may grant our prayer by denying us what we ask. We must always pray in accordance to the divine plan. Our Lord gave us the example in the Garden of Gethsemani, when He prayed: "Father, if it is possible, let this cup pass away from Me; yet, not as I will, but as Thou willest" (Matt. 26, 39).

⁴ If sickness were to bring us close to God, and health make us forgetful of Him; if failure were to humble us, and success puff us up with pride and arrogance; if poverty were to make us followers of the poor Christ (2 Cor. 8, 9), and riches cause us to abandon the faith, ought not God in His mercy and love refuse us what we in our ignorance crave? A loving mother will not give her child her husband's razor to play with, no matter how hard he cries for it. A good physician will not grant a change of diet to his patient, if he knows he is thereby causing his death.

Why do Catholics adore images and pray to them? Did not God prohibit the carving of idols (Ex. 20, 5)? Did not Catholics suppress the second commandment because it forbade the making of images? Why do you divide the commandments in a different manner?

[1] Catholics do not adore images or pray to them. The Council of Trent says: "The images of Christ and the Virgin Mother of God, and of the other saints, are to be had and to be kept especially in churches, and due honor and veneration are to be given them; not that any divinity or virtue is believed to be in them, on account of which they are to be worshipped, or that anything is to be asked of them, or that trust is to be reposed in images, as was done of old by the Gentiles, who placed their hope in idols; but because the honor which is shown them is referred to the prototypes which these images represent; in such a way that by the images which we kiss, and before which we uncover the head, and prostrate ourselves, we adore Christ, and we venerate the saints whose likeness they bear."

[2] The early Christians adorned their catacombs with many frescoes of Christ, the Blessed Virgin and the saints, which recalled incidents in the Sacred Scriptures. The most common paintings were Moses striking the rock, Noe in the ark, Daniel in the lion's den, the Nativity, the coming of the Wise Men, the marriage feast of Cana, the raising of Lazarus, and Christ the Good Shepherd. Statues were rare only because they were costly and difficult to make. When the first Christians came up from the catacombs, they began to decorate their churches with costly mosaics, carvings, paintings and statues. No one can honestly accuse these early Christians of idolatry, for they died in protest against it, and wrote treatise after treatise condemning it.

[3] The Church has never suppressed the second commandment. She has abridged it occasionally in her children's catechisms following thereby the good example set her in the Scriptures (4 Kings 17, 35). The Old Testament tells us that there are ten commandments (Exod. 20, 1-17; Deut. 5, 6-21), but gives no indication whatever how they are to be divided. The more logical Catholic division, following St. Augustine (*Quest. in Hept.*, 2, 71), has the first commandment prohibiting false worship and idolatry, and the ninth and tenth the separate sins of lust and covetousness. The Protestant division makes one command-

ment of the two distinct sinful desires of adultery and theft, while it makes two of the one prohibition of false worship. This division is based on Philo, Josephus and Origen.

Is it not superstitious to venerate the relics of the saints? What efficacy can there be in the bones of a dead man or woman, or in the garments belonging to them?

[1] The Council of Trent teaches "that the holy bodies of holy martyrs and others now living with Christ—which bodies were the living members of Christ and the temples of the Holy Spirit—and which are by Him to be raised to eternal life and to be glorified, are to be venerated by the faithful; for through these bodies many benefits are bestowed by God on men, so that they who affirm that veneration and honor are not due to the relics of the saints, or that these and other sacred monuments are uselessly honored by the faithful, and that the places dedicated to the memory of the saints are in vain visited with the view of obtaining their aid, are wholly to be condemned."

[2] The Catholic Church does not teach that there is any magical virtue or any curative efficacy in the relic itself. The Church merely says, following the Scriptures that they are often the occasion of God's miracles. In the Old Law we read of the veneration of the Jews for the bones of Joseph (Exod. 13, 19; Jos. 24, 32), and of the prophet Eliseus which raised a dead man to life (4 Kings 13, 21); in the New, of the woman cured by touching the hem of our Lord's garment (Matt. 9, 20-21), of the sick healed by the shadow of St. Peter (Acts 5, 15-16), and of the handkerchiefs and aprons that had touched the body of St. Paul (Acts 19, 12).

[3] The veneration of the relics of the saints can be traced as far back as the 2nd century. After St. Polycarp had been burned at the stake, his disciples "took up his bones, which were more valuable than precious stones and finer than refined gold, and laid them in a suitable place, where the Lord allows us to assemble in gladness and joy to celebrate the birthday of his martyrdom" (*Mart. Poly.*). Many of the early Fathers, while strongly repudiating the charge of idolatry or "cinder-worshipping," extol highly the cultus

of relics, among them St. Augustine, St. Ambrose, St. Jerome, St. Gregory of Nyssa, St. Gregory of Nazianzus, and St. John Chrysostom. St. Jerome (340-420) writes: "We do not worship, we do not adore, we do not bow down before the creature rather than to the Creator, but we venerate the relics of the martyrs in order the better to adore Him whose martyrs they are."

⁴ The same spirit that prompts a mother to treasure carefully a lock of her dead baby's hair; the same spirit that prompts Americans to treasure the pen of the signers of the Declaration of Independence, the Liberty Bell, or the sword of Washington, has ever prompted the Christian people to venerate whatever belonged to the saints of God.

The Catholic Church has never declared that any particular relic is authentic, but she takes the greatest pains to see that no public honor is paid to any relic, unless she is reasonably convinced of its genuine character. It matters little if the relic be not authentic, for the reverence we pay is to the saint. Since World War I the nations of the world have erected monuments to the Unknown Soldier, in order to foster the spirit of patriotism, The particular soldier thus honored may have been a coward in war time, or an unworthy scoundrel. The honors we pay are given to the soldiers who died for their country.

Is not the wearing of medals a superstitious practice, akin to the pagan custom of wearing amulets or charms to ward off disease and danger?

¹ No, there is no superstition in the wearing of medals. The pagans attributed to the amulets they wore, a magical power to ward off disease and death. Catholics wear medals to honor God and His saints, to bring to their minds some doctrine of the faith, or to attest their membership in some pious confraternity. They do not attribute any virtue to the medal itself, but they wear it to foster devotion. Would you call a man superstitious, because he wore a locket containing a portrait of his wife?

² Modern medals of devotion became popular in the 15th century, when the papal Jubilee medals were spread all over Europe; a century later the Popes gave them special blessings, and enriched them with many indulgences.

If it is superstitious to believe in dreams, why does God make use of dreams to make known His will to men, both in the Old Testament and the New?

¹ A rightly instructed conscience should guide our daily conduct. The Scriptures frequently warn us "not to observe dreams," and teach that "dreams have deceived many and they have failed who put their trust in them" (Lev. 19, 26; Deut. 18, 10; Sirach 34, 7). Ordinarily, dreams have a natural cause; our imagination forms "pictures" from the scattered events of our life. They are usually illogical and grotesque. Psychologists tell us that the contents depend on the state of our health, our nerves, our fears, and sleeping-postures. Interpretation of dreams (we really have many more than we remember) is an important technique in the treatment of mental illness. Dreams sometimes offer clues to the discovery of subconscious factors that are abnormally influencing the daily behavior of mentally and emotionally disturbed people.

² On the other hand, God has communicated with people by means of dreams. Abimelech, Jacob, Solomon, Nabuchodonosor, Daniel, St. Joseph, and St. Paul experienced prophetic dreams (Gen. 28, 12; 31, 10; 3 Kings 3, 5-15; Dan. 2, 19; 7, 1; Matt. 1, 20; 2, 13; Acts 23, 11; 27, 23). We should not forget, however, that these persons were also experiencing natural dreams to which they paid no attention.

³ When, instead of an upset nervous stomach, God is the cause of dreams, He always takes care to make their supernatural character evident.

Why does the Catholic Church condemn astrology? Is it sinful to have one's horoscope taken?

¹ᵃ Astrology is a superstitious practice which encourages fatalism. It belittles human freedom and divine Providence. The stars exercise no determining influence on human lives or human affairs. The casting of a horoscope or diagram of the heavenly bodies at the birth of a child in order to foretell its future is downright folly. St. Augustine attacked it strongly in his *City of God* (Bk. 8; Chap. 19) and St. Thomas writes, "If anyone applies the observa-

tion of the stars in order to know with certitude future human actions, his conduct is based on a false and vain opinion" (*Summa*, IIa. IIæ., q. 45, a. 5).

[2a] Astronomy is not to be confused with astrology. It is a valid science of the heavenly bodies and many Catholics are outstanding astronomers.

Did not Christ (Matt 5, 33-37) and St. James forbid the taking of oaths in any form?

[1] No, the literal interpretation of Christ's words held by the medieval Cathari and the modern Quakers is contrary to the Church's divine tradition and practice from the beginning. In counseling His followers "not to swear at all," Christ desired them to be so truthful and sincere that all oaths confirming their words would be unnecessary. Our Lord Himself replied to the solemn adjuration of the High Priest at His trial (Matt. 26, 63). St. Paul often called God to witness what he said (Rom. 1, 9), and declared that an oath for confirmation ends all controversy (Heb. 6, 16).

[2] St. Jerome, citing Jeremias 4, 2, asserts that three conditions are required for a lawful oath; it must be truthful, stating things as they are, and honestly intending to keep the promise made; it must relate to a matter of some importance for the welfare of either soul or body, whether it be public or private; it must not go counter to moral law.

[3] Perjury of its very nature is always a grievous sin, for it is contrary to divine precept (Lev. 19, 12), and implies contempt of God (St. Thomas, *Summa*, IIa. IIae., q. 98, a. 3).

Do not the Knights of Columbus take an oath in their Fourth Degree, in which they swear to extirpate all heretics and heresies, declaring at the same time that the Pope has the power to depose all heretical rulers? Is not this oath to be found in the Congressional Record?

[1b] No, this oath is a malicious invention, the falsity of which has been proved in many an open court, here and in Canada. A history of the various prosecutions for criminal libel in printing and publishing this alleged oath may be found in a pamphlet, published by the Supreme Board of

Directors of the Knights of Columbus at New Haven, Connecticut. It is entitled *Knights of Columbus vs. Criminal Libel and Malicious Bigotry.*

[2] In the *Congressional Record* of February 15, 1913 (3215 *et seq.*) appears a Report of the Committee on Elections No. 1, on the contested election case of Eugene C. Bonniwell against Thomas C. Butler. The contestant had alleged that the circulation of this bogus oath against him was libelous. After reciting this bogus oath, the committee says: "This committee cannot condemn too strongly the publication of the false and libelous article referred to in the paper of Mr. Bonniwell, and which was the spurious Knights of Columbus Oath, a copy of which is appended to the paper."

[3] The real pledge—not oath—taken by the Knights of Columbus in their Fourth Degree runs as follows: "I swear to support the Constitution of the United States. I pledge myself, as a Catholic citizen and Knight of Columbus, to enlighten myself fully upon my duties as a citizen, and to conscientiously perform such duties entirely in the interest of my country, regardless of all personal consequences. I pledge myself to do all in my power to preserve the purity and integrity of the ballot, and to promote reverence and respect for law and order. I promise to practise my religion openly and consistently, but without ostentation, and so to conduct myself in public affairs and in the exercise of public virtue, as to reflect nothing but credit upon our Holy Church, to the end that she may flourish, and our country prosper to the greater honor and glory of God."

Is suicide ever lawful; namely, to save one's honor? Is it not at times a courageous act as in the case of the martyrs?

[1] Suicide, which is the deliberate causing of one's own death either directly—by taking poison—or indirectly—by exposing oneself to certain death without just cause is never lawful. It violates the natural law of self-preservation. It is contrary to the divine law, "You shall not kill." (Ex. 20, 13). As Wisdom 16, 13 teaches, God alone "has power of life and death," and He alone has the authority to determine the life-span of an individual. The person

who freely commits suicide is stigmatized as a coward because he shirks the duties he owes to God and society. The brave man is ever ready to suffer the trials and humiliations of this life, after the example of Christ, in order to win the crown of justice reserved for those who fight the good fight and keep the faith (see 2 Cor. 4, 17), He abhors suicide.

2 It is true that some of the martyrs did not wait for their executioners to put them to death. They voluntarily leaped into the fire and died in the flames, like St. Apollonia of Alexandria in 249. In such cases, they were obeying God who clearly commanded them to perform this extraordinary act.

3 Before denying Christian burial the Church carefully examines the circumstances of a suicide. She does not penalize the insane but only "those who deliberately kill themselves" (Canon Law) "from despair or in wrath." (Decree of the Holy Office, May 16, 1866). And even in this latter case, the Church does not sentence them to hell or pass judgment on their eternal lot. That belongs to God alone.

Why does the Church condemn mercy-killing? Why should not a person who suffers from a painful incurable disease be allowed to relieve his suffering?

1 It is God alone who gives and takes away life. Euthanasia, popularly known as mercy-killing, violates the natural law. God has given each person an *inviolable* right to life and in revealing the 5th commandment God explicitly forbids a person to take his own life (suicide) or the life of another (homicide). Euthanasia is always a grave sin regardless of the motives.

2a The Church is neither harsh nor heartless in this matter. She does not oppose the relief of suffering nor does she insist on the unnecessary prolongation of life. Although she can never approve suicide or murder, she does permit doctors, when they prudently judge a case hopeless, to abstain from the use of *extraordinary* measures to prolong life. She leaves the application of medical therapy to the professional judgment of the attending physician. It is one thing to inflict death directly; it is quite another thing to allow a natural death. The former is immoral; the latter is permissible when the patient is beyond cure. We cannot treat people in the same way we do animals. People are not simply animals. Euthanasia also deprives the medical profession of the stimulus of research. There would be little incentive for new discoveries in the treatment of disease, for doctors are strongly moved to greater efforts by the sight of suffering and pain in their patients. Mercy-killing is an easy solution but it is all wrong. The Oath of Hippocrates states, "I will give no deadly medicine to anyone if asked, nor suggest any such counsel." We should also remember that our Blessed Lord endured intense pain which He offered to the heavenly Father for the redemption of man. Sick people in the throes of death should offer their pain to God that He may have mercy on their souls and that they may obtain eternal salvation.

Why is the Catholic Church opposed to the modern science of eugenics? Does it object to the betterment of the race? Ought not the State sterilize the physically unfit, the mentally defective and the criminal? No person has a right to beget children who will be a burden upon the community.

[1] The Church is not opposed to the science of eugenics but she strongly condemns those modern eugenicists who equate "betterment" with "physical betterment" and who have a fixation on sterilization as the "simple easy way" to improve the race. To better people physically has always been one of the objectives for which the Church incessantly labors. She is, however, also gravely concerned about their intellectual, moral, and spiritual development. And she vigorously proclaims that sterilization is an immoral means which, by debasing human dignity and denying individual God-given rights, would harm rather than benefit the human race.

[2] Sterilization is any operation designed to prevent a man or woman from producing children. It is a serious mutilation depriving a person of a natural organic function, namely the power to procreate. It is effected through surgery or radium.

[8] Catholic teaching distinguishes three types:

1. Therapeutic sterilization which is performed to preserve the total health of the body is morally permissible, for example, the removal of diseased genital organs.

2. Punitive sterilization is a punishment imposed by the government on certain criminals convicted of sexual crimes or other grave offenses. It seems unjust for several reasons: Criminal tendencies are not inheritable. Moreover, sterilization is ineffective as a penalty because it does not remove sexual desire. The sterilized criminal can satisfy his sex drives without fear of producing offspring. He can enjoy all the pleasure without incurring parental responsibility. This certainty will encourage him in his perversion.

3. Eugenic sterilization which deprives the physically unfit and the mentally defective of fruitful intercourse.

[4] Whether it is voluntary or imposed by the State, eugenic sterilization is immoral and unjust. Pope Pius XI warns private individuals that they are not free "to render themselves unfit for their natural functions, except when no other provision can be made for the good of the whole body" (as in therapeutic sterilization), and he cautions public officials that they "can never directly harm, or tamper with the integrity of the body for reasons of eugenics." (Encyclical, *On Christian Marriage,* 1930, Paulist Press, New York.) By enforcing compulsory eugenic sterilization, the government stands accused as an unjust aggressor violating the natural rights of the innocent.

[5] Advocates of eugenic sterilization base their position on the popular but unscientific assumption that physical and mental feebleness is ordinarily passed on by heredity. They forget that the State has no direct power over the life, liberty, and physical integrity of its innocent subjects. And they obstinately blind themselves to the fact that there are other means to prevent those who should not have children from propagating.

Is not capital punishment, murder? Why punish crimes by committing another crime?

[1] The Catholic Church has always taught that the State has the right to inflict death for serious crimes which

threaten its existence as a political society. Just as an individual has the right to defend himself against an unjust aggressor, so the State has the right to defend itself against external and internal enemies. Although the Church declares that capital punishment is morally just, she does not teach that the State has the duty to impose the death penalty. As an individual is not bound to slay his aggressor to preserve his own life neither is the State bound to slay the criminal to maintain public order. It may, by legislation, abstain from exercising its right of capital punishment and decree other forms of punishment for the preservation of the common good.

[2] Although there are some people who deny that the State has the authority from God through the people to inflict the death penalty for specified crimes, the debate over capital punishment centers on the need to exercise this God-given right. There are many people, including Catholics, who argue that the State can achieve its ends without capital punishment. They cite cases in which innocent men have been hanged and electrocuted. They present facts to show that the crime situation has improved where the death sentence has been abolished. On the other hand, those who favor capital punishment insist that it is a more effective deterrent to crime than life imprisonment. They believe the criminal fears death more because the "lifer" can always look forward hopefully to a possible escape or a possible pardon.

[3] Today the trend is toward abolition of the death sentence. Thirty-five countries have abandoned it. Nine states have outlawed it—Alaska, Delaware, Hawaii, Maine, Michigan, Minnesota, North Dakota, Rhode Island, and Wisconsin. Similar legislation is pending in several states. A recent poll showed a majority of persons in the United States opposed capital punishment.

[4] Does the State possess the *right* of capital punishment? The Catholic Church answers in the affirmative. "It is reserved to the public power to deprive the condemned person of the enjoyment of life in expiation of his crime when, by his crime he has already deprived himself of his *right* to live" (Pius XII, *Address at First International Congress on the Histopathology of the Nervous System,*

September 14, 1952). Should the *infliction* of capital punishment be abolished? The Church leaves it to the people through their legislative representatives to determine what crimes, if any, are to be punished by death.

Does not the Bible declare that all war is immoral? Did not Christ rebuke Peter for using the sword? Did not the early Fathers denounce the military profession?

[1] The Bible never declares that war is intrinsically evil. On the contrary, God approves war (Num. 21, 3); commands war (Judges 4, 6-7); and even works miracles to ensure victory for the chosen people (Judges 4, 15). God also sometimes sends war as a chastisement for men's sins (Deut. 28, 32-34).

[2] Christ repeatedly urges us to love God and our neighbor. If the world were faithful to this teaching, there would be no need for war. But pride and greed often set at nought the principles of justice and charity. Our Lord rebuked Peter for an impetuous act of violence which could easily have turned the Garden of Prayer into a slaughterhouse of blood. His action was folly, for Christ could have summoned twelve legions of angels to protect him (Matt. 26, 51-53).

[3] The early Fathers did not denounce the military profession for they knew that John the Baptist had given advice to the soldiers of his day (Luke 3, 14) and that Christ had praised the faith of the Centurion (Matt. 8, 10). Neither John nor Christ asked the soldiers to abandon their profession as immoral. However, the Fathers did object to Christians serving in pagan armies because of the danger of apostasy. At any moment the Christian soldier might be commanded to perform an act of public idolatry for the sake of the Emperor. Today members of our Armed Forces are not subject to such dangers for Catholic chaplains are assigned to care for their spiritual needs.

[4] While recognizing that war is a horrible evil that must be avoided, if at all possible, the Catholic Church has always taught that a *just* war is licit and moral. She condemns the pacificism of those who claim that all wars are incompatible with Christianity and the bellicism of those

who declare that aggressive wars are a nation's right and duty.

[5] Today we distinguish three kinds of war: aggressive, preventative, and defensive. Pope Pius XII stigmatized "war of aggression" as "a sin, an offense, and an outrage against the majesty of God" (*Christmas Message,* 1948). He pointed out that in the present historical moment in which we live, recourse to force cannot be a moral means for the redress of violated rights, because of the immeasurably increased violence that results from such wars. Neither does he allow a purely preventative war. A nation cannot resort to force simply because it suspects or fears an enemy attack. There must be an actual attack or clear factual evidence of its imminence.

[6] On the other hand, a defensive war to repress injustice and to preserve national security and freedom is morally admissible both in principle and in fact. The right to self-defense is man's by nature. To deny him this right would violate human nature itself. "Defense against an unjust aggression is without doubt fully justified" (Pius XII).

[7] Nevertheless, certain conditions must be fulfilled before a nation may licitly engage in defensive war.

1. There must be moral certitude that the nation is unjustly attacked and menaced in its vital rights. The war must be "imposed by an obvious and extremely grave injustice" (Pius XII, *Allocution to the World Congress of Women's Organizations,* 1952).

2. Every peaceful method of settlement must have been sincerely tried and proved inadequate. War is the last extreme solution because of the depths of manifold agony into which it may plunge humanity as a whole.

3. There must be a proportion between the damages inflicted by the grave injustice and the damages inflicted by war. This proportion must be evaluated in tough-minded fashion on the moral level.

4. There must be solid probability of success.

5. The use of force must be limited and controlled. When force "entirely escapes from the control of man, its use ought to be rejected as immoral. Here it is no longer a question of defense against injustice and of the necessary safeguard of legitimate possessions, but of the annihilation,

pure and simple, of all human life within its radius of action. This is not permitted on any account" (Pius XII, *Allocution to the World Medical Congress,* 1954).

[8] The morality of a modern nuclear defensive war is a complex problem. Some Catholic theologians assert that the use of atom and hydrogen bombs cannot be morally justified. They argue that the destruction of human life cannot be limited to the combatants and that the devastation would necessarily extend far beyond the military objectives. Furthermore, the ravages and ruins wrought by nuclear war would far outweigh the human suffering caused by violated rights. These moralists contend that it would be better to accept the loss of freedom and retain the hope of its restoration than to engage in a war of annihilation which would destroy not only freedom and hope but human life itself. Other Catholic theologians, however, claim that a nation can have recourse to nuclear warfare as a defensive measure. They argue that there are greater evils than the physical destruction of human life. They declare that there are human goods, like freedom, for which immense sacrifices, even that of death, should be borne in their defense. They would rather choose to have a shambles of civilization which could be reconstructed in justice and freedom than to accept by surrender an inhuman civilization of servitude.

[9] No sane person wants any kind of war, much less a nuclear war. All of us shudder at the tinderbox character of our world in which a spark may set off a conflagration. Individuals should constantly pray that the spirit of the Prince of Peace will inspire all hearts, and statesmen should eagerly explore every avenue of conciliation, in order that all nations may exist and work together in friendship to the end that peace may always reign over the earth. We should remember that war has never solved any human problem in the long history of man. In the words of an American General, "War is hell."

What is your opinion of present-day professional boxing? I think this brutal sport which caters to the lower human instincts should be outlawed. It has become a dirty business run by hoodlums.

[1] Most moral theologians and medical authorities agree with you. And the evidence uncovered by recent investigations conducted by law enforcement agencies proves that it is a sordid business.

[2] Although there is no official teaching of the Catholic Church, modern theologians generally teach that professional boxing as it exists today is immoral and should be condemned. They argue that by its very nature boxing tends to result in serious and unjustifiable injury to the participants and that each contestant intends to "floor the bum," if at all possible. There is no denying the fact that winning by a knock-out (K.O.) rather than by a technical knock-out (T.K.O.) or by points is the intended goal of the prizefighter. And the fans become emotionally bloodthirsty shouting encouragement to the contestants to slug it out until one drops to the canvas unable to rise before the count of ten. Such spectator behavior is a deordination of reason.

[3] Medical evidence shows that blows to the body and particularly to the head inflict damage that causes irreparable harm to the fighter. These injuries are sometimes crippling for life or even fatal. In New York City alone, from 1918 to 1950, there were 21 fatalities in the ring. And when statistics reveal that 60% of boxers develop neurologic and psychic changes in the brief span of five years, we must brand this sport as an unreasonable brutal form of recreation which offends the dignity and decency of man.

Why doesn't your Church forbid Catholics to drink intoxicating beverages? Is not alcoholism a sin? Why then call it a disease?

[1] The Bible does not forbid drinking wine or liquor. Jesus Christ never forbade it. In fact, He changed water into wine and the guests were delighted with it at the marriage feast of Cana (John 2, 1-10). There is nothing morally wrong with moderate and controlled drinking. For many people, however, drinking has its dangers as well as its pleasures. It can easily become excessive and it may often lead to sin. Irresponsible drinking has brought sorrow and tragedy to individuals and families, has broken

up happy homes, has blighted promising careers and has destroyed merited success.

[2] Psychologists distinguish three classifications:

1. There is the temperate drinker who controls his appetite for drink. He keeps his drinking within reason. It has no bad effect on his health or his behavior. He does not allow it to interfere with the fulfillment of duty or the performance of work.

2. There is the gluttonous drinker. He always takes too much, though he may not drink often. He knows he drinks to excess, yet he deliberately drinks. It produces a hang-over, makes him moody, cry, shout, or laugh to an unreasonable degree, and weakens his resistance to temptation. This person should not drink.

3. There is the compulsive drinker. He is unable to resist the urge to drink and to keep on drinking. This person is sick physically, spiritually and psychologically. He needs help from God, from doctors and from friends, if he is to be cured. He is an alcoholic.

[3] Despite comprehensive research on alcoholism we still do not know its specific origin or exact nature. Evidence indicates that it is a disease to which any person who drinks is susceptible. It seems to comprise both physiological and psychological elements. It may or may not be sinful depending on the freedom-capacity of the individual. On the moral side, all we can say is that anyone who knowingly and freely drinks to excess is guilty of sin against the virtue of temperance, and he is responsible in cause for any other sins he may commit while under the influence of liquor.

[4] To abstain completely from intoxicating beverages is most commendable, especially when it is done out of love for God, and Catholics are urged to make this laudable sacrifice. If a person knows he drinks too much and falls into sin, he is obliged to control his drinking or abstain completely. The alcoholic must never take a drink.

[5] Statistics reveal an alarming increase in excessive drinking among men and women and among students in high schools and colleges. Automobile accidents caused by drunken drivers and resulting in painful deaths are snuffing out hundreds of human lives each year. Everyone should seriously heed the wise advice of the Book of Proverbs,

"Consort not with winebibbers, nor with those who eat meat to excess; for the drunkard and the glutton come to poverty, and torpor clothes a man in rags" (Prov. 23, 20-21).

Have not the Bible, the early Fathers, and your Church generally until most recent times condemned the taking of interest as unjust and immoral? Why does she allow today what she condemned as a sin in the past?

¹ The Bible has very little to say about the taking of interest. The Old Testament forbade it among the Jews (Ex. 22, 25; Lev. 25, 36), but it made an exception in the case of a Jew dealing with a Gentile (Deut. 23, 21). Economic conditions and practices among the ancient Jews differed greatly from those of modern times, and the countless rules and laws observed by the Jews in those days have long been abandoned, especially since the time of Christ. We can offer no argument on such obscure references.

² The New Testament does not treat the question at all. Although a few men have seen a condemnation of taking interest in St. Luke's Gospel (Luke 6, 34f.), they have misinterpreted the text. Christ is giving a lesson in charity.

³ The early Fathers had no explicit teaching on the problem. They were more concerned with sins against justice and charity when they attacked unscrupulous money-lenders who took advantage of the poor.

⁴ It was not until the later Middle Ages that the councils and the theologians of the Church formulated a theory of interest and usury. In the first place, they condemned profit-making on a loan of something that was unproductive, that was only consumable or had limited use. The theologians felt that simple repayment was all the lender could ask. This attitude most likely originated in the system of acquiring goods by trading. Equality of exchange in trading was basic in medieval economics. When money became important as a substitute for goods in trading, it had only that single value as a medium of exchange. Theologians, therefore, applied the same principles to money which they had applied to the goods replaced by money for the sake of convenience in trading. Money, then, had no more productive powers than the commodities traded,

so they condemned the making of an extra charge or collecting interest on a loan of money. Repayment was all the lender could ask even in this case. The condemnation for taking interest on a loan of money may very well have been too general and strict. It must be admitted, however, that medieval and early modern economics were radically different from those of today.

⁵ Money, especially since the Industrial Revolution, has taken on a new value. Money has become productive. Its use can produce more money. If a man makes a loan of money today, he surrenders his opportunity to use his money productively. The borrower has the right to use the money as he wishes and to profit from the advantage the loan provides. In such a situation it is justice to allow the lender some compensation for giving up his right to use his money profitably. Justice allows him to charge interest.

⁶ The reason for a change in position by the Church, therefore, lies primarily in the changes in economics and in the value of money. The economic changes may have occurred faster than the changes in the policy of the Church, so individual theologians may have erred in their later condemnations of charging interest. Often these prohibitions were made to safeguard against the unscrupulous lender. The basic answer to the problem of change still rests on the changed nature of money.

Is it not lawful to lie in some cases as Luther taught? Do we not all tell lies to children, to the sick, and to those who have no right to know the truth?

¹ No, it is never lawful to lie under any circumstances, for a lie is intrinsically bad and unnatural. Father Cronin well defines a lie as: "Any speech, statement, communication or representation made to another person, which really purports to represent what one believes to be true, but which the speaker knows to be untrue" (*The Science of Ethics,* ii., 74).

² St. Thomas teaches that every lie is a sin, slight or grievous according to circumstances, because "a lie is of its nature evil, as bearing on undue matter. For as words

are naturally the sign of thought, it is unnatural and undue to signify by words what one has not in his mind"
(*Summa*, IIa. IIae., q. 110, a. 3).

[3] Some moralists, aware that in most cases men lie only
to deceive others, have included this intention of deceiving
in their definition of a lie. They are wrong because instances of lying occur in which there is no such intention.
The desire to deceive belongs to "the perfection" of a lie
(*Ibid.*, q. 110, a. 1), but it is not a constituent of the lie
itself.

[4] Lying is condemned in both the Old Testament and
the New. The 8th commandment orders: "Thou shalt not
bear false witness against thy neighbor" (Ex. 20, 16; Deut.
5, 20; Matt. 19, 18). The Old Testament says repeatedly
that lying is hateful to the Lord (Prov. 6, 17; 12, 22;
Sirach 7, 14; 20, 26-28), and merits divine chastisement (Ps.
5, 7). Our Lord attributes lying to the devil, the father of
lies (John 8, 44), and challenges the Jews to convict Him
of any sin against the truth (John 8, 46). St. Paul and St.
James warn the early Christians against lying (Eph. 4, 25;
Col. 3, 9; James 3, 14), and St. John declares that unrepentant liars will suffer the eternal torments of Hell (Apoc.
21, 8; 22, 16).

[5] We are not guilty of the sin of lying when we present
to children information beyond their years in a childish
dress suited to their mentality, or when we tell them beautiful legends of the saints or charming fairy tales about Santa
Claus, or the Easter Bunnie.

[6] Keeping a bit of news from a sick person, when we
are confident that the shock of its telling might endanger
his life, is permissible, as St. Augustine (*Contra Men.*, x.)
and St. Thomas teach (*Summa*, IIa. IIae., q. 110, a. 3,
ad. 4). But lying to the sick is a most grievous sin when it
prevents the sick person from making his peace with God
on a deathbed. I once attended a sick person who had
been told by his physician and his relatives that he would
be up and about in a few weeks. He refused at first to go
to confession, although he went at once when I told him
he might be dead before midnight. The well-meant but
cruel lies of his friends might possibly have been the occasion of his eternal damnation.

Is it not true that whereas you theoretically condemn lying, you allow it in practice by your teaching of equivocation and mental reservation?

[1] No, this is not true. It is good for us at the outset to define our terms, so that as St. Paul puts it, we may not fight as one "beating the air" (1 Cor. 9, 26).

[2] Mental reservation is an act of the mind which restricts the natural meaning that the spoken words appear to bear. If I give no outward clue to my mental limitation of the spoken phrase, either in the peculiar wording I use, or in the circumstances of person and of place, I am using a pure mental reservation, or, in plain English, a lie. If I do indicate externally my mental limitation according to the usages of language and of social custom, I am using a broad mental reservation, which is always lawful.

[3] Non-Catholics often confuse these totally different things, and translate the Latin term, *aequivocatio* (broad mental reservation), by the English word equivocation (pure mental reservation, or lie). If our questioner keeps this distinction in mind, he will readily grasp the doctrine of Catholic moralists.

[4] An example will illustrate our teaching. An importunate visitor, who has called repeatedly at my home, and borrowed money from me which he never dreamed of repaying, is told by my intelligent servant, "My master is not at home." Do not the usages of modern society make it clear that I am not at home *to him?*

[5] Our Lord gave us a striking instance of a mental reservation, when He declared that the Son of God did not know the Day of Judgment (Mark 13, 32). He certainly did know it, as all the Fathers maintained in their controversies with the Arians, the Apollinarists, the Nestorians, the Monophysites, etc. Like the priest-confessor just mentioned, He did know the fact, but the divine secret of the Day of Judgment belonged to God the Father, and formed no part of the mission He gave either to Christ or to His holy angels. In this sense He did not know it.

[6] Catholic moralists divide secrets into three classes: the natural secret, which concerns our own private life, or the hidden faults of our neighbor; the entrusted secret, which

refers to matters communicated to us under promise of secrecy; the professional secret, which pertains to facts told to priests, lawyers, doctors, and public officials.

[7] It is not only lawful, but it is in most instances, obligatory for us to keep these secrets inviolate. When impertinent people, either maliciously or stupidly, endeavor to wrest these secrets from us, we are perfectly justified in using a mental reservation to meet their rude and ill-bred questioning.

[8] Apart, however, from the confessional secret, which binds always and under all circumstances, because of the divine law, there are certain cases when secrets must be divulged. A natural or an entrusted secret, for example, must be told, if a legitimate court authority demands it, to prevent injury to a third party or to the community in general. Even the professional secret loses its binding force, if keeping it implies the violating of a higher precept. Thus a doctor, who knows privately that a boy at a boarding school has a serious case of smallpox that will infect the other students, is bound to inform the city's health board.

What is the difference between detraction and calumny?

[1] A person commits the sin of detraction when, without a good reason, he makes known the hidden faults of others. We must respect the good name and reputation of people. Only when there is a sufficiently grave reason may we reveal their hidden faults, for example, to save someone from becoming involved in a crime. However, it is not detraction to speak of faults publicly known in a community, although it is more charitable not to do so.

[2] On the other hand, a person commits the sin of calumny or slander when by lying he injures the good name of others. Calumny is opposed not only to justice and charity but also to truth. We should remember that "a good name is more desirable than great riches" (Proverbs 22, 1) and that God will destroy the slanderer.

[8] We should not forget that a person who has sinned by detraction or calumny, or who has needlessly revealed a secret must repair the harm he has done his neighbor, as far as he is able. This obligation is binding even if the guilty one thereby suffers some harm.

SELECTED BIBLIOGRAPHY

CARAMAN, PHILIP (ed). *Saints and Ourselves.* Garden City, N. Y.: (Image Books) Doubleday & Co. 1958.

COLLINS, JOSEPH B. *Teaching the Sixth Commandment.* Milwaukee: Bruce Publishing Co. 1953.

CONNELL, F. J. *The Ethics of War.* Huntington, Ind.: Our Sunday Visitor Press. 1954.

DEMPSEY, BERNARD W. *Interest and Usury.* Washington, D. C.: American Council on Public Affairs. 1943.

FABREGUES, JEAN DE. *Christian Marriage.* New York: Hawthorn Books. 1959.

FORD, J. C. and KELLY, G. A. *Contemporary Moral Theology.* Westminster, Md.: Newman Press. 1958.

GUARDINI, ROMANO. *Prayer in Practice.* New York: Pantheon. 1957.

KELLY, G. A. *Medico-moral Problems.* St. Louis: Catholic Hospital Association of U. S. and Canada. 1958.

KELLY, G. A. *Overpopulation.* New York: Paulist Press. 1960.

MCCARTHY, JOHN. *Problems in Theology, II: The Commandments.* Westminster, Md.: Newman Press. 1960.

MCSORLEY, JOSEPH. *A Primer of Prayer.* New York (Deus Books) Paulist Press. 1961.

NAGLE, W. J. (ed.) *Morality and Modern Warfare.* Baltimore: Helicon Press. 1961.

STRATMANN, FRANZIKUS M. *War and Christianity Today.* Westminster, Md.: Newman Press. 1957.

TREACY, GERALD C. *The Ten Commandments.* New York: Paulist Press. 1941.

PERIODICALS

"Artificial Insemination and the Law." *Catholic Mind.* (Sept.-Oct.) 1960.

"Birth Control and Foreign Aid." *Catholic Mind.* (May-June) 1960.

"Boxing, Medicine and Morals." *Catholic Mind.* (Jan.-Feb.) 1959.

"Remarks on the Moral Problem of War." *Theological Studies,* Vol. 20, No. 1, March 1959.

PART X

The Commandments of the Church

By what right does the Catholic Church make laws which bind Catholics under pain of sin?

[1] The Catholic Church has the right to make laws from Jesus Christ who founded the Church and who said to the first Bishops of His Church, "Whatever you bind on earth shall be bound also in heaven" (Matt. 18, 18). This legislative authority of the Church is known as "the power of the keys" and it includes everything necessary for the government of the Church and for the guidance of the faithful. The primary purpose of Church laws is the eternal salvation of men.

[2] Unlike the Commandments of God, promulgated on Mount Sinai, which treat of the basic unchangeable truths relevant to man's relationship to God and to his fellow-men, the Commandments of the Church apply the truths of revelation to current conditions existing in the world. They can be modified or abrogated should changes in the social situation render them ineffective, useless, or even harmful. Christ gave His Church the power not only to bind but also to loose (Matt. 18, 18).

[3] Besides the Commandments there are many other laws regulating the government of the Church and the administration of its affairs. The collection of laws binding the Latin Church is contained in an official book called the *Code of Canon Law*.

Why and when was the Sabbath changed from Saturday to Sunday? Who gave the Pope the right to change the Sab-

bath? Why must Catholics go to Mass every Sunday under penalty of hell?

[1] The third Commandment of the Old Law: "Remember thou keep holy the Sabbath day" (Exod. 20, 8) was partly moral, the natural law obliging all men to devote some time exclusively to the worship of God, and partly ceremonial in as much as it determined the time and the details of its observance.

[2] It is true that the Church could not abrogate the natural law, but the Apostles, as the divine infallible teachers of Christ's Church, could and did change the time, the motive and the details of the Sunday observance. They substituted the first day of the week, Sunday, for the seventh, Saturday; they made it commemorate the Resurrection of Christ instead of the Creation of the world (Exod. 20, 11).

[3] The Church commands us to hear Mass under grievous sin, because she considers the deliberate refusal to attend public worship on Sunday an insult to Christ, who is really and objectively present upon our altars, and who as priest and victim in the Sacrifice of the Mass, carries on the work of Calvary by appeasing the divine wrath, and obtaining mercy and forgiveness for us sinners.

[4] Could you honestly claim to love your mother dearly, if, married and living near her, you failed to visit her at least once a week? The living Christ of the Eucharist is our nextdoor neighbor, who loves us with an infinite love, and requires us to love Him above all things. Even if there were no obligatory law, Catholics would deem it the greatest privilege to visit Christ once a week, and thereby share in His infinite Sacrifice. The great fervor of the early Christians made an obligatory law unnecessary. It was not until the year 300 that we discover a decree of the Council of Elvira: "If anyone remains three Sundays in a city without going to church, he shall be deprived of Communion for a time."

[5] The obligation of hearing Mass ceases for weighty reasons. For example, the Church excuses the sick and convalescent, those caring for the sick, soldiers or servants on duty and mothers who cannot leave their children.

Why do Catholics break the Sabbath by playing golf and baseball on Sunday? Do Catholics believe that if they go to Mass, they can do as they like the rest of the day? I'm scandalized at Catholics working on Sundays.

[1] God wants us to pray, rest, and relax on Sundays more than we do on the other days of the week. He wants us to abstain from our regular occupation and to keep away from the shop, the store, the office and the plant. A person does not have to spend all day in church and in bed in order to make Sunday a day of worship and rest.

[2] Catholics keep Sunday holy by attending Mass, by reading religious books, by saying extra prayers, by visiting the sick, etc. And they are entitled to some wholesome relaxation and recreation after working hard all week. There is nothing wrong in their taking a drive, playing golf or tennis, watching a baseball or football game, or hiking over the countryside—it may be their only opportunity for such innocent pleasures.

[3] In a short talk to 53 European sports writers on April 2, 1960, Pope John XXIII said, "Every Sunday, tremendous crowds, find healthy distraction in sports. We are pleased to believe that many athletes and spectators are able to fit such diversion into a day consecrated to the Lord without neglecting their religious duties. This is in line with divine law whereby, after giving to God what is due to God, man may also on this day allow himself legitimate relaxation for his body and spirit."

[4] Some persons have to work on Sunday and they please and serve God as well as their neighbor—mothers in preparing meals, policemen and firemen in protecting people and property, doctors and nurses in caring for the sick, etc. What is forbidden is the doing of unnecessary work. Too often business goes on "as usual" on Sunday. Merchants are keeping their stores open on Sunday. Surely, they and their customers are violating the spirit of Sunday by selling and buying.

What do you mean by abstaining from servile work on Sunday?

¹ The abstention from servile work, like Sunday Mass attendance, was a tradition in the Church long before it became a law. Its original purpose was to provide for the Christian a rest from his week-day labors in order to attend Sunday Mass. The Sunday repose has often been mistakenly regarded as an outgrowth of the sabbatarian observances of the Jews. Historically this cannot be defended. Though the Sabbath and the Sunday are comparable as weekly days of worship, the early Fathers do not appear to have adverted to any direct historical relation between them as days of rest. Liturgical necessity alone accounts for the Christian repose. By the end of the 2nd century it was an accepted Christian tradition, and in 321 A.D. it received status in civil law through an edict of Constantine ordering the observance of a general civic and industrial repose on "the day of the sun."

² The Sunday law forbidding servile work was for centuries phrased in general terms and made no distinction between servile and liberal occupations. It simply forbade on Sunday the kind of activity one normally did during the week to earn one's sustenance. In most cases that activity amounted to rural or manual labor. The term "servile" does not appear in ecclesiastical literature until the early Middle Ages when some writers, instead of attributing the Sunday law to Apostolic tradition, mistakenly based it expressly on the third Commandment and regulated it mainly in accordance with the prescriptions of Exodus and Leviticus regarding servile work on the Sabbath.

³ Until recent decades theologians were still defining servile work in the sense it had when all manual labor was reserved to serfs and menials. This ancient definition has proved dissatisfying to 20th-century Christians because it does not fit modern conditions of working and living. From the 6th to the 18th century when the whole basis of society was agricultural, servile work in the sense of strenuous farm labor was precisely the kind of bondage the Sunday law sought to relieve.

⁴ Today, however, mechanization and automation have introduced a new kind of bondage. People are beginning to realize that the common label of servile work does not make much sense when most of the manual labor is being

done by machines. Thus there is a widespread and justifiable tendency to provide a more realistic interpretation of the term "servile" which puts the stress on the bondage rather than the manual element of the work. Accordingly, theologians are now defining servile work as that work which one does for a livelihood. Such work, which in relatively few cases is strictly manual, is the work he should avoid on Sunday. This applies even to non-manual activities, such as bookkeeping, salesmanship and typing. On the other hand, custom justifies drawing a line between manual work that is a trade and light manual activity done for a hobby. The latter does not violate the Sunday rest. Nor does common estimation consider recreational activities contrary to the Sunday law.

5 Of course, some of the old categories of servile work have not changed and probably never will, such as ploughing one's field or laying bricks. Others will always remain liberal, like reading and creative writing. The classification of others must depend on common consensus and custom, which is usually based on such norms as the motive behind the work, whether it brings pay, or whether it is one's usual occupation. In cases where one must work out of necessity he is excused from the law.

6 Until such time as the Church officially specifies the nature and extent of the term "servile," Catholics are free to abide by the traditional interpretation given that word and still be within the letter of the law. But to perform non-manual gainful activities on Sunday is clearly against the spirit of the law, which aims at setting one free from the routine daily cares of the world in order to devote oneself more perfectly to God and the things of God.

Why do Catholics fast before receiving Holy Communion? Why did Pope Pius XII dispense Catholics from fasting from midnight? Is it right for a Catholic to offer his Communion for someone else? What are some of the effects of Holy Communion?

1 To receive worthily the true Body and Blood of Jesus Christ in Holy Communion a Catholic must be in the state of grace and have fasted according to the law of the Church. Until recently the law of Eucharistic Fast obliged Catholics

to fast from midnight. Pope Pius XII, as the Supreme Legislator, modified this law considerably in order to lighten the burden of those who have difficulty in fasting, and to give more Catholics the opportunity of receiving more frequently. However, he urged those who can easily do so to continue to fast from midnight as something most pleasing to Christ.

² The essentials of the present legislation can be thus summarized. Priests and faithful, before Holy Mass or Holy Communion respectively, must abstain for three hours from solid foods and alcoholic beverages, and for one hour from non-alcoholic beverages. Water never breaks the fast; it can be taken at any time. The infirm, even if not bed-ridden, may take non-alcoholic beverages and that which is really and properly medicine, either in liquid or solid form, before Holy Mass or Holy Communion without any time limit.

³ Because in Holy Communion the Body and Blood of Christ is the spiritual food for our soul, only the person who actually receives can benefit. In this sense one's own Communion cannot be offered for another's sustenance. Nevertheless, to receive Holy Communion is to perform a prayerful and meritorious action which can be offered so that someone else may be granted God's grace and blessing.

⁴ Some of the effects of Holy Communion are: an increase of habitual or sanctifying grace in our souls, a special intimate union with Christ, our Savior, forgiveness of venial sins, and the right to actual graces by which we shall be able to overcome our daily temptations and to fulfill faithfully the daily duties of our state in life. Meditate often on the promise of Christ, "He who eats My flesh and drinks My blood has life everlasting, and I will raise him up on the last day. For My flesh is food indeed, and My blood is drink indeed. He who eats My flesh and drinks My blood, abides in Me and I in him" (John 6, 55-57).

Does not the Catholic Church ask too much of human nature by her laws of fast and abstinence? What is the difference between abstinence and fasting?

¹ Church laws are always reasonable and easy to observe; and the Church does not hesitate to modify them when the

pressures, habits, and conditions of modern living make them too burdensome for the faithful. The laws of fast and abstinence do not imply that meat and other foods are evil in themselves. Rather they help the Catholic to develop his will power, to practice temperance, and to do some penance for his personal sins.

[2] On *fast days* Catholics are allowed to eat one full meal, including meat; they may also have, at two other times of the day, a small amount of nourishment, exclusive of meat. Eating between meals is prohibited, although liquids, such as milk and fruit juices, are permitted. Besides the weekdays of Lent and the Ember Days there are only a few other fast days. Every Catholic between his twenty-first and sixtieth birthday must observe this law of fast on the appointed days. However, those who are sick, convalescent, or pregnant are excused; also those who would not be strong enough to fulfill the duties of their state of life, if they were required to fast.

[3] On days of *complete abstinence* Catholics are not allowed to eat any meat, for example on Fridays; on days of *partial abstinence* they are permitted meat at the principal meal, for example, on Ember Wednesdays. Every Catholic who has reached his seventh birthday must observe the law of abstinence. But again there are people who are excused: those who are ill or who cannot obtain food other than meat.

[4] The Pope, the Bishops, either singly or collectively, and pastors can dispense Catholics from the obligation of fast and abstinence. Here in the United States, for example, Catholics are dispensed when a national holiday, such as the Fourth of July, is celebrated on Friday.

What do Catholics mean by the Ember Days?

[1a] The Ember Days are the Wednesdays, Fridays and Saturdays at the beginning of the four seasons, which the Church appointed as special days of fasting and abstinence. The word is derived from the Latin, *Quatuor Tempora,* the four times.

[2a] While their origin is uncertain, it is generally believed that they were instituted to offset the pagan customs of the

5th century in Rome. The Romans, at the beginning of the time of seeding and harvesting, performed certain religious ceremonies to implore the help of their gods: in June for a good harvest, in September for a rich vintage, and in December for the seeding. The Church Christianized this pagan custom, and set aside these seasons as special times of prayer and thanksgiving.

Is the Eucharist necessary for salvation? How often are Catholics bound to receive Holy Communion? Is a Catholic obliged to go to Confession before he receives Communion?

[1] The Holy Eucharist is not absolutely necessary for salvation. It is, however, necessary in the sense that Christ commanded us to receive His Body and Blood (John 6, 54). And the Church has always heeded this divine command.

[2] The early Christians customarily received the Eucharist each time they assisted at Mass and carried it to those who were sick at home or confined in prison. From the 3rd to the 11th century it was the custom to give Communion to children immediately after Baptism and Confirmation. In 1215 the 4th Lateran Council prescribed that all Catholics are obliged to receive Communion at least once a year during the Easter time. Catholics in the United States, by special permission, may fulfill this duty between the First Sunday of Lent and Trinity Sunday. Although this is the present law of the Church, Catholics show their love for the Eucharistic Christ by frequent reception of Holy Communion. Pope Pius X in his Decree on Holy Communion (1905) encouraged this devotional practice by urging all the faithful who are "in the state of grace" and who have "a right and devout intention" to receive frequently, even daily.

[3] Catholics are obliged to confess all their mortal sins once a year, as soon as they have reached the age of discretion, that is, about the seventh year. This law, like that of annual Communion, dates from the 4th Lateran Council (1215) and was reaffirmed at the Council of Trent. It only applies to those guilty of mortal sins. So long as a Catholic is not in the state of mortal sin he may receive Communion

without first going to Confession. It is the usual practice for Catholics, however, to discharge their duty of Confession as a preparation for their Communion at Easter time. Most Catholics confess periodically and receive frequently because these two Sacraments increase God's grace and supernatural life in their souls.

How much money is a Catholic supposed to contribute to the support of his church and pastor? May a priest refuse his services to those who refuse to pay the usual fee or to the poor who can contribute nothing?

[1] Catholics in the United States are very generous in their contributions because they realize that their free offerings are almost the only source of Church revenue. The many Catholic churches, schools, and hospitals present striking evidence of their practical faith.

[2] Catholics are bound to support their parish church and pastor according to their means. The amount contributed depends upon the needs of a particular parish and the income of the particular parishioner. No tithe or percentage is levied. St. Paul tells us that "The Lord directed that those who preach the Gospel should have their living from the Gospel" (1 Cor. 9, 14).

[3] The Church forbids a priest to refuse his services or to deny the sacraments to anyone who fails to fulfill this precept. The mission of the priest is regulated by the command of Christ and not by the amount of contributions.

Why are Catholics forbidden to marry in Advent and Lent?

[1a] They are not forbidden to marry in Advent or Lent. Marriage may be contracted at any time of the year. The solemnities of marriage, that is, the solemn blessing, the ringing of bells, the playing of the organ, the use of a carpet, etc., are forbidden from the First Sunday of Advent till Christmas day inclusively, and from Ash Wednesday till Easter inclusively. The Bishop, however, may permit the nuptial blessing, although he should urge the marriage couple to refrain from any excessive display during the Church's season of penance.

SELECTED BIBLIOGRAPHY

DAVIS, HENRY. *Moral and Pastoral Theology* (Vol. II). New York: Sheed & Ward. 1957.

FORD, J. C. and KELLY, G. A. *Contemporary Moral Theology.* Westminster, Md.: Newman Press. 1958.

FRANKE, HERMANN. *Lent and Easter.* Westminster, Md.: Newman Press. 1955.

KELLY, J. P. *What the Church Gives Us.* New York: P. J. Kenedy & Sons. 1955.

LIPTAK, DAVID Q. *All About Fast and Abstinence.* New York: Paulist Press. 1960.

RIPLEY, FRANCIS J. *This Is the Faith.* New York: Golden Press. 1960.

VANN, GERALD. *Morals and Man.* (Rev. ed.) New York: Sheed & Ward. 1960.

PART XI

Catholic Worship

Where do you find the Mass in the Bible or in primitive Christianity? Is it not really a product of medieval thought?

[1] The Mass is foretold by the prophet, Malachias, "for from sunrise to sunset My name is great among the Gentiles, and in every place there is sacrifice, and there is offered to My name a clean oblation" (Malachias 1, 10-11).

[2] Christ fulfilled this prophecy when He offered the first Mass the night before He died and commanded His Apostles to change bread and wine into His Body and Blood. As the Old Testament of the Jews had its religious sacrifice so Christ saw to it that the New Testament of Christians would have its own special sacrifice.

[3] The sacrificial character of the Mass is evident from Christ's words in consecrating the chalice. St. Luke's narration, "This cup is the new covenant in My Blood, which shall be shed for you" clearly means that the Blood contained in the chalice is shed at the present time for you (Luke 22, 20). The words of St. Matthew, "This is My Blood of the new covenant, which is being shed for many unto the forgiveness of sins" (Matt. 26, 28) and those of St. Mark, "This is My Blood of the new covenant, which is being shed for many" (Mark 14, 24) also declare that Christ's Blood is being shed for us. The shedding of blood for remission of sins is a real sacrifice. "Since the life of a living body is in its blood, I have made you put it on the altar, so that atonement may thereby be made for your own lives, because it is the blood, as the seat of life, that makes atonement" (Lev. 17, 11).

⁴ The consecration of the bread affords another proof of the sacrificial character of the Mass. The words, "This is My Body which is being given for you" (Luke 22, 19) or "which shall be given up" (1 Cor. 11, 24) patently manifest that Christ truly offered Himself in sacrificial death.

⁵ The Mass was the official act of worship for the early Christians as it is today for Catholics. The Teaching of the Twelve Apostles (100 A.D.) tells us that they "assembled together on the Lord's day" (Chap. 14) to offer Mass as the "clean oblation" of Malachias (St. Justin, *Dial. cum Trypho.*, 41) and to present Christ as Victim to the Creator (St. Irenaeus, *Adv. Haer.*, 4, 18, 4). St. Cyprian in the 3rd century sets forth the Catholic doctrine on the Mass as clearly as a theologian of the 20th. He teaches (*Epis.* 63) that the Eucharist is a true and complete sacrifice; it contains an immolated victim; it was founded by Christ; that it is a commemoration of the Lord's passion and is even identical with that passion; that in it the Blood of Christ is offered; that it is offered for the living and dead; that it is a symbol of the communion of the people with Christ. He writes, "Christ is the Teacher and Founder of this sacrifice . . . if Jesus Christ, our Lord and God, is Himself the Chief Priest of God the Father, and has first offered Himself a sacrifice to the Father, and has commanded this to be done in commemoration of Himself, surely that priest discharges the office of Christ who imitates what Christ did; and he then offers a true and full sacrifice to God the Father in the Church, when he proceeds to offer it according to the manner in which he sees Christ to have offered" (*Epis.* 63).

⁶ History testifies that Christ Himself established the Mass and that His true followers, in obedience to His command, have offered this same sacrifice from the earliest years of Christianity. And it is the Catholic Church which guarantees its being offered until the end of time.

Why do Catholics have so many silly and meaningless ceremonies? Was not the early worship of the Christians simple, in utter contrast to the ceremonial of the Roman Church today? Cannot Christians worship God without so much ceremony?

[1] If our ceremonies appear silly and meaningless to you, it is because you do not understand their beautiful symbolism, or because you are ignorant of their origin. Not a word is said, nor a gesture made, not an action performed in a Catholic church, but is intended to raise the soul to God, and to foster and increase our love for Him.

[2] We could indeed worship God without ceremony, if we were wrecked on a desert island, far from the haunts of civilized men. Catholics were compelled to dispense with ceremony during the penal days, when Mass was said in a barn or a mountain cave. That is why ritual was most simple in Apostolic days, for Mass was said in private houses, or in the Catacombs, with the constant threat of death before the eyes of the faithful. The absence of ceremonial was due to necessity, and not to choice.

[3] Ceremony is natural to man. We are not disembodied spirits, but creatures composed of body and soul. The soul is always under the influence of the senses, which are apt to draw it away from the contemplation of the things of God. Does it not seem natural that a Church that appeals to the whole man, as God's Church alone does, should make the senses aid in the awakening of spiritual ideas, and the driving away of worldly distractions?

[4] The average man expresses outwardly what he feels interiorly. His handshake expresses friendship, his kiss expresses love, his blow evidences his anger. Should we not then give outward expression to our friendship and love of God, and our hatred of all things opposed to Him?

[5] Ceremonies are to be found in the Gospels, as well as in the Old Law, wherein they were prescribed to the minutest detail. Christ *knelt* in prayer (Luke 22, 41); He *fell flat* on the ground (Mark 14, 35); *He raised His eyes* to heaven in giving thanks (Mark 6, 41); He cured the deaf and dumb man by putting His finger into his ears, and spitting He touched his tongue (Mark 7, 33-34); He cured the blind man, spitting on the ground, and making a clay of the spittle (John 9, 6); He *breathed* upon the Apostles (John 20, 22); He *blessed* the disciples when He ascended into heaven (Luke 24, 50). We find the Apostles anointing the sick with oil (Mark 6, 13), baptizing with water (Acts 2, 41), imposing hands in ordination (1 Tim. 4, 14), using

relics to work miracles (Acts 19, 12), and performing symbolic actions (Acts 21, 11).

[6] Is it not strange that the very man who objects to the ritual of the Catholic Church, will take special delight in the ritual of some society like the Masons, the Elks, or the Pythians? Deprived of the old-time Christian ceremonies by the 16th century Reformers, non-Catholics today frame ceremonies of their own to satisfy the natural instincts of the human heart.

Why do not Catholics pray as the heart dictates, instead of always repeating a number of set prayers? Did the early Christians have set prayers which they read out of a book, as the priests do at Mass?

[1] In Apostolic times the Mass prayers were not all written down and read from a missal as the priest does today, but they were in part composed by the officiating Bishop. But it is generally admitted by liturgical scholars that the set prayers of the liturgy go back as early as the 2nd century. Our Lord had told His Apostles to do what He did at the Last Supper (Luke 22, 19), so that His words of consecration were naturally repeated in every Mass from the beginning, as we read in St. Justin Martyr (*Apol.*, i., 65). The lessons, psalms, prayers, and preaching which accompanied these sacred words were really a Christianized form of the synagogue service. St. Paul mentions readings from the Scriptures (1 Tim. 4, 13; Col. 4, 16; 1 Thess. 5, 27), the recitation of psalms and hymns (1 Cor. 14, 26; Col. 3, 16; Eph. 5, 19), the answering of Amen (1 Cor. 14, 16), and St. Luke the prayers which followed the consecration (Acts 2, 42).

[2] When one of the disciples said to Christ: "Lord, teach us to pray," He answered the request by teaching us the most perfect set prayer, the Lord's Prayer (Luke 11, 1). The Catholic Church, therefore, merely follows His divine example, when she approves the many prayers in honor of the Lord, the Blessed Virgin and the saints, such as the Creed, Confiteor, Hail Mary, Angelus, the Rosary.

[3] But Catholics may also pray as the heart dictates, making profession of their faith, hope, love, and sorrow for

sin. The Church has always approved mental prayer, where-by the soul is brought in union with Christ by offering to Him acts of adoration, and love, prompted by the thought of some doctrine or some fact of divine revelation.

Why do not Catholics say the Lord's Prayer in full? I notice that they omit the words: "For Thine is the kingdom and the power and the glory, forever. Amen" (Matt. 6, 13)?

[1a] Catholics say the Lord's Prayer as the Lord Himself taught it to His Apostles. The words cited above are a marginal gloss, interpolated by some copyist, who had in mind words borrowed from the Greek liturgy (*Cf.* 1 Par. 29, 11). They were rejected as unauthentic by St. Jerome in the 4th century, as they have been rejected by the authors of the Revised Version of 1881. The King James Version, as well as the more recent Revised Standard Version, omits this gloss in Luke 11, 4.

How do you know that Masses will take souls out of purgatory? Do you pretend to know the secrets of God? Why do you take money for Masses? Is not this the sin of simony? Why do you exact a fixed sum to get people out of purgatory by your Masses? Does not a rich man thereby have an unjust advantage over a poor man, simply because he leaves a priest money to pray him out of purgatory?

[1] The Council of Trent, which voices the teaching of the early Fathers and all the ancient liturgies, Eastern and Western, teaches that "the Mass is a propitiatory sacrifice for the living and the dead, and that the souls in purgatory are helped by the suffrages of the faithful, but chiefly by the acceptable Sacrifice of the Altar."

[2] There is no simony in accepting stipends of money for Masses. St. Thomas says (*Summa* IIa. IIæ., q. 100, a. 2, ad. 2), the priest accepts them as payment for his support, but not as the price of his Mass. Canon Law forbids simony, which it defines as "a deliberate eagerness to buy or sell for a temporal price anything intrinsically spiritual."

[3] In the primitive Church the faithful offered bread and wine at each Mass they attended, often placing money upon the altar for the use of the clergy and the poor. The prac-

tice of giving the priest a money alms for a Mass dates from the 7th or 8th century, and became a universal practice in the 12th.

4 The Church allows the priest to receive money for but one Mass a day, except on Christmas, and legislates severely against all trading in Masses. If more Masses are asked for than a priest can say, he is bound to send them to priests in poor parishes where few offerings are made, or to priests in the foreign missions.

5 The Scriptures prove that by divine law the Church has the right to demand from the people the support of the clergy (Matt. 10, 10). But the custom of accepting stipends for Masses is proved only by tradition, that is, the Church's approval for the past twelve hundred years. As the divine teacher of Christ's revelation, it cannot make any universal law contrary to the natural or positive divine law.

6 Non-Catholics generally suppose that five hundred Masses have five hundred times the efficacy of one. This is not the case. The value of the Mass is infinite, because Christ is the Minister of the Eucharistic Sacrifice. He delegates the priest to act in His name, and actually performs Himself the sacrificial action in each Mass. But while the merits presented to God in the Mass are infinite, their application to individuals is finite, and only to be measured by the acceptance of God. We know in a general way that God will answer our prayers, but how He will apply the fruit of a particular Mass, we do not pretend to know. The Church at every Mass remembers all her children, living and dead; the particular application of the infinite merits of Christ are known to God alone. The rich in giving alms have no advantage over the poor, for each one is bound to give alms in proportion to his means. If he were to neglect giving alms, he would be in a far worse position than the poor man, who cannot give what he does not possess.

What purpose do Catholics serve in celebrating Advent, Epiphany, Lent and Pentecost?

1 As our calendar year has its special seasons—spring, summer, autumn, and winter—so, too, the Church's liturgical year has its special seasons. They relate to certain events in the life of our Lord.

²ᵃ *Advent*—the four weeks immediately preceding Christmas—symbolizes the long centuries during which the Jews awaited the coming of the Messias promised by God. It is a time of prayer and penance in anticipation of the joyful feast of Christ's birthday and prepares us to open our hearts to the Savior.

³ *Epiphany*—the six weeks beginning on January 6th—commemorates the manifestation of the Infant Child to the Wise Men who traveled from the East to adore at the stable of Bethlehem. It reminds Catholics of their obligation to show forth Christ by a holy life. They are to pray and work that all men may come to know and love Christ and that there may be "one fold and one shepherd."

⁴ *Lent*—the forty days before Easter—highlights our redemption from sin by the passion and death of Christ. Catholics meditate on what our innocent and sinless Savior suffered for us guilty sinners: the agony in Gethsemane, the scourging at the pillar, the crowning with thorns, the death-march to Calvary, and the crucifixion. Such meditation stirs up love and urges us to fast as penance for our sins. By sorrowing with Christ during Lent we are better prepared to rejoice at His glorious resurrection on Easter Sunday.

⁵ *Pentecost*—the twenty-four weeks which begin on Pentecost Sunday—is a period of rejoicing that the Holy Spirit has descended upon the Church and is sanctifying us. We celebrate the birthday of the Church, renew our faith in her teachings, and strive to shape our lives in accordance with her instructions.

What is meant by the Forty Hours' Devotion?

¹ It is a devotion in honor of the Holy Eucharist, the people praying in adoration before It for forty hours continuously, in memory of the forty hours Christ's body remained in the tomb. It begins and ends with a Solemn High Mass, accompanied by a procession of the Blessed Sacrament, and the chanting of the Litany of the Saints.

² It originated in Milan at the beginning of the 16th century, and its purpose, according to Pope Paul III (1534-1539), was "to appease the anger of God provoked by the

offences of Christians, and to bring to nought the machinations of the Turks, who are pressing forward for the destruction of Christendom." It was popularized in Rome by St. Philip Neri and St. Ignatius, who urged its observance as an act of reparation for the sins committed during the carnival. It was introduced into the United States by Archbishop Kenrick of St. Louis in 1854.

What is the origin and meaning of the Stations of the Cross?

[1] The Stations of the Cross are a series of pictures or tableaux, placed on the walls of churches, or in the open air as in the Colosseum at Rome, representing scenes in the passion of our Lord. They may be said privately or publicly by Catholics, who go from one to another of the fourteen stations, singing hymns and reciting prayers, while they meditate on the Savior's sufferings and death.

[2] Pilgrimages to the Holy Land have been popular since the time of Constantine. St. Jerome mentions the crowds of pilgrims who came to Jerusalem in his day. To satisfy the devotion of Catholics, who could only make this pilgrimage in spirit, St. Petronius, in the 5th century, erected in St. Stephen's monastery at Bologna a number of chapels, modeled on the chief shrines of Jerusalem. Blessed Alvarez in the 15th century, on his return from the Holy Land, built a number of chapels in the Dominican friary of Cordova, on the walls of which were painted the chief scenes of the passion.

[3] The erection of Stations in the churches as we have them today did not become widespread until the close of the 17th century, when Pope Innocent XI granted special indulgences to the faithful, who would follow Christ in the Way of the Cross.

Why do Catholics make the sign of the cross? Is it not idolatry to "adore the cross," as Catholics do on Good Friday?

[1a] Catholics begin their prayers and sanctify their actions by the sign of the cross, because it is the symbol of our Redemption by Jesus Christ. They say with St. Paul: "God

forbid that I should glory save in the cross of our Lord Jesus Christ" (Gal. 6, 14). Catholics have used this sacred sign from the earliest times. We read in Tertullian: "In all our travels and movements, in all our coming in and going out, in putting on our clothes and shoes, at the bath, at the table, in lighting our lamps, in lying down, whatever employment occupies us, we mark our forehead with the sign of the cross" (*De Cor. Mil.*, 3).

2a If Catholics adored the mere wood or metal of the cross in itself, they would be guilty of idolatry. They do not. They give a reverence to the cross as representing something else, Jesus Christ the Lord. They adore Him who died upon it for our salvation.

Why do Catholics sprinkle themselves with holy water in their homes and before entering church? Is this not a superstitious practice without warrant in the Bible?

1 Catholics use holy water to drive away evil spirits, and to call to mind the purity of heart with which they should come into the presence of Christ, really present upon the altar. In blessing it, the priest adds some salt to symbolize incorruption and immortality. The use of holy water is in no way a superstitious practice, because Catholics do not believe that it has any virtue in itself; its efficacy depends entirely upon the devotion of those who use it, and upon God's acceptance of the prayers of His Church. St. Paul tells us that "Every creature of God is good . . . for it is sanctified by the word of God and prayer" (1 Tim. 4, 4-5).

2 Reason suggested to the Greeks and Romans that water, the natural element for cleansing, was symbolical of interior purity. They used it frequently in their religious ceremonies, to bless their fields, their cities and their armies. The Jews used holy water extensively in their ritual: in the ordination of priests and levites (Exod. 29, 4; Lev. 8, 6), before offering sacrifice (Exod. 30, 17), in the accusation of adultery (Num. 5, 17), and in the ablutions before meals and prayers (Mark 7, 13). A brazen laver for ablutions was specially blessed (Lev. 8, 11) and placed between the altar and the tabernacle (Exod. 30, 18). There were ten lavers in Solomon's Temple (3 Kings 8, 38).

[3] The holy water font of today goes back to the 6th century.

Why are ashes placed on the foreheads of Catholics on Ash Wednesday?

[1] Ashes have always been regarded as a sign of mourning and repentance. The priest on Ash Wednesday places ashes on the foreheads of the faithful with the words: "Remember man that thou art dust, and unto dust thou shalt return," to remind them that they are about to enter into the penitential season of Lent. This custom arose from the desire of the people to participate out of devotion in the humiliation of the public penitents of the early Church, who were dressed in sackcloth and marked with ashes, and expelled by the Bishop from Church until Holy Thursday.

Why do you bless palms in your Church the Sunday before Easter?

[1a] This ceremony recalls the triumphal entrance of Christ into Jerusalem on the first Palm Sunday (Mark 11, 8). The Spanish pilgrim Egeria, who visited Jerusalem in 380, has given us a good description of the Palm Sunday procession. She writes: "And when after long prayers it begins to be about six o'clock, that passage in the Gospel is read aloud in which the children with branches and palms greeted our Lord, crying, 'Blessed is He who comes in the name of the Lord.' And immediately the Bishop rises, and all the people with him, and thence they go to the summit of Mount Olivet, the whole way on foot, the people walking before him with psalms and antiphons, and continually singing the refrain: 'Blessed is He who comes in the name of the Lord.' And all the children in these places, even those who cannot yet walk, are carried in the arms of their parents, all with boughs, some of olive, some of palm and in that way they bring the Bishop to the city, just as the crowds escorted our Lord."

Is not the Agnus Dei a pagan charm or amulet?

[1] On the contrary, it was most probably a Christian substitute for the pagan charms current in Rome in the 5th century.

[2] Agnus Deis are small discs of wax, bearing on one side the imprint of a lamb bearing a cross, and on the other the arms of the Pope, or the figure of a saint. They are blessed by the Pope the first year of his pontificate, and every seventh year afterwards. The wax symbolizes the virgin flesh of Christ, and the cross Christ's Death for our salvation. The prayers of blessing make special mention of the prevention of perils from fire, flood, storm, pestilence, and childbirth. They urge Catholics to turn to Christ in every danger, and promise that He, the Lamb of God (*Agnus Dei*), "who takes away the sin of the world" (John 1, 29), will protect them, as of old the blood of the Paschal Lamb saved the children of Israel from the hands of the destroying angel (Exod. 12, 13).

Why do you burn fragrant spices during your services? What is incense? Why do you have candles lighted on your altar in the day time? Why are candles burned before the shrines of the saints, and around the bodies of the dead?

[1a] Incense is an aromatic substance obtained from resinous trees found in Eastern tropical countries. Placed upon a burning piece of charcoal in a thurible, it gives forth a heavy smoke of a most fragrant odor. It is symbolical of a good Christian's prayer, which ascends on high to the throne of God, and is pleasing in His sight. The Psalmist sings: "Let my prayer come like incense before You" (Ps. 140, 2).

In Christian tradition the clean wax of the candle is symbolic of the pure flesh of Christ, the wick an image of the soul of Christ, and the flame a figure of the divine personality of the Word made Flesh, "the true light that enlightens every man" (John 1, 9; 8, 12).

[2a] The candles that burn before the shrines of saints are symbolical of prayer and sacrifice. Those that burn around the dead, symbolize the faith of the Catholic, manifested before men by his good works. "So let your light shine before men, in order that they may see your good works, and give glory to your Father who is in heaven" (Matt. 5, 16).

What is the difference between a sacrament and a sacramental? What are some of your sacramentals?

[1] A sacrament is an outward sign instituted by Jesus Christ to give grace. A sacramental, on the other hand, is any blessing, ceremony, or religious article instituted by the Church for use in order to increase our devotion and to aid in our salvation. The sacraments contain and confer grace of themselves whereas the sacramentals, by reason of the intercession of the Church and of our own personal devotion, are helps to grace.

[2] Some of the sacramentals are:

1. *Blessings* as when the Church blesses the bride at her wedding and the mother after childbirth, people who are injured or sick, our homes, our food and drink, our fields and crops, our ships, automobiles, and airplanes.

2. *Blessed articles* such as ashes and palms, candles and holy water, crucifixes and pictures, medals, scapulars and rosaries.

3. *Ceremonies* as the consecration and dedication of churches.

[3] When the Church calls down God's blessing upon us and the things we use, she usually asks from God some benefit for soul or body, or protection against the world, the flesh and the devil. Thus the sacramentals are to help us live holy lives on earth and to use the things of this world for God's glory and for our own salvation.

Why are women required to wear a hat or a veil in a Catholic church?

[1a] Because it is an Apostolic custom, as we learn from St. Paul's letter to the Church of Corinth (1 Cor. 11, 3-16). He strongly denounces the Christian women of Corinth for presuming to come to church unveiled, accusing them of pride and arrogance unsuited to their sex. For he argues that by nature and God's law, woman is subject to her husband, and that the wearing of a veil is a sign of her dependence. "The head of the woman is the man"; "woman is the glory of man"; "man was not created for woman, but woman for man" (1 Cor. 11, 3. 6. 7. 9). To pray in church unveiled is insulting to the angels, and equivalent to hav-

ing the head shaved, a custom followed only by slaves in Greece, and by dancers and courtesans in Rome. After discussing the matter at some length, he ends by saying: "If anyone is disposed to be contentious, we have no such custom, neither have the Churches of God" (1 Cor. 11, 16). That is, if you cannot follow my subtle reasoning, let this suffice that you are going counter to the practice of all the other Churches.

What is meant by the churching of women?

[1] The churching of women is a blessing given by the priest to Catholic women after childbirth. The rite was probably suggested by the Jewish rite of purification of women after childbirth (Lev. 12). The contrast between the two rites is most striking, for whereas the Jewish mother was blessed to be freed from a legal defilement, the Christian mother comes before the altar to give thanks to God for her safe delivery. The ceremony consists of the recitation of Psalm 23, a special blessing with the sprinkling of holy water, and the beautiful prayer: "Almighty, Eternal God, who through the childbirth of the Blessed Virgin Mary has turned the sorrows of those who give birth into joy, look kindly upon Your handmaid, who has come to Your temple to give joyful thanks to You: and grant that after this life, through the merits and intercession of the same Blessed Virgin, she and her child may deserve to attain the joys of eternal blessedness. Through Christ our Lord."

[2] There is no church law requiring the churching of women, but the ritual calls it "a pious and laudable custom," that goes back to the earliest days of Christianity.

What is the difference between the Jewish Pasch and the Christian Easter? Why is Easter not kept on the same day every year?

[1a] The Jewish Pasch commemorated the Jewish Exodus from Egypt under Moses. It was kept on the fourteenth Nisan, and fell by turns on each day of the week.

[2a] The Christian Easter from Apostolic times commemorated the Resurrection of Christ, and was always kept on

a Sunday (Eusebius, *Hist. Eccles.*, v., 23). The Council of Nice decreed that this Sunday must follow the fourteenth day of the Paschal moon, that is, the moon whose fourteenth day followed the spring equinox. According to this rule, Easter Sunday is the first Sunday after the full moon which occurs on or next after March 21. The earliest possible date for Easter is March 22, the latest April 25.

Why do Catholics spend thousands and even millions on the building of their churches, when all around them are thousands of poor people sadly in need of even the necessaries of life?

[1] Because they know that their churches are really Houses of God, where Jesus Christ is really present. If men of the world who love their wives build magnificent homes for them when they can afford it, ought not the Catholic people build beautiful dwelling places for Christ, their Lord and King?

[2] The Jews in the Old Law were lavish with their gold and precious stones for the adorning of the Temple of Solomon (2 Par. 3, 4), which was merely a figure of the churches of the New Law.

This objection is on a par with the objection of Judas Iscariot, who found fault with Mary Magdalen for wasting the precious ointment on the feet of Jesus (John 12, 3-8). Our Lord praised her for her kindness and generosity, while St. John adds that Judas objected, "not that he cared for the poor, but because he was a thief."

[3] The Catholic Church has always been the great lover of the poor, and the Catholic priest, ever their truest friend, as the universal love of the poor for him abundantly proves. The money spent in church building is money well spent, for it is a practical, substantial proof of the Church's love of Christ, and of the poor, who are always welcome within her sanctuary.

[4] The modern non-churchgoer who says he can pray to God anywhere, as a matter of fact never prays at all. And the modern unbeliever is often the most hard hearted of mortals, believing with the old time pagan that it is silly to give monies in charity, for thereby you keep the poor longer in their misery.

SELECTED BIBLIOGRAPHY

AMIOT, FRANCOIS. *History of the Mass.* New York: Hawthorn Books. 1959.

CHEVROT, GEORGES. *Our Mass Explained from the Viewpoints of History, Theology, Piety.* Collegeville, Minn.: Liturgical Press. 1958.

ELLARD, GERALD. *The Mass in Transition.* Milwaukee: Bruce Publishing Co. 1956.

JUNGMANN, JOSEF A. *The Sacrifice of the Church.* Collegeville, Minn.: Liturgical Press. 1956.

———— *The Mass of the Roman Rite.* New York: Benziger Bros. 1959.

MERTON, THOMAS. *The Living Bread.* New York: Dell. 1959.

MILLER, JOHN H. *Fundamentals of the Liturgy.* Notre Dame, Ind.: Fides. 1960.

PARSCH, PIUS. *The Liturgy of the Mass, 3rd ed.* St. Louis: Herder Book Co. 1958.

———— *The Church's Year of Grace,* 5 Vols. Collegeville, Minn.: Liturgical Press.

PIUS XII, POPE. "The Sacred Liturgy" in *Four Great Encyclicals.* New York: (Deus Books) Paulist Press. 1961.

REINHOLD, HANS A. *Bringing the Mass to the People.* Baltimore: Helicon Press. 1960.

SULLIVAN, JOHN F. *The Externals of the Catholic Church. 2nd ed.* New York: P. J. Kenedy & Sons. 1959.

PART XII

The Blessed Virgin Mary

Can you prove from the Scriptures that the Virgin Mary was miraculously conceived? Does not your doctrine of the Immaculate Conception of the Virgin contradict the Scriptures, which teach that all men died in Adam (1 Cor. 15, 22; see Rom. 5, 12)? Is this not a new teaching of your Church, first proclaimed in 1854?

[1] We do not believe that the Virgin Mary was miraculously conceived. Her Son was born miraculously of a virgin Mother, but she herself had a real father and a real mother, St. Joachim and St. Anne. The doctrine means that at the very first instant when her soul was infused into her body, the Virgin Mary was sanctified by God's grace, so that her soul was never deprived of the sanctification, which all other creatures had forfeited by the sin of Adam. Her soul was never displeasing to God, because it had never been stained with original sin.

[2] On December 8, 1854, Pope Pius IX defined that "the doctrine which declares that the most Blessed Virgin Mary, in the first instant of her conception, by a singular grace and privilege of almighty God, in view of the merits of Jesus Christ, the Savior of the human race, was preserved exempt from all stain of original sin, is a doctrine revealed by God, and therefore must be believed firmly and constantly by all the faithful" (*Ineffabilis Deus*).

[3] The Scriptures nowhere expressly teach this doctrine, but Pius IX cites two passages, from which it may be inferred, if they are considered in the light of Catholic tradition. They are: "I will put enmity between you and the

woman, between your seed and her seed; he shall crush your head, and you shall lie in wait for his heel" (Gen. 3, 15). "Hail, full of grace, the Lord is with thee. Blessed art thou among women" (Luke 1, 28). Christ and His Mother are both spoken of as enemies of Satan and of sin: He, absolutely sinless as the Son of God, and she sinless, or full of grace, by God's special prerogative and gift.

⁴ The Blessed Virgin holds a unique position of dignity and pre-eminence in the writings of the early Fathers, many of whose statements would be exaggerated or untrue, had she been conceived in Original Sin. They imply her freedom from all sin by their insistence upon her perfect purity, and her position as the second Eve.

⁵ Of all the testimonies that might be given, St. Ephrem's (306-373) words of praise can only mean that Mary was immaculately conceived. He says that "she was as innocent as Eve before her fall, a Virgin most estranged from every stain of sin, more holy than the Seraphim, the sealed fountain of the Holy Ghost, the pure seed of God, ever in body and in mind intact and immaculate" (*Carmina Nisibena,* first discovered and published in 1866).

Why do you call the Virgin Mary the Mother of God instead of the Mother of Jesus? Can a human being be the Mother of the eternal God?

¹ Because the Sacred Scriptures plainly declare in many passages that the Blessed Virgin is the Mother of God. The angel Gabriel said to Mary: "Behold thou shalt conceive in thy womb, and shalt bring forth a Son, and thou shalt call His name Jesus. . . . The Holy Spirit shall come upon thee and the power of the Most High shall overshadow thee; and therefore, the Holy One to be born shall be called the Son of God" (Luke 1, 31-35). The saintly Elizabeth greeted Mary with the words: "And how have I deserved that the Mother of my Lord should come to me" (Luke 1, 43)? St. Paul says that "God sent His Son, born of a woman" (Gal. 4, 4).

² The Apostles' Creed professes: "And in Jesus Christ, His only Son our Lord, who was conceived by the Holy Spirit, born of the Virgin Mary." This belief was so firmly

accepted as divinely revealed, that the Council of Ephesus in 431 made it the standard of orthodoxy, excommunicating the Nestorian heretics who denied it.

[3] Non-Catholics who make Mary the Mother of Jesus do so, because they do not accept the true doctrine of the Incarnation, namely, that Jesus Christ possesses a divine and a human nature in one divine personality. Jesus was never a human person; He was a divine person who assumed our human nature in the womb of the Virgin Mary. She was the Mother of the Second Person of the Blessed Trinity, and therefore the Mother of God.

[4] As our mothers are not called the mothers of our bodies, but simply our mothers, because the soul directly created by God is united with the body in a human personality, so the Blessed Virgin is not called the Mother of the human nature of Christ, but simply the Mother of God, because the divine nature, eternally begotten of God the Father, is united with the human nature in the divine personality of Jesus Christ.

[5] Many Protestants do not know that both Luther and Calvin admitted the dogma of the divine maternity. Luther writes: "There is no honor, no beatitude, capable of approaching an elevation which consists in being, of the whole human race, the sole person, superior to all others, unequaled in the prerogative of having one Son in common with the heavenly Father" (*Deutsche Schriften,* xiv., 250). Calvin writes: "We cannot acknowledge the blessings brought us by Jesus without acknowledging at the same time how highly God honored and enriched Mary in choosing her for the Mother of God" (*Comm. sur l'Harm., Evang.,* 20).

Was not your dogma of the Virgin Birth taken over from paganism? Were not the gods of Mithra of Persia, Adonis of Syria, Osiris of Egypt and Krishna of India all virgin born?

[1] No, for although there are points of similarity between Christianity and the various pagan religions, the Virgin birth is certainly not one of them. The rationalist Harnack says: "The conjecture of Usener, that the idea of

the birth from a virgin is a heathen myth which was received by the Christians contradicts the entire development
of Christian tradition" (*History of Dogma,* i., 100).

[2] Mithra had no human mother at all, but was invariably
regarded as "rock-born," imaged by a conical stone which
represented the sky vault in which the light-god first appeared. Adonis, or Tammuz (Ezech. 8) was a demi-god,
representing the light of the sun. Various myths make
him the son of Cinyras, of Phoenix, and of King Theias of
Assyria and his daughter Myrrha. Osiris is either the son
of Seb (the Earth) and Nuït (the Sky), or begotten of the
heart of Atûm, the first of the gods and of men. Krishna,
the most popular of the avatars or incarnations of Vishnu,
was not virgin born, for the black god's mother had borne
several children to her husband Vasudeva, before he was
born. The legends that liken him to Christ are taken from
documents that post-date the Gospels by seven centuries.

[3] The ancient pagan myths are taken from nature, representing the succession of day and night, or of the seasons,
and the mystery of life and its transmission from one creature to another. They are undated, and unlocated, and
generally belong to a vaguely imagined period before the
coming of man. But the account of our Lord's birth has
the form, not of myth, but of history; place, date and contemporary persons and events are specified, and it is inter-
woven not only with the texture of general history, but
also with the events of our Lord's life in such a way as to
be inseparable from the Gospel account of them. As Martindale says: "Conscious adaptation of myth by the Gospel
writers is a grotesque supposition, neglected by reputable
scholarship; there was no time for an unconscious deforma-
tion of historical events in view of the early date now
generally admitted for the composition of the Gospels"
(*The Virgin Birth,* 30).

*Did not Christ speak harshly to the Virgin, saying to her
at the marriage of Cana: "What wouldst thou have me do,
woman" (John 2, 4)?*

[1] According to Father Lagrange the Arabs of Palestine
still use a similar expression: "What to thee?" It has a

twofold meaning, either "attend to your own affairs," or when said smilingly, "Do not worry, all will turn out well." This second meaning is certainly the meaning here, for Christ immediately works the miracle of changing water into wine at His Mother's request.

² The use of the word "woman" does not in the slightest degree imply any disrespect, or even emphasize as some have falsely held, the infinite distinction between Mary, the creature, and her divine Son. It is simply a solemn mode of addressing anyone, as we know from our Lord's use of it on the cross (John 19, 26).

Did not Christ disown His Mother, when He said, "My Mother and My brethren are they who hear the word of God, and act upon it" (Luke 8, 21)?

¹ᵃ Not at all. He is simply taking occasion of the presence of His Mother and cousins to teach the people the necessity of keeping the word of God, as Mary did (Luke 1, 38. 45; 2, 19. 51), and the necessity of detachment from even one's relatives for the love of God. Tertullian writes: "Christ is wont to do everything that He enjoins upon others. How strange then would it certainly have been if, while He was teaching others not to esteem mother or father or brother as highly as the word of God, He were Himself to leave the word of God as soon as His Mother and brethren were announced to Him. He denied His parents, therefore, in the same sense in which He has taught us to deny ours—for God's sake" (*De Carne Christi*, 7).

How can you claim that Mary was always a virgin, when the Scriptures often speak of the brethren of Jesus (Matt. 12, 46-50; Mark 3, 31-35; Luke 8, 19-21; John 7, 3-10; Acts 1, 14)?

¹ᵇ The dogma of the Virgin Birth was defined as an article of faith by the Fifth General Council held at Constantinople under Pope Vigilius in 553, and again by the Lateran Council held by Pope Martin I at Rome in 640. It is a dogma held unanimously by the Fathers of the Church from the very beginning, and taught explicitly in both the Old Testament and the New.

[2] The New Testament teaches the Virgin Birth in the Gospels of St. Matthew and St. Luke. "Do not be afraid, Joseph, to take to thee Mary thy wife, for that which is begotten in her is of the Holy Spirit" (Matt. 1, 20). "The angel was sent from God . . . to a virgin betrothed to a man named Joseph" (Luke 1, 26. 27).

[3] The Fathers of the first four centuries all teach the Virgin Birth: St. Justin Martyr (*Apol.,* xxxi., 46; *Dial. cum Tryp.,* 85); Aristides, (*Apol.*); St. Irenaeus (*Adv. Haer.,* v., 19); Origen (*Hom.,* vii., *In Lucam*); St. Hilary (*In Matt.,* i., 3), St. Epiphanius (*Adv. Haer.,* lxxviii., 1-7; St. Jerome (*Adv. Helv.*). They argue that "the brethren of the Lord" were not Mary's children: (1) her virginity was implied by her answer to the angel, "How shall this happen, since I do not know man" (Luke 1, 34)? (2) If Mary had other children, why is Jesus so emphatically called, *"the* Son of Mary" (Mark 6, 3) and why is Mary never called the Mother of the brethren of the Lord? (3) If Mary had other children, why should Jesus, at His crucifixion, have entrusted His Mother to the care of St. John? (John 19, 26-27.)

[4] The word "brother" in itself proves nothing, for it had a very wide meaning among the Jews. It is used in the Old Testament for relatives in general (Job 19, 13—14), nephews (Gen. 29, 15), distant cousins (Lev. 10, 4), and first cousins (1 Par. 23, 21. 22). Besides there was no word in Hebrew or Aramaic for cousin, so that the Old Testament writers were forced to use the word *AH,* brother, to describe different degrees of kindred. For example, Jacob, speaking of his cousin Rachel, calls himself her father's brother, rather than style himself the son of her father's sister, the only way he could in Hebrew describe his real relationship (Gen. 29, 12). It is certain, therefore, that if Jesus had cousins, especially if they were born of the same mother, they had to be called in the Aramaic tongue, His brethren.

Why do Catholics claim that the Virgin Mary never committed sin, when the Bible says: "If we say that we have no sin, we deceive ourselves, and the truth is not in us" (1 John 1, 8)?

[1] Catholics believe that the Blessed Virgin was free from all actual sin because of divine tradition confirmed by the Council of Trent. St. Augustine says: "Except, therefore, the Holy Virgin Mary, about whom, on account of the honor of our Lord, I will not allow the question to be entertained, when sins are under discussion—for how do we know what increase of grace was bestowed on her, to enable her to overcome sin in every way" (*De Natura et Gratia*, 36).

[2] The Council of Trent defines: "If anyone says that man once justified can during his whole life avoid all sins, even venial ones, as the Church holds that the Blessed Virgin did by special privilege of God, let him be anathema" (Sess. vi., can. 23).

[3] Is it not reasonable to suppose that our Blessed Lord, by the bestowal of special graces, would surely preserve His own Mother from the smallest sin?

Is the Assumption of the Blessed Virgin into heaven a dogma of the faith? Did Mary die? Is there any historical or Biblical proof for this dogma?

[1a] On Nov. 1, 1950, Pope Pius XII solemnly declared: "We pronounce, declare, and define it to be a divinely revealed dogma: that the Immaculate Mother of God, the ever Virgin Mary, having completed the course of her earthly life, was assumed body and soul into heavenly glory." (Four Marian Encyclicals, *Munificentissimus Deus*, par. 44, p. 42. New York, N. Y.: Paulist Press, 1959.)

[2a] Catholics, then, must believe that Mary was taken up to heaven, body as well as soul, at the end of her life on earth. The dogma carefully avoids the question as to whether Mary died or not. The more common and more probable opinion is that she did, both because she had a mortal body and, in order to be like her divine Son, by offering her sufferings and death for us. Thus, her death would not have been as a punishment for sin. However, we must admit that God *could* have granted her the gift of immortality.

[3a] The Assumption, since it is a dogma, must belong to the deposit of revelation. How are we sure? Pius XII says the best guarantee (before the infallible definition) was the

fact that it was believed with a moral unanimity by all Catholics—faithful and Bishops alike—as part of revelation. This unanimity "in an entirely certain and infallible way, manifested this privilege as a truth revealed by God, and contained in that divine deposit. . . ." (*ibid*. par. 12, p. 23). That is, since the Holy Spirit is keeping the Church from error, such a belief is only understandable if it conforms with the facts.

⁴ There is no historical testimony to the Assumption before the middle of the 6th century, at which time the testimonies and devotion to the Assumption begin to multiply rapidly. This simply means that a teaching, implicitly and obscurely contained in the deposit of revelation, now, under the guidance of the Holy Spirit and the maturing consciousness of Christ's message in the living Church, began to grow more manifest and explicit.

⁵ Scripture contains no explicit testimony to the fact of the Assumption, but several texts give a legitimate and solid foundation—especially when viewed in the light of Patristic interpretation and other Church teachings regarding Mary. Genesis 3, 15 taken together with several texts of St. Paul (*e.g.* Rom. 5) and the constant tradition of Mary as the new Eve, show us Mary closely associated with Christ in His victory over sin and death. Does it not also indicate her personal triumph over death by being taken to heaven? Luke 1, 28 testifies to Mary's "fullness of grace" and may well indicate that final grace and perfection of being assumed body and soul into heaven. Finally, Apocalypse 12, 1. 14-17: "And a great sign appeared in heaven: a woman clothed with the sun, and the moon was under her feet and upon her head a crown of twelve stars. . . ." There is a growing agreement today that this vision of St. John refers in the literal sense not only to the Church, but also to the Blessed Virgin.

⁶ By themselves, these texts would probably never have led to the belief in the Assumption. But viewed in the living Tradition of the Church they take on new depth and meaning. Pius XII sums up the best scriptural argument for the Assumption in the following words: "Just as the glorious resurrection of Christ was an essential part and the final sign of this victory, so that struggle which was

common to the Blessed Virgin and her divine Son should be brought to a close by the glorification of her virginal body, for the same Apostle (Paul) says: 'when this mortal thing puts on immortality, then shall come to pass the word that is written: Death is swallowed up in victory' (1 Cor. 54f.)." (*Ibid.* par. 39f.) Thus, by her Assumption, body and soul, into heaven, does Mary achieve that final degree of triumph over sin and death mentioned by St. Paul and willed for her by God.

How can Catholics call the Blessed Virgin "Queen"? Is it meant in the metaphorical or real sense? Does it imply some equality with Christ the King?

[1] The queenship of Mary is not a dogma of the faith, but all Catholics accept it. It has been a traditional title in the Church as far back as the 6th century, and similar titles such as "sovereign lady" go back even further. St. Andrew of Crete (d. 740) calls her "Queenly Mother of God." St. Bernard (d. 1153): "All generations shall call you blessed, O Mother of God, O Queen of the world, O Queen of heaven." Examples could be multiplied indefinitely. And many ancient prayers of the liturgy are addressed to Mary as Queen. Great numbers of Popes have spoken explicitly of her as Queen, *e.g.* Pius IX: "She has been appointed by God to be the Queen of heaven and earth, and is exalted above all the choirs of angels and classes of saints" (*Ineffabilis Deus,* 1854). The confirmation of this title has been traditionally found in Apoc. 12, 1 which speaks of "a woman clothed with the sun, and the moon was under her feet, and upon her head a crown of twelve stars." Many scholars today think that this vision of St. John refers in the literal sense to Mary as well as to the Church.

[2] A woman might be given the honorary title "queen" for her beauty, and a ship metaphorically styled "queen of the sea" for its speed. And in this sense, too, Mary could be called queen by reason of her excellence, being "full of grace" (Luke 1, 28).

[3] But Mary's queenship is not limited to this. She is queen in the real and proper sense—and by two different claims to the title.

1. She is Mother of Christ the King, of whose "kingdom there will be no end" (Luke 1, 31-33). And every mother of a king merits the title of queen by *natural* right.

2. Just as Christ, king already by birth, has another claim to kingship by His conquest of sin and the devil, so Mary by sharing with her divine Son in this victory, merits by an *acquired* right her name as queen (implied in Gen. 3, 15, especially as seen in the tradition of the early Fathers: Mary is the new Eve who helps the new Adam, Christ, undo the harm wrought by the first Adam and his co-helper Eve).

4 Thus, theologians teach that just as Christ is King by birth as Son of God incarnate, and by right of conquest in the Redemption; so also Mary is Queen by natural right as Mother of God, and by acquired right by reason of conquest.

5 However, Catholics firmly hold that although this queenship has the same extension as our Lord's kingship—namely, over all angels and men—nevertheless, Mary's role is always *subordinate* to that of Christ, and there is no sharing of equal authority. Whatever power and rule Mary has as Queen is given her by her divine Son.

6 Exactly how does she exercise her queenship over us? All agree that she exercises this power and rule by her unique role of intercessor on our behalf, obtaining graces for us by her powerful intercession. Any queen mother would be most influential with her son the king, and Mary most of all.

7 Many theologians, stressing in addition Mary's queenship by acquired right also insist on the rights she has, under Christ, by reason of conquest; whereby she would have the right—though always conformed to the divine will —of distributing graces to whom she wills. Some would even concede her a certain place alongside Christ at the last judgment; but this is a matter of opinion.

Do Catholics adore the Virgin Mary, and consider her omnipresent, so that she can answer their prayers?

1 No, Catholics adore God alone, Father, Son and Holy Spirit. They love and reverence the Blessed Virgin, be-

cause God honored her above all creatures by choosing her to be the Mother of His only Son. St. Epiphanius in the 4th century condemned the Collyridians, the only sect in history, who gave her divine honors, saying: "We do not adore the saints. . . . Let Mary then be honored, but the Father, Son and Holy Spirit alone be adored" (*Adv. Collyrid.*, 29).

[2] God alone is omnipresent. The power of the Blessed Virgin to know our particular wants, and to answer our prayers no more implies omnipresence than my power to grant the request of a friend thousands of miles away implies my presence in that place.

Why do Catholics pay so much honor to Mary, when she was only an ordinary woman? Does not Catholic devotion to her detract from the worship due to Christ?

[1] The Catholic Church has always paid special honor to the Blessed Virgin, because God honored her above all creatures by bestowing upon her the highest dignity He could confer—the divine maternity. The Scriptures tell us that Jesus honored her by dwelling with her under the same roof at Nazareth for thirty years until He began His public ministry, and that He showed His love to her on the cross, when He left her to the kindly care of His beloved disciple, St. John (John 19, 26). How can intelligent men hope to extol the Son of God by making little of the Mother of God. We do not win the affections of our fellow men by despising or making little of their mothers.

[2a] How can you call Mary an ordinary woman, and at the same time pretend that you have studied the Scriptures? Would God choose an ordinary woman to be the Mother of His only Son, when He had countless millions of women to choose from? The prophet Isaias spoke of her coming centuries before (Isaias 7, 14), and God sent from heaven a special ambassador to announce her supereminent dignity (Luke 1, 26), and another to comfort St. Joseph in his doubting (Matt. 1, 20). Both the angel and St. Elizabeth called her "blessed among women" (Luke 1, 28), and her own prophecy that "henceforth all generations shall call me blessed" (Luke 1, 48) is fulfilled to the letter every day by Catholics the world over.

[3] Instead of detracting from the love of Christ, devotion to Mary increases our love for Him. The devout client of Mary is ever the strong defender of the divinity of Jesus Christ, her Son. The divine maternity, as the Council of Ephesus clearly recognized in 431, has ever been the standard of orthodox belief in the true doctrine of the Incarnation.

[4] Love for Mary, the masterpiece of God's creation, by its very nature leads us to the love of Christ her Son. He cannot be jealous of the praise we give her, for every one of her privileges and prerogatives are His own free gift. Is the artist jealous of the praise you give his masterpiece? Is the author jealous of the praise you give his book?

Are not some of the expressions used by Catholic writers in speaking of the Blessed Virgin inaccurate and blasphemous?

[1] An intelligent Catholic always distinguishes carefully the language of devotion from the language of dogma, and instinctively interprets an exaggerated expression of some pious writer by the exact wording of the creed, the catechism or a manual of theology.

[2] St. Alphonsus, for example, wrote his *Glories of Mary* for the simple, uneducated, and imaginative peasant of Southern Italy. You may reject the legends he records if you will, but do not forget that his doctrine regarding the Blessed Virgin is thoroughly Catholic from start to finish. Let me quote a few passages. "No one denies that Jesus is the only Mediator of justice, who alone by His merits reconciles us with God." . . . "It would be a serious error to believe that God could not give us grace without the intercession of Mary." . . . "We acknowledge that God is the only Source of good, and that Mary is only a creature; all she has received is due to the grace of God."

Why do Catholics pray to the Virgin and the saints? Is not Christ the one Mediator of God and men (1 Tim. 2, 5) and our one Advocate with the Father (1 John 2, 1)?

[1a] The Church's teaching on the invocation of the saints is thus defined by the Council of Trent. "The saints, who reign together with Christ, offer up their own prayers to

God for men. It is good and useful suppliantly to invoke them, and to have recourse to their prayers, aid and help for obtaining benefits from God, through His Son Jesus Christ, who alone is our Redeemer and Savior. Those persons think impiously who deny that the saints, who enjoy eternal happiness in heaven, are to be invoked; who assert that they do not pray for men; who declare that asking them to pray for each of us in particular is idolatry, repugnant to the word of God, and opposed to the honor of the one Mediator of God and men, Christ Jesus."

² The Old and New Testament plainly teach the principle and the practice of asking the prayers of our brethren, especially of the just (James 5, 16-18). God commanded Abimelech to ask Abraham's prayers: "He will pray for you that you may live" (Gen. 20, 7. 17). God had mercy on the sinful children of Israel in the desert because Moses interceded for them (Ps. 15, 23). God said to the friends of Job: "My servant Job shall pray for you; his face I will accept" (Job 42, 8). St. Paul in his letters continually asked the brethren to pray for him (Rom. 15, 30).

³ Is it reasonable to suppose that the Christian, who prayed for his brethren while upon earth, will lose all interest in them, once he reaches the kingdom of heaven? The Christian tradition from the beginning declares that the interest of the saints in heaven will be increased a hundredfold, because they will realize then more fully our needs and necessities, and God's willingness to hearken to their intercession. St. Jerome (340-420) is a striking witness to this fact. He writes: "If Apostles and martyrs, while still in the flesh and still needing to care for themselves, can pray for others, how much more will they pray for others after they have won their crowns, their victories, their triumphs. Moses, one man, obtains God's pardon for six hundred thousand armed men, and Stephen prays for his persecutors. When they are with Christ will they be less powerful? St. Paul says that two hundred and seventy-six souls were granted to his prayers, whilst they were in the ship with him. Shall he close his lips after death, and not utter a syllable for those who throughout the world have believed in his gospel? (*Adv. Vigil,* 6.)

⁴ Catholics firmly believe in the unique mediatorship of Jesus Christ (1 Tim. 2, 5), and the Council of Trent emphasizes this very doctrine when declaring her teaching on the invocation of saints. Catholics believe that Jesus Christ alone redeemed us by His death upon the cross, thus reconciling us to God, and making us partakers of His grace here and His glory hereafter. No divine gift can reach us except through Christ and the merits of His sacred passion. Therefore, every prayer we pray, and every prayer in heaven of the Blessed Virgin, the angels and the saints, have their efficacy only through Jesus Christ our Lord. The saints simply add their prayers to ours, and, although specially pleasing to God because of their greater holiness, they aid us only through the merits of the one Mediator.

Is not Christ the Redeemer of the whole human race and the one Mediator between God and men? Why then do Catholics make Mary equal to Christ by calling her "coredemptrix" and "mediatrix of all graces?" I cannot accept this idolatrous teaching.

¹ Mary is a creature totally dependent upon God for all that she is and for all that she possesses. God created Mary; Christ redeemed her; the Holy Spirit sanctified her. Christ is a divine person; Mary is a human person. This is the belief of all Catholics. And anyone who would say that Mary is divine (idolatry) or that she is equal to Christ (blasphemy) would immediately be branded a heretic. Nevertheless, it is Catholic doctrine that Mary is truly "coredemptrix" and "mediatrix of all graces."

² We can properly understand Mary's role in redemption by reflecting on what Christ, by redeeming us, enabled us to do. On Calvary Christ made satisfaction for all sin, merited salvation for all men, and offered to His Father a sacrifice infinitely pleasing which has been accepted in favor of all mankind. But the Council of Trent reminds us that "although He died indeed for all, not all, however, profit by His death, but only those to whom the merit of His passion is communicated." Men receive redemption, not as a gift merely coming from Christ, but as grace incorporating them into Christ. They receive it by becoming

one with Christ who saves them. When we receive justification, by baptism into the death of Christ, we receive the power of meriting and of making satisfaction. "He is the vine, we are the branches; and as the branches cannot bear fruit unless they remain in the vine, so we can do nothing unless we abide in Christ. And as no one would be so foolish as to say that this detracts from the glory of the vine that its branches bear much fruit, so no one, unless altogether stupid, can say that it detracts from the glory of Christ if His servants, by His grace, through His Spirit, and through faith and charity inspired by Him should do works of such worth that the just Judge owes them a crown of glory. . . . The merits of men are required not because of the insufficiency of Christ's merits, but because of their greater efficacy. . . . He merited for us the power of meriting" (St. Robert Bellarmine).

[3] If all the redeemed can do this, namely, merit and make satisfaction, why not Mary who was perfectly redeemed by Christ? If our merit and satisfaction can be offered for others, accepted by God for others, then Mary's merit and satisfaction which, performed as the Mother of Christ, are much more abundant than ours can also be offered for others. Father Mersch sums up this beautiful teaching clearly, "Christ alone is the Redeemer. But in communicating His life to His members, He communicates to them something of His quality as Redeemer. This quality He communicates especially to her who is united to Christ's members more closely than any other, that is, to His mother, who thus becomes the co-redemptrix. This title which is attributed to the Blessed Virgin shows clearly that the fact of being redeemed does not prevent one from redeeming" (*The Theology of the Mystical Body*).

[4] In Christ is the source of all graces. But just as God willed that Christ should come to all men through Mary so Christ willed that all His graces should come to all men through Mary. Being the Mother of Christ and the Mother of men she deserves to be the proper channel of all grace between her Son and His members. As Christ is the one Mediator between God and men so Mary is the one "mediatrix" between Christ and all those whom He has redeemed.

SELECTED BIBLIOGRAPHY

ATTWATER, DONALD. *A Dictionary of Mary.* New York: P. J. Kenedy & Sons. 1956.

BERNARD, ROGATIANUS. *The Mystery of Mary.* St. Louis: B. Herder Book Co. 1960.

CAROL, JUNIPER B. *Mariology. 2 Vols.* Milwaukee: Bruce Publishing Co. 1957.

CYRIL, BERNARD. *Mother of God.* New York: Macmillan. 1957.

DANIELOU, JEAN. *The Angels and Their Mission, According to the Fathers of the Church.* Westminster, Md.: Newman Press. 1957.

DANIEL-ROPS, HENRI. *The Book of Mary.* New York: Hawthorn Books. 1960.

FLICOTEAUX, EMMANUEL. *Our Lady in the Liturgy.* Baltimore: Helicon. 1959.

FRIETHOFF, CASPER. *A Complete Mariology.* Westminster, Md.: Newman Press. 1958.

LAURENTIN, RENE. *Our Lady and the Mass.* New York: Macmillan. 1960.

LOCHET, LOUIS. *Apparitions of Our Lady.* New York: Herder & Herder. 1960.

MCNAMARA, KEVIN. (ed.) *Mother of the Redeemer.* New York: Sheed & Ward. 1960.

NEUBERT, EMILE N. *Life of Union With Mary.* Milwaukee: Bruce Publishing Co. 1959.

PIUS XII, POPE. *Four Marian Encyclicals.* New York: Paulist Press. 1959.

REGAMEY, PIE R. *What Is An Angel?* New York: Hawthorn Books. 1960.

SCHORSCH, ALEXANDER P. *Our Lord and Our Lady.* New York: Philosophical Library. 1957.

PART XIII
Religious Orders

Are there not many divisions and sects in the Catholic Church such as the Franciscans, the Dominicans, the Jesuits?

[1] No, religious orders are not, like the denominations of Protestantism, independent sects with creeds of their own devising. They are bodies of men that have arisen at different ages of Church history to give men the example of a particular virtue like the poverty of the Franciscan or the obedience of the Jesuit, and while living the life of the counsels of Christ, to carry on a special work of charity, education, or missionary activity. Every order believes in every teaching of the Catholic faith; they differ only in matters of opinion, wherein every Catholic is free. As Cardinal Newman says: "Augustinians, Dominicans, Franciscans, Jesuits and Carmelites, have indeed their respective homes and schools, but they have, in spite of all that, a common school and a common home in their Mother's bosom; . . . Quarrels, stopping short of divisions, but prove the strength of combination; they are the token, not of the languor, but of the vigor of life. . . . The doctrines of faith are the common basis of the combatants, the ground on which they contend, their ultimate authority, and their arbitrating rule" (*Difficulties of Anglicans*, i., 261).

I do not find religious orders mentioned in the Bible. Are they essential to Christianity? Why should so many Catholics retire from the world and live a cloistered life, refus-

*ing to bear their burdens of the world's responsibilities,
when Christ said: "Let your light shine before men, in
order that they may see your good works" (Matt. 5, 16)?*

[1] There is indeed no mention of religious orders in the
Bible, but the ideas and principles that prompted their
founding are clearly set forth in the life and teaching of
Christ, whom they endeavor to follow in the way of perfection. While the vast majority of Christians are content to
keep the Ten Commandments, there will always be an élite
few in the true Church who will endeavor to observe the
counsels of perfection which the Lord commended so
highly. "You therefore are to be perfect, even as your
heavenly Father is perfect" (Matt. 5, 48), said Christ, and
He expressly pointed out to His followers the two special
counsels of perfection, chastity and poverty. "Let him accept it who can" (Matt. 19, 12). "If thou wilt be perfect,
go, sell what thou hast, and give to the poor, and thou
shalt have treasure in heaven; and come, follow Me" (Matt.
19, 21).

[2] The religious orders are not essential to Christianity,
for the Pope could suppress them all tomorrow, as Pope
Clement XIV suppressed the Jesuits in 1773, and the
Church would still exist in all her divine doctrine, law
and worship. But the religious orders are the natural
flower and fruit of the tree of God's planting. Men and
women join them in response to a divine call, whereby
they pledge themselves to strive after perfection, living
under an approved rule that helps them to love God more
perfectly and all men for His sake.

[3] The text cited is irrelevant. Our Lord was simply
teaching His disciples that a good Christian life gives the
world the best possible proof of the truth of the Christian
Gospel. The many saints of the religious orders have indeed let the light of their good works shine amid the darkness of a world of sin, and have thus glorified their Father
who is in heaven.

*Are not religious vows contrary to evangelical freedom?
Are not vows a degrading slavery, men promising God
something they know is impossible?*

[1] No. The religious vows of poverty, chastity and obedience are means which a person freely takes to help him follow Christ more closely. They free him from the slavery of greed, lust and pride, and unite him more intimately to his Savior. No person is more free to love God wholeheartedly than a person who has taken religious vows. He has joyfully surrendered his possessions, his body and his will to serve God heroically from whom he received these things as gifts.

[2] The Church does not permit a person to take religious vows except after a long period of severe training and testing in virtuous living. It then remains for the person to decide for himself if he is convinced God wants him to follow the more perfect way. To take the vows is to exercise an act of the highest freedom—freely to give up all for love of Christ.

[3] This consecration is something difficult but not impossible. The grace of God is always at hand to strengthen us along the way to complete spiritual freedom. Those who so dedicate themselves are the most carefree and happy people in the whole world. Visit a monastery or convent and you will find out for yourself that these people are truly free, with hearts filled with love of God and neighbor.

Were not the monks of the Middle Ages a lazy, ignorant and immoral set of men?

[1a] The medieval monks reclaimed millions of acres of desert and marsh land in every country of Europe; they copied thousands of manuscripts of the Bible, the early Fathers, the Greek and Latin classics; they founded many famous schools — Lerins, Marmoutier, Tours, Clonard, Clonmacnois, Bangor, Fulda, St. Gall, Reichenau, Jarrow, Wearmouth and York; they gathered together valuable libraries; they practiced every possible form of charity toward the poor, the sick, the leper, the prisoner; they won to the Church by their missionary labors England, Ireland, Scotland, France, Germany, Flanders, and the greater part of Italy. Our Lord told us to judge a tree by its fruits (Matt. 7, 17).

[2] It of course happened at times that monasteries declined in fervor, especially when kings and nobles put their

unworthy favorites in charge, but the Popes and the Bishops were ever on the alert, and reform, often inaugurated by a saint, soon became the order of the day. Civilization owes the monks a debt it never can repay.

Why are not your convents open to public inspection? Are not nuns detained in your convents against their will?

[1] Because they are private homes. The State has the right to inspect its schools, its penitentiaries, its hospitals and its institutions for the insane, the mentally defective, etc., in order to see that its appropriations are well spent, and to correct abuses that occur from time to time. It has no right whatever to invade the privacy of a man's home, unless there is grave suspicion of a crime. Convents are regularly inspected by the Bishop of the diocese, and by the superiors of the various communities. They may be visited by anyone who is properly authorized.

[2] No one is obliged to enter a convent; no one is detained therein against her will. In many communities the sisters renew their vows from year to year; and even in the strictest orders the nuns may obtain a dispensation from their solemn vows, once they discover they have no vocation. Convent life is not a refuge for emotional women, disappointed in love or overwhelmed with some great sorrow, as many non-Catholics seem to think. Some of the liveliest and most attractive young women, blessed with everything this world holds dear, have given up their homes and kindred despite the bitterest opposition, to labor among the people in China or Japan, or to care for the abandoned children of the African natives. It is a divine vocation to spend one's life in the service of Christ's brethren; it is a mark of the true Church that she is able in every age to fill her cloistered convents with women, who, by their constant prayers and ascetic life, make up for the sins and worldliness of the outside world.

Were not unchaste nuns walled-up alive in the Middle Ages?

[1a] No, this is a stock calumny of anti-Catholic lecturers, whose only authority is the episode introduced into Sir

Walter Scott's poem, *Marmion*. Father Thurston, who has studied this matter thoroughly writes: "To anyone who honestly looks into the matter, it will be clear that no statutes of any religious order have yet been brought forward which prescribe such punishment; that the few traditions that speak of the discovery of walled-up remains crumble away the moment they are examined; that the growth of the tradition itself can be abundantly accounted for; that the few historians or antiquaries of repute whether Catholic or Protestant, either avowedly disbelieve the calumny, or studiously refrain from repeating it" (*The Myth of the Walled-up Nun*).

Did not Henry VIII dissolve the English monasteries because of their gross immorality?

[1a] No, this was merely a pretext for confiscating their properties. The chief accusers of the English monks—Layton, Leigh, Ap Rice and London—were men whom no one could believe under oath. As the *Athenæum* remarked in a critique of Gairdner's Letters and Papers (November 27, 1886): "Seldom in the world's history has a tyrant found baser instruments for his basest designs than Henry found for carrying out the visitation of the English monasteries. That any monastery in England contained half a dozen such wretches as the more prominent visitors who came to despoil them is almost inconceivable. The reader is in danger of disbelieving everything that these men report, in his indignation at the audacious and manifest lying which characterizes their reports."

Does not the Jesuitical system of casuistry with its immoral doctrine of probability undermine the ethics of the Gospel? Did not Pascal ridicule the moral teaching of the Jesuits? Do not the Jesuits teach that the end justifies the means?

[1b] There is nothing in the teaching of moral theology that undermines the ethics of the Gospel. The Ten Commandments and the fundamental Christian virtues have always been clearly taught and fully explained by the Catholic Church in the light of a divine and infallible tradition, so that the Catholic conscience has never been the

slave of a shifty, unethical public opinion. While the way of perfection is set forth in our ascetical and mystical writers, the moral theologians are concerned with the minimum of duty, writing as they do for confessors, who are bound to insist only upon that which is of absolute obligation.

² Casuistry in morals corresponds to case law and precedent in our law courts. It is merely the application in a particular case of the general principles of Catholic ethics. It has always existed in the Church, and is in no sense a creation of the Jesuits, although they have done much to systematize its findings. St. Paul, for example, was a casuist, when he decided many a moral question in his Epistles, such as the eating of meat sacrificed to idols, the fact of women wearing veils in church, and the right of separation. Many moral questions were discussed by the early Fathers, the Popes and the Bishops, the particular and general councils of the Church.

³ Pascal's satirical charges consisted of "an almost complete misrepresentation of Jesuit teaching, a conglomeration of interpolations, omissions, citations lifted from their contexts, and falsified texts" (Harney, *The Jesuits in History*). His tirades against probabilism were most unfair, for the doctrine is plain common sense. Suppose, for instance, that I have a serious, outstanding doubt about the existence of a certain law, obliging me to act in a particular case. Although I know it exists, I honestly doubt whether it touches my case. I have done my best to obtain certainty, and cannot obtain it; I have carefully weighed all the circumstances; I find I have good arguments from reason, and grave authorities against the law. I certainly then have a probable opinion that this law, being doubtful, has no binding obligation. What could be more reasonable?

⁴ The Jesuits have never held that the end justifies the means. In common with all Catholic moralists they teach that an end, no matter how good, can never justify a means that is morally evil. One cannot do evil that good may come (Rom. 3, 8). For example, I cannot steal to give to the poor, because this is to serve a good end with bad means.

⁵ If this calumny were true, why is it that bitter anti-Jesuits, like Pascal in the 17th and Döllinger in the 19th century, never dared mention it in their charges against Jesuit morality? If this calumny were true, why is it that no one has been able to point out this teaching in any approved author? The thousand florins offered by the Jesuit Father Roh in 1852, and the two thousand florins offered by the German deputy Dasbach in 1903 to anyone who would prove that this immoral principle was stated in any Jesuit book, has never been forfeited. The apostate Jesuit, Count von Hoensbroech took up the challenge in his book, *Der Zweck heiligt die Mittel,* and even appealed to the courts to claim the reward. The Court of first instance and the Cologne Court of Appeals both ruled against him, on the ground that the passages adduced from Jesuit authors did not contain the sentence, "the end justifies the means, either formally or materially" (Mausbach, *Catholic Moral Teaching*).

I was shocked to learn that Pope Pius XII favored Secular Institutes. Have you Catholics abandoned us Protestants in fighting secularism? I thought you considered Secularism even more dangerous than Communism.

¹ Pius XII urged the establishment of Secular Institutes to combat secularism. They are societies of lay men and women who profess and practice the evangelical counsels of poverty, chastity and obedience while *remaining in the world,* (hence, the word *secular* meaning world). These men and women are not monks or nuns. They do not live in monasteries or convents. They do not wear a religious garb. More than ten such Institutes have already been formed in the United States. The members, staying in the world, pray and work for their own holiness and for the sanctity of others. Just as there are secular (belonging to a diocese like Brooklyn or Chicago) and religious (belonging to a Community like the Jesuits or Paulists) priests so there are Secular (members live in the world) and Religious (members live in monasteries and convents) Institutes.

² The Catholic Church is the avowed enemy of secu-

larism which would remove God from the American scene and keep Him from having any influence on the daily lives of people. The policy of secularists is to ignore God as if He did not exist. They would have heaven or hell on this earth with nothing beyond death. Secular Institutes, on the other hand, try to make people more conscious of God, more aware of His loving care, and more alert to obey His law.

[3] Secularism is more dangerous than Communism because it pretends to cherish the Constitution and to promote the American way of life. It infects "nice" people who abhor Communism, who detest violence, and who readily defend freedom and the rights of man. Secularism is a creeping, crippling disease which eats away the spiritual foundations of America without our realizing its deadly effects. As termites topple big structures which appear strong, so Secularism can destroy our country. Communism is more open in its purpose and attack. We clearly see it as an enemy and we fortify ourselves against it. But secularism is sometimes hard to detect and, for this reason, we must be more vigilant to forestall its harm. Unless we are dedicated to God and faithful to our religious duties, our nation cannot be morally strong and spiritually healthy.

SELECTED BIBLIOGRAPHY

BURKE, THOMAS J. *Catholic Missions.* New York: Fordham University Press. 1957.

CANALS, SALVADOR. *Secular Institutes and the State of Perfection.* Chicago: Scepter. 1959.

CANU, JEAN. *Religious Orders of Men.* New York: Hawthorn Books. 1960.

MERTON, THOMAS. *The Silent Life.* New York: Dell. 1959.

MOORE, THOMAS VERNER. *Heroic Sanctity and Insanity.* New York: Grune & Stratton. 1959.

MOSS, DOLEY C. *Of Cell and Cloister.* Milwaukee: Bruce Publishing Co. 1957.

NIGGS, WALTER G. *Warriors of God.* New York: Alfred Knopf. 1959.

PERINELLE, JOSEPH. *God's Highways.* Westminster, Md.: Newman Press. 1958.

PART XIV
The Future Life

How do you know this world will come to an end? Did Christ prophesy when this would happen? Will not God warn us? Does not the "secret" of Fatima concern the time of the world's dissolution?

[1] We know that the world will come to an end because such is part of divine revelation. Christ said: "Behold, I am with you all days, even unto the consummation of the world" (Matt. 28, 20). He did not prophesy when the end will come; rather He stressed the fact that "of that day and hour no one knows, not even the angels of heaven, but the Father only" (Matt. 24, 36). There will be certain warnings or signs however, such as the preaching of the Gospel to the whole world (Matt. 24, 14), the conversion of the Jews (Rom. 11, 26), the appearance of an anti-Christ (2 Thess, 2, 3), and many widespread catastrophies (Matt. 24, 24-29). The world, as we know it, will be destroyed but will exist again in a new manner: " 'And I saw a new heaven and a new earth. For the first heaven and the first earth passed away, . . . the former things have passed away.' And he who was sitting on the throne said, 'Behold, I make all things new' " (Apoc. 21, 1-5).

[2] In view of the fact that God has reserved this knowledge to Himself, it is not likely that the "secret" of Fatima makes such a revelation.

Is there a probation after death? How do you prove from the Bible that there is a Judgment immediately after death? If there is, what need is there of a General Judgment?

¹ Death brings to an end a person's probation. It excludes the possibility of further merit or demerit. "Night is coming when no man can work" (John 9, 4).

² Immediately after death there takes place what we call the Particular Judgment. "Call no man happy before his death, for by how he ends, a man is known" (Ecclus. 11, 28). Our Lord illustrates this fact with His story of Dives and Lazarus (Luke 16, 19-31) and He promised the dying good thief, "this day you shall be with Me in paradise" (Luke 23, 43). St. Paul warns us that after death comes the judgment (Heb. 9, 27). Jesus Christ judges us and His sentence is definitive and final. As Pope Benedict XII defined in 1336, the souls of those who depart this life in the state of mortal sin descend into hell immediately after death and suffer infernal torments while those who die in the state of grace either enter heaven to behold God face-to-face or purgatory to be purified (Bull, *Benedictus Deus*).

ᴸ On the last day there will take place the General Judgment. "The Son of Man is to come with His angels in the glory of His Father, and then He will render to everyone according to His conduct" (Matt. 16, 27). All our thoughts, words, and actions will be revealed to the whole human race (Matt. 12, 36; I Cor. 4, 5). This Judgment will show forth God's power, mercy, and justice; it will manifest the triumph and exaltation of Christ as Redeemer; it will mark the public vindication of the just and the public humiliation of the wicked.

⁴ It is fitting that there be two judgments because man is both a personal and a social being. He is not only an individual person but a member of human society. It is also fitting that man's body share in the judgment of his soul. The General Judgment simply confirms and makes public the Particular Judgment.

Can you prove an eternal hell from reason alone? Did the Jews believe in hell? Does not the Jewish word sheol *mean the grave? Why do Catholics believe in an eternal hell? Were not many early Fathers Universalists?*

¹ Reason cannot prove that hell is eternal; it can merely show that the doctrine does not involve any contradiction. We can learn of eternal punishment solely from divine revelation.

² The Catholic Church has always taught that those who die in mortal sin are condemned by God to hell forever. The Fourth Lateran Council (1215) and the Council of Trent both speak of the lot of the impenitent as "everlasting and eternal punishment" and "eternal damnation."

³ It is true that the Hebrew word *Sheol* in the Old Testament generally means the grave, or the other world of either the good (Gen. 37, 35) or the bad (Num. 16, 30). It has that meaning sometimes even in the New Testament (Acts 2, 27; Apoc. 20, 13). The Jews had at first a very vague idea of the hereafter, although God protected them always from falling into the current pagan errors of pantheism, dualism and metempsychosis. They believed in the other world, but their minds were chiefly on this one, intent upon personal happiness and national prosperity. In the Pentateuch, Josue, Judges and Kings there is no explicit distinction between the lot of the good and the wicked in the hereafter (Vigouroux, *La Bible et les Découvertes Modernes,* iv. 585). Job is the first to assert the reward of the just in the other life, thus implicitly proclaiming the punishment of the wicked (14, 16, 8). The Psalms (48, 72, 91, 95, 109); Ecclesiastes (11, 12); Proverbs (10; 11; 14; 24), and the minor prophets (Joel 3, 1-21; Soph. 1, 3) speak of a divine universal judgment, clearly implying the punishment hereafter of the wicked. Isaia (76), Ezechiel (32) and Daniel (12) mention the eternal punishment of the wicked.

⁴ The New Testament teaches the doctrine of hell clearly on its every page. St. John the Baptist insists upon it to urge his hearers to do penance for their sins (Matt. 3. 10. 12; Luke 3, 7. 9. 17; John 3, 36). In asking men to follow Him and believe His Gospel, Christ continually tells them that their eternal salvation is at stake; that if they die in their sins they will merit eternal punishment. Thus He warns them of the sin against the Holy Spirit (Matt. 12, 32), and the sin of scandal (Matt. 18, 8); He urges the duty of fraternal charity (Matt. 5, 32), and

the virtue of chastity—all under the penalty of hell. The kingdom of heaven is for those who do His Father's will, the penalty of hell for the workers of iniquity (Matt 7, 21-23).

⁵ In His description of the Last Judgment our Lord pictures the final separation of the good from the wicked, to whom He will say: "Depart from Me, accursed ones, into the everlasting fire" (Matt. 25, 41).

⁶ Universalists have held that the Greek word *aionios* does not mean everlasting, but age long, that is, a long period, but not an unending one (Matt. 25, 46). But the same Greek word is used for "everlasting life" and for "everlasting punishment." As no one holds that the reward of the just will come to an end, is it not unreasonable to suppose that Christ meant the punishment of the wicked to cease after a time.

⁷ It is true that some of the early Christian Fathers denied the eternity of hell, led astray by the errors of Origen (185-255), who believed in "a restoration (*apokatastasis*) of all things"; St. Gregory of Nyssa (395) and probably St. Gregory of Nazianzus (330-390). But Origen was condemned by a synod of Constantinople in 543, and again by the Fifth General Council of Constantinople in 553. With these few exceptions all the Fathers teach with the Scriptures the doctrine of an eternal hell.

⁸ "The denial of an ultimate sanction," writes Father Arendzen, "would lead to the absurd statement that a man might blaspheme and hate God, and fling up to heaven his deliberate preference of some loathsome pleasure to the possession of Him, and that he might do so with the calm certainty that God was bound to forgive him. Thus God would betray helplessness toward His own creatures" (*What Becomes of Our Dead?*, 61).

What does your Church teach regarding the torments of hell? Are they eternal?

¹ The teaching of the Church in this matter is summed up in the words of Christ who upon the last day will say to some: "Depart from Me, accursed ones, into the everlasting fire" (Matt. 25, 41). Hell is everlasting and there

is a twofold punishment—the pain of loss which consists in the eternal separation from God and the realization that one has only himself to blame (*see* Luke 13, 27; 1 Cor. 6, 9; Apoc. 22, 15); and the torment of fire, so often mentioned in the Scriptures (Matt. 13, 30-50; 18, 8; Luke 16, 24; Heb. 10, 27. etc.). Speculation as to the form and effect of the "unquenchable fire" (Mark 9, 44) cannot be conclusive, for the simple reason that God has not revealed its nature.

Is it not unjust to punish a few years of sin with an eternity of punishment?

[1] No, it is not unjust. The comparison should be made not between this short life of ours and eternity, but between a sinner eternally obdurate in sin and a God all Holy, "whose eyes are too pure to behold evil" (Hab. 1, 13).

[2] Even if we had a thousand years of probation, would that in any way alter the problem? What indeed would ten thousand years be in comparison with eternity? In fact we should thank God that the time of our probation and danger is so short. We can make a definite choice of God in one minute, as many a deathbed repentance proves. God says to us: "I have set before you life and death, the blessing and the curse. Choose life, then" (Deut. 30, 19).

Is not man punished enough in this life, without God putting him in hell thereafter? Would not a limited punishment in the world to come be sufficient?

[1a] "It is not true," writes Balmes, "that the culprit experiences already in this life chastisement enough for his faults. Gnawing remorse indeed torments him; the infirmities produced by his irregularities grow on him, and the disastrous consequences of his perverse conduct weigh him down; but neither is he wanting in means to blunt the sharp sting of his conscience; neither is he devoid of artifices to neutralize the evil effects of his revels, nor short of resources to come clear out of the false positions in which his excesses have involved him" (*Letters to a Skeptic*, ch. 3).

[2a] One of the proofs of immortality lies in the fact that the unpunished wickedness of many in this life, calls upon God to render just judgment upon them in the next. Our Lord teaches plainly that the wicked may be perfectly content in this life, but that punishment will await them hereafter. "Woe to you rich! for you are now having your comfort" (Luke 6, 24). "Son, remember that thou in thy lifetime hast received good things; but now here he is comforted whereas thou art tormented" (Luke 16, 25).

Does your Church teach that all pagans are damned? Your Council of Trent teaches that after the promulgation of the Gospel no one can be saved without Baptism. What about the millions of pagans who before and after Christ never heard of Baptism? Are they not all kept from heaven by their original sin?

[1] The Catholic Church does not teach that all pagans are damned. On the contrary, it teaches that God wishes all men to be saved and to come to the knowledge of the truth" (1 Tim. 2, 4); that God gives sufficient grace to all men to be saved; that unbelief is never sinful unless it is free.

[2] The question does not appraise the Council of Trent accurately. It teaches "that no one can be brought from original sin into the grace of God, unless by Baptism *or the desire for it.*" The pagan may never have heard of Baptism, and therefore the Gospel has not been promulgated as far as he is concerned. He can only be saved by "the desire of Baptism." St. Thomas clearly teaches that a pagan "obtains the remission of his original sin through grace, once he has turned (has ordered himself) to God his Last End" (IIa. IIæ., q. 89, a. 6).

[3] The pagan must have faith as a necessary means of salvation, for "without faith it is impossible to please God" (Heb. 11, 6). The Apostle immediately adds that he must accept two fundamental articles of faith, namely, the existence of God, and His rewarding providence. "For he that comes to God must believe that God exists, and is a rewarder to those who seek Him."

[4] This divine gift of faith will be given to every well disposed soul, who is invincibly ignorant of the Gospel.

Pope Clement XI condemned as heretical the teaching of Quesnel, who said that "no grace is given outside the Church." On the contrary, just as all fell in Adam, so all were elevated to the supernatural order through Christ, as St. Paul teaches (Rom 5, 18; see 1 Cor. 15, 22). This implies that the saving grace of Christ's redemption is given to all men, illuminating their minds, and moving their wills, so that they turn to God as the True End of their being. If they are responsive to the divine inspiration, they receive sanctifying grace which remits their Original Sin, and if they offend grievously afterward, the grace of perfect contrition.

[5] The pagan, however, is not saved by his good faith, but by divine faith; that is, he must accept the revealed truths of God, explicitly with regard to God's existence and His rewarding providence, implicitly with regard to all other dogmas.

Does not your teaching "Outside the Church there is no salvation" imply that all non-Catholics go to hell?

[1] It implies nothing of the kind. We believe that the Catholic Church is the one society for man's salvation instituted by Christ and that men must be affiliated with her in some way to be saved. We also believe that people who are invincibly ignorant of the Catholic Church, of its claims and teachings, or of their obligation to join it may attain to eternal life by leading an honest and upright life with the help of God's grace.

[2] Pope Pius IX states the Catholic doctrine clearly, "We must hold as of faith, that out of the Apostolic Roman Church there is no salvation; that she is the only ark of safety, and whosoever is not in her perishes in the deluge. We must also, on the other hand, recognize with certainty that those who are in invincible ignorance of the true religion are not guilty in the eyes of the Lord." (Allocution, 1854)

[3] The Church has never taught that all non-Catholics go to hell—in fact, she has condemned individual Catholics for so teaching—but she is always urging non-Catholics to pray for God's light, to search diligently for the truth,

and to examine carefully and seriously her own claims to be God's Church on earth.

Does not your practice of excommunicating and anathematizing people imply condemning them to eternal perdition? Were not the medieval bishops too prone to use this weapon against their enemies?

[1] Neither excommunication nor anathemas imply the Church's condemning anyone to hell. That is the prerogative of God alone. Excommunication is a Church law, excluding a notorious sinner from the communion of the faithful. Its purpose is to warn the sinner of the danger he runs of incurring eternal ruin, unless he repent of his sin.

[2] It is true that excommunication was enacted too frequently, and in some cases without just cause, for the Council of Trent, aware of these abuses, solemnly warned the Bishops to be more moderate in its use. It declares: "Although the sword of excommunication is the very sinews of ecclesiastical discipline . . . yet it is to be used with sobriety and great circumspection; seeing that experience teaches that if it be wielded rashly and for slight causes, it is more despised than feared, and works more evil than good."

[3] When St. Paul said "let him be anathema" who preaches an heretical gospel (Gal. 1, 8), he did not condemn the heretic to hell, but stigmatized the willful teacher of false doctrines as a rebel against the Gospel of Christ. The Church, in the anathemas which accompany the canons of her councils, merely imitates the example of the Apostle.

How could a good God predestine anyone to an eternal hell? Does not this divine decree do away with our freedom of choice? If God foreknew that I was to be lost forever, why then did He create me?

[1a] The Catholic Church has never taught that God predestined anyone to hell. On the contrary the Council of Trent condemned the heresy of Calvin, who held that an absolute divine decree predestined part of mankind to hell, and, in order to attain that end effectually, to sin. No in-

telligent man could worship a God who was the author of evil, or a God who did away with our free will, thus making all merit or guilt on our part impossible. Calvin's teaching, which many of his followers today reject as unreasonable, is plainly against the Scriptures, which insist upon God's mercy being ever ready to pardon the most hardened sinners (Rom. 2, 4; 2 Peter 3, 9), and which teach that Jesus Christ died for all men (2 Cor. 5, 15; John 1, 29; 1 John 2, 2), and that God "wishes all men to be saved" (1 Tim. 2, 4).

2a Suppose for an instant that God could not create a soul whom He foresaw would be lost by the abuse of his free will, and his stubborn resisting of God's grace. It would follow then that every man, by the very fact of his creation and without any effort or striving on his part, would be infallibly certain of heaven. Virtue and vice then would be on a par. The moral law would then be without any sanction.

How can an infinitely good and merciful God condemn us whom He loves to the everlasting torments of hell? Does not hell imply a cruelty on God's part that we would hesitate to impute to the most heartless of men? Would a human father or mother so torment even a most worthless son? Does not hell imply the final triumph of Satan over Christ the Redeemer?

1 Hell is indeed a great mystery, and, like every other mystery of Christianity, is infinitely beyond the scope of any finite mind. The Catholic knows it to be a dogma divinely revealed, and he accepts it humbly and without question on the word of Jesus Christ, the Son of God. As the Apostle says: "How incomprehensible are His judgments and how unsearchable His ways" (Rom. 11, 33). Do scientists reject a known fact, simply because they are unable to explain it?

2 Is it honest for the unbeliever to ask in one breath: "How can a good God punish His creatures in hell?," and in the next, "How can a world so full of wretchedness and misery be the creation of an infinitely wise and good God?" God is either too good or too evil, according as the un-

believer feels inclined to deny either hell or divine providence. And yet in God all is one—His mercy, justice, power and love. It is only the limited character of our intellects that makes us set one attribute of God against the other. He cannot defeat His mercy by His justice, nor His justice by His mercy. He cannot deviate from the right without ceasing to be God. He is justice; He is mercy.

[3] The Church always has taught that if a man is condemned to hell, he certainly has deserved it. If he can say honestly I did not know God's law, or I could not help sinning, God cannot and will not punish him. For God "wishes all men to be saved" (1 Tim. 2, 4). If a man dies with his will rebellious to God, *he puts himself in hell.* Why blame God, when he alone is responsible?

[4] I have met men who deliberately chose to corrupt the innocent, and have numbered their victims as sharpshooters in war time count their successful hits. I have known men who have deliberately broken up the happy home of a friend out of pure malice. I have known men who have defrauded minors out of every cent of their property. Can God, Jesus Christ, justly say to such men, if they die unrepentant: "Come blessed of My Father, take possession of the kingdom prepared for you from the foundation of the world?" (Matt. 25, 24.)

[5] Satan would indeed triumph over Christ, if he could promise heaven to those who had led perfectly sinful lives. Hell implies his defeat, for it vindicates the supremacy of Christ and the divine law, which cannot be defied with impunity.

What is the meaning of the words of the Apostles' Creed, "He descended into hell?" Did Christ really go to the hell of the damned? What do Catholics mean by Limbo?

[1] "We profess," says the Catechism of the Council of Trent, "that immediately after the death of Christ His soul descended into hell, and dwelt there as long as His body remained in the tomb; and also that the one Person of Christ was at the same time in hell and in the sepulcher. . . . Hell here signifies those secret abodes in which are detained the souls that have not obtained the happiness of heaven."

[2] This was not the "hell of the damned" but the place where souls were awaiting entrance into heaven which had been closed to the human race because of original sin. Our Lord calls it "Abraham's bosom" (Matt. 25, 10) and "paradise" (Luke 23, 43). Theologians refer to it as the "Limbo of the Patriarchs."

[3] It was a place of happiness, for those souls were supernaturally perfect and confirmed in grace. They could neither sin nor suffer. Yet their happiness still had to be consummated by admission into heaven as a place.

[4] Since Christ ascended into heaven only the souls of those, mostly children, who die in original sin without ever having been guilty of personal mortal sin, are in this place of happiness. These souls enjoy a positive happiness being united to God and to their parents, if they are in heaven, by a *natural* knowledge and love. It is commonly called the Limbo of Children.

Where do you find Purgatory or praying for the dead in the Bible? Did primitive Christianity believe in an intermediate state? Is it not more reasonable to suppose that at death a man goes directly to heaven or to hell?

[1] The Catholic Church has defined the existence of purgatory in the Decree of Union drawn up at the Council of Florence in 1439, and again at the Council of Trent which says: "The Catholic Church, instructed by the Holy Spirit, has from Sacred Scriptures and the ancient traditions of the Fathers, taught in Sacred Councils, and very recently in this Ecumenical Synod that there is a purgatory, and that the souls therein detained are helped by the suffrages of the faithful, but principally by the acceptable sacrifice of the altar."

[2a] The same Council taught, in accordance with the Scriptures (Num. 20, 12; 2 Kings 12, 13. 14) that God does not always remit all of the temporal punishment due to forgiven sin. The Scriptures teach that nothing defiled can enter heaven (Wisd. 7, 25; Isa. 25, 8; Hab. 1, 13; Apoc. 21, 7), and that Christians often die with venial sins upon their souls. All, therefore, who die in venial sins, or with the temporal punishment of their sins still unpaid must atone for them in purgatory.

[8] The teaching of the Bible is found in 2 Machabees 12, 43-46. After Judas had defeated Gorgias, he came with his company to bury the Jews who had been slain in the conflict. He found under their coats some of the donaries, that is, votive offerings, which they had, contrary to the Law (Deut. 7, 25), robbed from the idols of Jamnia. Judas at once prayed God that their sin might be forgiven (12, 37-42), and "making a gathering, he sent twelve thousand drachms of silver to Jerusalem for sacrifice to be offered for the sins of the dead." He did not consider their sins grievous, "because he considered that they who had fallen asleep with godliness, had great grace laid up for them." The sacred writer then adds: "It is, therefore, a holy and wholesome thought to pray for the dead, that they may be loosed from sins" (2 Mach. 12, 43-46).

[4] It is true that Protestants consider the books of Machabees apocryphal, but they rest upon the same authority as Isaias or St. John—the divine infallible witness of the Catholic Church. Even prescinding from the fact of their inspiration, we may cite them as an historical witness of the Jewish belief centuries before Christ.

[5] All the Fathers of both East and West mention the Apostolic custom of praying for the dead. Tertullian (160-240) speaks of anniversary Masses: "We make on one day every year oblations for the dead, as for their birthdays" (*De Cor. Mil.*, 3).

[6] All the ancient liturgies of both East and West contain prayers for the dead. The prayer of the Roman liturgy runs as follows: "Be mindful, O Lord, of Thy servants who are gone before us with the sign of faith, and sleep in the sleep of peace. Grant them, we beseech Thee, O Lord, a place of refreshment, light and peace, through the same Christ our Lord." The phrase "refreshment, light and peace" is found in many of the Catacomb inscriptions. The formula *In Pace* (In Peace) like our modern *Requiescat in Pace* (May he or she rest in peace), and the words, "mayest thou have eternal light in Christ," and "may God refresh you," are found over many a Christian's tomb in the the first three centuries.

[7] The Catholic doctrine is most reasonable. It follows logically from the fact that many die with the burden of

venial sins on their conscience, or die with the temporal punishment due to their forgiven sins still unpaid. The average Christian commits many a venial sin in his lifetime, for which he never craves pardon. The sinner of many years standing, who in God's mercy is pardoned on his deathbed, must in the hereafter, unless given a plenary indulgence, satisfy to the last farthing his debt of temporal punishment.

⁸ I have more than once met Protestants who admitted to me that they prayed for their dead, despite the teaching of their ministers, on the principle that their beloved dead were neither bad enough for hell nor good enough for heaven. I recall especially a Lutheran woman in Baltimore, who prayed daily for her husband. She had never read a line of St. Augustine, and probably never had heard his name. Yet out of the natural instinct of her heart she knew his teaching, namely, that "there are some who have departed this life, not so bad as to be deemed unworthy of mercy, nor so good as to be entitled to immediate happiness" (*De Civ. Dei.,* xxi., 24).

Is heaven a place or a state of the soul? What do we really know about heaven? Will we know our relatives and friends there?

¹ Heaven is both the eternal happiness and the eternal dwelling place of the just in the life to come. It is called the kingdom of heaven (Matt. 5, 3), the kingdom of God (Mark 9, 46), the kingdom of the Father (Matt. 13, 43), the kingdom of Christ (Luke 22, 30), the city of God (Heb. 12, 22), paradise (2 Cor. 12, 4), life everlasting (Matt. 19, 16), the crown of life (James 1, 12), of justice (2 Tim. 4, 8), of glory (1 Peter 5, 4), and our eternal inheritance (Heb. 9, 15).

² The supernatural happiness of heaven consists in the intuitive vision of the divine essence. "We see now through a mirror in an obscure manner, but then face to face. Now I know in part, but then I shall know even as I have been known" (1 Cor. 13, 12). This doctrine was defined by Benedict XII in 1336. and by the Council of Florence in 1439. To enable the intellect to see God, it is supernatu-

rally perfected by *the light of glory,* as the Council of Vienne defined in 1311.

No one can enter heaven unless he is free of sin (Apoc. 21, 27), in the state of justice and friendship of God. Its supreme happiness excludes all evil, physical or moral. "And God will wipe away every tear from their eyes. And death shall be no more; neither shall there be mourning, nor crying, nor pain any more, for the former things have passed away" (Apoc. 21, 4).

[3] The eternal happiness of heaven (Luke 22, 33) admits of various degrees. "He who sows sparingly will also reap sparingly, and he who sows bountifully will also reap bountifully" (2 Cor. 9, 6).

[4] The soul's intimacy with God in heaven, its relationship with the saints, its immunity from sin, are joys that the human mind cannot grasp. "Eye has not seen nor ear heard, nor has it entered into the heart of man, what things God has prepared for those who love Him" (1 Cor. 2, 9).

[5] We shall certainly know our relatives and friends in heaven, and know them more intimately and love them more ardently than we did upon earth. One of man's greatest joys here is the love of kinsfolk and friends. God will supernaturalize this affection, but He will not destroy it. Everything in heaven is supernatural, but not unnatural. Love and friendship on earth are frail things at best, and no quarrels are greater than quarrels among kinsfolk. In the hereafter, when all souls are confirmed in sanctity, the natural affections of the human heart will be intensified and increased a hundredfold. We will love our own in God and for God.

Is not the dogma of the resurrection of the body unreasonable? How is it possible that we shall all rise again with the same bodies we possessed while upon earth? Are not our bodies constantly changing?

[1] The resurrection of the body, while eminently reasonable, is a miraculous event, due solely to the omnipotence of God. Human reason of itself could never know it with certainty; we believe it firmly, because the Catholic Church, the infallible teacher of divine revelation, in the name of

the Bible and tradition, has declared it an article of faith in her Creeds—the Apostles', the Nicene and the Athanasian—and in her Councils, namely, the Council of Constantinople (553), and the Fourth Lateran in 1215. The last named Council declares that "all men shall rise again with their own bodies, which they now bear, to receive according to their works."

² Our Lord taught the resurrection of the body frequently, and attributes the denial of the Sadducees to their ignorance of the Scriptures (Matt. 22, 29). His own resurrection (Luke 24, 39-43; John 20, 27. 28) in His identical body confirms His teaching of our bodily resurrection.

³ St. Paul preached the resurrection from the dead as one of the fundamental doctrines of Christianity at Athens (Acts 17, 18. 31. 32), at Jerusalem (Acts 23, 6), before Felix (Acts 24, 15), and before Agrippa (Acts 26, 8), besides mentioning it in many passages of his Epistles (Rom. 8, 11; 1 Cor. 6, 14; 15, 12; 2 Cor. 4, 14; 6, 1; Phil. 3, 21; Thess. 4, 12; 2 Tim. 2, 11; Heb. 6, 2). He proves the resurrection of the dead from the resurrection of Christ, declaring that "if there is no resurrection of the dead neither has Christ risen" (1 Cor. 15, 13; see St. Thomas III., q. 56, art. 1).

⁴ The dogma of the resurrection of the dead implies more than the immortality of the soul; it teaches a real and complete resurrection of man in the fullness of his nature. There is a threefold identity in the risen man, which makes him the same human person he was from birth; identity of soul, identity of bodily life, and identity of the ultimate material substance of his body. All Catholic theologians agree that there is complete identity of soul, for the soul is the chief factor in determining personal identity. All agree also in holding that the giving back of man's bodily life is the very heart of the resurrection miracle and mystery. But while the majority of theologians are in favor of the identity of matter in man's natural and risen state, a minority hold that such material identity is unnecessary. We are well aware that the material substance of which the body is composed is continually changing, but reason and experience tell us that this ever continuing process in no way interrupts the vital identity of the body from infancy to old age.

⁵ Catholics believe with St. Paul (1 Cor. 15, 42-44) that the risen body will possess added qualities, which in no way interfere with their substantial sameness. It will be impassible, that is, immortal and incorrupt. It shall "rise in incorruption." "Neither shall they be able to die any more" (Luke 20, 36). It "shall rise in glory," that is, "shine forth like the sun in the kingdom of their Father" (Matt. 13, 43). It "rises in power," that is, no longer subject to the limitations of space, like our Lord's resurrected body. It "rises a spiritual body," that is, endowed with spiritual and supernatural qualities.

What is the meaning of the words: "Heaven and earth will pass away, but My words will not pass away" (Mark 13, 31)?

¹ The meaning of the Savior's words are clear. He had been speaking of the future destruction of the temple of Jerusalem, and the end of the world. He then adds that, whereas this world and all earthly things are perishable, His gospel is eternal.

² At the end of the world the form of our earth with its rivers, lakes, fields, valleys and mountains, and of our sky with its sun, moon and stars shall be completely transformed. In the passage quoted, the word "heaven" is not the everlasting "heaven of the blessed." Rather, it signifies the heavenly bodies we see in the sky.

³ The prophet Isaia expresses the same idea, "The heavens shall vanish like smoke, and the earth shall be worn away like a garment, and the inhabitants therein shall perish in like manner. But my salvation shall be forever, and my justice shall not fail" (Isaia 51, 6).

What is meant by "the Communion of Saints"?

¹ᵃ This phrase is rich in meaning and expresses a beautiful inspiring doctrine of the Catholic Church. It is found in the Apostles' Creed and it means that the faithful on earth, the saints in heaven, and the souls in purgatory are united together in love and prayer.

²ᵃ The faithful on earth help each other by prayers and good works. For example, the faithful, who enjoy health and freedom, by their prayers and penances truly aid those

who are sick and persecuted. The works and sufferings of each redound to the spiritual welfare of all.

³ Then, too, the faithful on earth are in communion with the saints in heaven. We celebrate their memory with feastdays, ask for their prayerful intercession, and strive to follow their example and to practice their virtues. In turn, they praise God with us and pray to Him for us.

⁴ The faithful on earth are also united to the souls in purgatory. We speed their entrance into heaven by offering prayers and Masses for them. In turn, they are grateful to us and pray to God for us.

⁵ The faithful on earth—still struggling to win the victory of salvation—form the "Church Militant." The saints in heaven—enjoying the fruits of final victory—make up the "Church Triumphant." The souls in purgatory—still suffering in order to be perfectly purified from the effects of sin—constitute the "Church Suffering." On the last day Christ will bring this great family together in the everlasting City of God.

⁶ At each Holy Mass—and they are continually celebrated from the rising to the setting sun—the Church prays for all the faithful on earth, asks God to hear the prayers of all the saints in heaven, and petitions God to usher the souls in purgatory into the beatific vision.

SELECTED BIBLIOGRAPHY

ARENDZEN, JOHN P. *Purgatory and Heaven*. New York: Sheed & Ward. 1960.

BECQUE, MAURICE. *Life After Death*. New York: Hawthorn Books. 1960.

CHAPMAN, DOM JOHN. *Spiritual Letters*. New York: Sheed & Ward.

GARRIGOU-LAGRANGE, REGINALD. *Life Everlasting*. St. Louis: B. Herder Book Co. 1952.

GLEASON, ROBERT W. *The World to Come*. New York: Sheed & Ward. 1958.

GREENSTOCK, DAVID L. *Death: The Glorious Adventure*. Westminster, Md.: Newman Press. 1956.

GUARDINI, ROMANO. *The Last Things*. New York: Pantheon Books.

LUBAC, HENRI DE. *Catholicism*. New York: Sheed & Ward. 1950.

LUNN, ARNOLD. *Within that City*. New York: Sheed & Ward.

McCARTHY, JOSEPH P. *Heaven*. New York: P. J. Kenedy & Sons. 1959.

PEERS, E. ALLISON (trans.). *The Works of St. Teresa of Avila*. New York: Sheed & Ward.

PERRET, A. S. *Toward our Father's House*. St. Louis: B. Herder Book Co. 1959.

ULANOV, BARRY. *Death, a Book of Preparation and Consolation*. New York: Sheed & Ward. 1959.

WICKLOW, WILLIAM. *Life After Death*. Westminster, Md.: Newman Press. 1959.

ZOLLI, EUGENIO. *Before the Dawn*. New York: Sheed & Ward.

PART XV
The Church and the Bible

What do Catholics mean when they say the Bible is inspired? Is the Pope inspired when he speaks infallibly?

[1] The Vatican Council, after declaring that God's revelation to man is preserved by the living Magisterium in her Bible and her Tradition, and that the canon or list of the Sacred Books is guaranteed in the authentic Latin Vulgate translation, teaches, "The Church holds these books as sacred and canonical, not because, composed by merely human industry, they were thereupon approved by her authority; nor alone because they contain revelation without error; but because, written under the inspiration of the Holy Spirit, they have God for their Author, and as such were delivered to the Church herself."

[2] Mere approval of a book by the Church, absolute inerrancy in its contents, or the fact that it contains revelation do not make that book inspired. No action of the Church *causes* a book to be inspired. She simply exercises her infallibility to judge that a particular book is inspired. Only the fact that God is the Author makes a book inspired and the Holy Spirit prevents the Church from erring in judging what books have God as their Author. A book is actually inspired prior to any judgment of the Church. Her decision confirms the fact of its divine author.

[3] Pope Leo XIII in his Encyclical, *Providentissimus Deus,* explains the meaning of inspiration. "God by His supernatural power in such a way incited and moved them (the sacred writers) to write, in such a way assisted them in writing, that they should rightly conceive in the mind, and should desire to write faithfully, and should express

fitly with infallible truth, all those things and only those things which He Himself should command."

⁴ Although "the inspired writer, in composing the sacred book, is the living and reasonable instrument of the Holy Spirit" (Pius XII, Encyclical, *Divino Afflante Spiritu*), he retains his own personality, idiomatic expressions, and literary style. It is not necessary for God to inspire the words and phrases used. In fact, the writer may not even know that he is being inspired. Subject to the divine action, he remains intelligent, free, and active in his composition. How he writes depends on his vocabulary and literary skill, "for as the substantial Word of God became like to men in all things, except sin, so the words of God, expressed in human language, are made like to human speech in every respect, except error" (Pius XII, *ibidem*). What he writes down is not necessarily something that God has directly revealed to him; for example, St. Luke consulted documents and gathered facts from eyewitnesses. But what he writes down must be true, for "inspiration not only is essentially incompatible with error, but excludes and rejects it absolutely and necessarily, for it is impossible that God, the Supreme Truth, can utter what is not true" (Leo XIII, Encyclical, *Providentissimus Deus*).

⁵ The Pope is not inspired when he speaks infallibly. Unlike the sacred writer who is moved and directed to write what God wants written, the Pope, after he himself decides to speak *ex cathedra,* is protected by God from falsehood in all matters of faith and morals. However, both these gifts, inspiration and infallibility, are given primarily for the public good. They do not add to the holiness either of the writer or of the Pope. Their aim is the instruction and exhortation of the people in the ways of God.

Does not the content and the literary form of the Bible prove its inspiration? Does not the Bible contain miracles and prophecies, holy and sublime doctrines? Does it not appeal to the heart of man by its peculiar beauty and simplicity?

¹ No, the book itself does not guarantee its own inspiration. Such a criterion is useless, because at most it would

prove that some parts of some books are inspired, but not that any book is divine in its origin. The writings of many of the Fathers and saints of the Church contain topics just as sublime, and written in just as sublime and simple a style. And yet no one ever considered St. Augustine, St. Bernard or Thomas à Kempis inspired. Some books like Numbers are in many portions as interesting as the multiplication table, while others like Esther do not mention any religious topic whatsoever. Literary taste, moreover, is variable and subjective, and, therefore, useless as a test of inspiration.

Can we not prove the inspiration of the Bible from "the inward testimony of the Spirit"? Does not the Bible produce in the reader sentiments of devotion, faith, hope, and love of God and one's neighbor?

[1a] Such a criterion is purely subjective. The impression received from reading the Bible varies with each individual reader, and as happened in Luther's case, may give rise to arbitrary denials of whole books of the Bible. For example, he eliminated the Second Book of Machabees because he rejected the doctrine of purgatory; he considered the Apocalypse "neither Apostolic nor prophetic"; he called the Epistle of St. James an "Epistle of straw," and declared the Apostle was "mad with his crazy doctrine of good works" (Grisar, *Luther,* v., 521, 522).

[2] Moreover, there are many portions of the Bible which do not arouse devotion, and many non-inspired books that do. On this false test we would have to reject the inspiration of Exodus 35, Leviticus 11, or 2 Kings 11, and maintain the inspiration of the *Interior Castle* of St. Teresa and the *Dark Night of the Soul* of St. John of the Cross.

How can anyone be absolutely sure what books in the Bible are really inspired? Does not the Catholic Bible contain more books than the Protestant Bible?

[1b] "As the inspiration of the sacred books," writes Father Gigot, "is a divine operation, not necessarily known even to the mind that is acted upon by the Holy Spirit, it necessarily follows that the testimony of God Himself is required to make men perfectly sure of its existence; but this divine

testimony comes to their knowledge, and is the absolute ground of their faith, only by the voice of that infallible and living Church, which He has commanded us to hear" *(Bibical Lectures).*

[2] Catholics believe that God revealed to the Apostolic Church the divine authorship of certain books, that He entrusted their preservation and promulgation through the centuries to this divinely-guided Church, and that He commissioned this same infallible Church to interpret and teach their true meaning without fear of error. The Catholic Church alone can with certainty tell us what books are inspired and written by God. Her infallibility is our sure guarantee for the inspiration of the Bible. Whereas Protestants depend upon the human and fallible arguments of literary criticism for their list of inspired Biblical writings, Catholics depend upon the divine and infallible witness of the teaching Church founded by Christ.

[3] The Council of Trent (1546) declared that all the books of the Old and New Testament contained in the Catholic Bible are sacred (inspired) and canonical. This canon is identical with the lists of sacred books promulgated by the Councils of Florence (1441), Carthage (397), Hippo (393), Laodicea (363), and by Popes Hormisdas (514-523), Gelasius I (492-496), Innocent I (402-417), and Damasus I (366-384). The Tridentine definition includes books rejected by Protestants as apocrypha, for example, Tobias, Judith, Wisdom, Ecclesiasticus, Baruch, and the two Books of Machabees, along with fragments of Esther 10, 4; 16, 24 and Daniel 3, 24-90; 13; 14.

[4] For Catholics, the term apocryphal means writings falsely attributed to the prophets of the Old Law or the Apostles of the New Dispensation, whose claim to inspiration was rejected or at least ignored by the Church. Such, for example, were the Book of Enoch, the Assumption of Moses, the proto-Evangel of St. James, the Acts of St. Peter and St. Paul, and the Letter of Christ to Abgar.

Do Catholics regard the Bible as absolutely inerrant? Is it not incorrect on scientific matters and historical data? Are there not many errors and contradictions to be found in the text of both the Old and New Testaments?

[1] Catholics believe that the original text of the Bible as it was written down by the inspired writers contains no error. As God, who can neither deceive nor be deceived, is its divine Author, the Bible is necessarily true. Pope Leo XIII declared, "This is the ancient and unchanging faith of the Church" (Encyclical, *Providentissimus Deus*).

[2] We must remember that the original text was copied many times and that the Bible has been translated into every known language. Neither the copyists nor the translators were inspired or immune from error. Consequently, variations of the text, additions, omissions, and other errors have been found in succeeding versions and editions of the Bible. By means of textual criticism scholars are constantly correcting these mistakes. Pope Pius XII praised and encouraged the science and art of textual criticism, "for its very purpose is to ensure that the sacred text be restored, as perfectly as possible, be purified from the corruptions due to the carelessness of the copyists and be freed, as far as may be done, from glosses and omissions, from the interchange and repetition of words and from all other kinds of mistakes, which are wont to make their way gradually into writings handed down through many centuries" (Encyclical, *Divino Afflante Spiritu*).

[3] The Bible is neither a scientific treatise nor a history book. It is a popular narration of God's dealings with men. The sacred writer employs words and phrases that the ordinary person of his time would understand; he was not writing for scientists nor for historians. "What is the literal sense of a passage is not always as obvious in the speeches and writings of the ancient authors of the East, as it is in the works of the writers of our own time. For what they wished to express is not to be determined by the rules of grammar and philology alone, nor solely by the context; the interpreter must, as it were, go back wholly in spirit to those remote centuries of the East and with the aid of history, archaeology, ethnology and other sciences, accurately determine what modes of writing, so to speak, the authors of that ancient period would be likely to use, and in fact did use. For the ancient peoples of the East, in order to express their ideas, did not always employ those forms or kinds of speech, which we use today; but rather

those used by the men of their times and countries. What those exactly were the commentator cannot determine, as it were, in advance, but only after a careful examination of the ancient literature of the East" (Pius XII, *ibidem*).

⁴ In reading the Scriptures we must not be disturbed by the objections and charges of the scientists and the historians. God has handed over the sacred writings of which He Himself is the Author to the Catholic Church for preservation and interpretation. It is the Church alone who can authentically and officially tell us the true meaning of any scriptural passage. We should emulate the wholesome attitude of St. Augustine, "When in the pages of Sacred Scripture I come upon anything that is contrary to the truth, I judge that the text is faulty, that the translator did not strike the right meaning, or simply that I do not understand it" (Letter to St. Jerome, 82, 3).

Does not modern science plainly show that the Bible's chronology with regard to the age of the human race is very faulty and inaccurate?

¹ It does not, because it has not yet solved the problem of the antiquity of man. Besides, the Bible makes no pretense of giving us a scientific chronology and we have not yet discovered what systems of chronology the various sacred authors employed. Father Pope's comments are worth noting, "It is well to bear in mind that the Biblical chronological system is in no sense a scientific one, that its details are often conflicting, that starting as it does from the beginning when there can have been no means of dating events—it is possibly only meant as a guide to the memory, and not as a clue to history. On the other hand, none of the dates assigned by scholars to the events of this early period can be regarded as more than approximate, and should not be regarded as solid means of testing the Biblical statements" (*Catholic Student's Aids to the Bible*).

² The Church has never interfered with the freedom of scientists in determining the age of the human race from the data of prehistory, geology, anthropology, and allied disciplines. In the name of common sense, however, she rightly asks scientists not to give forth their guesses as proved facts or absolute truths.

Is the history of creation in the first chapters of Genesis scientific history? Are Catholics bound to believe that the world was created in six days of twenty-four hours each?

[1] "The first eleven chapters of Genesis, although they do not, properly speaking, conform to the historical method used by the best Greek and Latin writers or by competent authors of our time, nevertheless do pertain to history in a true sense, which, however, must be further studied and determined by exegetes; the same chapters, in simple and metaphorical language adapted to the mentality of a people but little cultured, state both the principal truths which are fundamental for our salvation, and also give a popular description of the origin of the human race and the chosen people. If, however, the ancient sacred writers have taken anything from popular narrations (and this may be conceded), it must never be forgotten that they did so with the help of divine inspiration, through which they were rendered immune from any error in selecting and evaluating those documents" (Pius XII, Encyclical, *Humani Generis*).

[2a] The author of Genesis teaches the fact that God is the Creator of the world and all things in it. His purpose is not to teach when or how God created the world, plants, animals, or man. He is neither a historian nor a scientist, but a religious teacher. And he employs a literary form to teach the religious truth that all things owe their existence to God. He is not narrating events in chronological order or in scientific fashion. He is simply teaching ordinary people in language familiar to them, that God created all things, and that He rested on the Sabbath.

[3] Catholics need not accept the literal interpretation of "day" as "24 hours." The writer is presenting salvation-history and not history in the modern sense of the term. He places the events within the framework of the Jewish 24-hour day which was measured from sunset to sunset, and he employs this literary form as a cleverly arranged memory device to foster Sabbath observance. He is thus teaching the Jews that as God rested from work on the 7th day they should cease all work on the Sabbath.

Are Catholics compelled to believe the book of Jonas as literal history?

[1] Many modern critics and a few modern Catholic scholars, for example, Jean Steinmann, regard the composition of the book as symbolical, allegorical or parabolic with or without a historical background. They hold *only* that the book has an important message to teach, namely, the loving mercy of God includes also the Gentiles.

[2] However, the historicity of the narrative has always been maintained by Jewish and Christian tradition. Christ alludes to the story of the sea-monster and Jonas as an historical fact, to serve as a type of His own death and resurrection (Matt. 12, 31-41; 16, 4; Luke 11, 21-32).

[3] The fact that the book has an important lesson to teach is not necessarily a sufficient proof of its being figurative or parabolic. Nor is the account of the stupendous miracle of Jonas being swallowed by a sea-monster and after three days being vomited out upon the dry land to be considered bizarre and unworthy of the wisdom of God. Then, too, the period described in the book perfectly coincides with the historical conditions prevailing at that time in Nineve.

[4] Nevertheless, in most Catholic circles it is admitted that Jonas is a long parable. Either position is possible for the believing Catholic. The parable position may easily be an example of the harmony with intelligence which the Church has always proclaimed to be necessary.

Is not the story of the deluge a legend or a nature myth? Does not modern science prove that it was not universal?

[1a] The deluge described in Genesis 6, 5—8, 22 is an historical fact. It was one of several floods that occurred in antiquity—perhaps, the most disastrous. Geologists are not able to give us a date, but they estimate that it took place earlier than 4000 B.C.

[2a] It is true there are similarities between the Biblical narrative and some Babylonian legendary accounts, but this fact does not necessarily posit a connection between them. The Biblical account has no polytheism in it and a much more sober tone marks its presentation. Our Lord speaks of the flood as being no less real than His second

coming (Matt. 24, 37-39). St. Peter twice refers to the deluge as an historical fact (1 Peter 3, 20; 2 Peter 2, 5).

[3] In describing the details of the flood the writers were not interested in its scientific aspects, but in using it to inculcate helpful lessons such as the malice and ugliness of sin and God's mercy and justice. They stressed its religious implications rather than its historical setting.

[4] We do not doubt that there was a flood, but we think it was a local serious flood which inundated a particular area. It was not world-wide or universal. If it covered the entire earth, how are we to explain what happened to the vast quantity of water, especially in view of the saucer-like conception the ancient people had of the earth. The Hebrews falsely believed that the earth was already floating like a saucer on waters of bottomless depth. Their whole picture of the universe—so different from ours today—was non-scientific and based on naked-eye observation and appearances.

How do you explain the so-called miracle of Josue in commanding the sun to stand still (Josue 10, 12)?

[1] We must remember that "the sacred writers did not seek to penetrate the secrets of nature, but rather described and dealt with things in more or less figurative language, or in terms which were commonly used at the time" (Pope Leo XIII, Encyclical, *Providentissimus Deus*).

[2] In this instance, the author adapted his language to his contemporaries and recorded the remarkable occurrence in terms of the current popular belief that the sun moved daily across the sky and that the prolongation of sunlight was a temporary cessation of that movement. His astronomy was false, but the fact that the sun continued to shine was true. His purpose was not to teach astronomy or to describe the mechanics of the miracle. He simply testified that there was light when according to nature there should have been darkness. With gratitude he was reporting that God had bestowed the light necessary for the victory; he did not attempt to explain *how* God had stayed the darkness.

[3] Scientists and theologians have offered many explana-

tions of what actually happened that day. Unfortunately, those of the 17th century tried to make the Biblical passage conform to the current Ptolemaic system and insisted that the sun literally stood still. When the Copernican theory supplanted the Ptolemaic, the scientists rejected the miracle and the theologians condemned the Copernican system. Both sides, of course, were wrong. For the truth of the passage does not depend upon any scientific theory. There was a miracle even though we cannot explain how it occurred.

⁴ Even today scholars are not sure of the exact meaning of the inspired passage. The interpretation of the learned Jesuit, Father Hummelauer, is plausible. He suggests that while the Amorrhites were fleeing from the Israelites, the clouds containing the death-dealing hailstones (Josue 10, 11) covered the whole sky and hid the sun in absolute darkness. Josue, confiding in God, commanded the sun to reappear (Josue 10, 12). Immediately, the sun reappeared (Josue 10, 13) and the Israelites were able to continue the attack.

⁵ Although the miracle of Josue is only of secondary importance in the conquest of Chanaan, the sacred writer mentions it because it was a remarkable fact that had struck the popular imagination, and had been a recurring theme for years with the poets of Israel.

Your account of Christ depends on the Four Gospels. How can you be sure that they are genuine history? May they not have been written long after the events they record? May they not be mere legends or myths?

¹ It is certainly possible to prove by historical criticism that the four Gospels are authentic history. Any criticism undertakes the task of comparing the content of a book with the evidence of history, geography ethnology and archaeology. In this way, one can prove the high degree of historicity of a work such as Caesar's "Gallic Wars," or even take a document without historical foundation such as "The Song of Roland" and give an immensely valuable insight into early feudalism.

² However, it must be seen that the Gospels were meant

to be catechisms rather than history books. They were preceded by an oral catechism and were formed in large measure by the Church.

[3] The evangelists' faithful depiction of the Judean-Palestinian background to Jesus' life, a background which disappeared after the suppression of the revolt against Rome in 70 A.D., is all the more remarkable. The modern reader cannot fail to be impressed by the authentic Galilean peasant and Jewish tone of the Gospels. Such local color, quite alien to the Greek or Roman, could never have been created by the imagination of slaves living at Corinth, Rome or Alexandria.

[4] The minor inexactitudes one finds in the Gospels are not a serious problem since it is unreasonable to expect exactitude in matters which did not bother any writer of that time. Rather, the confrontation of the divergence in unimportant details bears witness that we are getting history very nearly at first hand. There is no evidence that the Gospel texts have been modified and glossed by later generations. It is practically certain that having regard to the wide diffusion of the Gospels and the number of ancient ones we still possess, any doctoring of this kind would have come to light.

[5] While there is much reinforcement by external criticism for the historical validity of the Gospels, the real proof is interior knowledge. No one can read the Gospels without the conviction that Jesus was a living person. This authenticity is especially pointed out by the different view the then Jewish world had of a glorious Messias from the view presented in the Gospels; namely, a suffering Messias dying a shameful death quite contrary to the accepted tradition to which even His own disciples, at times, were attached.

[6] In addition, the words, parables and tone of Jesus are inimitable. The Apostles cannot command that quality elsewhere which indicates that the "word of Christ" has been faithfully transmitted; v.g. "Render to Caesar. . . .," "See how the wild lilies grow. . . ." Also, the teaching of Christ is itself a guarantee of this historical reliability. The great events of the Transfiguration, Resurrection and miracles are found in the most ancient testimonies. Not Paul,

but Christ starts the doctrine of Incarnation and Redemption. It is found in the Gospels, and only that can explain the great phenomenon which no one can refuse to admit, the birth of the Church, the visible projection into society of the faith of the early Christians. Christianity without Christ is unthinkable as an historical fact and as a testimony. The Church itself is a guarantee.

Is there not a fundamental difference between the Synoptic Gospels and the Gospel of St. John? Is not St. John's Gospel more of a theological treatise than a sober history? Can you prove that St. John really wrote it?

[1] No, there is no fundamental difference between the Synoptic Gospels and the Gospel of St. John. The only difference lies in the way the portrait of Christ is drawn. As Father Pope says: "In the Synoptic Gospels Christ's miracles and teaching speak for Him; in St. John, Christ speaks for Himself; the few miracles given serve as pegs on which hang Christ's discourses concerning His Nature and Person" (*The Godhead of Christ as Portrayed in the Gospels,* 22).

[2] The differences in style and content are readily understood, once we realize the purpose St. John had in view. While the Synoptists, writing before the fall of Jerusalem, aimed at converting the Jews of the Holy Land and of the dispersion by showing that Jesus was the promised Messias, St. John, writing thirty years after the destruction of the Temple, appealed directly to the pagan world. He desired to correct the false notions current about the *Logos* among Greek thinkers, and to refute the Gnostic and Docetic denials of Christ, the Son of God (John 20, 31). Useless indeed would have been his labors, if he had merely repeated the sayings of St. Matthew, St. Mark and St. Luke.

[3] Unbelieving critics lay great stress upon the differences between the Synoptic Gospels and St. John. But they fail to stress the facts they both record.

1. Christ claims to be the Son of God (Mark 14, 61-61; John 3, 16-18; 5, 18).

2. Christ shows an intimate knowledge of the Father's mind and will (Matt. 11, 25; 12, 50; John 8, 55).

3. Christ claims pre-existence (Luke 5, 13; John 8, 23).

4. Christ is the Judge on the Last Day (Matt. 10, 32; Mark 8, 38; Luke 17, 30; John 5, 27).

5. Christ is the Lord of the Sabbath (Matt. 12, 8; Mark 2, 28; Luke 6, 5; John 5, 17).

6. Christ forgives sin and delegates this power to His Apostles (Matt. 9, 5; 16, 19; John 8, 11; 20, 23).

7. Christ knows intimately the thoughts of men, and the future (Matt. 23, 36; 26, 13; John 1, 48; 2, 24; 6, 71).

8. Christ demands love and service even unto death (Matt. 10, 37-39; 11, 23-30; John 15, 12-21).

9. Christ's disciples are slow to believe in Him (Mark 16, 14; John 7, 5; 20, 9.

[4] On the other hand, the sacred author is aware that his readers are already familiar with the other Gospels. He says nothing about the institution of the Eucharist because the Synoptics contained full accounts of this event. Instead he describes the promise of the Eucharist (John 6, 22-72) which the Synoptics had omitted. He also fills in details concerning events described in the other Gospels. He adds to Mark's account of the multiplication of loaves the historical fact that it was Philip who remarked that enough bread would require more than "two hundred denarii worth" (John 6, 7; Mark 6, 37). And it is John who names Judas as the person who complained that the wasted perfume could have been sold for three hundred pence when the sinful woman washed the feet of Jesus (John 12, 1-9; Mark 14, 3-9). John shows himself a true historian who carefully distinguishes fact and theory.

[5] A study of the fourth Gospel reveals that it was written by an eyewitness who appeals to his own veracity, a Jew who was familiar with Palestine before its destruction, a disciple whom Jesus especially loved (John 1, 14; 20, 24; 1 John 1, 1). And by the end of the 2nd century it was universally known and undisputed that the author was St. John, the son of Zebedee (Arendzen, *The Gospels*).

What is the Gospel according to St. Thomas?

[1] The Gospel according to St. Thomas is not really a Gospel but simply a collection of 114 sayings which the Gnostics, a heretical sect of early Christianity, compiled

about the middle of the 3rd century. The Gnostics (*gnosis* is the Greek word for knowledge) falsely believed that salvation comes through hidden esoteric knowledge which is limited to the elect. St. Irenaeus and Origen vigorously refuted this heresy.

[2] The original manuscript was found near Luxor in southern Egypt in 1946. It consists of over 1,000 sheets of brittle papyrus paper wrapped in 13 leather portfolios and placed in jars for preservation.

[3] Some of the sayings in this "Gospel" are identical with passages from the New Testament, but most of them are phrased with a Gnostic slant. Because these sayings do not endanger the faith of Catholics today, they have not been placed on the Index of Forbidden Books. Moreover, they are of little value to the study of New Testament times and do not add much to the knowledge we already have.

Is not the Bible the only source of faith—the one means whereby the teachings of Christ have been handed down to us?

[1] No, the Bible is not the only source of faith. Without the intervention of a divine, infallible teaching apostolate distinct from the Bible, we could never know with absolute certainty what books constitute the inspired Scriptures, or whether the copies we possess today agree with the originals.

[2a] The Bible itself is but a dead letter calling for a divine interpreter; it is not arranged in systematic form like a creed or catechism; it is often obscure and hard to understand, as St. Peter says of the Epistles of St. Paul (2 Peter 3, 16; *Cf.* Acts 8, 30-31); it is open to many a false interpretation. Moreover, a number of revealed truths have been handed down by divine tradition only.

[3a] When Luther first put forth this false view of the transmission of divine revelation, he stated that the Bible could be interpreted by everyone, "even by the humble miller's maid, nay, by a child of mine," but when the Anabaptists, the Zwinglians and others denied his teaching, the Bible became "a heresy book," most obscure and difficult to understand. Even in his own day his false theory gave rise to many a new heresy. He says himself in 1525: "There

are as many sects and beliefs as there are heads. This fellow will have nothing to do with Baptism; another denies the Sacrament; a third believes that there is another world between this and the last day. Some teach that Christ is not God; some say this, some that. There is no rustic so rude but that, if he dreams or fancies anything, it must be the whisper of the Holy Spirit, and he himself a prophet" (Grisar, *Luther,* iv., 386-407).

[4] Protestants in practice set aside their theory either by appealing to an inward illumination of the Holy Spirit, or by making reason their one guide.

Did not Christ say: "You search the Scriptures, because in them you think that you have life everlasting. And it is they that bear witness to Me" (John 5, 39).

[1] Christ is not telling the Jews to read the New Testament, which did not exist, to find out His Gospel, but He is insisting upon the fact that they did read the Old Testament with no profit, because they failed to recognize Him as their Messias. The prophets of the Law taught that He was the Messias, the Son of God, in whom they were to believe in order to have eternal life *(See* John 3, 16).

How do Catholics answer this statement that appeared in a Church of Christ publication: "Here is an excerpt from an address by the Cardinals in the Roman Church to Pope Pius III, which is preserved in the National Library of Paris, folio No. 1068, Vol. 2, pp. 650 and 651: '. . . if one compares the teachings of the Bible with what takes place in our churches, we will soon find discord, and realize that our teachings are often different from the Bible, and oftener still, contrary to it.' "?

[1a] No such address was ever made by Cardinals to any Pope. Nor does the *Bibliothèque Nationale* contain any such entry as "folio no. 1068." The *Office de Documentation,* a research affiliate of the *Bibliothèque Nationale,* has drawn up a special report on the history of this address. The report is summarized in the following paragraphs.

[2] In 1536, Pope Paul II (not Pius III, who reigned for only a few months in 1503) named a commission of nine

Cardinals who were to prepare the needed program of Church reform. This commission, in March, 1537, presented to the Pope its famous report which was to be the basis of the Council of Trent's reform decrees: *The Advice of the Commission of Cardinals on the Reform of the Church Set Forth at the Command of Pope Paul III.*

[3] In the same year Luther translated this report on the Cardinals into German and published it with a critical preface. Other editions of *The Advice of the Commission of Cardinals* were published by Protestants who added to it their criticisms and objections. The Protestants were so successful in using this authentic Catholic document for their own cause that Pope Paul IV in 1559 placed all editions of *The Advice of the Commission of Cardinals,* Catholic and Protestant, on the Index of Forbidden Books. This prohibition remained until 1758 when the Index was modified so as to cover only the editions printed with heretical commentaries (Putnam, *The Censorship of the Church of Rome,* I, p. 169).

[4] It is important to note that in none of these editions of *The Advice of the Commission of Cardinals* does the alleged anti-Biblical statement of the Cardinals appear. But because of the profitable way in which some Protestants were able to use this authentic document, another opponent of the Church got the idea of fabricating a document similar to the report actually drawn up by the Cardinals in 1537. In the same Index of 1559 in which *The Advice of the Commission of Cardinals* was prohibited, an anonymous pamphlet was also listed entitled: *The Advice of Some Bishops Convened at Bologna Given to Pope Paul for the Strengthening of the Roman Church, 1549.* This meeting of Bishops was a pure invention. It is in this fictitious document that we find "some Bishops" admitting that the Church's teachings contradict those of Scripture.

[5] There is abundant evidence that this fictional "advice" to the Pope was written by the apostate Bishop, Petrus Paulus Vergerius, after he left the Church in 1549. On October 6, 1562, and in August, 1563, in letters to his protector, Christopher, Duke of Württemberg, Vergerius explicitly declares that he is the author of the fabricated document (this correspondence published by Schott, Tü-

bingen, 1875). The pamphlet can be found in Vergerius's collected works under the title: *Consilium quorundam episcoporum Bononiae congregatorum (Primus Tomus Operum Vergerii Adversus Papatum,* Tübingen, 1563).

[6] The purely fictional nature of *The Advice of Some Bishops* is seen in the fact that the *Office de Documentation* was able to locate three separate editions of the *same* "advice," all written by Vergerius, but addressed to three different Popes (Paul III, Julius III, Pius IV) signed by different groups of Bishops; and composed in different years (1549, 1553, 1555)!

[7] The question arises: "Why, if this 'advice' was a pure invention, did Vergerius admit that he was the author?" Father Herbert Thurston answers that the witty Vergerius never intended to pass off his *Advice of Some Bishops* as a true, factual document which Catholic Bishops actually sent to the Pope. Instead Vergerius wrote the pamphlet as a satire on reforms the Church was contemplating. Father Thurston writes: ". . . satirical compositions have often been taken seriously. An example is the 'Letter of the Three Bishops,' which, though written by an apostate of infamous character, Peter Paul Vergerius, and professing to be a letter of advice given by three Bishops to the Pope to help to strengthen the power of the Papacy, is obviously a skit rather than a forgery. But this letter has been quoted by hundreds of Protestant controversialists from Crashaw downwards" (C.E. vii, 702).

By what right do you teach doctrines not found in the Bible? Does not this practice put the Church above the Word of God? Did not Christ rebuke the Pharisees for "teaching as doctrine the precepts of men" (Matt. 15, 9), and "you make void the commandments of God by your tradition" (Mark 7, 13)?

[1] Because the Bible nowhere implies that it is the only source of faith. On the contrary St. Paul expressly teaches that Christians must believe not only what he *wrote* but what he *preached.* "So then, brethren, stand firm, and hold the teachings that you have learned, whether by word or by letter of ours" (2 Thess. 2, 15). "Hold to the form of sound teaching which thou hast heard from me, in the

faith and love which is in Christ Jesus. Guard the good trust through the Holy Spirit, who dwells in you" (2 Tim. 1, 13-14).

2 The Council of Trent "seeing clearly that this truth and discipline are contained in the written books and the unwritten traditions which, received by the Apostles from the mouth of Christ Himself, or from the Apostles themselves, the Holy Spirit dictating, have come down even unto us, transmitted as it were from hand to hand, following the example of the orthodox Fathers, receives and venerates, with an equal affection of piety, all the books of the Old and New Testaments . . . and also the said traditions . . . preserved in the Catholic Church by a continuous succession."

3 Christ in the text cited was rebuking the Pharisees for nullifying the fourth commandment by their casuistry (Mark 7, 11-12; Lagrange, *S. Marc,* 176). The tradition of the Church is not human opinion, but the divine teaching of an infallible Apostolate established by Christ.

4 The Bible in many passages tells us that the divine teaching of Christ is transmitted to us by teachers accredited by God. St. Matthew speaks of this Apostolate as a divinely authorized teaching of the whole doctrine of Christ to all men of all times, who are to accept it once they are baptized. "All power in heaven and on earth has been given to Me. Go, therefore, and make disciples of all nations, baptizing them in the name of the Father, and of the Son, and of the Holy Spirit: teaching them to observe all that I have commanded you; and behold, I am with you all days, even unto the consummation of the world" (Matt. 28, 18-19).

5 St. Mark speaks of the divine sanction given this "preaching": "Go into the whole world and preach the Gospel to every creature. He who believes and is baptized shall be saved, but he who does not believe shall be condemned" (Mark 16, 15-16).

6 St. Luke speaks of the Apostolate "preached in His name to all nations" (Luke 24, 47), and declares the Apostles authentic witnesses of a divine revelation, which is infallibly guaranteed by the Holy Spirit: "You shall receive power when the Holy Spirit comes upon you, and you shall

be witnesses for me in Jerusalem and in all Judea and Samaria and even to the very ends of the earth" (Acts 1, 8).

7 The teaching of Christ that His Gospel is to be learned not from the Bible alone, but from a divine, infallible Apostolate until the end of the world is clearly set forth by St. Paul: "For whoever calls upon the name of the Lord shall be saved. How then are they to call upon Him in whom they have not believed? But how are they to believe Him whom they have not heard? And how are they to hear, if no one preaches? And how are men to preach unless they be sent? . . . Faith then depends on hearing, and hearing on the word of Christ. But I say: Have they not heard? Yes, indeed, 'Their voice has gone forth into all the earth and their words unto the ends of the world'" (Rom. 10, 14-18).

8 The Apostles always represented themselves as the ambassadors of God (Rom. 1, 5; 15, 18; 1 Cor. 2, 16; 3, 9; 1 John 4, 6); they proved their divine mission by miracles (1 Cor. 2, 4; 2 Cor. 12, 12; 1 Thess. 1, 5); they required all the faithful to obey their divine message (Rom. 1, 5; 2 Cor. 10, 4-6); they anathematized those who refused to accept it. "But even if we or an angel from heaven should preach a gospel to you other than that which we have preached to you, let him be anathema" (Gal. 1, 8).

9 That men were to learn the Gospel not from their private interpretation of the Bible, but from this permanent Apostolate, is clear from the fact that the Apostles appointed successors to themselves, and ordered them in turn to appoint others to carry on their work. "Hold to the form of sound teaching thou hast heard from me. . . . Guard the good trust through the Holy Spirit, who dwells in you" (2 Tim. 1, 13-14). "The things that thou hast heard of me through many witnesses, commend to trustworthy men who shall be competent in turn to teach others" (2 Tim. 2, 2).

10 St. Irenaeus (140-205), Bishop of Lyons in the 2nd century, clearly taught that all Christians were to learn the Gospel from the tradition of the Apostles and their successors, especially from the tradition of the Apostolic See of Rome. He writes: "Therefore in every Church there is the tradition of Apostles made manifest throughout the

whole world; and we can enumerate those who were by the Apostles instituted Bishops in the Churches, and the successors of those Bishops down to ourselves." Then after mentioning Smyrna, which through St. Polycarp (d. 155) takes us back to St. John, he adds: "But it would be too long to enumerate here the successions of all the Churches; it suffices to point out the Apostolic tradition, the teaching that has come down to us by Episcopal succession in the Church of Rome, the greatest and most ancient of all known everywhere, and founded in Rome by the two glorious Apostles, St. Peter and St. Paul" (*Adv. Haer.,* iii., 3).

Do not Catholics reason in a circle when they prove a teaching Apostolate by the Bible, and then the Bible by this teaching Apostolate?

[1] We do not reason in a circle. If we were to prove the Apostolate from the inspired Scriptures, and then the inspired Scriptures from the Apostolate, we would be guilty of the fallacy of the vicious circle. On the contrary, we do not in any way pre-suppose that the books of the New Testament are inspired, but only that they are genuine, authentic documents written by honest men. We allow the words of Christ and His Apostles to speak for themselves, without appealing to the authority of the Church.

[2] The Bible proves that the Church's claims were the same in the beginning as they are now, while the Church pledges the authority it has received from Christ in support of the inspiration and inerrancy of the Bible. Thus both Bible and Church depend on the authority of our Lord. The Church also appeals to the Bible as a contemporary record of historical facts.

[3] When two independent witnesses confirm each other's evidence, the argument for the truthfulness of both is not circular, but cumulative.

Was not Luther the first to translate the Bible into the vernacular? Why did Catholics object to it so strongly at the time?

[1] No, Luther was not the first to translate the Bible into the vernacular. His translation of the New Testament was not published until 1522, and his version of the Old

Testament not until 1534. Catholics from 1466 to 1522 had already published fourteen complete editions of the Bible in High German at Augsburg, Basle, Strassburg and Nuremburg, and five in Low German at Cologne, Delf, Halberstadt and Lubeck (Janssen, *History of the German People*, xiv., 388). During this same period—from 1450 to 1520—Catholics had published 156 Latin and 6 Hebrew editions of the Bible, besides issuing complete translations in Italian (11), French (10), Bohemian (2), Flemish (1), Limousine (1), and Russian (1) (Falk, *Die Bibel am Ausgange des Mittelalters*).

[2] Catholics objected to Luther's German translation, because, as Emser wrote at the time, "He has in many places confused, stultified and perverted the old trustworthy text of the Christian Church to its great disadvantage, and also poisoned it with heretical glosses and prefaces. . . . He almost everywhere forces the Scriptures on the question of faith and works, even when neither faith nor works are thought of" (Janssen, *History of the German People,* xiv., 425). Emser points out 1,400 inaccuracies, while Bunsen, a Protestant scholar, mentions 3,000. Luther ridiculed Ecclesiastes, rejected the Epistle to the Hebrews and the Apocalypse as not Apostolic, omitted the two books of Machabees because they mentioned prayers for the dead, and called the Epistle of St. James "an epistle of straw," because it clearly contradicted his false doctrine on good works. He deliberately perverted the meaning of St. Paul in Romans, by adding the words "only" (nur) in Rom. 3, 20 and Rom. 4, 15, and "alone" (allein) in Rom. 3, 28. When this interpolation was pointed out to him by Catholic critics, he wrote: "If your new Papist makes much ado about the word 'alone,' just say straight out to him: 'Dr. Luther will have it so, and says, Papist and donkey are one and the same thing; thus I will and am determined to have it; my will is the reason'" (*Ibid.,* 419).

Was not the Bible practically unknown in the Middle Ages, when your Church was dominant?

[1] The priests used it in preparing their sermons, and knew it from their daily reading of the missal and the breviary. The monks copied the Scriptures in their *scrip-*

toria, and meditated upon them frequently. The laity, before printing was invented and when Bible manuscripts were rare and costly, knew the Scriptures from listening to sermons, and from studying the sculpture, paintings, frescoes and mosaics that filled their churches. What a comprehensive view of both the Old Testament and the New could be had by a parishioner of St. Mark's in Venice in the 13th century. As Ruskin says: "The walls of the church became the poor man's Bible, and a picture was more easily read than a chapter" (*The Stones of Venice,* ii., 99). "There is," writes Dr. Cutts, "a good deal of popular misapprehension about the way in which the Bible was regarded in the Middle Ages. Some people think that it was very little read, even by the clergy; whereas the fact is that the sermons of the medieval preachers are more full of Scriptural quotations and allusions than any sermons in these days; and the writers on other subjects are so full of Scriptural allusion, that it is evident their minds were saturated with Scriptural diction" (*Turning Points of English History,* 200).

Was not the Bible first translated into English by John Wyclif? Did not your Church show her hostility to any translation of the Bible into English by proscribing the translations of Wyclif and Tyndale?

[1a] No, Cardinal Gasquet has proved that the so-called Wyclifite Bibles in existence today are really the old English Catholic Bibles, mentioned by Blessed Thomas More, who wrote: "The whole Bible was long before his (Wyclif's) day, by virtuous and well-learned men, translated into the English tongue, and by good and godly people and with devotion and soberness, well and reverently read" (*English Works,* 233).

[2] Wyclif's translation was condemned by the Council of Oxford under Archbishop Arundel in 1408, because he introduced into it his heretical views. It ordered that no translation should be made, until "it shall have been approved by the Bishop of the place or by the provincial council." Blessed Thomas More thus comments on this law: "I trow that in this law you see nothing unreason-

able. For it neither forbiddeth the translation to be read that were already well done of old before Wyclif's day, nor damneth his because it was new, but because it was naught; nor prohibiteth new to be made, but provideth that they shall not be read, if they be made amiss, till they be by good examination amended."

[3a] Tyndale's translation of the New Testament was burned at St. Paul's by Bishop Tunstall in 1530 for the same reason. It was a faulty translation containing some 2,000 errors. The Bishops of those days banned it just as a modern State prohibits the circulation of counterfeit money; It did not represent the pure word of God.

Why did the monks of the Middle Ages chain the Bible in their libraries and churches?

[1] The Bible and other books were chained in the libraries and churches of the Middle Ages to preserve them from theft, and especially to make them accessible to students.

[2] The first mention of chained Bibles occurs in the catalogue of St. Peter's Monastery of Wiessenburg, Alsace, in 1040, which mentions four Psalters chained in the monastery church. Most medieval libraries stored their books in locked chests and presses. There is no other mention of chained libraries until the 15th century. All the books of St. Mark's Library in Florence (1441) and of the Malatesta Library in Cesena (1452) were chained.

[3] Throughout the Middle Ages it was deemed a pious work to bequeath Bibles, Psalters and Books of Hours to be chained in church for common use. Count Frederick of Heidelberg bequeathed his Book of Hours to the Church of the Holy Spirit in 1474; a Catholic of Leyden, Holland, his Bible to St. Peter's Church; and the Earl of Ormond his Psalter to be chained to his tomb at St. Thomas Acon.

[4] The Oxford College of Eton, Brasenose and Merton did not remove the chains until the 18th century, while some libraries removed them only in the 19th century.

Why does your Church forbid Catholics to read the Bible and at the same time claim that she champions the Bible as the inspired word of God?

[1] You have been misinformed. The Church encourages Catholics to read the Bible. In a letter to the Archbishop of Florence, Pius VI (1778) urges Catholics to read the Bible. He writes: "At a time when a great many books which grossly attack the Catholic religion are being circulated even among the unlearned, to the great destruction of souls, you judge exceedingly well that the faithful should be urged to read the Holy Scriptures; for they are the most abundant sources which ought to be left open to everyone, to draw from them purity of morals and of doctrine, and to eradicate the errors which are so widely spread in these corrupt times."

[2] Pius VII a few years later wrote in the same strain to the English Vicars-Apostolic, asking them "to encourage their people to read the Holy Scriptures; for nothing can be more useful, more consoling, and more animating, inasmuch as they serve to confirm the faith, support the hope, and influence the charity of the true Christian."

[3] Leo XIII, in his Encyclical on the Bible (1893), writes: "The solicitude of the Apostolic office naturally urges, and even compels us, to desire that this great source of Catholic revelation should be made safely and abundantly accessible to the flock of Jesus Christ. . . . (By reading the Scriptures) the intelligence will be illuminated and strengthened . . . and at the same time the heart will grow warm, and will strive with ardent longing to advance in virtue and divine love."

[4] Pope Benedict XV, in his Encyclical on St. Jerome, quotes St. Jerome's letter to Demetrias: "Love the Bible and wisdom will love you; love it and it will preserve you; honor it and it will embrace you" (*Epis.*, cxxx., 20).

[5] Pope Pius XII in his Encyclical, *Divino Afflante Spiritu* (1943), instructs Bishops "to lend help to those pious associations whose aim is to spread copies of the Sacred Letters, especially of the Gospels, among the faithful, and to procure by every means that in Christian families the same be read daily with piety and devotion."

[6] The Church, however, does forbid Catholics to read false translations of the Bible which are often accompanied by glosses and notes destructive of true faith. But she has

never prohibited versions in the vernacular which have been approved by the Bishops of the various countries.

⁷ The Church also objects to the reading of the Bible in the public schools because in some states where Protestantism is dominant, the reading of the Protestant translations has been made the occasion of introducing all the elements of a religious service, a practice contrary to the spirit of the American Constitution.

⁸ The Supreme Court of Illinois, June 29, 1910, held "that the stated exercises constituted sectarian instruction, and made the public school a house of worship in violation of the Illinois Constitution." The Supreme Courts of Wisconsin, Nebraska, and Louisiana have rendered similar decisions.

⁹ Catholics to whom the Bible is a "heaven-sent treasure" cannot approve its being used in state-supported schools as a means of proselytizing students.

How could the Council of Trent declare the Vulgate "authentic" when we know it contains many mistakes? Why did it set aside the Hebrew and Greek Bibles?

¹ In declaring the Vulgate "authentic," that is, officially guaranteed, the Council of Trent did not imply that it was in every respect an absolutely accurate rendering of the original text, but that it was free from error in faith and morals, and was substantially faithful to the original Scriptures. The disciplinary decree, *Insuper,* applies only to the Latin Church and to the public use of the Vulgate. It does not in any way diminish the authority and value of the original texts. The Council was not concerned about the Hebrew and Greek Bible. It simply judged that of the Latin versions, which were in circulation at that time, the Vulgate was to be preferred for public use.

² Pope Pius XII in his Encyclical, *Divino Afflante Spiritu,* succinctly explains the meaning of the Tridentine decree, "this special authority, or as they say, authenticity of the Vulgate, was not affirmed by the Council particularly for critical reasons, but rather because of its legitimate use in the Churches throughout so many centuries; by which use indeed the same is shown, in the sense in which the

Church has understood and understands it, to be free from any error whatsoever in matters of faith and morals; so that, as the Church herself testifies and affirms, it may be quoted safely and without fear of error in disputations, in lectures, and in preaching; and so its authenticity is not specified primarily as critical, but rather as juridical."

Would you kindly tell us something about the Dead Sea Scrolls? I have been told that they contain evidence against Christianity.

[1] Early in the spring of 1947, some Bedouins found a number of manuscripts in a cave near the Dead Sea. In February, 1949, scientific excavation of the cave yielded some manuscript fragments and fragments of jars in which the manuscripts were stored. It is considered to be the most important Biblical discovery of modern times.

[2] Among the manuscripts discovered were:

1. A complete text of Isaia with a few lacunae.

2. A Manual of Discipline used by an unknown Jewish sect.

3. A commentary on Habucuc.

4. What seems to be the long lost apocryphal book of Lamech in Aramaic.

5. Four scrolls containing hymns of thanksgiving.

6. A manuscript entitled, "The Battle between the Sons of Light and the Sons of Darkness."

7. A fragment with sections from Isaia.

8. Fragments of Daniel, Leviticus—and many other fragments that have not yet been identified.

They appear to have been written between 2 B.C. and 25 A.D., and scholars think that they were placed in the jars during the last half of the 1st century A.D.

[3] An immense amount of literature has been written on the meaning and effect of these Scrolls. Many people rushed into print to express their personal opinions. Some of them made irresponsible statements and drew unwarranted conclusions which they later retracted. The atmosphere gradually cleared and authoritative experts in paleology,

archaeology, philology and Biblical studies have been busy in serious painstaking research. Their efforts are being rewarded in uncovering new knowledge that strengthens the truth of Christianity. Catholics and Protestants welcome this discovery and the authoritative interpretations of these documents are proving a boon for the Christian religion.

[4] We would recommend your reading two books: *Meaning of the Dead Sea Scrolls* by Jean Danielou, Helicon Press, 1959, and *Dead Sea Scrolls and the Bible* by Roland E. Murphy, O.Carm., Newman Press, 1956, for a more detailed account of the discovery and interpretation of these important documents.

What do Catholics mean by the word, tradition? We Protestants know only Scripture.

[1] Tradition is the preaching of the Church. It is the communication by the teaching Church of the revelation made by Christ and His Spirit to the Apostles. It is not confined to the past for it involves continuous preservation and continuous presentation. In Tradition there is life; in Tradition there is growth of the Church's consciousness of her possession and of progress in her presentation of that possession to men. What makes Tradition a living thing is that the Church looks to her own living consciousness for the doctrines confided to her by the Spirit of Truth.

[2] God's revelation has been handed down to us in two ways, by inspired writings (Scripture) and by divinely-directed pronouncements of the teaching Church (Tradition). The Church transmits and communicates revealed doctrine by her living preaching and also by teaching Scripture. The Bible is the Church's book. She received it and she owns it. Only she can tell us what is Scripture and what is not; only she can tell us authoritatively what it means. Although she uses Scripture, the Church insists that in Tradition alone God's revelation has been integrally deposited. The Church is the one salvific teaching instrument founded by Christ, and she does not depend upon Scripture for her existence or for her doctrine.

SELECTED BIBLIOGRAPHY

AUZOU, GEORGES. *The Word of God.* St. Louis: B. Herder Book Co. 1960.

BARROSSE, THOMAS. *God Speaks to Men; Understanding the Bible.* Notre Dame, Ind.: Fides. 1960.

CASTELOT, JOHN JOSEPH. *Meet the Bible!* Baltimore: Helicon Press. 1960.

CHARLIER, CELESTIN. *The Christian Approach to the Bible.* Westminster, Md.: Newman Press. 1958.

DANIELOU, JEAN. *The Dead Sea Scrolls and Primitive Christianity.* Baltimore: Helicon Press. 1958.

DANIEL-ROPS, HENRI. *What Is the Bible?* New York: Hawthorn Books. 1958.

DANNEMILLER, LAWRENCE. *Reading the Word of God.* Baltimore: Helicon Press. 1960.

DOUGHERTY, JOHN J. *Searching the Scriptures.* Garden City, N. Y.: Hanover House. 1959.

GROLLENBERG, LUCAS H. *Shorter Atlas of the Bible.* New York: T. Nelson. 1960.

HESSLER, BERTRAM J. *The Bible in the Light of Modern Science.* Chicago: Franciscan Herald Press. 1960.

LUPTON, DANIEL E. *A Guide to Reading the Bible.* Chicago: Acta Publications. 1960.

McELENEY, NEIL J. (Gen. ed.) *Pamphlet Bible Series.* New York: Paulist Press. 1960.

MORIARTY, FREDERICK L. *Introducing the Old Testament.* Milwaukee: Bruce Publishing Co. 1960.

MURPHY, ROLAND E. *Seven Books of Wisdom.* Milwaukee: Bruce Publishing Co. 1960.

———— *The Dead Sea Scrolls and the Bible.* Westminster, Md.: Newman Press. 1956.

PIUS XII, POPE. "On the Promotion of Biblical Studies" in *Four Great Encyclicals.* New York: (Deus Books). Paulist Press. 1961.

RICCIOTTI, GIUSEPPE. *The History of Israel.* 2nd ed. Milwaukee: Bruce Publishing Co. 1959.

———— *Life of Christ.* Milwaukee: Bruce Publishing Co. (Popular Ed. 1952).

SULLIVAN, KATHRYN. *God's Word and Work.* Collegeville, Minn.: Liturgical Press. 1958.

VAWTER, BRUCE. *A Path Through Genesis.* New York: Sheed & Word. 1956.

PART XVI
The Church and Democracy

Is not the social question merely an economic question, with which the Church has nothing to do? Why don't your Pope, your Bishops, and clergy stick to the Gospel and stop meddling in social, economic, and political matters?

[1] The social question is not limited to economics. It also involves morals and religion. Pope Pius XII has stated, "The social question is undoubtedly an economic question, but even more than that it is a question which concerns the ordered regulation of human society. And, in its deepest sense, it is a moral and, therefore, a religious question." And, as Pope Leo XIII declared, it "must be settled by the principles of morality and according to the dictates of religion" (Encyclical on *Christian Democracy*).

[2] The Catholic Church believes that the ultimate solution of the social question depends upon the universal recognition of the moral and religious teaching of Christ. Like her divine Founder, she has a mission pre-eminently spiritual. Her task is to bring salvation to all men through the grace of Christ. She holds herself aloof from all particular forms of government or parties, and from all special theories of economic and social reform. Nevertheless, when sociologists, economists, and politicians offer theories and reforms which deny the Gospel and violate the natural rights of man, she cannot and does not remain silent.

[3] The Catholic hierarchy and clergy are duty-bound to examine and judge all social, economic, and political matters, in fact all human affairs, insofar as they relate to moral and religious issues. The Church believes that it would be wrong for her to interfere without just cause in

such earthly concerns; but she can never relinquish her God-given task of interposing her authority, not indeed in technical matters for which she has neither the equipment nor the mission, but in all those that have a bearing on moral conduct. (*See* Pius XI Encyclical on *Reconstructing the Social Order.*)

[4] Man's conduct in every sphere of life must be guided by the teachings of Christ. For the clergy to abandon the marketplace to the enemies of the Gospel would mean a betrayal of Christ whom they represent on earth. The experts are free to devise means of bettering the temporal welfare of people, but it is ever the duty of the Church to determine the morality of such means. She alone can judge whether they promote or hinder the salvation of man.

How can Catholics give the United States an undivided allegiance, when they are subjects of a foreign power? If the Pope were to command Catholics in purely civil matters to be disloyal to their country, would Catholics be bound to obey him?

[1] No. As Cardinal Gibbons once wrote, "The Pope will take no such action we know . . . but were he to do so, he would stand self-condemned, a transgressor of the law he himself promulgates. He would be offending not only against civil society, but against God, and violating an authority as truly from God as His own. Any Catholic who clearly recognized this would be bound not to obey the Pope" (*A Retrospect of Fifty Years,* p. 227).

[2] This view of the American Cardinal accords with the official teaching of the Popes. "All things that are of a civil nature the Church acknowledges and declares to be under the power and authority of the ruler" (Encyclical of Leo XIII on *Civil Government*).

[3] Catholics are obligated to be patriotic citizens because "the supernatural love for the Church and the natural love for our own country proceed from the same eternal principle, since God Himself is their Author" (Encyclical of Leo XIII on *Duties of Christians as Citizens*). History witnesses that the very martyrs to Elizabeth's unjust penal laws in *religious* matters frequently announced on the scaffold their loyalty to her in *civil* matters.

[4] The Church cannot interfere in purely civil affairs, nor the State in purely religious matters. "And in things where for different reasons the decision belongs both to the sacred and to the civil power, the Church wishes that there be harmony between the two so that injurious contests may be avoided" (Encyclical of Leo XIII on *Civil Government*). Catholics, like other citizens, are bound to obey the civil laws unless they are unjust, destructive of liberty, or contrary to the moral or divine law.

[5] An unjust law has no validity in morals nor any binding force in conscience. It must be rejected by every Christian in loyalty to Christ. When the Roman Emperors asked the martyrs to sacrifice to pagan gods and when the Mohammedans ordered Christians to deny the divinity of Christ, all loyal followers of Christ refused compliance in the name of freedom of conscience and defied these tyrants unto death. With St. Peter they declared, "We must obey God rather than man" (Acts 5, 29).

[6] The basic reason why Catholics can give full allegiance to the United States and to the Pope is that "the Almighty has appointed the charge of the human race between two powers, the ecclesiastical and the civil; the one being set over divine things, the other over human affairs. Each in its kind is supreme; each has fixed limits within which it is contained. . . . Whatever, therefore, is of a sacred character, whatever belongs to the salvation of souls or to the worship of God is subject to the power and judgment of the Church. Whatever is to be ranged under the civil and political order is rightly subject to the civil authority. Jesus Christ has Himself given the command that what is Caesar's is to be rendered to Caesar and that which belongs to God is to be rendered to God" (Encyclical of Leo XIII on the *Christian Constitution of States*). Between the duties these two powers, Church and State, respectively enjoin, neither can rightly come into collision with the other.

Did not the Popes, especially in the Syllabus of Pius IX, condemn the American principle of the separation of Church and State? Is it not always better for the two powers to remain separate?

[1] No Pope has condemned the present relation between the Church and State in America, nor has any Pope even expressed a wish that any change should be made. Many non-Catholics cite the Syllabus, without being possessed of the theological training necessary to interpret that document accurately. Cardinal Newman had to teach Mr. Gladstone its meaning in 1874 (*Letter to the Duke of Norfolk*), and Governor Smith of New York had to repeat the lesson, when his loyalty was challenged in 1927 by a bigoted New York lawyer (*Atlantic Monthly*, April, 1927).

[2] The Syllabus is merely an index of false doctrines, previously condemned by Popes Gregory XVI and Pius IX in various Apostolic letters, Briefs and Encyclicals. No one can understand the meaning of its condemned propositions, unless he reads the original context carefully.

[3] When the Syllabus condemns the proposition (No. 55): *"The Church must be separated from the State, and the State from the Church,"* all that the condemnation implies is that the Church need not *always* be separated from the State. Only the narrow bigot, who believes that the union of Church and State should under no circumstances be maintained, could logically find fault with this reasonable condemnation, or maintain that it involves a conflict of loyalties.

[4] Catholics, while holding firmly the Church's theoretical teaching regarding the ideal State, do not identify this ideal with the actual situation which prevailed throughout the Middle Ages. As Dr. Pohle writes: "The intimate connection of both powers during the Middle Ages was only a passing and temporary phenomenon, arising neither from the essential nature of the State, nor from that of the Church. The Church is free to enter into a more or less close association with the State, but she can also endure actual separation from the State, and, given favorable circumstances, may even prosper under such conditions, as for example in the United States" (*C. E.*, xiv., 769).

[5] Cardinal Gibbons, a true Catholic and a loyal American, could write: "American Catholics rejoice in our separation of Church and State; and I can conceive of no combination of circumstances likely to arise, which should make a union desirable either for Church or State. We

know the blessing of our present arrangement; it gives us liberty and binds together priests and people in a union better than that of Church and State. We do not believe our system is adapted to all countries; we leave it to Church and State in other lands to solve their problem for their own best interests. For ourselves, we thank God we live in America, 'in this happy land of ours,' to quote Theodore Roosevelt, 'where liberty and religion are natural allies' " (*A Retrospect of Fifty Years*, p. 234).

Why is the Catholic Church so strongly opposed to communism?

[1] Because the doctrine of modern communism is by its very nature anti-religious. This doctrine states that there is in the world only one reality, matter, the blind forces of which evolve into plant, animal and man. Even human society is nothing but a phenomenon and form of matter, evolving in the same way. By a law of inexorable necessity and through a perpetual conflict of forces, matter moves toward the final synthesis of a classless society. In such a doctrine, there is no room for the idea of God; there is no difference between matter and spirit, between body and soul; there is neither survival of the soul after death nor any hope in a future life. There is no recognition of any right of the individual in his relations to the communist State; no natural right is accorded to human personality, man becomes a mere cogwheel in the communist system. Thus communism attacks the very foundations of all religious belief.

How does the Catholic Church answer the communist charge that religion is the "opium of the people"?

[1a] Communists call religion the opium of the people to emphasize the idea that the nature and purpose of religion is to ease the physical and mental sufferings of this life by promising greater happiness in a future life. Like opium, religion intoxicates the minds of men and prevents them from viewing life and the universe as they really are.

[2] The effects of this drug called religion is threefold:

1. It teaches the rich their rights, thereby strengthening the rich in their determination to exploit the poor.

2. It teaches the poor their duties to the ruling class, thereby aiding in their being exploited by the rich.

3. It is by its very nature, passive and destructive of any activity on man's part which would tend toward his economic betterment.

The Church answers these objections in the following way:

[3] 1. Never in the history of the Catholic Church has there been one single official declaration to substantiate this charge. On the contrary, the Catholic Church has been the one great force in the world—centuries before communism ever existed—which has always protested against the exploitation of the poor. From the very beginning of Christianity, the Founder stated that it would be as difficult for the rich to enter heaven as for a camel to pass through the eye of a needle. In our own day numerous encyclicals of the Popes such as *Quadragesimo Anno* and *Rerum Novarum* have rebuked the ruling classes for practices of exploitation. In the words of Leo XIII, "the rich man must remember that to exercise pressure for the sake of gain upon the indigent and destitute and to make one's profit out of the need of another is condemned by all laws human and divine."

[4] 2. Communists again can be challenged to bring forward a single official statement in the entire history of the Church in which she has urged the poor to submit to exploitation. Down through the ages, the Church has been the one great champion of the poor. Through hospitals, schools, orphanages, etc. the Church has worked for the material as well as the spiritual welfare of the poor. To counter this charge, we quote the words of Pope Leo XIII in *Rerum Novarum*, "It is the duty of the State to promote in the highest degree the interests of the poor. . . . It is the desire of the Church that the poor should rise above poverty and wretchedness and should better their condition in this life, and for this it strives."

[5] 3. Religion, instead of being passive, is essentially dynamic. The very symbol of Christianity, the Cross, testifies to the activity of man in religion. The Christian is told to be a man of action, if he is given ten talents, he must earn ten more to gain the kingdom of God; he must

ot merely run the race or fight the good fight but must
win; he must help his neighbor, keep the commandments,
carry his cross daily. This is action in the fullest sense of
the word as any saint could readily testify.

*Were not Christ and the early Christians in Jerusalem
communists? Did not the Fathers of the 4th and 5th centuries deny the right of private property: John Chrysostom,
Basil, Ambrose, Augustine, Jerome?*

[1] Christ never condemned private ownership as unjust.
While insisting upon the dangers of riches (Matt. 19, 24),
and picturing in a parable the heartless rich man in hell
(Luke 16, 22), He admits the possibility of the rich man,
who is faithful to God's law, attaining the kingdom of
heaven (Matt. 19, 26). If Christ had regarded private ownership unlawful He would not have counseled the rich
young man to *sell* what he possessed (Matt. 19, 21), nor
would He have been content with Zacchaeus giving only
one-half of his goods to the poor (Luke 19, 8). Instead of
condemning private property, our Lord insists upon its
proper distribution in works of mercy, as one of the conditions of gaining the kingdom of heaven (Matt. 25, 35-36).

[2] The communism of the Jerusalem Christians (Acts 2,
44-45) was similar to the common life of our religious
communities, but it in no way implied a denial of private
ownership. It was a purely voluntary agreement, as we
learn from St. Peter's words to Ananias, "While it yet remained, did it not remain thine; and after it was sold was
not the money at thy disposal?" (Acts 5, 4.)

[3] The late Msgr. John A. Ryan has ably refuted the
charge of socialism or communism brought against the
early Fathers. He proves conclusively that not one of them
denied either explicitly or implicitly the right of private
property. While they denounced many of the rich men
of their day for having acquired their wealth unjustly, and
insisted upon a Christian devoting his superfluous goods
to the poor, they themselves retained personal ownership
of part of their estates (St. Basil, St. Ambrose), and taught
with St. Jerome that "wealth is not an obstacle to the rich
man, if he uses it well" (*Alleged Socialism of the Church
Fathers*).

Is not all authority vested in the people? Are they n
free to establish their own forms of religious and politic
government? Why does your Church claim to be exem
from popular sovereignty?

[1] All authority is rooted solely in God. He confe
political authority on the people as a whole and they a
free to establish any form of *civic* government based o
justice. He did not, however, vest any *religious* authori
in the people but only in Jesus Christ who was free
establish any form of *religious* government He chose.

[2] Pope Pius XII declares that "the ecclesiastical pow
is essentially different from the civil power." In explai
ing, he writes, "The origin of the Church, unlike t
origin of the State, is not to be found in the Natural La
The most complete and accurate analysis of the human pe
son offers no ground for the conclusion that the Churc
like civil society, was naturally bound to come into exis
ence and to develop. Its existence is derived from a po
tive act of God beyond and above the social nature of ma
though in perfect accord with it; therefore, the eccles
astical power is born of the will and act by which Chri
founded His Church. It remains true, however, that one
the Church was constituted, as a perfect society, by the a
of the Redeemer, not a few elements of resemblance t
the structure of the civil society sprang from her ver
nature.

[3] "In one point, however, the fundamental differenc
between the two is particularly manifest. Christ who i
His Church set up on earth the Kingdom of God which H
had announced and destined for all men and all times, di
not vest in the community of the faithful the mission o
Priest and Pastor but He transmitted and communicate
it to a college of Apostles or messengers, in order that the
by their preaching, by their priestly ministry, and by th
social authority of their office, bring into the Church th
multitude of the faithful to be sanctified, enlightene
and led to the full maturity of followers of Christ" (*Act*
Apostolicae Sedis, 1945, p. 256).

[4] The members of the ecclesiastical hierarchy have a
ways received and do receive their authority from abov

and are responsible for the exercise of their mandate immediately to God only, to whom the Roman Pontiff is subject, or as far as the other grades are concerned, to their hierarchical superiors. They have no account to render to the people.

[5] In the State the primordial subject of power is the whole people to whom its rulers are accountable, but in the Church the prime subject is never the community of the faithful. It is God and not the people who demands that ecclesiastical rulers wield their delegated power not to enslave the human person but to assure its liberty and perfection, redeeming it from the errors and aberrations in spirit and heart, which sooner or later always end in dishonor and servitude.

Did not modern democracy originate with the Reformation, which did away forever with the medieval idea of the divine right of kings?

[1] No. The Reformation both in England and on the continent based the authority of the Tudor kings and the German princes upon divine right, the better to combat the divine authority of the Pope.

[2] St. Robert Bellarmine, the learned Jesuit theologian and apologist of the 16th century, defended popular sovereignty against the divine right theory of the absolutist James I of England. He argued that God, the source of all authority, vested political power directly in the people as a political unit, and not in any individual person. It is the right of the people to choose their own form of society and to select the ruler or rulers who shall govern them. They are free to establish any form of legitimate government: monarchy, aristocracy, or democracy. Another famous Jesuit, Suarez, of the same period, denounced the divine right theory as something "new and singular, invented to exaggerate the temporal and to minimize the spiritual power," and he insisted that authority comes to rulers from God only through the people.

[3] The 17th century witnessed a reaction against despotism by divine right and a return, at least partial, to the

medieval idea of natural human rights, popular sovereignty, and the liberties of municipal and corporate bodies. As Gierke testifies, "Political authority and absolute power by divine right was wholly foreign to the Middle Ages" (*Political Theories of the Middle Ages*, p. 38). In the 13th century St. Thomas had succinctly stated, "Human dominions and princedoms are by human, not by divine right" (*Summa*, IIa-IIæ, q. 10, a. 10).

[4] The teaching of the Church is clearly expressed by Pope Leo XIII, "So long as justice is respected, the people are not hindered from choosing for themselves that form of government which suits best either their own disposition or the institutions and customs of their ancestors" (Encyclical *On Civil Government*).

Was not Cardinal Bellarmine's theory of popular sovereignty responsible for the French Revolution as much as Rousseau's theory of the social contract? Is rebellion ever lawful?

[1] No. The French Revolution was inspired by the political idea of Rousseau, and more directly by the tyranny, extravagance, and absolutism of Louis XIV and Louis XV. There is a fundamental difference between the doctrines of Bellarmine and Rousseau.

[2] Bellarmine held that political authority is a natural and God-given power necessary for the good of society while Rousseau held it was a mere human convenience existing solely by the agreement of men. Bellarmine derived political power immediately from the people as a whole but ultimately from God while Rousseau rested it solely on the contract between ruler and people. Bellarmine held that men are bound to obey legitimate rulers while Rousseau contended that "each one is invited to all, but obeys only himself, and remains as free as before." It was Rousseau who offered principles which inspired the French Revolution while Bellarmine laid the solid foundations for true democracy.

[3] Rebellion is lawful when rulers abuse authority granted by the people or usurp the people's authority to set up a tyranny. People, however, are to resort to rebel-

lion only after all peaceful means for changing the government have been seriously tried and have proven useless. Morever, a rebellion must be approved by the large majority of the people and it must have a reasonable chance of success. Rebellion is always an extreme measure and, if possible, should be avoided.

Does not the Catholic Church in defending the right of property take the side of the rich against the poor? Why is the Catholic Church opposed to Socialism? Is it not the most hopeful remedy for the evils of our modern industrial system?

[1] Socialism essentially refers to community ownership of the means of production. In its most radical form, the socialist State would own and control all sources of productive wealth—lands, mines, machinery, raw materials, utilities, communications, banking facilities, etc. In less extreme forms, the State would allow a certain amount of private ownership, but it would take over all basic industries, so as to control the entire economy effectively. What distinguishes the socialist State, therefore, is its complete or preponderant ownership of the means of production.

[2] It is possible to have considerable State ownership without having socialism. Thus, if certain vital industries are folding because of lack of capital, or other problems that private initiative cannot solve, then it might become necessary for the State to nationalize the industry for the sake of the common good. In these cases, the owners must be fairly compensated. Such ownership would be perfectly consistent with the State's office, for it would be doing something for the common good, that private individuals and groups could not do for themselves. The State should also provide services such as health insurance, social security and the like. These services are not to be labelled socialistic.

[3] Both Leo XIII and Pius XI, in their social teachings, declared that socialism cannot be reconciled with the teachings of the Catholic Church. The Popes object to socialism mainly because it attacks the sacred and inviolable right of the individual to possess private property in

the form of productive goods. Yet, man needs productive goods to provide for the present and future necessities of his family. Without such ownership, he is subject to others in a manner that insults his dignity and independence. In the socialist State, a man would be completely dependent on the State. Such State paternalism is unnatural and undesirable. On this point, Leo XIII says, "The socialists in setting aside the parent and introducing the providence of the State, act against natural justice and threaten the very existence of family life."

[4] In the socialist State, vast power is concentrated in the hands of government, for economic power tends of its nature to State absolutism. The State could control all wages and prices. It could dictate jobs, assign places to live, even force labor if necessary for its ends. Laborers would have little chance to assert their rights against the State, for the State would be the only employer. The socialist State runs the danger of becoming dominated by utilitarian values, for concentration upon economic necessities leaves the door open to materialism and secularism.

[5] Since the State would control communications, freedom of speech could be seriously jeopardized. Even our schools could be entirely State-controlled. All of these abuses need not be present in a socialist society but the danger is always there. Socialism, then, is clearly not the remedy for the evils of our industrial system.

[6] In defending the right of private property, the Church is not taking the side of the rich against the poor. The Church clearly teaches that every man is entitled to a living wage—one that will support him and his family in decency and comfort. On the other hand, the Popes teach that there is a certain natural inequality among people as regards capability, diligence, health, etc., and consequently unequal fortune is a natural and necessary result. While the free enterprise system has its abuses, it fundamentally respects the natural rights of man, and labor has demonstrated its ability to secure its rights through legitimate organization. In the capitalist system, the State exercises its proper function by protecting and actively promoting by wise legislation, the rights of both capital and labor.

Do you Catholics favor a World Government and a World Court? Would not such international organizations nullify our nation's autonomy and constitute a threat to our national security? What is your opinion of the U.N.?

[1] Catholics do favor a World Government and a World Court in principle. If it is said that such a principle violates national sovereignty, the answer is that only God is truly sovereign and all nations must obey His moral law. To prevent a recurrence of the terrible world war of 1941-45 caused by so-called "sovereign" nations, Pope Pius XII in 1945 advocated the formation of "an organ invested by common consent with supreme power to whose office it would also pertain to smother in its germinal state any threat of isolated or collective aggression." He reiterated his position in an address to the World Federalists on April 6, 1951 in which he said: "Your movement dedicates itself to realizing an effective political organization of the world. Nothing is more in conformity with the traditional doctrine of the Church. . . ." On other occasions, Pope Pius stated that Catholics are specially well-equipped to collaborate in projects for a better organized world since they belong to a supra-national organization and should entertain no "nationalistic narrowness." In fact, the Pope's pro-Secretary of State, Monsignor Giovanni Montini, in July, 1953 rebuked Catholics who were slow to follow the Papal directives in this matter: "How many . . . continue to shut themselves up within the narrow confines of a chauvinistic nationalism incompatible with the courageous effort to start a world community demanded by recent Popes."

[2] The principle underlying the United Nations organization is that all the peoples of the world form one human family, one community of peoples. This principle accords with Catholic teaching. In his Christmas message of 1948, Pope Pius XII said: "The Catholic doctrine on the State and civil society has always been based on the principle that, in keeping with the will of God, the nations form together a community with a common aim and common duties." Such a community of nations should have a governing body to which each State must necessarily surrender

some of its power. The United Nations is not a true governing body of the world but is merely an alliance of States bound together by treaty. It is a step toward the creation of a governing body.

[3] Ever since the beginning of the United Nations in 1945, the Holy See has not only manifested its interest in the United Nations but has even associated itself with a number of United Nations agencies such as UNESCO. Pope John XXIII in 1960, speaking to a world-wide gathering of delegates to the Food and Agricultural Organization, publicly gave thanks to God "that an enterprise like the F.A.O. was able to come to life."

[4] Pope Pius XII, addressing the minister of San Salvador in 1947, said that no dedicated worker for world peace should renounce the use of the world forum of the United Nations "in order to prod the conscience of the world from so high and open a place." Bishop James H. Griffiths, chairman of the U. S. Bishops' Committee for the Pope's Peace Plan, speaking to Catholic editors in New York City on March 18, 1960, reminded them that while the United Nations may be used as a sounding board for atheistic communism, it is also a forum in which Catholics can state their views. What is needed is not less but more Catholic interest in the United Nations.

Do we have an obligation to vote? Doesn't your Church order you to vote for Catholic candidates? Isn't it true that the Church demands that Catholics form a united front on political issues?

[1] The Constitution guarantees qualified citizens, regardless of race, creed, or color, the right to vote. It is the duty of each citizen to exercise this right and vote for the candidate he sincerely believes will best fulfill the office.

[2] The Church never commands Catholics to vote for any particular candidate. It urges Catholics to study the issues, to appraise the candidates, and to cast their vote according to their individual conscience. The fact that a candidate is a Catholic does not necessarily qualify him as the best man for the office. On the other hand, the fact that a candidate is a Catholic should not disqualify or

bar him from office, even the office of President of the United States. Robert Michaelsen, writing in the Protestant magazine *The Christian Century*, (Feb. 10, 1960) says that just as independents recommend voting for the man, not the party, he would recommend voting for the man, not the Church. He points out that two men of the same religious affiliation may be poles apart politically. The Catholic Church heartily endorses his wise maxim, "Vote for the man, not the Church."

³ It is impossible for the Church to demand that Catholics form a united front on political issues. You will find Catholics in every political group. They are Democrats and Republicans, Conservatives and Liberals, Laborites and Independents. Sometimes, however, a moral issue is injected into the political arena, for example, Communism with its doctrines of atheism, totalitarianism, and violence or artificial birth prevention. When this happens, Catholics, irrespective of party, will vote in accordance with their faith and morals. No reasonable person would want them to do otherwise. In such matters they are morally obligated in conscience to uphold their religious convictions.

⁴ The image of a united "Catholic vote" or "Catholic front" is a fantastic invention of people suffering from political hallucinations and illusions. Various polls over the years and especially election returns have clearly demonstrated that the votes of Catholics are widely scattered among candidates and issues. Catholics are inseparably united in faith and morals but not in politics.

Can the government draft "conscientious objectors" into the Armed Services against the dictates of their conscience? Does not your Church permit Catholics to refuse to defend their country?

¹ It is the right of the State to arm itself for self-defense and it is the duty of citizens to respond to legitimate legislation enacted for this purpose. Pius XII stated that such a government is "acting in a manner that is not immoral and that "a Catholic citizen may not make appeal to his own conscience as ground for refusing to give his services

and to fulfill duties fixed by law" (*Christmas Message*, 1956).

[2] Citizens whose religious principles forbid them to bear arms and engage in combat have a duty to follow their conscience. In such cases, the government usually assigns them to "auxiliary services" as their contribution to the national defense. They need not directly "kill the enemy" but they are obliged to aid their country against an unjust aggressor. How they are to do this the government has the right to decide.

What laws are subject to change? What is Penal Law?

[1] Civil laws, which are made by human legislators to govern the local community or the State, can change and must change to meet constantly changing circumstances. Tax laws, commerce laws, national defense laws—these are continually being revised.

[2] All civil law, however, must be rooted in the natural law and have some relation to it, however remotely. If civil law clearly contravenes the natural law, it is in reality no law at all. Laws in communist countries, for instance, which forbid the worship of God violate the principles of the natural law. No one is morally obliged to obey such unjust laws.

[3] Penal law is a civil law which does not oblige in conscience either to perform or omit the human action covered by the law. Nevertheless, it morally obliges a person who disobeys to accept the penalty for violation. Usually, penal laws facilitate good order, for example, parking regulations. It is to be noted that penal law violations often carry moral fault when their violation includes an offense against some virtue.

SELECTED BIBLIOGRAPHY

ABBO, JOHN A. *Political Thought; Men and Ideas.* Westminster, Md.: Newman Press. 1960.

ABELL, AARON I. *American Catholicism and Social Action.* Garden City, N. Y.: Hanover House. 1960.

BOUSCAREN, ANTHONY T. *A Guide to Anti-Communist Action.* Chicago: H. Regnery Co. 1958.

CHAMBRE, HENRI. *Christianity and Communism.* New York: Hawthorn Books. 1960.

D'ARCY, MARTIN C. *Communism and Christianity.* New York: Devin-Adair. 1957.

FANFANI, AMINTORE. *Catechism of Catholic Social Teaching.* Westminster, Md.: Newman Press. 1960.

—— *Catholicism, Protestantism and Capitalism.* New York: Sheed & Ward. 1955.

GARDINER, HAROLD C. *Catholic Viewpoint on Censorship.* Garden City, N. Y.: Hanover House. 1958.

KERR, WALTER. *Criticism and Censorship.* Milwaukee: Bruce Publishing Co. 1954.

KERWIN, JEROME G. *Catholic Viewpoint on Church and State.* Garden City, N. Y.: Hanover House. 1960.

LECLERCQ, JACQUES. *Christianity and Money.* New York: Hawthorn Books. 1959.

LEO XIII, POPE. *The Christian Constitution of States* (Encyclical). New York: Paulist Press.

—— *On Civil Government* (Encyclical). New York: Paulist Press.

—— *The Chief Duties of Christians as Citizens* (Encyclical). New York: Paulist Press.

MURRAY, JOHN C. *We Hold These Truths.* New York: Sheed & Ward. 1960.

PIUS XI, POPE. *The Church and the Reconstruction of the Modern World.* New York: (Image Books.) Doubleday & Co. 1957.

RAHNER, KARL. *Free Speech in the Church.* New York: Sheed & Ward. 1960.

SHEED, FRANCIS J. *Society and Sanity.* New York: Sheed & Ward. 1953.

SHIELDS, CURRIN V. *Democracy and Catholicism in America.* New York: McGraw-Hill. 1958.

WARD, BARBARA. *Faith and Freedom.* Garden City, N. Y.: Doubleday & Co. 1958.

PART XVII

The Church and Education

Why are Catholic nations less prosperous than Protestant ones? Why is it that every country in which Romanism prevails, the people are most backward and unprogressive?

[1] Jesus Christ never made material prosperity a mark of His true Church; He never declared worldly success a sign of divine favor. On the contrary, He is so outspoken against the sins incident to riches, that some unthinking socialists have claimed Him for their own.

[2] Christ says that no man can serve both God and Mammon (Matt. 6, 24), and asserts that riches may often prove an insuperable obstacle to a man's gaining the kingdom of heaven: "Woe to you rich! for you are now having your comfort" (Luke 6, 24). "It is easier for a camel to pass through the eye of a needle, than for a rich man to enter the kingdom of heaven" (Matt. 19, 24). He insists upon the fact that His "kingdom is not of this world" (John 18, 36), and adds: "What does it profit a man, if he gain the whole world, but suffer the loss of his own soul?" (Matt. 16, 26.) Hell was the portion, not of the poor Lazarus, but of Dives (Luke 16, 19-31).

[3] Material prosperity is no guarantee of the divine favor, for otherwise the unchangeable God would be as changeable as His creatures. Did God sanction the idolatry of pagan Egypt, Assyria, Babylon, Greece or Rome in the days of their political prosperity? Did God declare the religion of the Jews when they were slaves under Pharao, or Christianity untrue when the early Christians were persecuted to the death by the mighty, prosperous Romans?

[4] A criterion that works both ways is evidently false. Did God sanction the Catholicism of Spain in the days when Philip II ruled the world, and does He reject it today when Spain has lost most of her colonies and her monies? Did God sanction the Protestantism of Holland in the 17th century when she fought England as an equal, and did the carrying trade of Europe, and does He denounce it today, because she has lost her rank among the first-class powers?

[5] No, material prosperity has nothing to do with a nation's religion. It never is a sign of God's favor. A country's progress and development depend on the fertility of its soil, the wealth of its mines of gold, silver, coal, copper and iron; on the inventions of machinery, steam and electricity; on the energy and industry of its people. A pagan can make money out of a large wheat farm in the Northwest as well as a Catholic; a Jew can make a fortune out of an oil-well in Texas as well as a Protestant.

Why are Catholics hostile to the public school? Why do they have separate schools? Is this not un-American? Do Catholics recognize the State's right to educate its citizens? Has the Parent or the State the primary duty in education?

[1] Hostile is not the word to use in describing the Catholic attitude toward public schools. Critical might describe the Catholic feeling, but many non-Catholics share this kind of attitude today. Even the word tolerant would fit better than hostile. In 1890, when the public school system was much less developed than now, Archbishop John Ireland of St. Paul expressed a tolerant view on Catholics' using the public schools. "America is not a 'Protestant State,' and if Catholics pay school taxes they should receive benefit from them. The burden upon our Catholics to maintain parish schools up to the required standard for all the children of the Church is almost unbearable. There is danger that we shall never have schools for all Catholic children, or that Catholics will grow tired of contributing. At present nearly half the Catholic children of America do not attend parish schools. The true solution, in my judgment, is to make the State-school satisfactory to Catholic consciences, and to use it."

² Nevertheless, Catholics cannot approve wholly of the public school system, nor can they accept public schools as equals to the parochial schools. Catholics will admit a child can obtain at least as good an academic training in the public school as in the parochial. Learning the arts and sciences, however, is a small part of a child's education. He cannot exist in a vacuum and learn such subjects. The child will necessarily pick up many non-academic ideas from his teachers and fellow-students. The child does not go to school with his mind blocked off except for parts capable of learning the arts and sciences. He is a complete person, and only as a complete person does the child learn.

³ During the years a child is trained in the arts and sciences, he must learn how to live as a man and as a member of society. He has to receive proper direction in this learning also, and more necessarily. A child is intellectually supple, so that his early education molds him for later life. As the school subjects become a part of the youth, at the same time a knowledge of God and of morality must develop in him. The failure of the public schools to educate the whole child in such a way is the reason Catholics prefer to give their children a Catholic education in a parochial school.

⁴ The Catholic Church, being convinced of man's destiny for a life with God after death, does all in its power to make the goal obtainable. It has a teaching it believes is best suited for men to follow in seeking that end. The Church will, therefore, do all it can to give its children that teaching. The parochial school can best provide the children with Church teachings. If this were the only advantage of the parochial school, however, Catholics would be happy to send their children to public schools and teach religion outside, during released time classes, for instance. But the lack of Catholic religious training is not the only objection Catholics have against the public school. A child learns much more than what he is taught in class. The entire school atmosphere has a tremendous influence on his training. The public school has traditionally had a Protestant atmosphere, although today its atmosphere tends to be more irreligious than Protestant because of modern fears to have any religious influences in State-supported

schools. Catholics feel they must protect their children from this Protestant and irreligious atmosphere, especially in the precious formative years. It is a religious belief of Catholics that they must so protect their children, and this belief is defended by the American Constitution, which guarantees religious freedom. The parochial school teaches not only the arts and the sciences and religion, but it also helps to instill in the child the understanding of its direction in life toward God—an understanding free American parents want in their child.

[5] Parochial schools are certainly not un-American, for education in America began and long remained in the hands of various private groups, primarily religious. The public schools in America began as schools for the poor and orphaned children. Eventually the system included less needy children, and it spread throughout the United States. It was not the original form of education though. The Catholic parochial school in America has a longer American history than the public school, so it could accurately be called more American than the public school, if closeness to United States origins makes a thing more American.

[6] In 1955 the Catholic bishops of America gave an official viewpoint on the place of the non-public school in the United States. "Historically and actually our nation has been blessed with educational freedom. Her school system is not a closed, unitary creation of the State, a servile instrument of governmental monopoly, but one which embraces, together with the State-supported schools, a whole enormous cluster of private and Church-related schools, including many of the most honored names in the entire educational world, and devoted to the education of many millions of the nation's youth. . . . Let this be fully understood: Private and Church-related schools in America exist not by sufferance but by right. The right is implicit in the whole concept of American freedom and immunity from totalitarian oppression and in the constitutional framework of our Federal Government and of the several States. . . ."

[7] A child is born into a family, and it is to the family that it first of all looks for sustenance. The parents have

both the duty and the right to provide as well as they can for the needs of their children. The State enters to help the family to care for its members when the family lacks the means—as when the State provides such things as police and fire protection. Although the parents have the primary right to educate their children, the State may interfere to help when the parents cannot or will not complete the work of education. A State must set standards of education for its own good. Of course most parents cannot themselves educate their children to reach such standards, so outside assistance is needed. The State itself may be the the source of the help, but it does not have to be. So long as the State sees its standards maintained, it has no right to dictate the means by which the standards are achieved in educating a child. No matter what the parents choose to help them to educate their children, they still retain the duty and right to see their children receive the full education they need in order to live as good men and as good citizens.

⁸ First consideration must go to the child to be educated. No matter what conflicting ideas Americans hold on the educational problem they must be waived if they threaten to hurt any child intellectually, emotionally, or morally. The child cannot decide for himself what is the best way to learn. His parents have to make the decision, and if the parents are Catholics, the United States Constitution defends their right to decide according to their religious beliefs.

Is it not the duty of the State to educate? Why then do you Catholics have your own parochial schools? Would it not be more American and economical for all children to attend the public schools?

¹ The primary end of marriage is the procreation *and* education of offspring. Parents are primarily responsible for the education and discipline of their children. As Pope Pius XI taught, "the family holds directly from the Creator the mission and hence the right to educate the offspring, a right inalienable because inseparably joined to the strict obligation, a right anterior to any right whatever

of civil society and of the State, and therefore inviolable on the part of any power on earth" (Encyclical, *Christian Education of Youth*). The duty on the part of the parents continues up to the time when the child is in a position to provide for himself.

2 Parents, rather than the State, are under a grave obligation to see to the religious, moral, civic and physical education of their children. They must, as Pope Leo XIII pointed out, "make every effort to prevent any invasion of their rights in this matter, and to make absolutely sure that the education of their children remains under their own control" (Encyclical, *Sapientiae Christianae*). Basing its decision on the natural law, the Supreme Court declared that it is not in the competence of the State to fix any uniform standard of education by forcing children to receive instruction exclusively in public schools (*Oregon* case, 1926).

3 In the matter of education it is the duty of the State to protect the rights and freedom of families. It has, of course, the right to establish its own schools and to make sure that all its citizens have the necessary knowledge of their civic and political duties as well as a certain degree of physical, intellectual and moral culture necessary for the common good. But it would be unjust and unlawful— even a violation of the Constitution—to force children to attend public schools. The State must respect the freedom of parents to send their children to any independent accredited school.

4 Catholics construct and staff their own parochial schools because they honestly believe that such schools are necessary for the proper training of their children. They save the taxpayer money because they not only finance parochial schools but they also pay their share of taxes for public schools. It would certainly be more economical for *Catholics* to send their children to public schools. The religious training of their children, however, is more important to them than money. On the other hand, to demand that all children attend public schools would require higher taxes. A legislated uniformity in education would be un-American—it would be abhorrent to true Americans.

Why don't you Catholics send your children to the public schools if you want financial aid from the government? Why should my tax money be used to provide free lunches, transportation and health services for Catholics who are opposed to the public schools?

[1] Freedom of education, which is guaranteed by the 1st and 14th Amendments of the Constitution, means that parents have the right to choose to what accredited school they will send their children. Yet, those who desire to send their children to private or parochial schools are either forced to relinquish this freedom of choice or their children are deprived of educational benefits provided by the government. To make attendance at public schools a condition for receiving governmental benefits is to penalize parents for exercising their freedom and to ostracize their children as second-class citizens.

[2] If the government provides free lunches, transportation and health services for public school children, it should also provide the same benefits for independent-school children. Such benefits are given to the *children* and not to the *school*. The Supreme Court declared that in transporting children to Church-related schools "the State contributes no money to the schools. Its legislation . . . does no more than provide a general program to help parents get their children, regardless of religion, safely and expeditiously to and from accredited schools" (*Everson case, 1947*). Veterans under the G. I. Bill of Rights were given financial help no matter what accredited school they chose to attend. The happy result was that they were educated not only as doctors, teachers, lawyers and engineers, but also as Protestant ministers and Catholic priests. This law was fair because it guaranteed freedom of education and equal rights for *all* veterans. It is also the duty of government to guarantee equal rights for *all* school children.

[3] Catholics are not opposed to the public schools. After all, they pay taxes to help support them. But as citizens they demand the right to select the school in which their own children shall be educated without being unjustly penalized. And they rightly claim that the government

should not discriminate against their children in distributing social welfare benefits to school children. They and their children in parochial schools are as worthy of aid as are the parents and children in public schools. Their money as well as that of all parents makes such benefits possible.

What is the attitude of Catholics regarding federal aid to education? I understand that some are opposed while others desire it. Is there an official Catholic position?

[1] The Church has taken no official stand on this controverted question. And you are right in saying that there is a difference of opinion among Catholics.

[2] Many Catholics, including members of the hierarchy, oppose, or question the wisdom of federal aid to education. They charge that such aid constitutes a step in the direction of socialized education, and that it involves the growth of a monolithic structure favorable to dictatorial control of the free processes of education. They claim that education is the responsibility of the state and local governments, and that it would be folly for such agencies to relinquish control to the federal government.

[3] On the other hand, there are Catholic educators among the laity and clergy who believe that federal aid is necessary if our school system is to keep pace with rapidly changing world conditions. They argue that it is too expensive for state and local governments to finance and that these agencies do not have access to sufficient funds. Of course, they do not favor federal *control* and they are convinced that the state and local governments can maintain their autonomous authority over education while receiving federal aid.

[4] All Catholics, however, agree that all current federal aid proposals which ignore the needs of those children who freely choose to attend non-public schools are to be vigorously opposed. These proposals unjustly discriminate against children attending private or parochial schools. Public-school children are favored over independent-school children and this condition is grossly unfair. The latter are counted in determining the amount of federal aid to be

allocated to each state but they are counted out as objects of the aid which the federal government would allot. Such discrimination is a patent violation of the freedom inherent in American education and deprives countless citizens of rights guaranteed by the Constitution.

Is not the Roman Index a clear proof of clerical intolerance? Should not Catholics be allowed to read both sides of a disputed question? Ought people of mature years be treated as children? Has not the Church often made mistakes in condemning certain books?

[1] The Roman Index proves, not the Church's intolerance, but her zealous care for the salvation of men. As Christ's representative she is bound to safeguard by every means in her power the faith and morals of her members. Centuries of experience have convinced her that many people make shipwreck of their faith and give themselves over to uncleanness because of indiscriminate reading. The State protects the public health of its citizens by combating epidemics, by isolating men and women afflicted with contagious diseases, and by restricting the sale of narcotics and poisons. Similarly, the Church protects her members from the deadening and poisoning influence of irreligious and immoral literature.

[2] The Index was first published in 1559 by order of Pope Paul IV. In 1571 Pope Pius V created a Congregation of the Index which is now under the Congregation of the Holy Office. There have been 31 editions, the latest appearing in 1948. The Index is printed in Latin, has an Italian preface, and is available only in a few bookstores. Most of the 6,000 works which are listed were written by authors of the 17th, 18th, and 19th centuries.

[3] Although it is true that many of the authors condemned are unknown today, their works out of print, and their ideas insignificant, the Church had good reason to place them on the Index when she did. Perhaps, they are innocuous today but they were dangerous to faith and morals in respect to the social climate of the period in which they were written. We must beware of transplanting our 20th century into previous centuries. When the Church judges that particular condemned books are no longer a

danger for Catholics, she will remove them from the Index. A Congress on literary criticism held at Rome in 1959 recommended a study and revision of the Index. Its proposals are now under consideration by the Holy Office.

[4] People of mature years are not immune from the evil effects of pernicious and indecent literature, as the lives of many prove. A steady diet of literary poison will weaken and finally destroy the religious health and life of the most ardent Christian. We gradually become what we read.

[5] It is not enough for the faithful Catholic to by-pass books on the Index. He must put aside any reading that his individual conscience judges to be harmful to his spiritual welfare. On the positive side, he should read worthwhile books that will afford him wholesome pleasure, improve his mind and enrich his life as a human person created in the image of God.

SELECTED BIBLIOGRAPHY

DAWSON, CHRISTOPHER. *America and the Secularization of Modern Culture.* Houston: U. of St. Thomas Bookstore. 1960.

DUNN, WILLIAM K. *What Happened to Religious Education?* Baltimore: Johns Hopkins Press. 1958.

ELLIS, JOHN T. *American Catholics and the Intellectual Life.* Garden City, N. Y.: Hanover House. 1956.

FICHTER, JOSEPH H. *Parochial School.* Notre Dame, Ind.: University of Notre Dame Press. 1958.

MCCLUSKEY, NEIL G. *Catholic Viewpoint on Education.* Garden City, N. Y.: Hanover House. 1959.

MCHUGH, LAURENCE C. *Education for Time and Eternity.* Washington, D. C.: N. C. C. M. 1954.

NUTTING, WILLIS D. *Schools and the Means of Education.* Notre Dame, Ind.: Fides. 1959.

PIUS XI, POPE. *Christian Education of Youth* (Encyclical). New York: Paulist Press.

PIUS XII, POPE. *Pope Pius XII and Catholic Education.* St. Meinrad, Ind.: Grail Publications. 1957.

REDDEN, JOHN D. *A Catholic Philosophy of Education.* Milwaukee: Bruce Publishing Co. 1956.

PERIODICALS

"What Is the Aim of Catholic Education?" *Catholic World*, October 1959.

"The Baptists Revive Parochial Schools." *Ibid.*, July 1960.

"The Right to Choose Your Own School." *Ibid.*, October 1959.

PART XVIII
The Church and Science

Has not your Church, by striving to maintain an absolute uniformity of belief, always been the determined enemy of science? Have not most scientists been atheists or agnostics — a positive proof that religion and science are incompatible?

[1] The Catholic Church has no quarrel with science because there can be no real contradiction between her teaching and true science. The truths of religion and science have exactly the same ultimate source, namely, the one true God. His revelation cannot contradict his creation. Moreover, "faith and reason are of mutual help to each other; by reason well applied, the foundations of faith are established, and in the light of faith, the science of divinity is built up. Faith, on the other hand, frees and preserves reason from error, and enriches it with knowledge. The Church, therefore, far from hindering the pursuit of the arts and sciences, fosters and promotes them in many ways. . . . Nor does she prevent sciences, each in its own sphere, from making use of their own principles and methods. Yet, while acknowledging the freedom due them, she tries to preserve them from falling into error contrary to divine doctrine, and from overstepping their own boundaries, and throwing into confusion matters that belong to the domain of faith." (Vatican Council)

[2] The Church gladly accepts the proved facts of science, but she refuses to accept the erroneous guesses of some scientists as established truths. She cautions scientists not to make rash assertions and she warns theologians to be

accurately informed of the latest scientific findings. And to promote more sympathetic and better understanding among scientists and theologians she has founded the Academy of Science. The leading scientific authorities of the world—Catholic, Protestant, and Jew—belong to this august body of experts. In 1605 Kepler, a Protestant astronomer, praised "the wisdom and prudence of the Roman Church" for its public encouragement of scientific research.

[3] Most scientists have not been atheists and agnostics. Poggendorf, after listing 8,847 scientists covering the period from antiquity to 1863, stated that ten per cent were priests. He pointed out that the Jesuits had 42 astronomers and 14 observatories in Europe. Eymieu, who confined his data to the 19th century, listed 432 names. Setting aside 34 whose religious views were not known, he tabulated them as follows: atheists 16, agnostics 15; believers 367. Father Kneller, a German Jesuit, also compiled a similar list of 19th century scientists. Sir Bertram Windle edited a series of biographies of scientists who had no difficulty whatever in being loyal Catholics and recognized science-experts. As for the 20th century the vast majority are believers. (Poggendorf, *Dictionary of the Exact Sciences*— Eymieu, *La Part des Croyants dans les Progres de la Science au XIX Siecle*—Kneller, *Christianity and the Leaders of Modern Science*—Windle, *Twelve Catholic Men of Science*)

[4] Catholic scientists are not afraid of fresh discoveries, for their faith in the Creator of all things is strong. Because they hear the voice of God in the Church, they are eager to catch every whisper of that same voice in the world of nature.

The case of Galileo clearly shows that your Church is opposed to scientific progress. Was not Galileo condemned as a heretic, imprisoned in a dungeon, and tortured?

[1] In the 16th century the scientists as well as the theologians firmly yet falsely believed that the sun revolved around the stationary earth. They accepted the Ptolemaic system as a fact and applied its teaching to explain the miracle of Josue recorded in the Bible (Josue, 10, 13f.).

² Nikolaus Copernicus, a Polish astronomer, while conducting his experiments discovered that the earth and not the sun was really moving in orbit. He knew that his novel theory would arouse heated opposition, and he hesitated to publish his findings. In 1543, however—Copernicus meanwhile had died of a stroke—his book was printed under the title, *De Revolutionibus Orbium Caelestium.* To forestall public controversy Copernicus had dedicated it to Pope Paul III and had stated in the Preface that the book should not be taken seriously because it was simply an exercise in Logic. Consequently, the book caused no immediate widespread outraged reaction.

³ In the 17th century, however, a storm of controversy deluged science and theology when Galileo, a famous and respected scientist, publicly championed the Copernican system. Called before the Inquisition in 1616 he promised not to teach Copernicanism. In 1632 he broke his promise by publishing his book, *Dialogues on the Two Great Systems of the World,* in which he ridiculed the authority of the Church. Again summoned before the Inquisition he was condemned as "violently suspect of heresy." He was not tortured nor confined in a dungeon. The truth is that he was detained in an apartment for about three weeks and then permitted to live comfortably and to carry on his studies in the houses of his friends. Galileo remained a faithful Catholic and when he was dying, Pope Urban VIII sent him his special apostolic blessing.

⁴ We must not forget that the scientists, as well as the theologians, were bitter against Galileo. They rejected the Copernican system for scientific reasons. They argued that Galileo had not adduced a single valid proof for the novel thesis. To them his arguments failed to disprove the Ptolemaic theory. As the astronomer Laplace put it, Galileo defended his views with analogical theorizing rather than with positive facts. The theologians, on the other hand, feared Galileo's meddling in Scripture. He stubbornly insisted that they immediately change the traditional interpretation of the Bible to conform with his unproved hypothesis.

⁵ Cardinals Barberini (who became Pope Urban VIII), Conti, del Monte, and Bellarmine assured him that the

literal interpretation of Josue, 10, 13f. was not official infallible Church teaching, and they tried to explain how unreasonable he was in demanding a new exegesis before his hypothesis was proved a fact. Cardinal Bellarmine conceded that if a valid proof were found that the sun is fixed, "it would be necessary to acknowledge that the passages in Scripture which appear to contradict this fact have been misunderstood." Galileo erred in becoming involved in a Biblical problem; he should have stayed in the field of science. The theologians erred in assuming that Ptolemy's hypothesis was a fact of nature—they should have remembered that science advances by substituting one theory for another. The scientists erred in being "dogmatic" about the Ptolemaic system.

6 No one at the time regarded the decisions of the Inquisition or the Congregation of the Index (in 1617 it forbade the reading of Copernicus' book) as infallible pronouncements or doctrinal definitions. As Riccioli wrote in 1650, "it is by no means of faith that the sun turns and the earth is at rest." Their decisions prescribed disciplinary measures, commanding what one *must do* and not what one *must believe*.

7 It is only fair to remember that there was Protestant opposition to the scientific opinions of Copernicus and Galileo. Luther, Melancthon and other Protestant theologians voiced objections to Copernicus' book as an attack on the Bible. And in 1679—over forty years after the Galileo controversy—the theological faculty of Upsala condemned Nils Celsius for proposing and defending the Copernican system in his doctoral dissertation.

8 We should not be too harsh in judging the theologians of that era, Catholic or Protestant, when we realize that among the scientific elite some continued to hold and teach the false Ptolemaic system even after Newton, in 1682, had discovered the law of gravitation. Modern scientists and theologians, we hope, will learn from this unfortunate episode not to censure opinions and reject theories hastily. Today we know that the Copernican theory is a demonstrated fact and yet it in no wise contradicts the teaching of Scripture. The true facts of nature and the truths of the Bible are always in perfect harmony.

Did not Pope Boniface VIII forbid dissection, thus manifesting the Church's opposition to the advance of medical science?

[1] No, Pope Boniface VIII (1294-1303) in his Bull on Burials, issued in 1302, did not prohibit dissection for medical purposes, but legislated against a barbarous custom of the crusading nobles, who, dying in foreign lands, were anxious to be buried in their native land. "The custom," says the Pope, "consists of disemboweling and dismembering the corpse, or chopping it to pieces and then boiling it, so as to remove the flesh before sending the bones home for burial." The bodies of Louis IX of France and of the German Emperor, Frederick Barbarossa, had been shipped home in this way, and the practice had become prevalent toward the close of the 13th century. The Pope stigmatized this custom as "revolting" and "abominable," and forbade it henceforth under penalty of excommunication (*Extravagantes,* iii., ch. 1).

Is not vivisection immoral, involving as it does great cruelty to animals? Have we no duties toward them?

[1] No, vivisection is licit and moral, for animals were created for the service of man (Gen. 9, 3). To talk about their rights and our duties toward them is nonsense. Cardinal Newman well says: "You know we have no duties toward the brute creation; there is no relation of justice between them and us. Of course, we are bound not to treat them ill, for cruelty is an offense against that holy law which our Maker has written on our hearts, and it is displeasing to Him. But they can claim nothing at our hand; into our hands they are absolutely delivered. We may use them, we may destroy them at our pleasure, not our wanton pleasure, but still for our own ends, for our own benefit and satisfaction, provided that we can give a rational account of what we do" (*Omnipotence in Bonds*).

[2] There is no branch of medical science that has not benefited from vivisection. It has led to many important scientific discoveries; it has taught us the effects of many a poison and drug; it has advanced surgery by testing new methods of sewing up wounds; it has saved many human

lives by its experiments in serum treatments. The true scientist never inflicts more pain than is necessary, and, wherever possible, he anaesthetizes the animals on which he experiments.

Why does your Church teach cruelty to animals? Recently some forty Catholics ceased to attend church because they could not reconcile the cruel views publicly expressed by a priest with the mercy of God.

[1] The Catholic Church has never taught cruelty to animals. In 1950 in an interview with representatives of 200 Animal Welfare societies Pope Pius XII asserted, "Any reckless desire to kill animals, all unnecessary harshness and callous cruelty toward them are to be condemned. Such conduct is baneful to a healthy human sentiment and only tends to brutalize it."

[2] The animal world, as all creation, is a manifestation of God's power, wisdom, and goodness. Although we are not *bound* to love any animal whatsoever, we do have an obligation to treat them with kindness. Where cruelty is tolerated, man becomes brutalized and no longer protests against it, especially if there is money or blood-lust attached to it. Witness bull-fighting in Spain, cock-fighting and dog-fighting in America, bull-baiting and bear-baiting in England.

[3] Sentimentality, however, must not blind us to the fact that God has created animals to serve man who because of his intelligence is essentially superior to the entire animal world. We must not pretend, or make-believe, that animals are our equals and that their companionship and affection are to be preferred to the companionship and affection of our fellow-men. It is not rational to heap upon them excessive affection or to bestow on them what we deny to men and women and children.

[4] We have no *duties* to animals but we do have duties to God to accept them as His creatures, to treat them as God's gift to man, and to use them for the perfection of man and the glory of God.

Although we abhor and justly condemn the atrocious human experiments which were carried on during World

War II, is it not true that doctors today are permitted to perform experiments on healthy people for the purpose of scientific research and progress? Is it not unethical and immoral for a doctor to treat his patient with dangerous drugs that may cause harm or death? God made us persons of dignity but the medical profession seems to regard us as "guinea pigs."

[1] The postwar trials brought to light terrifying evidence of individuals who were sacrificed in the "medical interests of the community." The testimony shows how, with the consent and command of public authority, certain research centers systematically demanded to be furnished with persons from concentration camps for their medical experiments. The detailed descriptions of the conduct and results of such experiments are nauseous. One cannot read these reports without feeling profound contempt for the officials involved and deep compassion for the victims, and without being frightened by such cruel torture and inhuman behavior. The whole world has trembled with horror at this devilish aberration of the human mind and heart. And it has rightly punished this unscrupulous invasion and violation of the rights of innocent people.

[2] We must, however, be careful not to identify this patently immoral practice with current medical experimentation which respects human dignity and strives to promote the physical and psychic welfare of the individual and society. Nevertheless, experiments on human beings constitutes a serious problem which causes grave concern among moralists.

[3] No medical experiments can be made on any man or woman without the consent of the patient or on any child or feeble-minded person without the consent of the legal guardian. The State has no authority in this matter, nor do research workers and doctors. Pope Pius XII declared, "the doctor can take no measure or try no course of action without the consent of the patient. The doctor has no other rights or power over the patient than those which the latter gives him, explicitly or implicitly and tacitly" and "public authority has no power in this sphere. It cannot, therefore, pass it on to research workers and doctors"

(*Address to First International Congress on the Histopathology of the Nervous System*, September 14, 1952).

⁴ Although free consent is absolutely necessary, "the patient has no right to involve his physical or psychic integrity in medical experiments or research when they entail serious destruction, mutilation, wounds or perils" (*ibidem*). Nevertheless, there are situations in which a person may freely consent without demanding "that all danger or risk be excluded" (*ibidem*). To forbid him to do so in such cases "would paralyze all serious scientific research, and very frequently be to the detriment of the patient" (*ibidem*).

⁵ Human experimentation in its strict sense implies the use of treatments or procedures as yet not fully established scientifically for the purpose of discovering some medical truth or validating some hypothesis. The subject is asked to submit freely, after he knows the danger to self, in order to serve the common good by co-operating in the advance of medical science. When risk of harm is insignificant, he may choose to undergo the treatment. When the risk is unpredictable but it is certain that the experimental procedure will not seriously and permanently impair his functional integrity or gravely endanger his life, the subject may submit for the benefit of others. In such circumstances, he must have assurance that the procedure has already been adequately tested on cadavers and animals, that it promises reasonable hope of achieving a good proportionate to the danger, that there is a necessity here and now for employing human subjects, and that care will be taken to avoid even unintended harm. When the risk is predictable and certain to result in death, the subject cannot submit to the procedure, no matter how valuable this testing might be for the acquisition of useful medical knowledge. As Pope Pius XII reminded us, "science is not the highest value" (*ibidem*). Human life is much too precious to be subordinated to the quest for knowledge. We cannot commit suicide for the sake of science; a good end cannot justify immoral means. If the subject were a criminal already justly condemned to death, he might licitly choose this form of execution. But this is the only possible exception.

[6] On the other hand, human experimentation in its broad sense implies the use of uncertain remedies in order to cure or control a malady for which no sure remedy is available for the sick person. This experiment has for its immediate and primary purpose some benefit for the individual patient who would otherwise be beyond help. To forbid him this opportunity for recovery, if he wishes to gamble, would be unjust, a violation of his freedom, and a repudiation of common sense.

[7] Medical experiments on human beings are necessary and worthwhile. When safeguarded by moral principles as well as medical skills they have resulted in marvelous benefits to the human race. It is only out of love, however, either for himself or for others, that a person is permitted to be a subject of experimentation. And the doctor must always respect the dignity of the person by strict observance of the moral law.

Many medical Foundations which carry on needed research for the cure of disease report they are hampered in their work because Catholics are not allowed to will their bodies for autopsies. Is this true?

[1] There is no Catholic law forbidding post-mortem examinations and the study of diseased organs after death. Autopsies performed for the advancement of science and the betterment of health are permitted by the Church. An autopsy, properly conducted, is in no way disrespectful of the dead, and the medical knowledge obtained may save the lives of other people.

[2] A Catholic is free to have his body after death turned over to a medical center for the purpose of scientific research. He may specify that certain organs, like the brain or eyes, be donated to a particular scientific Foundation.

In what way does Christian Science conflict with the teachings of the Catholic Church? Is a Catholic allowed to go to Christian Scientists for treatment, provided he does not accept their views?

[1a] The Catholic Church regards Christian Science as an essentially pagan cult; an illogical, incoherent hodge-podge of Pantheism, Manicheism and Idealism.

² It is very difficult to summarize the teachings of Christian Science, because the Bible of the cult, *Science and Health,* is a book full of incoherence, contradictions, illogical reasoning, arbitrary exegesis of Biblical texts, and countless false statements. Many of its pages are unintelligible. As Mark Twain well says: "Of all the strange and frantic and incomprehensible and uninterpretable books which the imagination of man has created, surely this one is the prize sample" (*Christian Science,* 29).

³ A pantheistic concept of the universe underlies all Mrs. Eddy's (its founder) teachings. God alone is mind, she argues, and alone has true existence. The world, plants, animals and men are simply His ideas, without any real activity of their own. Since God alone is real, all that is opposed to the Divine is unreal. God is spirit; God is good. Matter and evil are opposed to Him; therefore matter and evil have no existence. By such amazing logic Christian Science solves the two great problems of sin and suffering by simply declaring them non-existent.

⁴ Christian Science denies every dogma of the Christian creed, while still claiming the Christian label. It denies the existence of a personal Creator, the divinity of Christ, the redemption, the freedom of the will, the fact of original and actual sin, the existence of a divine teaching Church, the sacramental system, the necessity of faith, grace, prayer, asceticism, the resurrection of the body, angels, demons and the eternal sanction of rewards and punishments.

⁵ Mrs. Eddy's claim that all sickness is mental and that all health cures are due to the direct action of God, in the sense that the Divine Mind is a negation of disease rather than a cause of cure, is a denial of established scientific facts. Although illness is sometimes mental or functional, it is also physical, organic, or somatic, and in many cases it is psycho-somatic or a combined mental-physical malady. Moreover, the modern techniques of medicine, psychology, and psychiatry have been effectively employed in the treatment and cure of all types of sickness. Evidence clearly proves that not all sickness is imaginary and that scientific treatment is not to be disdained.

⁶ Our analysis of Christian Science leads us to the fair and reasonable conclusion that, despite its name, it is neither Christian nor Science.

⁷ Catholics are forbidden to go to Christian Science healers for treatment, because such action would necessarily imply a recognition of an anti-Christian cult, and encourage a false, superstitious method of health cure. The Church, while urging humble prayer to God, forbids her children to neglect the ordinary means at their disposal for the cure of disease—medicines and the skill of doctor and surgeon—as irrational and sinful. She cries with approval the words of Holy Writ: "Honor the physician for the need thou hast of him; for the Most High has created him. . . . The skill of the physician shall lift up his head, and in the sight of great men he shall be praised. The Most High has created medicines out of the earth, and a wise man shall not abhor them. . . . My son, in thy sickness neglect not thyself, but pray to the Lord, and He shall heal thee" (Ecclus. 38, 1-9).

What is your opinion of psychiatry? I have been told that it is in conflict with Catholic philosophy and religion.

¹ Psychiatry is the relatively new branch of medical science and art of treating people afflicted with mental and emotional sickness as general medicine is the old established science and art of treating people suffering from physical and organic disease. In itself psychiatry has nothing to say about the existence and nature of God nor about the origin and nature of man. It rightly leaves these matters to theology and philosophy. Psychiatry devotes its attention to the operation of man's emotional apparatus and attempts to discover and correct the faulty hidden unconscious mechanism of human behavior.

² We owe a great debt of gratitude to the pioneers of this struggling science. Breuer, Freud, Adler, Jung, and their successors discovered the important truth that people can be mentally and emotionally ill as well as physically ill. They explored the complex reasons why persons think, feel, and act as they do—reasons that are hidden from the individuals themselves. They originated effective treatment

for the neurotic and psychotic maladies of human nature. It is because of their dedicated research and scientific labors that "odd" people are no longer regarded as possessed by the devil and in need of religious exorcism, as criminally maladjusted and deserving of being flogged and locked in chains, as "hereditary victims" frantically confined to attics and cellars, or as "freaks" exploited in traveling shows.

[3] The Catholic Church desires that people seek relief from their physical, mental, and emotional suffering with the help of competent physicians, psychiatrists, and clinical psychologists. She teaches that "grace builds on nature" and that faith, hope, and love will operate more effectively and fruitfully in the mature, well-adjusted, right thinking, and emotionally healthy individual. The Church acknowledges the value and welcomes the benefits of all the recognized psychiatric methods—wonder drugs, electric and insulin shock therapies, and the increasingly popular psychotherapeutic techniques of "talking it out."

[4] Catholic hospitals have impressive psychiatric departments and the welfare organizations of most dioceses employ specialists in the mental health field. Workshops on psychotherapy are conducted at a number of Catholic educational centers and the faculties of such programs include both psychiatrists and priests. It should also be noted that a number of priests are qualified practicing psychiatrists and clinical psychologists.

[5] On April 13, 1953, Pope Pius XII addressed the 5th International Congress of Psychotherapists and Clinical Psychologists and encouraged them in their labors. "Be assured that the Church follows your research and your medical practice with a warm interest and with her best wishes. You labor on a terrain that is very difficult. But your activity is capable of achieving precious results for medicine, for the knowledge of the soul in general, for the religious dispositions of men and for their development." These words of the Holy Father should dispel all fear of accepting psychiatry as a respected science and art and should assure us that psychiatry has no quarrel or conflict with Catholic philosophy and religion.

Is psychoanalysis the same thing as psychiatry? Should not a Catholic seek the wise counsel of a priest rather than the professional advice of a psychiatrist?

¹ In psychiatry, as in philosophy, there are various systems and schools of thought. Psychoanalysis is one of the systems of psychiatry and within psychoanalysis there are several schools. Despite their wide disagreements over theories and techniques all psychoanalytic schools trace their inspiration to Sigmund Freud and attribute to man's unconscious drives a large, active, and dynamic role in his behavior, both normal and abnormal. These schools analyze the influence of emotional experience in the distant past to release the tensions and solve the conflicts underlying mental illness. Although they cannot subscribe to many of Freud's philosophical and religious views, Catholic authorities in the field of psychiatry generally agree that the fundamental psychoanalytic techniques constitute a sound therapeutic method. Contrary to popular impressions, such therapy need not make use of irreligious or immoral means to cure a patient.

² When a Catholic is troubled about faith and morals, he should seek help from an understanding priest. But when his inner disturbances create personal and social conflicts which he can neither understand nor control, he may need the professional help of a psychiatrist. Psychological and psychiatric problems should not be confusedly identified with religious and moral problems. They are distinct although sometimes related. Moreover, the competence of a psychiatrist, as with that of a physician or surgeon, is not to be judged on the basis of his religion or lack of it. So long as he sticks to his science, it matters not if he be Catholic, Protestant, Jew, or even atheist. The well-trained psychiatrist does not attack or undermine the religious and moral convictions of his patient. Rather he works for a cure within the patient's religious framework. In fact, the competence of a psychiatrist is indicated by his unwillingness to enter into a purely religious discussion in therapy. He will rather advise the patient to seek such information from a priest, minister, or rabbi.

³ Sin and sickness are not the same, though at times

they may seem to be. A person subject to inner conflicts may act in ways contrary to the moral law. But the reasons for such behavior is often rooted, not in free choice, but in the frightening thoughts and disordered emotions of the patient. Catholics should not, in such cases, resent the fact that the psychiatrist, rather than the priest, must assume the responsibility for helping the person solve his problem. A false reliance on spiritual aids as a cure for mental "tics" and emotional "quirks" confuses the person and does an injustice to both religion and psychiatry.

What is the Church's attitude toward hypnosis? May a Catholic patient submit to hypnotism in the treatment of illness?

[1] Hypnosis derives its name from the Grecian god of sleep, Hypnosis. It is an artificially induced state of sleep during which time the patient remains under the complete control of the hypnotist. What the nature of hypnosis is; whether a person under hypnosis can be induced to act contrary to his moral principles; whether it is possible by suggestion to induce an hypnotic state in an unwilling subject—these are controverted issues among the doctors and psychiatrists.

[2] Hypnosis has proved valuable as a therapeutic technique in psychiatric practice. It is helpful in revealing unrecognized motives and conflicts in psychosomatic and psychoneurotic disorders, in removing symptoms and in altering morbid habits of thought and behavior, and, especially, in effecting a proper rapport between the patient and the doctor. It is also successfully employed as an analgesic or anesthetic agent. It alleviates pain without the need of habit-forming drugs and, in surgery, it improves the patient's outlook, eases tension and produces relaxation before the operation, and minimizes post-operative shock.

[3] Although hypnosis has its dangers, and its permanent therapeutic effects are widely questioned, the Church regards it as a valuable contribution to medical and psychiatric practice. The Church allows Catholics to be hypnotized provided the following conditions are satisfied:

1. The hypnotist must be competent and trustworthy and have received professional training. He must possess

deep respect for the dignity of the person who surrenders temporarily his mind and will.

2. A sufficient reason must be present, for example, restoration or preservation of physical or mental health. Hypnosis is not a party-game and it can never be attempted for amusement. "The use of hypnosis for entertainment purposes is vigorously condemned" (*Journal of American Medical Association,* Sept. 13, 1958).

3. Consent of patient or guardian must be procured.

4. Patient must be protected from unjustifiable risk of harm.

5. Information obtained during hypnotic spell falls under professional secrecy.

I have read that doctors are performing a brain operation called lobotomy to cure psychotics. What is this operation and does your Church permit it?

[1] Lobotomy is an operation in which the brain is opened and some of the association fibers connecting the frontal lobes and the thalamus are severed. It offers relief from emotional tension by separating unhealthy emotional responses from the knowledge causing them. For example, a thought which before the operation induced a state of dread or panic in the patient scarcely troubles him after the operation. Unfortunately, there are dangerous side effects in such operations: the patient manifests inertia and lack of ambition; he becomes indifferent to the opinions of others; he tends to be satisfied with no work or with a little work of inferior quality. For these reasons, doctors have stressed the importance and necessity of extended post-operative care and training. Patients are able to be re-educated to somewhat normal behavior.

[2] Catholic moral teaching allows this operation as a last resort in mental cases that have resisted all other medical techniques. Only a competent brain surgeon may perform the operation and he must have the consent of the patient or guardian. Moreover, the doctor must have reasonable hope that the effects will be more beneficial than harmful, and he must provide for post-operative guidance and treatment.

May "truth drugs" be used in criminal investigations and in the treatment of mental illness?

[1] Before administering a so-called "truth drug" in a criminal investigation, the doctor must inform the patient that what he might say under narcosis might be used in evidence against him. No one can be forced to give evidence against himself. It is to be noted that people may easily indulge in the wildest fantasy during a narcoanalysis and that people susceptible to suggestion may confess a crime of which they are truly innocent.

[2] In mental treatment the drug is not to be administered without the consent of the patient or his guardian. Measures must also be taken to safeguard the patient from any harmful effects. Any information obtained comes under professional secrecy.

SELECTED BIBLIOGRAPHY

BALTHASAR, HANS URS VON. *Science, Religion and Christianity.* Westminster, Md.: Newman Press. 1959.

BRACELAND, FRANCIS, ed. *Faith, Reason and Modern Psychiatry.* New York: P. J. Kenedy & Sons. 1952.

CHENU, M. D. *Is Theology a Science?* New York: Hawthorn Books. 1959.

CHAUVIN, REMY. *God of the Scientists, God of the Experiment.* Baltimore: Helicon Press. 1960.

FLOOD, PETER. *New Problems in Medical Ethics.* Westminster, Md.: Newman Press. 1960.

HAGMAIER, GEORGE and ROBERT W. GLEASON. *Counseling the Catholic.* New York: Sheed & Ward. 1959.

MARSHALL, JOHN. *Medicine and Morals.* New York: Hawthorn Books. 1960.

O'DONNELL, THOMAS J. *Morals in Medicine.* Westminster, Md.: Newman Press. 1959.

PIUS XII, POPE. *Guide for Living.* New York: Acme News Co. 1960.

VAN DER VELDT, JAMES H. and ROBERT P. ODENWALD. *Psychiatry and Catholicism.* New York: McGraw-Hill Co. 1957.

WIESINGER, ALOIS. *Occult Phenomena, in the Light of Theology.* Westminster, Md.: Newman Press. 1957.

ZILBOORG, GREGORY. *A History of Medical Psychology.* New York: W. W. Norton & Co. 1941.

PART XIX
The Church and Labor

What is the Catholic theory of a living wage? Are not employers and workmen free to agree on whatever wages they like? Is not a free contract a just contract?

[1] Pope Leo XIII, in his encyclical, *Rerum Novarum,* describes a living wage as "remuneration sufficient to support the wage earner in reasonable and frugal comfort." Pius XI in his great social letter, *Quadragesimo Anno,* clarified this idea, insisting that a worker must be paid a wage sufficient to support him and his family—in other words, a family living wage. The Popes were not advocating a mere subsistence wage, enough for a minimum of food and clothing. Man was so endowed by his Creator that he must have the opportunity to develop not only physically, but also intellectually and morally. Such fully human development is impossible without a living wage.

[2] A living wage is also a saving wage. In 1940, the American Hierarchy issued the statement, "A living wage means sufficient income not merely to meet the present necessities of life, but those of unemployment, sickness, death and old age as well."

[3] Since God intended the earth for the sustenance of all His children, and since labor is the means whereby man earns this sustenance, an employer has a duty in justice to pay a living wage. There may be individuals in the laboring force who cannot make a normal contribution to production, for example, the aged and the handicapped. In such cases, the Popes teach it is the duty of the State to subsidize them, for it aids the common good to relieve the

needs of the poor. This can be done by providing low-cost housing, insurance, family allowances, and like means.

[4] While the Popes have insisted on the payment of a living wage, they have not specified how this should be achieved. Some Catholic moralists hold that a man should be paid according to the size of his family. Others contend it is more practical for an employer to pay a living wage sufficient for the support of an average family. Fathers of unusually large families should be compensated by company insurance, fringe benefits, or some kind of family allowance.

[5] If women are hired to do the same job as men, they must be paid the same wages, lest they compete with family men for jobs. However, it would not be unjust for a lower wage level to exist in classes of work usually reserved for single women and minors.

[6] Since labor is necessary for a man to provide adequately for himself and his family, he cannot agree, even freely, to accept any arbitrary sum for his labor; for he cannot deprive himself and his family of decent living conditions. A contract to work for less than a living wage would be manifestly unjust, unless certain conditions, economic or personal, made it impossible to receive a just wage.

Is it lawful for workmen to strike? Does your Church condemn the sympathetic or the general strike?

[1] A strike is an organized stoppage of work by a number of workers trying to compel an employer to give in to certain demands for better wages or improved conditions or union recognition. Men are free to work or not to work, so a strike is not immoral in its nature. Workers are morally justified to strike for a just and good cause, provided they do not use violence against the employer, non-strikers, or strike-breakers, in an attempt to make their demands more readily accepted. A good and just cause for a strike would be low wages, bad hours without adequate compensation, unsanitary or unsafe working conditions, increased retirement benefits, and acceptance of a union desired by a majority of the workers.

[2] In every strike the cause should be proportionate to

the gravity of its effects. Workers should not strike until all other means have been tried unsuccessfully, producing no good results. Nor should they strike unless there is a fairly good chance of getting a satisfactory solution by taking such action. An unsuccessful strike harms not only the employer, but it may seriously hurt the worker and the family depending upon him for support.

[3] Pope Leo XIII spoke of the harm a strike may do, and he suggested measures to make the strike unnecessary. "When workers have recourse to a strike, it is frequently because the hours of labor are too long, or the work too hard, or because they consider their wages insufficient. The grave inconvenience of this not uncommon occurrence should be obviated by public remedial measures; for such paralysis of labor not only affects the masters and their workers, but is extremely injurious to trade, and to the general interests of the public; moreover, on such occasions, violence and disorder are generally not far off, and thus it frequently happens that the public peace is threatened. Laws should be enacted beforehand to prevent these troubles from arising; they should lend their influence and authority to the removal in good time of the causes which lead to conflicts between masters and those whom they employ." Pope Leo said this in 1891, but his words are worth listening to even today.

[4] The general strike, if it aims to destroy the capitalist system, is immoral in both its end and its means. Workers have no right to exclude private owners from industry. They may not justly try to ruin their employer's productive power, nor may they take action which cripples the social order.

[5] A limited sympathetic strike, in which men stop work in a certain industry in support of badly treated fellow workers, is not unlawful or immoral. A general sympathetic strike, in which all workers boycott entirely the products of a certain industry, is hard to justify. Such a strike often results in the breaking of just contracts, leads to general hardships among the nation's people, and errs in blindly refusing to consider the justice or injustice of the case.

[6] Pope Pius XII speaking of the workingman said that

it was "the natural right of each individual to derive from labor the means of providing for his livelihood and that of his children. . . ." If this is impossible for a man, he is justified to strike in order to force an employer to provide his rightfully demanded needs.

Is it moral for labor unions to insist on a "union shop," "closed shop," or "agency shop" in negotiating contracts with management? A tough labor law is the only way to control unions and to guarantee full production for American industry.

[1] The United States labor movement has never sought compulsory union membership by law. It is dedicated to freedom of election for workers and to free bargaining for employers. Before a labor organization can obtain a union shop in a particular plant or office, it is required by law (Taft-Hartley Act) to follow a lengthy procedure.

1. It must persuade a substantial number of workers to sign union membership cards before it can request an election from the National Labor Relations Board (NLRB).

2. In a secret-ballot election conducted by the NLRB, it must win a majority of votes of all workers to become the employees' legal representative in collective bargaining.

3. It must decide by democratic process whether to seek a union shop.

4. The union must convince the employer to sign a union-shop contract. There can be no real union shop unless both labor *and* management freely agree to its establishment.

[2] The different kinds of "shops" may be popularly distinguished as follows:

Open Shop: an employer can hire whomever he chooses.

Union Shop: an employer may hire whomever he chooses, but every new employee, after a certain trial period, must join the union and pay dues.

Closed Shop: an employer may only hire union members.

Agency Shop: an employer may hire whomever he chooses, but every new employee, although he need not join the union, is assessed his rightful share for "services" he receives from union representation.

All these "shops" are morally justified so long as public law is observed, workers freely express their choice, and employers freely sign contracts.

[3] Every reasonable person, including union leaders, favor the enactment of fair laws that are necessary to remove the abuses of both labor and management and that will contribute to the public welfare. Voters and legislators would do well to heed and ponder the wise counsel of Pope Pius XII, "Neither collective bargaining nor arbitration nor all the directives of the most progressive legislation will be able to provide a lasting labor peace unless there is a constant effort to infuse the breath of spiritual and moral life into the very framework of industrial relations." It is imperative that labor leaders and management executives frankly examine their consciences on the motives and tactics which presently govern and direct their actions. Both must be inspired by true justice and charity if our country is to prosper.

The Catholic Church teaches the importance of law and extols the dignity of the individual. Why then have some Bishops and priests taken the side of corrupt unions against the honest working man by opposing the "right to work" law?

[1] Labor unions are good for the working man, even necessary. They have won him many blessings: a living wage, safe and sanitary work-conditions, shorter hours, sick benefits, pension, and the like. Without unions individual workers would be exploited by unscrupulous employers. The unsavory practices of management in the past reduced decent working men to the unworthy status of "tools of industry." It was only by uniting together into unions that the laboring man was able to secure economic dignity and respectability. We should not quickly forget that it was only after years of bitter struggle that the God-given natural moral right of workers to organize in defense of their own welfare was legally recognized. Although Pope Leo XIII in his Encyclical, *Rerum Novarum* had pro-

claimed and proved this right in 1891, it was not until 1935 that legislation was enacted to guarantee freedom of organization to American workers.

[2] Neither labor nor management is "on the side of the angels." Both are guilty of grave injustices. The Catholic Church condemns the abuses of labor as well as those of management. She deplores the violent tactics and corrupt practices that characterize a segment of the labor movement. She urges members to take a more active interest in their unions, to participate in meetings, and to use prudently their voting franchise to elect responsible trustworthy leaders. Union members and their elected officials must "clean house" vigorously and effectively to preserve the "house of labor" and to render it ever more deserving of public support.

[3] The Catholic Church maintains that every man has a right to work. This is not the issue, however, in the controversy over the "right to work" law. The phrase is a misnomer calculated to deceive the unwary, because the real intent is to "outlaw" the union shop freely contracted by employees and employers. This legislation is a subtle technique of making the open shop legally compulsory. Such laws substitute government interference for free collective bargaining which has always been an essential principle of America's successful economic system. Their purpose is not to guarantee men the right to work; for example, they give no assistance to men over 40 who are trying unsuccessfully to find jobs or to Negroes who are denied jobs simply on the basis of the color of their skin. Their real aim is to strip labor of its rightful gains and to isolate the working man into a position of weakness at the negotiating table.

[4] Although the Supreme Court in 1957 ruled unanimously that the union shop does not violate the Bill of Rights or any basic constitutional freedom, more than 20 states have passed these so-called "right to work" laws. Ironically, 12 of these states have statutes compelling lawyers to belong to the Bar Association before they can practice legally. And in many areas a doctor cannot be placed on a hospital staff unless he is a member of the Medical Society. Why then should the owner of an industrial plant

and his employees be forbidden to make union membership a condition for working in that particular plant? To "outlaw" the union shop is to penalize unfairly a particular group of citizens. It smacks of unjust discrimination.

⁵ Most Catholics agree with the view expressed by Archbishop O'Brien of Hartford, Connecticut, "it is neither immoral nor unethical to require union membership for the greater good of the group" and with the statement issued by the Bishops of Ohio, "we are convinced that a 'right to work' amendment would not solve our problems, but might lead to a more intensified struggle for domination and thus postpone an era of peaceful co-operation." It is also encouraging to find many business executives opposing these laws as harmful to the establishment of proper stable labor-management relations.

What do you think of the practice, so common nowadays, of employing married women in business offices, factories and plants?

¹ Although we deplore the practice, we realize that industrial development and economic conditions have forced millions of married women to seek work outside the home. This distressing fact is part of modern life and we have to learn to live with it. We should, however, strive to minimize its bad effects, particularly as they relate to the family. The married woman must never forget that her first duty is to her husband and children, that she is the heart of the home, and that being a good wife and mother is much more important than being a good employee.

² When Pope Pius XII spoke to a convention of working women in Rome in 1945, he reminded them that they have a right to the same pay as men for the same work. It would be contrary to the public welfare, unjust to the men refused employment, and unjust to themselves if they accepted less. Female labor is not a cheaper commodity than male labor, for both are the work of human beings.

SELECTED BIBLIOGRAPHY

CRONIN, JOHN F. *Catholic Social Principles*. Milwaukee: Bruce Publishing Co. 1950.

—— *Social Principles and Economic Life*. Milwaukee: Bruce Publishing Co. 1959.

HIGGINS, THOMAS J. *Man As Man*. Milwaukee: Bruce Publishing Co. 1949.

HUSSLEIN, JOSEPH, (ed.). *Social Wellsprings, 2 Vols*. Milwaukee: Bruce Publishing Co. 1949.

KELLER, EDWARD A. *The Case for Right-to-Work Laws*. Chicago: Heritage Foundation. 1956.

KWANT, REMY C. *Philosophy of Labor*. Pittsburgh: Duquesne University. 1960.

LEO XIII, POPE. *Rerum Novarum* (The Condition of Labor) in *Five Great Encyclicals*. New York: Paulist Press. 1960.

LEROY, ALBERT. *The Dignity of Labor*. Westminster, Md.: Newman Press. 1957.

MESSNER, JOHANNES. *Social Ethics*. St. Louis: B. Herder Book Co. 1952.

PIUS XI, POPE. *Quadragesimo Anno* (Reconstructing the Social Order) in *Five Great Encyclicals*. New York: Paulist Press. 1960.

RYAN, JOHN A. *Distributive Justice*. New York: Macmillan. 1942.

PERIODICALS

BROWN, LEO C. "New Labor Law," *Social Order*, Vol. 9, No. 10 (Dec. 1959).

GRUENBERG, GLADYS W. *"Unionism at the Crossroads,"* *Social Order*, Vol. 5, No. 1 (Jan. 1955).

"Labor Unions In a Democratic Society." *Catholic World*, February 1960.

"Labor, Management and Human Dignity." *Catholic Mind*, July-Aug. 1959.

"What Labor Laws Can't Do." *Catholic Mind*, Nov.-Dec. 1959.

PART XX
The Church and Intolerance

Are not Catholics bound to defend the Inquisition with all its cruelty and injustice as an essential part of the Church's constitution? Were its rulings infallible? Would not Catholics be urged today to set it working again by the Pope, if he had the power to enforce its laws?

[1] "Catholics," writes Father Keating, "are by no means concerned to defend this tribunal in all the details of its activity. It manifested all the characteristics of administration of justice in those rude times, though generally in a milder form. That its processes, according to modern notions, were faulty; that, just like the secular courts of law, it often suffered from the abuses to which its procedure laid it open; that it was used to satisfy avarice and glut private enmities; that its officials were not always above suspicion in their motives; that its penalties were often arbitrary, unjust, cruel—these may be established facts; but the inference is not that the institution was unwarranted by the circumstances of the age or opposed to its mentality. The attachment of physical penalties to offenses largely spiritual, the use of torture to elicit evidence, the defects of the legal methods, the harshness of the sentences, these characterized the tribunal, not because it was Catholic, but because it was medieval. . . . There is nothing in the history of the Inquisition which invalidates the claim of the Church to be the Church of Christ. All that Christ guaranteed her in her institution was that, through His divine power, she should never cease to exist, should always be guided in her teaching by His Spirit, and should

never, therefore, lead His flock astray into false pastures. For the rest the Church is composed of human beings, and, therefore, outside the limits implied in these divine promises, is exposed to human frailties. History shows that she has not been protected against mistakes in policy and errors in administration" (*Does the Catholic Church Persecute?*).

[2] Blotzer writes in the *Catholic Encyclopedia:* "It is essential to note that the Inquisition, in its establishment and procedure, pertains not to the sphere of belief, but to that of discipline. The dogmatic teaching of the Church is in no way affected by the question whether the Inquisition was justified in its scope, wise in its methods, or extreme in its practice" (viii., 36).

[3] A fair-minded man ought not to view the 12th or the 13th century from the standpoint of the 20th. The very fact that the Church could call upon the civil power to repress rebellion against her teaching, proves conclusively that the men of that day considered the Church's teaching necessary for the well-being of society. Many non-Catholics today find this viewpoint difficult to understand, for with them religion is a matter of human opinion. They believe that a man is free to choose his religious beliefs, as he chooses the style of his coat, or his political opinions. They have ceased to regard religious truth as something objective; they have ceased to believe in a divine revelation.

[4] We must remember also that heresy in the Middle Ages was very often allied with some anti-social sect, which, like modern anarchism and communism, menaced the very existence of the State. By the very nature of things, therefore, the interests of both Church and State were identical.

Must we not thank the Reformation for the fact that men today are no longer tortured, imprisoned and put to death for heresy?

[1] By no means. The leading Reformers both in England and on the Continent taught without question the medieval doctrine of intolerance.

[2] Harnack says of Luther: "It is an altogether one-sided view, one, indeed, which willfully disregards the facts, to

hail in Luther the man of the new age, the hero of enlightenment and the creator of the modern spirit" (*Lehrbuch der Dogmengsch,* iii., 810). Catholics and Zwinglians in Saxony who did not conform to the Lutheran doctrine were to be exiled, and the Anabaptists, even though they did not openly teach seditious doctrines, were to be put to death (Grisar, *Luther,* v., 592; vi., 252). Melanchthon in a letter to Calvin in 1554 approved the burning of Servetus, saying: "I agree entirely with your sentence; I also declare that your authorities have acted wisely and justly in putting this blasphemous man to death" (Grisar, *ibid.,* iii., 358). Calvin burned Servetus for denying the Trinity, and wrote a treatise to defend his action. Farel wrote to Calvin in 1533: "Some people do not wish us to prosecute heretics. But because the Pope condemns the faithful (the Huguenots) for the crime of heresy, it is absurd to conclude that we must not put heretics to death, in order to strengthen the faithful." Theodore of Beza wrote in 1554: "What crime can be greater or more heinous than heresy, which sets at naught the word of God and all ecclesiastical discipline? Christian magistrates, do your duty to God, who has put the sword into your hands for the honor of His majesty; strike valiantly these monsters in the guise of men" (Vacandard, *The Inquisition,* 222-224).

[3] Hallam bears similar testimony. He writes: "Persecution for religious heterodoxy in all its degrees was in the 16th century the principle as well as the practice of every Church. It was held inconsistent with the sovereignty of the magistrate to permit any religion but his own, inconsistent with his duty to suffer any but the true. . . . Persecution is the deadly original sin of the Reformed Churches, which cools every honest man's zeal for their cause, in proportion as his reading becomes more extensive" (*Literature of Europe,* ii., ch. ii.; *Constitutional History,* i., ch. ii.).

[4] Lord Acton, an enemy of intolerance if ever there was one, while admitting the intolerance of both Catholics and non-Catholics in the past thus contrasts them: "Protestantism set up intolerance as an imperative precept and as a part of its doctrine, and it was forced to admit toleration by the necessities of its position. . . . The Catholic Church began with the principle of liberty, both as her claim and

as her rule, and external circumstances forced intolerance upon her" (*The History of Freedom,* 187).

[5] In the England of Elizabeth and the early Stuarts, there was no toleration of Catholics by Protestants. "Throughout the whole of the 16th century no other State in Christendom decreed such ignominious penalties for a purely religious offense. However horrible it was, death at the stake distinguished the heretic from other criminal types. But in England the complete confusion of spiritual and temporal, the result of an angry nationalism, first gave the king all the powers of the Church, and then allowed the same king to inflict identical punishments for loyalty to Rome and high treason" (Lecler, *Toleration and the Reformation,* Vol. 2).

[6] The history of the penal laws of Great Britain and Ireland under Henry VIII, Elizabeth, Edward VI, James I, Charles I, Cromwell, Charles II and William III is a history of fines, imprisonment, banishment, torture and death for the practice of the Catholic Faith.

Do you dare defend the cruelty of Pope Innocent III (1198-1216), in ordering the crusade against the Albigenses, and in mercilessly demanding that they be put to death?

[1] Yes we do defend his policy, for the laws he enacted were not at all excessive compared with the strict Roman law, or even with the practice then in vogue in France and Germany (Vacandard, *The Inquisition,* 46). Havet writes: "We must in justice say of Innocent III that, if he did bitterly prosecute heretics, and everywhere put them under the ban, he never demanded the infliction of the death penalty" (*l'Héresie et le Bras Séculier,* 165). Luchaire also shows that the laws and letters of Innocent III speak of banishment and confiscation of the property of the Albigenses, but *they never once mention the death penalty* (*La Croisade des Albigeois,* 57).

[2] The Albigenses of Southern France in the 13th century were a disturbing element in the Christian commonwealth, like the communists of today, who endeavor to stir up trouble everywhere for legitimate governments. They were an anti-Christian and an anti-social body, which denied marriage, questioned the lawfulness of oaths and refused

service on the plea that all war was unlawful. Their chief defender was Raymond VI, Count of Toulouse (1194-1222), who had for years oppressed the Church in his domains, expelling bishops from their sees, despoiling the monasteries, and devastating the country with his mercenaries.

[3] This anti-Christian heresy had been growing stronger and stronger for almost one hundred years, despite the condemnation of the Councils of Arras, Charreux, Vienne, Reims and the Third Lateran, and the condemnation of Popes Eugenius III (1145-1153) and Alexander III (1159-1181). The preaching of many a Papal legate—Cardinal Alberic, St. Bernard, the Bishop of Osma, and St. Dominic —had proved of no avail. The murder of Innocent's legate, Peter of Castelnau, brought matters to a crisis in 1208. The Pope, seeing that peaceful methods had failed, called upon the King of France, the sovereign of Toulouse, to use force, and the crusade began under the leadership of Simon de Montfort.

Was not the Spanish Inquisition one of the most cruel institutions the world has ever known? Was not the authority of the Popes used to urge Catholic Spain to repress and punish heresy?

[1] Inhumanity is not a special prerogative of Catholic Spain; it was characteristic of the cruel Inquisition of Lutheran Saxony, the Genevan Inquisition of Calvinistic Switzerland, and the English Inquisition of Elizabeth, James I and Cromwell.

[2] On November 1, 1478, Pope Sixtus IV empowered Ferdinand and Isabella to establish the Inquisition in Spain. In the beginning it was directed primarily against the many pseudo-Jewish converts (*Marranos*) who after popular uprisings against their usury and extortion, had accepted Baptism merely as the alternative to death.

[3] The successful Spanish war against the Moors (1480-1492) also resulted in a great number of nominal conversions for the sake of temporal advantage. These pseudo-Moorish converts (*Moriscos*), added another factor to the problem of national disunion, which the Spanish monarchs determined to fight, as the French kings fought the Hugue-

not separatists a century later, or Lincoln fought our Southern separatists in 1861. Later on under Philip II (1556-1598), the Inquisition was the weapon used successfully to prevent Protestantism from dividing the kingdom.

[4] It is beyond question that the Spanish monarchs often made the real danger that existed from these pretended Jewish and Moorish converts a mere pretext for prosecuting any powerful enemy of the crown, and for filling the treasury's empty coffers by the arbitrary confiscation of the property of innocent citizens.

[5] The old view that the Inquisition was purely a State institution was popularized in France by De Maistre (*Lettre à un Gentilhomme Russe*), Gams *Zur Gesch. der Span. Staatsinquisition*), Hergenröther (*The Church and State*) and by the Protestant historian von Ranke (*Fürsten und Völker*), but the majority of Catholic scholars today hold with Pastor that "it was a mixed, but primarily an ecclesiastical institution" (*History of the Popes,* iv., 402). The Pope established it, gave the Grand Inquisitor the necessary jurisdiction, and empowered the council to act only through his delegate. The fact that the condemned were always handed over to the secular arm proves the correctness of this theory.

[6] Catholics, while sympathizing with the Spanish kings in their desire for political unity, and with their hatred of heresy, are just as vehement as non-Catholics in their denunciation of the cruelties and the injustice of the Spanish Inquisition. They, however, ask fair-minded men not to judge the 15th century from the viewpoint of the 20th.

[7] The words of Cardinal Gibbons are indorsed by every Catholic: "I heartily pray that religious intolerance may never take root in our favored land. May the only king to force our conscience be the King of Kings; may the only prison erected among us for the sin of unbelief or misbelief be the prison of a troubled conscience" (*Faith of Our Fathers,* p. 259).

Did not Charles IX of France and his mother Catherine de Médicis, under orders from the Pope, slaughter one hundred thousand Huguenots on St. Bartholomew's Day, August 24, 1572? Did not Pope Pius V plot this crime with the French Court, and did not Pope Gregory XIII sing a Te Deum *for it in Rome?*

[1] The Popes had nothing to do with the massacre of St. Bartholomew's Day. Pius V did not plan the massacre with Catherine de Médicis, nor did he ever urge it upon the French court in any way; Gregory XIII never approved of the crime, but had a *Te Deum* sung in thanksgiving for the saving of the king and the royal family from death, according to advices sent him from the French court. The Pope's congratulations were on a par with the congratulation sent in modern times by one State to another, when informed that a king or a president has escaped an assassin's bullet or bomb.

[2] The massacre was a dastardly political crime of Catherine de Médicis conceived in panic after the failure of her attempted assassination of Coligny on August 22.

[3] Catherine had no zeal for the Catholic religion. She was a freethinker of the school of Machiavelli, bred in the worst traditions of the Italian tyrants, and ruling one of the most corrupt courts of Christendom. Her one aim in life was to govern France personally or through her puppet sons, and to strengthen her power by placing her children on the thrones of England, Spain and Poland. Jealous alike of both the Catholic and the Huguenot princes, she played one against the other to gain her ends. When Coligny began to overshadow her, and to undermine her influence with her son Charles, she deliberately planned his death.

[4] No one holds today that the massacre was premeditated. In fact it was planned and executed so quickly that the French court did not at first know what defense to manufacture for the other nations of Europe. On the very day it occurred Charles wrote his ambassador in England that it was due to a faction fight between the Duke of Guise and the friends of Coligny, whom he blamed for having murdered his father. When the Duke of Guise refused to accept the full infamy of the crime, the king wrote the following day that he himself assumed responsibility for all that had happened. He declared that he had ordered the massacre to frustrate a conspiracy of Coligny

and his followers to kill himself and all the royal family. With the exception of Germany and Switzerland, this diplomatic lie was accepted by all Europe, and congratulatory messages were received by Charles IX from the Venetian Senate, the Duke of Tuscany, Philip II of Spain and Elizabeth of England.

[5] It is true that Pius V frequently urged the French court to take the severest measures against the Huguenots, whom he rightly regarded as enemies of both Church and State. He wrote to Charles and Catherine "to fight the enemies of the Church openly and freely to their utter destruction," and "to grant no toleration to these rebels, lest the kingdom of France be the bloody scene of continual sedition." We are not called upon to defend the Pope's political views for the safeguarding of the French monarchy, although it is certain that a strong consistent policy would have saved France a great deal of turmoil and bloodshed. The Pope wished the war fought to a finish, and the rebels utterly subdued. He was indignant when he heard of royal victories ending in the profit of the vanquished. Open warfare, however, is one thing; assassination another.

[6] Not a Bishop of France was present at the meeting that planned the massacre; no Bishop ever gave it his approval. The Cardinal of Lorraine, who is often pictured blessing the daggers of the murderers of Paris, was actually in Rome when the massacre occurred. As one Protestant historian of Catherine says: "Upon Catherine de Médicis the chief responsibility for the deed must always rest." And he adds: "No one who knows anything of her character through her letters, or who had carefully studied her tortuous state policy, could suspect for one moment that there was in her anything resembling religious fanaticism" (Van Dyck, Catherine de Médicis, ii., p. 88).

[7] How many were killed in France during the six weeks of the massacre will never be accurately known. The estimates of over a score of contemporary and modern historians range all the way from 2,000 to 110,000, which proves that the figures given are mere guess work, like the figures of modern scientists estimating the age of the world.

[8] That France lied to the Pope about the facts in the

case, describing the massacre as the just punishment of conspirators, we know from the reports of the king's messenger, De Beauvillier, and from the letters of the French ambassador de Férals, the Cardinal de Bourbon, and the Papal nuncio, Brantôme, who, in his Memoirs, says that when the Pope learned the real facts, he shed bitter tears, and denounced the massacre "as unlawful and forbidden by God."

Did not Pope Innocent XI urge Louis XIV to revoke the Edict of Nantes (October, 1685), and to persecute the French Huguenots?

[1] Innocent XI did nothing whatever to bring about the revocation of the Edict of Nantes. As a matter of fact he asked his Nuncio in England to have James II intercede with Louis XIV in favor of the persecuted Huguenots. The Protestant historian, Ranke, in his *History of the Popes* (ii., 306), admits this. He writes: "It has been alleged that Pope Innocent XI was privy to and an abettor of the design; but in reality this was not the case. The Roman court would have nothing to do with a conversion affected by armed Apostles. Christ has not employed such means; men should be led, but not dragged into the Church."

[2] By the Edict of Nantes (April, 1598) Henry IV had granted toleration to the French Huguenots, hoping thereby to put an end to the long series of religious wars which had devastated France. The Edict accorded the Huguenots the liberty of private and public worship in two hundred towns and some three thousand seigneural domains. It endowed the Huguenot schools, permitted their churches to receive gifts and legacies, granted the right of holding synods and many other privileges. From a political standpoint it made the vital mistake of giving the Huguenots complete control of two hundred towns, including the important cautionary towns of La Rochelle, Montauban and Montpelier.

[3] If we remember that the Huguenots formed less than one-fifteenth of the population of France, it is certainly a remarkable fact that this Edict of toleration was observed

for nearly one hundred years. During this same period no Catholic in England or in the Scandinavian countries could openly practice his religion.

[4] From the very first days of his reign Louis XIV gave evidence that he regarded the very existence of the Huguenots—a party aloof from the national unity—as an open affront to his despotic sovereignty. If religion entered his mind at all, it was merely from a desire to atone for his many conflicts with the Pope, by manifesting his zeal for the faith. As one biographer says: "He judged religious questions from a purely political point of view—as King of France, not as a theologian. . . . If he considered Protestants enemies of the State, it was because, under the cover of religion, they were sowing dissension throughout the nation, and weakening it in the face of the enemy" (Bertrand, *Louis XIV,* 346). The Huguenots of his time were an unarmed and peaceful body, whose conversion, he wrongly thought, could be easily brought about. Their refusal to conform simply angered this despot, and led him to undertake an un-Christian policy of suppression, as in England the tyranny of an Elizabeth or a James I enacted the death penalty against Catholics. What his despotic grandfather had decreed, he could just as despotically revoke. The subservient Parliament of the day had merely to register his Edict, and his officers had merely to enforce it.

[5] Catholics are not called upon to defend the political policy of Louis XIV any more than they are bound to apologize for his impudent Gallicanism, his gross extravagance, his ruthless wars, or his flagrant immorality. In fact he was simply acting on the Protestant principle set forth by the Treaty of Westphalia in 1648, which the Popes had denounced: *Cujus regio, illius est religio*: "the kingdom must follow the religion of the prince."

[6] The revocation of the Edict of Nantes was a grave political mistake, for it drove from France about 200,000 of its citizens, cost France some twelve millions of dollars, injured her commerce and her industries, and furnished many a recruit to the armies and navies of her enemies. It was, moreover, carried out in violation of a fundamental human right, for as Tertullian says: "It is assuredly no part

of religion to compel religion. It must be embraced freely, and not forced" (*Liber ad Scapulam,* ch. ii.).

Did not the cruel and bigoted Catholic Queen, Mary Tudor (1553-1558), put thousands of Protestants to death at the stake, thus meriting the title of "Bloody Mary"?

[1] The title of "Bloody" might just as well have been given to Henry VIII, Elizabeth or Cromwell, had Catholicism and not Protestantism dominated English literature for the past four centuries.

[2] The portrait of Mary Tudor as a cruel and bigoted tyrant, first sketched by the lying Foxe in his *Book of Martyrs,* and slavishly copied by many an anti-Catholic English historian (Hume, *History of England,* iv., 404), has within the past fifty years been stigmatized as a caricature by Catholic and non-Catholic students of the Tudor period, namely, Gairdner, Innes, Pastor, Pollard, Stone, Zimmermann and others. Innes says of her: "From the time of her childhood she was exposed to unceasing hardness; a princess born, she was treated as bastard; despite all, her natural generosity survived. Royally courageous, loyal and straightforward; to her personal enemies almost magnanimous; to the poor, and afflicted, pitiful; loving her country passionately. She was blind to the forces at work in the world, obsessed with the idea of one supreme duty, and she set herself, as she deemed, to battle with Antichrist by the only methods she knew, though they were alien to her natural disposition, facing hatred and obloquy" (*England Under the Tudors,* 242).

[3] But while her personal life was chaste and pious, all admit that as a political ruler of a powerful kingdom she was utterly incompetent and inefficient. Her Spanish blood prompted her to lean upon the Emperor, Charles V, and to marry Philip II, his son, an unwise and foolish policy that angered her people, led to the war with France, and antagonized Pope Paul IV, who, toward the end of her reign, excommunicated Philip II. In her conscientious desire to restore the stolen Church lands, she failed to realize how much the wealthy English nobles dreaded the possible consequences of a reconciliation with the Papacy, although

Rome was far-sighted enough to point out her mistake. Her worst error was her failure to understand the England of her day, which had become religiously indifferent owing to the anti-Catholic reigns of Henry VIII and Edward VI.

[4] From the very beginning Mary Tudor had to fight for her life. The rebels under Northumberland, who attempted to place Lady Jane Grey upon the throne, were treated most leniently. Her mildness was mistaken for weakness, as Wyatt's rebellion the year afterwards proved (*Cambridge Modern History*, ii., 538). Considering her peril, the punishment she meted out to the rebels in this second uprising was severe, but it was certainly justified. Like most men or women of lowly origin who become possessed of limitless power, the Tudors were all despots. Mary was determined to restore the old religion of her mother, just as Elizabeth was determined to extirpate it. She was undoubtedly angered at the many scurrilous and seditious writings published against her government by the fanatical Protestants in England and on the continent, and she was naturally indignant at the many outrages committed daily against the Catholic faith.

Why have your Popes always so bitterly denounced Freemasons, and forbidden Catholics to join their lodges? Is it fair or just to condemn a social and charitable society, to which so many prominent and respectable citizens belong? Should not an exception have been made for English or American Freemasons, who have openly repudiated the atheism of the Grand Orient of France? Do not the Masons go back to King Solomon?

[1] Freemasonry was originally a Jacobite political society which repudiated the Pretender and founded the first Grand Lodge in London in 1717 under the patronage of the Prince of Wales. Its constitution and ritual were written by the Prince's Huguenot chaplain aided by a Scotch Presbyterian minister. Its aim was mutual assistance and the worship of "The Great Architect of the Universe" in which Jews, Christians and Mohammedans may equally participate. It was introduced into America before 1727.

[2] This secret society was first condemned by Pope Clem-

ent XII in 1738, even though many prominent Catholics of the time belonged to the lodges, such as the Duke of Wharton, the Duke of Norfolk and the Chevalier Ramsay. Pope Clement knew the real facts because Pritchard, in his *Masonry Detected,* had published their secrets to the world in 1730 and an English-speaking lodge had been formed in Rome as early as 1735. Eight other Popes have since condemned it. Catholics who become Masons are excommunicated. They are deprived of the sacraments and of Christian burial.

³ It is certainly unreasonable to suppose that the Catholic Church, the great advocate of charity down the centuries and the great defender of the natural right of association, would condemn any society on account of its charitable works or good fellowship. What then are the reasons for the Church's condemnation of Masonry?

1. It is a religion of naturalism which ignores Jesus Christ, our Savior. It has its own altars, vestments, prayers, worship, burial service, and the other elements for a religious ritual ceremony.

2. Its oath is immoral. Such a society has no right to exact an oath from its members—this right belongs only to legitimate ecclesiastical and civil authorities. Moreover, an oath, calling God to witness the truth of what we say, is a very serious affair and should concern important matters. But a Mason promises that he will not reveal such trivia as passwords, grips, symbols, and lodge rites under threat of having his tongue torn out or his throat cut. If a member takes his oath seriously he freely submits himself to possible mutilation; if he takes it as a joke he violates the first Commandment by taking the name of God in vain.

3. Masonry has been, and still is, the Church's enemy in spreading false propaganda and attacking Catholic faith.

⁴ The Church readily admits that some individual Masons are good holy people, that some join a lodge simply for social reasons, and that some are blissfully ignorant of the official tenets of Masonry. It also commends Masonic charitable undertakings such as hospitals for crippled children. But the Church is obligated by the mandate of its divine Founder to protect the faith and morals of its own members.

Why were the medieval Popes so remiss in allowing for centuries the cruel, unjust and superstitious trials by ordeal?

[1] The Roman tribunals never permitted trials by ordeal, and the Popes from the 9th century did their utmost to abolish this unjust and superstitious custom. The peoples of Northern Europe had inherited trials by ordeal from their pagan ancestors, and on their conversion demanded the intervention of the true God in their courts, as of old they had appealed to Woden. By a faulty, superficial reasoning, natural to an illiterate people, they appealed to the ordeal of "the waters of jealousy" in Numbers 5, 12-31, and to the intervention of God with reference to the sacrifice of Abel (Gen. 4, 4), the Deluge (Gen. 7), the destruction of Sodom (Gen. 19), the punishment of Core (Num. 16), and of Ananias (Acts 6, 5). They did not realize that miracles were extraordinary things, dependent entirely upon God's will and not on man's; that God graciously answered our prayers, but He was not bound to render a decision at our bidding. Ordeals were, therefore, rightly characterized by Popes Nicholas I (858-867) and Honorius III (1216-1227) as a sinful, superstitious "tempting of God" (Isa. 7, 12).

[2] Pope Stephen V (885-891), in a letter to the Archbishop of Mainz, forbids the ordeals of hot iron and of boiling water, declaring: "It is our duty to judge of crimes that are known either by the confession of the culprit or by the testimony of witnesses. What remains completely hidden, must be left to the judgment of Him, who alone reads the heart." Alexander II (1061-1073) tells us that "ordeals are not sanctioned by the canons of the Church"; Alexander III (1159-1181) denounces them as "detestable" (*execrabile judicium*); Celestine III (1191-1198) is outspoken in his condemnation of the ordeal as "superstitious judgments against God's law and the Church's canons." This decree became the formal and authentic teaching of the Church from the 13th century, and is recorded in Raymond of Pennafort's collection of the Decretals (Cf. *Council of Lateran* in 1215).

[3] The ordeal by mortal combat has been denounced by

the Church from the earliest times. St. Avitus of Vienne (518) protested against it in the 6th century; St. Agobard (840) and the Council of Valence (855) in the 9th. It was declared "contrary to Christian peace, and destructive of body and soul"; an absurd survival of the old pagan ordeal.

[4] The Catholic Church forbade "the detestable custom of dueling" at the Council of Trent, and Popes Benedict XIV (1752) and Leo XIII (1893) declared that nothing could ever justify it.

A Protestant acquaintance of mine claims that the Popes always persecuted the Jews. She says that delegates from different synagogues in 1807 entered a protest to Napoleon against the actions of the Popes. Is this true?

[1] The charge is false. The Jews themselves have offered testimony on this subject. In 1807 the rabbis and delegates from different synagogues were invited by Napoleon to meet in Paris and constitute a great sanhedrin. This was, perhaps, the first act of toleration and of justice toward the Jews on the part of a civil government. Exercising a sentiment of delicacy that did them honor, they seized the opportunity to praise publicly the only earthly power that had protected them in the previous centuries, namely, the Papacy. Here is the memorable resolution which was passed on February 5, 1807, and which is preserved in the Department of Public Worship:

[2] "It is in consequence of the sacred principles of morals that in different times the Roman Pontiffs have protected and received into their states the Jews—persecuted and expatriated from different parts of Europe. About the middle of the 7th century, St. Gregory defended and protected the Jews in the whole Christian world. In the 10th century the Bishops of Spain opposed with all their power the people who wished to massacre them. The Pontiff Alexander II wrote to those Bishops a letter full of felicitations on their conduct. St. Bernard, in the 12th century, condemned the fury of the Crusaders. Innocent II and Alexander III equally protected them. In the 13th century Gregory IX protected them when, in England, France, and Spain, they were threatened with great misfortune; he forbade, under pain of excommunication, to force their con-

science or trouble their festivals. Clement V did more than protect them—he facilitated for them the means of instruction. Clement VI gave them asylum at Avignon, when they were persecuted in all the rest of Europe. In the following centuries Nicolas wrote to the Inquisition to prohibit forcing the Jews to embrace Christianity."

[3] During World War II, the humanitarian efforts of Pius XII have been widely recognized and commended by the Jews. The Holy See established several offices devoted to rescue work. The three letters U.I.V. (Uffizio Informazioni Vaticano—Vatican Office of Information) are remembered by hundreds of thousands who first heard them in connection with news of relatives who had been missing, interned, or enslaved. Pius XII welcomed to the Vatican many Jewish citizens who were expelled from governmental and scientific positions. In fact, thousands of Jewish refugees poured into Vatican City; thousands of others sought shelter in the basilicas and buildings of the Holy See outside the Vatican wall.

[4] No less than 15,000 were cared for at Castel Gandolfo. And the Pope sent by hand a personal letter to the Bishops instructing them to lift the enclosure from convents and monasteries so that they could house the Jews. On one occasion, the Chief Rabbi of Rome was summoned by the German military and ordered to deliver by noon of the following day one million lire and 100 pounds of gold. Refusal or failure meant wholesale dispersal of Jews with consequent atrocities and death. Because the Jewish community of Rome could not fulfill this unjust command, the Chief Rabbi appealed to Pius XII for help. The Pope immediately instructed the Vatican treasurer to raise whatever was necessary. In less than a day, by melting down religious vessels, the stipulated amount was obtained. After the war, Pius XII addressed a group of European Jews who had come to the Vatican to thank him "for his generosity on their behalf during their persecution."

[5] History bears witness to the truth that the Catholic Church and the Popes have always befriended the Jews. Wherever there is human suffering the Church is ever ready and eager to employ all her influence and resources to alleviate it.

Does your Church give equal rights to Negroes? Does it recognize marriages between Negroes and whites?

[1] The Catholic Church recognizes that Negroes have the same God-given rights as any person. The fact that they are black does not make them less human than are the whites. Whatever rights the whites commonly enjoy, the Negroes also possess them. And neither the Church nor the State can deprive them of these natural rights without violating justice.

[2] One of these basic rights is the right to marry a person of one's choice, provided both parties are ready for marriage and freely willing to contract it. This is the reason the Church has no law forbidding interracial marriages.

[3] In the United States, however, prejudice and social customs present many practical difficulties to the success and happiness of such marriages and to the rearing of offspring. These should be given serious consideration because marriage is not for a day or a year but for life.

I admire the Catholic Church for defending the rights of Jews and Negroes. But can you tell me why there are so many Catholics who are bitter toward the Jews and who oppose racial integration?

[1a] The Church teaches Catholics what they ought to believe. She also urges them to pray and receive the sacraments so that God may give them the grace of light and strength to accept the truth and to manifest it in their conversation and behavior. Unfortunately, some Catholics are ignorant of particular teachings of the Church. They do not have the curiosity to inquire nor the industry to study. Then there are Catholics who are careless about what the Church teaches, who pray little, and who seldom receive the sacraments. The *perfect* Catholic thinks, speaks, and acts with the Church. But few Catholics are perfect— they fall in thought, word, and deed from the *ideal.*

[2] It is necessary to remember that Catholics are ordinary human beings displaying a wide variety of temperaments and personalities. They are influenced by their parental inheritance, their schooling or lack of it, and by the social and economic climate in which they have been reared and

in which they have lived. Like everyone else they are afflicted with phobias and prejudices which they have not controlled and overcome. Too often, feeling derived from and fed by unpleasant personal experiences blinds them to truth, engulfs their reason, and sweeps them into false judgments and bad conduct.

[3] I suspect that much of the opposition to Jews and Negroes stems from experiences with individuals of these two groups. The tragic consequence is that each group is judged and made to suffer because of the misbehavior of a few "unacceptable" individuals. The tendency is to see these "misfits" as the normal standard and to generalize that all Jews and Negroes are alike. Prejudice takes command and it becomes deep-seated and stubborn. It closes the mind to facts and the heart to love. A person so trapped by emotional bias is no longer reasonable. His injustice offends God and harms his neighbor.

[4] Christ Himself warned against this human fault of jumping to universal conclusions from particular cases by narrating the parable of the publican and the pharisee (Luke 18, 10). The pharisee proudly boasted that he was better than the publican whom he did not even know but upon whom he heaped all the misdeeds of a few publicans with whom he had had personal dealings. The pharisee blamed and condemned this humble man simply because he happened to be a publican.

[5] The one Christian doctrine that unifies the whole of Christian teaching and that must permeate all living of the Christian life is "oneness with Christ"—the oneness of the branches with the Vine, the unity of bodily members among themselves and with their Head. "There is neither Jew nor Greek; there is neither slave nor freeman; there is neither male nor female. For you are all one in Christ" (Galatians 3, 28).

Does the Catholic Church believe in the tolerance of other religions?

[1] By tolerance we mean a willingness to permit other religious beliefs, different from Catholic beliefs, to be held by individuals. The Church does believe in a practical

civil tolerance which allows other individuals to believe as they will, even though these religious beliefs are held to be erroneous by the Church. On the other hand, the Church does not believe in a theoretical, dogmatic tolerance. For it insists on objective truth in the religious sphere as in other areas of knowledge.

[2] Pope Pius XII in an address on "The World Community and Religious Tolerance" given to the National Convention of Italian Jurists on December 6, 1953, stated this doctrine. He said:

"Within its own territory and for its own citizens, each State shall regulate its religious and moral affairs according to its own laws; nevertheless, throughout the whole territory of the international community, the citizens of each member-State shall be allowed to exercise their own beliefs and ethical and religious practices, insofar as these practices do not violate the penal laws of the State in which they are residing.

". . . Now in regard to religious and moral interests, a twofold question arises:

"1. The first concerns objective truth and the obligation in conscience to follow what is objectively true and good.

"2. The second concerns the practical attitude of the international community toward the individual sovereign State, and the attitude of the individual sovereign State toward the international community insofar as religion and morality are concerned.

"The first cannot easily be the object of a discussion and ruling between individual States and the international community, especially in the case where a pluralism of religious beliefs occurs within the community itself. The second question, on the other hand, is of the greatest weight and urgency.

"This is the manner in which to answer the second question. Above all we must clearly state: no human authority, no State, no community of States, whatever be their religious character, can give a positive command or positive authorization to teach or to do that which would be contrary to religious truth or the moral good. . . .

"Another essentially different question is this: whether a norm may be established in a community of States, at east under certain circumstances, whereby the free practice of religious or moral beliefs which is valid in one of the member-States, be not impeded in the entire territory of the community of nations by means of State laws or coercive measures? In other words, we raise the question whether the 'non impedire' or toleration is permissible in these circumstances, and, as a consequence of this, whether positive suppression may (under these same circumstances) cease to be of binding obligation.

". . . Reality shows that error and sin are in the world in great measure. God reproves them; yet He permits them to exist. Therefore the affirmation that religious and moral error must always be impeded whenever possible, because to tolerate them is in itself immoral—is not valid *unconditionally and absolutely.*

"Moreover, God has not even given to human authority such an absolute and universal command, in matters of faith and morals. The common conviction of mankind, Christian conscience, the sources of revelation, and the practice of the Church have never recognized the existence of such a command.

". . . The duty to suppress moral and religious error cannot, therefore, be an ultimate norm of action. It must be subordinated to *higher and more general norms* which, *under certain circumstances,* permit and may even make it appear that the best choice for promoting *greater good* is the toleration of error.

"Thus we have clarified the two principles from which, in concrete cases, we obtain the answer to every serious question concerning the attitude to be adopted by the jurist, the statesman and the sovereign Catholic State with regard to a formula of religious and moral toleration described above, in consideration of the community of nations.

"1. That which does not objectively correspond to the truth and to the norm of morality, does not in turn have the right to exist, to be propagated or to be activated.

"2. Failure to impede this with State laws or by coercive measures can, nevertheless, be justified in the interests of a higher and more general good."

Why do Catholics label members of the Orthodox Churc "schismatics"? Why do you refer to Protestant sects « "heretical"? Why are some former Catholics called "apo tates"?

[1] Schism, heresy, and apostasy are technical words en ployed by Canon Law to describe the relation of certai baptized persons to the Catholic Church. Their meanin is based on the belief that every person who is validly ba tized by that very fact becomes a member of the Catholi Church, whether he knows it or not.

[2] A schismatic is a baptized person who actually accep all the defined teachings of the Catholic Church, yet r fuses to recognize and acknowledge the primacy of autho ity and power of the Bishop of Rome, as the Vicar of Chri on earth.

[3] A heretic is a baptized person who, retaining the nam Christian, refuses to accept one or more truths reveale by God and taught by the Catholic Church.

[4] An apostate is a baptized person who repudiates th name Christian, rejects entirely Christian teaching, an abandons the practice of his faith.

[5] These words, despite their harsh overtones, do n necessarily imply any moral guilt. God judges the ind vidual conscience in accordance with the person's know edge of truth, emotional state, freedom of decision, an circumstances of action.

Why does the Catholic Church forbid cremation? I se nothing evil in it. Do not cemeteries infect the air, an poison the wells of a community?

[1a] The Church does not forbid cremation because it intrinsically evil, but because it goes counter to the Jewis and Christian tradition, and was initiated by anti-Chri tians with the express purpose of destroying belief in th immortality of the soul and the resurrection of the body.

[2a] Cremation has been condemned by three Roman d crees. The first, May 16, 1886, forbids Catholics to joi cremation societies or to order their bodies cremated; th second, December 15, 1886, deprives such Catholics (Christian burial; the third, July 27, 1892, forbids pries

to give them the last sacraments. These decrees of the Holy Office condemn cremation, not as contrary to the divine or natural law, but as a "detestable pagan practice, introduced by men of doubtful faith," who aim at lessening Catholic reverence for the dead.

[3] The first attempt in modern times to revive cremation was made by the neo-pagans of the French Directory in the fifth year of the Republic. The project did not meet with any popular response at the time, although the spirit back of it was part of the Revolution's attack upon Christian doctrine, law and custom. The same scoundrels who put priests to death, abolished the Mass and the Sunday, and invented the new cult of reason, advocated cremation the better to destroy "the superstitions of the immortality of the soul and the resurrection of the body."

[4] The world had to wait nearly seventy-five years before unbelief in Europe made another and more successful attempt to introduce cremation. The first cremations occurred at Padua in 1872, and at once anti-Christians everywhere began to found cremation societies, and to defend the practice in hundreds of books and pamphlets.

[5] If cremation were adopted, many of the beautiful prayers and ceremonies of the Church would become altogether meaningless. Absolutely speaking, the Church could change her ritual in this respect, but it is not at all likely that she will. If, however, the State were to make cremation compulsory, the Church would readily adapt her prayers to the new method of disposing of the dead.

[6] Many jurists, physicians and insurance men are opposed to cremation, because it obliterates all traces of crime. Autopsies performed three months after death have more than once furnished proof of poisoning, sufficient to send a criminal to the gallows.

[7] Modern science denies that cemeteries cause infection either of the air, or of the wells and rivers. The origin of the plagues of history has been traced, not to the dead, but to the living.

SELECTED BIBLIOGRAPHY

ABBO, JOHN A. *The Sacred Canons.* St. Louis: B. Herder Book Co. 1960.

ADAM, KARL. *The Roots of the Reformation.* New York: Sheed & Ward. 1957.

CONGAR, MARIE J. *After Nine Hundred Years.* New York: Fordham University Press. 1959.

———— *Lay People in the Church.* Westminster, Md.: Newman Press. 1957.

DAWSON, CHRISTOPHER. *The Historic Reality of Christian Culture.* New York: Harper & Bros. 1960.

DENZINGER, HEINRICH J. *The Sources of Catholic Dogma.* St. Louis: B. Herder Book Co. 1957.

HALES, EDWARD E. Y. *The Catholic Church in the Modern World.* Garden City, N. Y.: (Image Books). Doubleday & Co. 1960.

———— *The Church and the Revolution.* Garden City, N. Y.: Doubleday & Co. 1961.

HARTE, THOMAS J. *Papal Social Principles.* Milwaukee: Bruce Publishing Co. 1956.

HUGHES, PHILIP. *A Popular History of the Reformation.* Garden City, N. Y.: Hanover House. 1957.

KREY, AUGUST CHARLES. *The First Crusade.* Gloucester, Mass.: Peter Smith. 1958.

LAFARGE, JOHN. *The Catholic Viewpoint on Race Relations.* Garden City, N. Y.: Hanover House. 1956.

LECLER, JOSEPH. *Toleration and the Reformation.* New York: Association Press. 1960.

LEO XIII, POPE. "Freemasonry" (Encyclical). New York: Paulist Press.

NEILL, THOMAS P. *A History of Western Civilization.* 2 Vols. Milwaukee: Bruce Publishing Co. 1960.

RICCIOTTI, GIUSEPPE. *The Age of Martyrs.* Milwaukee: Bruce Publishing Co. 1959.

SCHARP, HEINRICH. *How the Catholic Church Is Governed.* New York: Herder and Herder. 1960.

WATKIN, EDWARD I. *Roman Catholicsm In England From the Reformation to 1950.* New York: Oxford University Press. 1957.

WHALEN, WILLIAM J. *Christianity and American Freemasonry.* Milwaukee: Bruce Publishing Co. 1958.

WILLIAMSON, HUGH ROSS. *The Conspirators and the Crown.* New York: Hawthorn Books. 1959.

PART XXI
The Church and Ecumenism

What is an ecumenical council? Has it any power over the Pope? I read recently that Pope John XXIII has called a council to be held in Rome. Will Protestants and Orthodox Catholics be invited?

[1] An ecumenical or general council is the assembly of Catholic Bishops representing the whole Church. It is convoked to discuss and settle questions of faith, morals and discipline. It enjoys no power over the Pope because he is the Supreme Teacher and Ruler of the Universal Church established by Jesus Christ. The Pope must call the council, preside over its deliberations in person or through his appointed representative and confirm the decrees enacted.

[2] Pope John XXIII has announced that a general council will be held in Rome and preparations are now being made. Only Catholic Bishops in communion with the Holy See will be officially invited to participate in the sessions. It is possible that Protestants and Dissident (the term Orthodox is misleading) Catholics who do not accept the primacy of the Pope may attend as "observers" and take part in informal conversations with individual Catholic delegates outside the regular meetings.

[3] Pope John XXIII hopes that the council may deepen and strengthen the "union, unity, and concord in the holy Church of God" and serve as "an invitation to the separated brethren . . . that they may return to the universal sheepfold." He prays that the happy result will be a fuller knowledge of the teaching of the Church, a salutary progress in Christian morality, and an expansion of the united

kingdom of the divine Savior, a kingdom of truth and of justice, of love and of peace.

To what extent are Catholics permitted to participate in the ecumenical movement which is currently being sponsored by the World Council of Churches?

[1] "The Catholic Church takes no actual part in 'ecumenical' conventions and other assemblies of a similar character" (Instruction of the Holy Office, *Ecclesia catholica,* 1949). Nevertheless, it urges Catholics to pray for those engaged in non-Catholic ecumenism because such efforts have been awakened "under the inspiring grace of God" (*ibid.*). And in recent years Bishops have permitted priests to be present at inter-creedal meetings as unofficial observers.

[2] The Church is not opposed to collaboration of Catholics with non-Catholics on a cultural level. In fact, it is expedient that these diverse faith-groups unite in the defense of the natural law and in the promotion of Christian ethics. When, however, it is a question of interdenominational meetings that are devoted to a discussion of doctrine and worship, the Church is obliged to uphold its claim to be the one true Church established by Christ and to proclaim that reunion, for a Catholic, can only mean acceptance of Catholicism by non-Catholics. The Church can never compromise its faith or morals; it already possesses the fullness of revelation and perfect religious unity.

[3] In practice, any and all co-operation of Catholics with non-Catholics is subject to the authority of Bishops who are the Pope's appointed pastors and teachers of the flock of Christ. It is for them, guided by instructions from Rome, to decide if, when, where, and to what extent a Catholic, priest or layman, may participate in mixed meetings of a religious nature.

Why are you Catholics so intolerant of Protestants, Jews, and other groups who don't agree with your views? Should not all peoples unite in love? Why doesn't your Church join the Protestant ecumenical movement?

[1] Catholics are intolerant of no person or group of people. They are only intolerant of the teachings which oppose or contradict the faith and morals bequeathed by Christ to the Catholic Church. Our conscience, guided by God's revelation, will not permit us to agree with some of the teachings proposed by Protestants, Jews and other groups.

[2] It is true that all peoples should unite in love but this does not mean that they should compromise or deny their beliefs or pretend that truth is merely relative. It is truth which makes us free to love and live in peace.

[3] The Church has always condemned discrimination based on race or color or creed. Its love embraces all men because it wishes "all men to be saved and to come to the knowledge of the truth" (1 Tim. 1, 4). Cardinal Spellman, appearing before the Federal Civil Rights Commission in New York City in 1959, labeled discrimination as a "fatal disease" and as "the hangman of any free nation." He spoke the mind of Catholics by declaring, "Malice toward none, justice to all, should forever stand as the basic American formula and practice. No true American would nurture, promote, or incite anti-Semitic, anti-Negro, anti-Catholic, anti-any group of fellow law-abiding American citizens." The Cardinal told the Commission that those who "incite, participate, or connive against their fellow citizens through race or religious hatred, are disloyal Americans" who are "weakening the democratic structure of this great and glorious government."

[4] The Catholic Church refuses to join the Protestant ecumenical movement because its purpose is "to search for truth and unity." The Church is convinced that it already possesses full religious truth and perfect earthly unity. However, its theologians are permitted to attend ecumenical meetings as unofficial observers and to engage in informal discussion. In fact, the Church ever prays and strives, in union with its Divine Founder, to bring all peoples into the unity of one Lord, one faith, one Baptism.

Is it not inconsistent for you to invite Protestants to attend doctrinal lectures in your Church, and yet at the same time to forbid Catholics to attend lectures in our churches, or take part in our services?

[1] There is no inconsistency in our attitude. A Catholic would violate Catholic principles by attending services in a Protestant church, whereas a Protestant violates no principle of his religion by attending doctrinal lectures on Catholicism.

[2] Protestantism is essentially a religion based on private judgment; a Protestant is logically a seeker after truth. In view of the many doctrinal divisions among the sects, and the many different viewpoints of liberal thought, the logical thinker in the outside churches can never be certain of his position. He must at least admit that the Catholic Church may be the one Church of Christ.

[3] Catholicism is essentially a religion based on a divine, infallible teaching; a Catholic is logically a possessor of the truth. Why, therefore, should he seek for that which he already possesses? His faith precludes all possibility of doubt; it rests on the authority of God. He can never admit that other churches, liberal or orthodox, may possibly be right.

[4] A Congregationalist minister once said to the writer: "What is better than searching for the truth?" "Finding it" was my answer.

If, as you pretend, the claims of your Church are so strong, why is it that so many intelligent non-Catholics fail to see their force?

[1a] The reason is that they have never considered the claims of the Church in their entirety, or, if they have studied them fairly well, they have approached the study with prejudicial minds and sinful hearts. I have asked many an inquirer to devote at least a half hour a day for a year to a study of the Church's teaching, praying earnestly in the meanwhile for God's grace and guidance. All who faithfully followed this advice received the gift of faith in the end. Even when the journey home lasted from three to five years—the first year's study and prayer made the final victory possible.

[2a] More people are kept out of the Catholic Church by

prejudice than by intellectual difficulties. The Jews, who were looking for a political Messias, found it hard to accept the meek and humble Jesus, who was continually prophesying His death upon the cross. They might admit His miracles, but they denied their proving power, ascribing them to the devil (Matt. 12, 24; 16, 21). The same prejudice against the supernatural will make a rationalist today admit as a fact a well authenticated miracle at Lourdes, but negate its proving power by ascribing it to some unknown law of nature. A Methodist or Baptist of Mississippi or Alabama, who has been taught from childhood by parents whom he loves, and by teachers and friends whom he respects, that the Catholic Church is an unreasonable, unscientific, unscriptural, superstitious, intolerant, and foreign system of priestly imposture, must fight valiantly the prejudices of a lifetime, before he can weigh carefully the divine claims of Catholicism.

[3] Our Lord and His Apostles tell us that worldliness and sensuality frequently blind men's minds to the light of truth. "The sensual man," says St. Paul, "does not perceive the things that are of the Spirit of God, for it is foolishness to him, and he cannot understand" (1 Cor. 2, 14). Even fairly good living people at times find it difficult to see the force of the Catholic claims, because they realize that conversion will mean for them the loss of an inheritance, the estrangement of relatives and friends, and the blighting of their political prospects.

[4] On the other hand, however, Catholics can point to the thousands of converts who are coming to the Catholic Church every year from paganism, unbelief and Protestantism, at the cost of sacrifices that often amount to a practical martyrdom. We recommend our questioner to read the adventure of some of these spiritual pilgrims on their road to the City of Peace.

What are the differences between the Orthodox Eastern Church and the Catholic Church?

[1] The term "Eastern Orthodox Church" refers to that part of historic Christianity in the Near East which followed the lead of Constantinople in the break with Rome in 1054.

² Today, the Orthodox Church numbers 150 million souls and consists of 17 independent Churches. The five main ones are the patriarchates: Constantinople, Alexandria, Antioch, Jerusalem and Moscow. Independent Churches of lesser dignity serve the Orthodox populations of Cyprus, Bulgaria, Serbia, Rumania, Georgia, Yugoslavia, Finland, Poland, Czechoslovakia, Albania and the United States. The monastery on Mount Sinai is an independent Church. In the United States there are over 2 million Orthodox Christians.

³ The fundamental difference between the Eastern Orthodox Church and the Roman Catholic Church is the uncertainty as to where her infallible, doctrinal authority resides. In the Catholic Church it resides ultimately in the Pope who is the supreme head of the Church. The Orthodox Church consists of a number of autonomous Churches which lack a supreme head. The Patriarch of Constantinople has only a primacy of honor and not of jurisdiction. And even this nominal leadership is being disputed by the Russian patriarch who is forced to serve the aims of the Soviet government.

⁴ Whereas, under the authority of the Pope, Roman Catholicism is ever reaching a richer understanding of the apostolic truths, Eastern Orthodoxy is at a standstill in its dogmatic development. It does not regard as binding any doctrinal decisions of councils held since 787. Thus the Orthodox have great reverence for the Virgin but do not recognize the Immaculate Conception; pray for the dead but are vague about purgatory and indulgences; grant the Pope a primacy of honor over all the Churches, but reject his infallibility in matters of faith and morals.

⁵ The historic dispute where Roman Catholics believe that the Holy Spirit proceeds from God the Father and God the Son as against the Orthodox teaching that the Holy Spirit proceeds directly from God the Father is not seen today to be as grave a disagreement as it once was.

⁶ The Orthodox have seven sacraments. Baptism is conferred by a threefold immersion while the legitimacy of other modes is admitted. Infants receive Confirmation immediately after Baptism. The Real Presence of our Lord on the altar takes place not only through the words of

Consecration but through a prayer to the Holy Spirit (the *Epiklesis*) which is added to them. Leavened bread is used in the celebration of the Eucharist. Communion is administered under both species and is received only a few times a year.

[7] Bishops are celibate, but priests may be married.

[8] In Orthodox churches there is only one altar. The sanctuary is separated from the rest of the church by a picture-wall (*iconostasis*) behind which the sacred actions of the liturgy are performed out of sight of the congregation.

[9] Divorce with remarriage is allowed for reasons of adultery, apostasy, insanity and desertion.

[10] The Eastern Orthodox Church is nearer to Catholicism than any other religious body. Along with the Roman Church, it holds to Scripture and Tradition as the sources of faith; accepts all the doctrinal decisions of the seven councils before 787, including the dogmas of the Incarnation, of the Trinity, and of the two natures in the one person of Jesus Christ. Its Bishops are true Christian Bishops; its priests are true priests; its divine Liturgy (the Mass) is a true sacrifice; its sacraments (mysteries) are true sacraments. It has preserved Apostolic succession and the essentials of Christian worship.

[11] Besides the Orthodox Church there are the lesser Eastern Churches—the Coptic, Jacobite, Nestorian and Armenian—which all sprang from the two great heresies of the 5th century: Nestorianism, condemned at Ephesus in 431, and Monophysitism, condemned at Chalcedon in 451.

[12] At various times in Church history members of these three main classes of Eastern Churches, the Orthodox, the Nestorians and the Monophysites, have repented of their schism, and joined again the true Church. These are known as Uniates and are counted among Catholics of the Eastern rite. They number about 9 million.

What was the origin of the schism between the Orthodox Eastern Church and Rome?

[1] It is not possible to point to any one person or to any single event as the origin of the schism between the Ortho-

dox Eastern Church and Rome. The schism as we know it today is the result of a progressive alienation between the East and the West, dating back to the establishment of Constantinople as the "new Rome," early in the 4th century. We can point to certain events as decisive in the progressive alienation: the Acacian schism, the Photian schism, the schism of 1054. None of these, however, may be called the origin of the schism.

In this progressive separation, political, cultural and ecclesiastical factors tell the most complete story.

2 Politically, these factors are important. In the East, the emperor assumed a sovereign role in Church matters, accordingly as the patriarchate of Constantinople took a primary place over Antioch and Alexandria. In the West, where the Pope was actually the only effective authority until the coming of Charlemagne, there was no imperial power to intervene in Church affairs. The Eastern emperors in time gave the decisions of Church councils the value of imperial law, so that the authority of the Church became identified with the authority of the emperor. As this bond between Church and emperor became closer, the notion arose in the East that a transfer of the empire meant a transfer of the ecclesiastical primacy.

In the West, the ecclesiastical primacy was always identified with the Apostolic succession of the Popes at Rome. It was in rejection of the principle that ecclesiastical importance depended on civil importance that Pope Leo I annulled the 28th canon of the Council of Chalcedon, which listed the patriarchate of Constantinople as second only to Rome.

3 One of the most important cultural difficulties was the difference in language between East and West, and the mutual misunderstanding that this difference created, especially in theological terms. Of special note is the question of the *Filioque,* a word added to the Creed in the 7th century, which the East later rejected as heretical. The early objections, however, were not so much questions of dogma as questions of adding to the established Creed. The Orientals maintained that it was not permissive to add to a Creed established by a General Council.

4 Ecclesiastical difficulties were the most important of

all. There were two fundamental approaches to the notion of the Church. In the East, the emphasis was on the local Church as the center of the mysteries and the sacraments. In the West, the emphasis was on the Universal Church, centered on the mystical and sacramental life of the Church, with universal powers of judgment from the Apostles. This ecclesiastical diversification dates from the Council of Sardica (Sofia) in 342. The differences in theological thought and religious feeling that stem from that time grew wider through the centuries, so that between the years of 323 and 867 (the date of the Photian break), there were five separate breaks, totaling 203 years of separation.

[5] The East clarified its approach by stressing the administrative authority of the local Churches. The West centered administrative authority in Rome. These two canonical traditions came into conflict in the grievances between East and West over rites, custom and discipline, especially at the times of the patriarchs, Photius and Cerularius.

[6] The reign of Emperor Michael III (842-867), which opened with the final defeat of the Iconoclasts, was to close with the beginning of a most serious breach—the Photian schism. In 867, the patriarch of Constantinople, Photius, became the first man in history to pass an official judgment against the Pope, when he formulated his case against the Papacy. Photius was excommunicated, and he went into schism. Although this schism lasted only ten years, Photius was such a powerful figure in Constantinople that his action set a precedent that was invoked or imitated by all those who later were to break the unity of the Church. Photius was re-established as patriarch in 879. Forced to resign in 886, Photius died in exile in 891.

[7] In the 150 years between the time of Photius and the time of Michael Cerularius, both East and West hardened into a state of mutual mistrust and misunderstanding. In Rome there were 43 Popes between 896 and 1049, none of whom made any significant attempts at reconciliation with the East. In Constantinople, there was a strengthening of the efforts to establish "de jure" autonomy.

[8] In 1054 the fatal blow to unity fell. Just prior to this

date, relations between East and West seemed to be improving. When the patriarch, Cerularius, and the Pope's legate, Cardinal Humbert, met, however, the culminating point of the schism was at hand.

⁹ Cerularius was a man of ambition who sought to preserve the power of the Eastern empire, especially the power of the patriarch. When the rise of the Normans in southern Italy threatened to unite the Pope and the emperor, he countered by closing the Latin churches in Constantinople and by forbidding all use of the Latin rite. In 1053, he dispatched a list of grievances to the Pope, a dispatch implying that any union between Rome and Constantinople had long ceased. A series of letters between Rome, the emperor and the patriarch followed. Finally, in 1054, Cardinal Humbert arrived in Constantinople with two other Papal legates. Cerularius seems to have been against both the legates and the emperor in an effort to break off relations between Rome and Constantinople and win complete independence for the East.

¹⁰ The patriarch's ambition was matched by the Cardinal's lack of understanding and tact. Pope Leo IX had been dead for several months when the Cardinal placed the bull of excommunication on the main altar of Santa Sofia on July 16, 1054. Although affecting only Cerularius and his partisans, it was just what Cerularius needed to raise anti-Roman fever in Constantinople. Later, he drew up a manifesto of the Eastern case against Rome, again implying that disunity had existed for centuries and that unity was in no way necessary or desirable.

¹¹ The events of 1054 were not merely the actions of two men. They represent the clash of the two ecclesiastico-cultural traditions, the climax of the progressive alienation between the East and the West. Although not the date of a total alienation, it was a fatal one, for since that time, except for a brief attempt at Lyons in 1274 and another at Florence in 1439, no effort has succeeded in uniting the two parts of the Christian world in an enduring form.

Why do you apply the term "Catholic" exclusively to your Church? Have not Anglo-Catholics a rightful claim to the name? and Easterns also? Do not all Christians profess

*that they believe in the Catholic Church, when they recite
the Apostles' Creed? Are there not more Protestants than
Roman Catholics in the world today?*

[1] Our Church alone is Catholic or universal in time,
doctrine and extent. She has existed in perfect continuity
from the time of Christ and will last until His Second
Coming. She teaches all His gospel, and administers all
His divine means of salvation. She is not confined to any
particular region or nation, but is widespread among all
the nations of the world. The word Catholic does not de-
note a quality. One cannot be Anglo, Eastern or Liberal
Catholic; one cannot be more or less Catholic. One either
is a Catholic or he is not.

[2] The Eastern schismatics are not Catholic in time, for
they date only from the 5th (the Lesser Eastern Churches)
or from the 11th century (the Orthodox Eastern Church).
The Protestant churches are not Catholic in time because
they date from the 16th (Lutherans and Anglicans), the
17th (Baptists), the 18th (Methodists), or the 19th century
(the Disciples of Christ). The outside Churches are not
Catholic in faith, because they have broken away from the
center of unity, the Roman See, and question many of
Christ's laws and doctrines. They are not Catholic in extent, for, from the beginning of their secession, they have
identified themselves with some particular nation — Germany, the Scandinavian countries, England, Russia, Bulgaria, Roumania, Serbia, Greece.

[3] Mere profession of a Creed does not constitute one a
Catholic, for the different separatist Churches read into it
their own peculiar opinions. A number of different sects
scattered all over the world do not constitute a Catholic
Church. Catholicism implies a divine unity of government,
faith and worship.

[4] "The Church," says Karl Adam, "is not one society or
one Church alongside many others, nor is she just a Church
among men; she is the Church of men, the Church of
mankind. It is this claim that gives her action its persever-
ing determination and its grandeur. Her members belong
to this or that nation, and national interests are bound to
exert some influence on the Church's action. There have

even been times when the Church seemed to be no more than a handmaid of the German Emperor or the French King. But these were only episodes, only brief and passing checks in her world-wide mission. She had to fight hard for it again and again, in bitter struggles, but she won for herself, in virtue of her mission to all mankind, her spiritual freedom from princes and peoples, and so secured the sovereignty of the Kingdom of God, and the independence of Christian faith and morals" (*The Spirit of Catholicism,* 146).

⁵ The Catholic Church is Catholic in time, because while we can accurately fix the date of every heresy and schism, no one can assign any date to her origin save the day of Pentecost. The admission of her perpetuity is often made unconsciously. I remember years ago, an old Methodist minister who, introducing a young Catholic priest to a public audience, said: "It gives me great pleasure as an *old* member of a *new* Church to introduce a *young* member of the *old* Church."

⁶ "The Church is called Catholic by all her enemies, as well as by her own children. Heretics and schismatics can call the Church by no other name than Catholic, for they would not be understood, unless they used the name by which the Church is known to the whole world" (*De Vera Religione,* 7, St. Augustine).

You claim that your Church alone is Apostolic. We believe it to be a corruption of the Primitive Church, and that Luther by sending us to the Bible for our religion, restored the Church to its primitive purity. Is he not a true successor of the Apostles who holds to the Apostles' Creed, preaches Christ, and manifests Christ's love to the brethren?

¹ Apostolicity implies that the true Church is the Church which Christ commissioned His Apostles to establish under the supremacy of St. Peter. He Himself chose the twelve Apostles, made St. Peter their head, and commissioned them to transmit infallibly all His divine revelation to all nations till the end of the world (Matt. 4, 18-22; Mark 16, 15).

² The true Church is Apostolic in origin, doctrine and

ministry. The true Church must trace its origin in unbroken line to Jesus and the twelve Apostles. Before giving His divine commission to the Apostles, Christ insists upon His divine commission from His heavenly Father. "As the Father has sent Me, I also send you" (John 20, 21). "The very works that I do, bear witness to Me that the Father has sent Me" (John 5, 36). "All power in heaven and on earth has been given to Me. Go, therefore, and make disciples of all nations" (Matt. 28, 18-19). No individual has the right to associate himself with the Apostles; he must be "sent" or "commissioned" with divine authority. "How are men to preach," asks St. Paul, "unless they be sent?" (Rom. 10, 15.)

[3] A comparison may make this clear. If, for example, a body of twelve men receive from the owner of a large wheat farm in the Northwest the contract to gather in the whole harvest, they receive at the same time the right to hire as many other workers as are necessary to fulfill their contract. But no one can lawfully work in that field expecting payment, unless he has been empowered to do so by one of the twelve, or someone else acting in their name and with their authority. So the Lord of the harvest (Luke 10, 1-12) has given the harvesting of the nations to the twelve Apostles and their legitimate successors until His Second Coming. No intruder or usurper outside the legitimate succession can have any jurisdiction. A break with the past proves that apostolicity of origin has been lost. As our Lord put it: "He who enters not by the door into the sheepfold, but climbs up another way, is a thief and a robber" (John 10, 1).

[4] Apostolicity of origin is proof of apostolicity of doctrine. God's Church cannot become corrupt, because He has promised to preserve it from error: "The gates of hell shall not prevail against it" (Matt. 16, 18). "I am with you all days" (Matt. 28, 20). Christ never said that the Bible would contain all His divine revelation; Christ never said that critical estimates of certain early documents would be a sufficient guarantee of His Gospel. The mere appeal to the Bible or to history is therefore beside the point. He did guarantee to keep His one true Church free from error until the end of the world.

[5] Apostolicity of ministry implies the authority to teach, to rule and to sanctify, which has been handed down from the Apostles. Valid Orders alone do not guarantee an Apostolic ministry, for they may be conferred by men who are in heresy and schism. Valid Orders must be accompanied by legitimate jurisdiction, which comes only through union with the head of the Apostolic body, the See of Peter.

[6] The only Church that can rightly claim that its origin is not due to a break with the past is the Catholic Church. The Eastern Churches broke with the past and lost the Apostolic succession when Cerularius was excommunicated by the Papal legates in 1054. The continental Protestants broke with the Apostolic Church at the time of Luther's revolt in 1520, and the English Protestants in 1559, when the State made Parker the first Protestant Archbishop of Canterbury.

Is not the Church of England and her offshoot, the Protestant Episcopal Church of the United States, continuous and identical with the Church in England prior to the Reformation? Did not the pre-Reformation kings and Bishops of England deny in many an instance the supremacy of the Pope?

[1] No, the continuity theory of modern High Churchmen is a myth, for the Established Church of England which dates from Elizabeth differs totally in government, doctrine and worship from the Catholic Church. No English king or Bishop prior to the Reformation ever denied the primacy of the Pope.

[2] The archbishops of Canterbury, primates of the English Church, were never recognized until their appointment had been confirmed by the Pope. When consecrated and invested with the pallium, which the Pope always sent them as a symbol of their rightful jurisdiction in union with him, the Church's supreme head, they swore "to defend the Roman Papacy against all men, to obey the commands of the Holy See with their whole strength, and to cause them to be obeyed by others" (Stubbs, *Const. Hist.*, iii., 305). In their letters they continually style themselves the "legates of the Holy See," and declare "their service

and obedience" to the Pope (Letter of Archbishop Chichely to Pope Martin V in 1426).

[3] The English Bishops before the Reformation were never recognized without the Pope's confirmation, and as a rule were directly appointed by him. The oath taken at their consecration ran as follows: "I will be faithful and obedient to St. Peter, to the Holy Apostolic Roman Church, to my Lord Pope N— and his successors canonically entering. . . . I will give aid, saving my order, to defend and to maintain against every man the Papacy of the Roman Church and the Royalty of St. Peter. . . . So may God help me and these holy Gospels" (Wilkins, *Concilia*, II, 199). Rome was always the supreme court of appeals in all important trials (Stubbs, *Cont. Hist.*, iii., 315). The kings of England always recognized the Pope's supremacy in the matter of episcopal appointments, the granting of dispensations in the prohibited degrees, the receiving of Papal legates, and the accepting of Papal interdicts and excommunications.

[4] All the disagreements between England and Rome prior to the Reformation were concerned with temporal, and not spiritual matters. For example, William the Conqueror (1066-1087), while fully acknowledging the primacy of Gregory VII (1073-1085), refused, as he had a perfect right to do, feudal homage for his kingdom.

[5] From the 6th to the 16th century the Catholic Church in England flourished and grew, as every other country of Christendom, in union with the divine center of unity, the Pope.

[6] Under Henry VIII (1509-1547), England for the first time in her history denied the supremacy of the Pope, and thereby lapsed into schism. This grossly immoral Tudor despot, after trying in vain to persuade Pope Clement VII (1529-1534) to annul his valid marriage with Catherine of Aragon, determined to take the matter into his own hands. On January 25, 1533, he was married privately to his mistress, Anne Boleyn, by one of the Court chaplains without even the pretense of a divorce. Henry chose a married priest, Thomas Cranmer, to be Archbishop of Canterbury, deceiving the Pope, who would never have sent the bulls, had he been aware of this marriage and of his Protestant

views. Within seven weeks (May 17) this time-serving apostate obediently declared Henry's marriage with Catherine null and void in order to satisfy "the conscience of the King." Two years later he was just as willing to declare Henry's marriage with Anne invalid, for had not Henry, who now wished to marry Jane Seymour, seduced Anne's sister Mary? In November, 1634, a subservient Parliament enacted that "the King, his heirs and successors, should be taken and reputed *the only supreme heads on earth of the Church of England,* with full power to visit, reform and correct all such errors, heresies, abuses, contempts and enormities, which by any manner of *spiritual* authority ought to be reformed and corrected" (Lingard, *History of England,* v., 33).

[7] Most of the cowardly English Bishops proved recreant to their trust, and the new nobility, enriched by the plunder of the Church lands, followed Henry in his schism. Saints like Sir Thomas More and Bishop John Fisher together, with some Franciscans and Carthusians, went gladly to the scaffold rather than acknowledge the King's supremacy in spiritual matters. "I cannot conform my conscience," said More, "to the counsel of one kingdom against the general consent of Christendom."

[8] In this way the national Protestant Church of England came into existence, and the English sovereigns and their Parliaments became the origin of all that Church's jurisdiction, and the sole arbiters of its laws, doctrines and worship. The idea of the Catholic Church as the Kingdom of God upon earth, independent, sovereign, universal and supernatural was lost, and a State Church substituted which was dependent, local, national, and purely natural.

[9] Is it not strange, that some men of that Church which for hundreds of years gloried in its Protestantism, and persecuted to the death five hundred martyrs who professed loyalty to the Pope and love for the Mass, should today repudiate the Reformation, and attempt to defend the unreal, unhistorical myth of continuity. As Cardinal Bourne well said in his Pastoral Letter for Lent, 1928: "No one who has really studied and understood the history of the English martyrs in the 16th and 17th centuries can honestly maintain that there is any real continuity between

the Elizabethan Church, still legally established in this country, and the Catholic Church set up among us by St. Augustine in 597, of which we Catholics, in union with the Apostolic See, are the sole legitimate representatives today."

Was not the early British Church independent of Rome? Did not the British Church refuse to accept St. Augustine for its archbishop, proving that it denied the Papal supremacy, and differed doctrinally from the Roman Church?

[1] The early British Church was not independent of Rome, nor did its teaching differ in any way from the beliefs held by the Universal Church.

[2] The speech of the hermit Dinoth in Bede's *Ecclesiastical History* (II, 2), is regarded by many non-Catholic scholars as "spurious" (Bright, *Early English History,* 96) or "apocryphal" (Haddan and Stubbs, *Conc.,* I, 142). But even if it be substantially correct, it certainly does not prove that the British Church was independent of Rome. The British Bishops refused to obey St. Augustine, because he came to them as the friend of their most bitter enemies. Had they been heretics or schismatics, would the Roman Augustine have dreamed of inviting them to help him convert the hated Saxons?

[3] The early British Church owed its existence to Rome. Its chief bishoprics were in the towns occupied by the Roman legions; its earliest martyrs bore Roman names; the earliest antiquarian remains of British Christianity were found in Canterbury, Dover and Richborough, where Roman soldiers had been stationed. In the 2nd and 3rd centuries we find mention of British Christians in Tertullian (*Adv. Jud.,* viii., 2) and in Origen (*In Luc,* xiii.). British Bishops attended the Councils of Arles in 314, Nice in 325, Sardica in 347; they were also present at the French Councils of Tours in 461, Vannes in 465, Orleans in 511, and Paris in 555. This proves that they agreed doctrinally with the Universal Church.

[4] The logic of our "continuity" theorists is greatly at fault. As Matthews puts it: "If the British Church refused to have anything to do with the English Church, how can

the latter be in continuity with the former? And if the Briton's opposition to St. Augustine, amounted to a rejection of Papal jurisdiction, is not this admitting that St. Augustine, the first Archbishop of Canterbury, the first hierarchical head of the Church in England, was neither more nor less than a Papal emissary? But then what becomes of the independent national character claimed for the Church of England, if it was so Popish as its birth?"

What do Catholics mean by unity? Is not the so-called unity of your Church a veneer, impossible to realize, considering the claims of reason to think for itself?

[1] Catholics, taught by Christ, and the divine tradition handed down from the beginning of Christianity, believe that the Catholic Church alone possesses a unity of divine government, divine faith and divine worship.

[2] Jesus Christ never spoke of a plurality of Churches, but of "My Church," when He first promised Peter, chief Apostle, that He would make him the rock foundation of the divine society He was about to establish. When He referred to the Kingdom of God prophesied in the Old Testament, He called it the kingdom of heaven, the city on the hill, the net containing good and bad fishes, the field of the wheat and the tares, the pearl of great price, the one fold of the One Shepherd. The Church is always pictured in the New Testament as visibly one, presided over by the shepherd Peter, who represents Christ, the Good Shepherd, a kingdom of God, telling all men until the last day to *believe* only what He and His Apostles taught, to *obey* His and their commands, to *worship* as He ordered (Matt. 16; 3, 24).

[3] Christ plainly foretold that the gates of hell would never prevail against His Church, and that He would provide for its unity by His abiding presence, and the power of the Holy Spirit. For "every kingdom divided against itself is brought to desolation, and house will fall against house" (Luke 11, 17). We readily grant that the private judgment of the individual, and the selfish nationalism of the nations would *naturally* bring about disunion

in the Church, but the Divine builder ensured its unity by a special *supernatural* grace, which He asked of His Heavenly Father the night before He died. There can be no doubt of the meaning of our Lord's prayer: "That all may be one, even as Thou, Father, in Me and I in Thee; that they also may be one in Us . . . and the glory which Thou hast given Me, I have given to them; that they may be one, even as We are One" (John 17, 21. 22). The unity Christ prays for is to be the most striking mark of His true Church, for it is founded on the mutual love of Father and Son in the unity of the Most Blessed Trinity.

⁴ St. Paul insists upon the unity of the Church in his every Epistle. Although he mentions individual local churches in certain cities (Col. 4, 15. 16), he teaches clearly that they are parts of the one Church in every place (1 Thess. 1, 8; 1 Cor. 1, 2; 2 Cor. 2, 14). The Church is not a mere organization that may divide and subdivide like a nation or a club, but a divine organism with its own inherent principle of life. It is Christ's Mystical Body, of which He is the Head and all Christians the members. It is founded by *One* Lord, animated by *One* Spirit, entered into by *one* Baptism, ruled by a *united* episcopate, and having *one* aim, the glory of God and the salvation of men's souls (Acts 10, 28; Rom. 12, 4-8).

⁵ "For as the body is one, and has many members, and all the members of the body, many as they are, form one body; so also is it with Christ. For in one Spirit we were all baptized into one body, whether Jews or Gentiles, whether slaves or free . . . you are the body of Christ, member for member" (1 Cor. 12, 12-27). "Careful to preserve the unity of the Spirit in the bond of peace: one body and one Spirit; even as you were called in one hope of your calling: one Lord, one faith, one Baptism; one God and Father of all, who is above all, and throughout all, and in us all" (Eph. 4, 3-6).

⁶ We often hear non-Catholics say that men are free to worship God according to the dictates of their conscience. No one who grasps the full meaning of Christ's words can believe this. Our Lord told the Apostles to baptize "in the name of the Father and of the Son and of the Holy Spirit," and said: "Unless a man be born again of water

and the Holy Spirit, he cannot enter into the kingdom of God" (Maatt. 28, 19; John 3, 5). He said again that we must partake of His Body and Blood to have divine life. "Unless you eat the flesh of the Son of Man, and drink His blood, you shall not have life in you" (John 6, 54). The Mass, the clean oblation foretold by the prophet Malachias (1, 11), He instituted the night before He died, saying: "This is My Body. This is My Blood. Do this for a commemoration of Me" (Matt. 26, 26-28; Luke 22, 19).

[7] The Catholic Church is distinguished from all other Churches by the mark of unity. The Churches that are in communion with the See of Rome are all agreed in matters of faith. Ask any Catholic Bishop or priest the world over to explain any Catholic doctrine, and he will give you substantially the same answer. "Mere tradition will not account for it; for human traditions vary, and tend to become contradictory, especially as they spread. Mere authority will not account for it, or written declarations or decrees. For why should so many millions freely and gladly submit to this authority, and as freely and gladly reverence and obey these decrees. There must be some guiding Spirit, which animates the whole, and inspires alike teachers and taught. A complex organism can remain one only so long as there is a vital force within it" (Walker, *The Problem of Reunion,* 232). The same holds good for worship. In every Catholic church in the world the same Mass is offered daily, and the same seven sacraments administered to the people. That unity of faith and worship are safeguarded by the Pope, who rules the whole flock in Christ's name and with His authority is admitted even by non-Catholics who have declared: "We have in the Roman Catholic Church a realized ideal of unity" (C. H. Matthews, *Faith or Fear,* 190).

Is not the Universal Church one, inasmuch as it is made up of the Roman, Anglican and Eastern Churches, which are entirely independent, yet bound together as branches of the one Church?

[1] By no means. This Branch Theory held by certain members of the High Church party of the Church of England is a visionary, illogical, incoherent theory, repudiated

alike by both Rome and Constantinople, and possessing not the slightest warrant either in the Sacred Scriptures or in the writings of the Fathers.

[2] Our Savior indeed uses the symbol of Christians as branches in a vine, but they are branches joined to each other visibly and really by their common life in the trunk, which is Christ the Lord. It is a symbol of *united* branches. The schismatic, or separated branch, as Christ says, "shall be cast outside as the branch and wither; and they shall gather them up, and cast them into the fire, and they shall burn" (John 15, 6).

[3] According to the Fathers of the Church, who frequently discuss the point, a schism is not merely "an unfortunate misunderstanding" among Christians, but "an invention of the devil," as St. Cyprian calls it (*The Unity of the Church*), implying a real breach of intercommunion and "a stealing of men from the Church." That a man could separate from the Church and at the same time be a Catholic, was to them inconceivable.

[4] One can easily understand the Catholic position. There is one visible Church in communion with herself the world over, forming one universal divine society under the Pope. One can understand the Protestant theory: there is no visible Church, but everyone is a Christian or a Catholic who follows Christ. But this compromise opinion of a union of utterly antagonistic bodies cannot be understood nor satisfactorily explained.

[5] Moreover this theory supposes, contrary to facts, that there is one great Eastern Church, united in the same primitive faith, that ever agreed in denying the Papal claims. This is a mere figment of the imagination. No such body ever existed. The East has been from the beginning, and it is today, full of heresies and schisms. Besides the sixteen branches of the Eastern Orthodox Church (Fortescue, *The Orthodox Eastern Church*, 273), there are other Eastern Churches, the Nestorian, the Coptic, the Jacobite, and the Armenian, who are no more in communion with her than with us Catholics. The Orthodox regard them as heretics and schismatics. Do our Anglican friends regard them as real branches? How can they do so in the face of the Councils of Ephesus and Chalcedon?

"When we mention the Church of England, what do we mean? What are its doctrines? What are its laws? What is its worship? Every sort of answer will be given the inquirer. No one part can honestly claim to speak for the whole body, which is a "comprehensive" medley of the most divergent opinions. On the other hand, the Catholic Church alone is truly one and undivided in doctrines, in laws and in worship. It is the Pope who speaks for all true Catholics.

SELECTED BIBLIOGRAPHY

BAUM, GREGORY. *That They May Be One.* Westminster, Md.: Newman Press. 1958.

BROWN, ROBERT McAFEE. *An American Dialogue.* Garden City, N. Y.: Doubleday & Co. 1960.

CRISTIANI, LEON and JEAN RILLIET. *Catholics and Protestants: Separated Brethren.* Westminster, Md.: Newman Press. 1960.

DALMAIS, IRENEE H. *Eastern Liturgies.* New York: Hawthorn Books. 1960.

DUHAMEL, PIERRE A. *Essays in the American Catholic Tradition.* New York: Rinehart. 1960.

DUMONT, CHRISTOPHER J. *Approaches to Christian Unity.* Baltimore: Helicon Press. 1959.

HANAHOE, EDWARD F. *One Fold.* Garrison, N. Y.: Chair of Unity Apostolate. 1959.

HARDON, JOHN A. *Christianity in Conflict.* Westminster, Md.: Newman Press. 1959.

———— *The Protestant Churches of America.* Westminster, Md.: Newman Press. 1956.

JEDIN, HUBERT. *A History of the Council of Trent.* Vol. 1. St. Louis: B. Herder Book Co. 1957.

LEEMING, BERNARD. *The Churches and the Church.* Westminster, Md.: Newman Press. 1960.

MURPHY, JOHN L. *The General Councils of the Church.* Milwaukee: Bruce Publishing Co. 1960.

RAAB, CLEMENT. *The Twenty Ecumenical Councils of the Catholic Church.* Westminster, Md.: Newman Press. 1959.

THIELEN, THORALF T. *What Is An Ecumenical Council?* Westminster, Md.: Newman Press. 1960.

TODD, JOHN M. *Catholicism and the Ecumenical Movement.* London, New York: Longmans, Green. 1957.

WEIGEL, GUSTAVE. *A Catholic Primer on the Ecumenical Movement.* Westminster, Md.: Newman Press. 1957.

INDEX OF SUBJECTS

440 INDEX OF SUBJECTS

446 INDEX OF SUBJECTS